PAST LIVES

ALSO BY HEATHER DAVIS-FISCH

Canadian Performance Histories and Historiographies: New Essays on Canadian Theatre Volume 7

Loss and Cultural Remains in Performance: The Ghosts of the Franklin Expedition

PAST LIVES
PERFORMING CANADA'S HISTORIES

EDITED BY HEATHER DAVIS-FISCH

PLAYWRIGHTS CANADA PRESS
TORONTO

Library and Archives Canada Cataloguing in Publication
Past lives : performing Canada's histories / Heather
Davis-Fisch, editor. -- First edition.

Includes bibliographical references.
ISBN 978-1-77091-776-7 (softcover)

1. Canada--History--Drama. 2. Canada--Drama.
3. Canadian drama. I. Davis-Fisch, Heather, 1979-, editor

PS8309.H5P37 2017 C812.008'035871 C2017-901362-9

We acknowledge the financial support of the Canada Council for the Arts, the Ontario Arts Council (OAC), the Ontario Media Development Corporation, and the Government of Canada through the Canada Book Fund for our publishing activities.

Canada Council for the Arts Conseil des arts du Canada

ONTARIO ARTS COUNCIL
CONSEIL DES ARTS DE L'ONTARIO
an Ontario government agency
un organisme du gouvernement de l'Ontario

Canada

Ontario
Ontario Media Development Corporation

For Jasper and Quinn

CONTENTS

INTRODUCTION

HEATHER DAVIS-FISCH

> *In the space between the meaninglessness of the present and the unknowable past is the entertainment of history.*
> —Greg Dening, *Performances*

Since Marc Lescarbot's masque, *The Theatre of Neptune in New France*, was performed at Port-Royal in 1606, Canadian dramatists have been invested in not only representing but also generating the entity we might term "Canadian history." Lescarbot's masque celebrated the return of Jean Biencourt, Sieur de Poutrincourt, to Port-Royal and featured, in its cast of characters, not only the eponymous Neptune, but also four "savages," likely portrayed by French performers. As de Poutrincourt and his crew rowed ashore, they were welcomed back to the settlement by the masque's characters in their own vessels. De Poutrincourt and his crew were cast as both spectators and impromptu participants in the performance. French settlers and their Mi'kmaq neighbours joined the returning men in watching the spectacle. Lescarbot also published a text of the masque upon his return to France. The "target" audience for the performance, then, was a dual one, including de Poutrincourt, settlers, and Indigenous spectators in the performance's present moment and French readers who would encounter the masque after the fact. The performance, in other words, was not only for the present audience at Port-Royal on that November day but also for posterity, for a future, and—in the moment of performance—still only imaginary audience. The performance marked de Poutrincourt's return *as* historical; that is, as significant enough to be remembered, but it was not a retroactive recreation of a history that had already passed: it was an active creation, through embodied performance and textualization, of a history of the present. Alan Filewod perceptively remarks that the masque "offers a recessive hall of mirrors which promises a glimpse into a moment of history but which in the end offers only images of images, each incrementally distorted from the assumed original. Lescarbot's play was an image of an image itself, a virtualized simulation of an imagined real."[1]

The Theatre of Neptune in New France reveals two simple but significant points about Canadian historical drama: first, that the relationship between written drama, performance, and history is a foundational one; and second, that historical drama is not just about the past, but is about both present and future moments as well. There is an obvious fraught-ness to discussing Canadian drama. This is, perhaps, most apparent when referring to the pre-Confederation period, as considering texts from this time as "Canadian" underlines the historical anachronism of the notion of Canada. This also becomes clear when one attempts to characterize Canadian drama in relation to either Canada's historical construction as both French and English or Canada's relationship to Indigenous peoples as a settler colony. I simply flag the strangeness of "Canadian" drama here, as I discuss it in detail in the introduction to this anthology's companion, *Canadian Performance Histories and Historiographies.*

Despite—or perhaps because of—persistent and constantly re-forming anxieties concerning Canadian identity, literary critics, dramatists, and performance historians have repeatedly identified the creation of a "native" dramatic tradition as essential to the formation of national culture. This triangular relationship between national identity, literature, and history is exemplified in Harcourt Farmer's 1919 definition of Canadian playwrights as "persons of Canadian descent, or adoption, who have written plays the subject-matter of which deals with some intrinsic part of Canadian life, past or present; and whose plays are directly artistic representations of Canadian life, or interpretations of Canadian temperament."[2] Almost fifty years later, Murray Edwards drew a similar connection by framing Canadian drama, both discursively and concretely, in relation to notions and realities of indigeneity:

> Although it might be true that the history of this country is not studded with many dramatic moments, there are sufficient areas that stand out as material for the dramatic artists and are, even more importantly,

1 Alan Filewod, *Performing Canada: The Nation Enacted in the Imagined Theatre* (Kamloops, BC: UC of the Cariboo P, 2002), xii. For more information about the performance and its textual history, see Jerry Wasserman's introduction to *Spectacle of Empire: Marc Lescarbot's* Theatre of Neptune in New France (Vancouver, BC: Talonbooks, 2006).

2 In Don Rubin, ed., *Canadian Theatre History: Selected Readings* (Toronto: Playwrights Canada, 2004), 44–45.

> indigenous to this country. The early relations with the Métis, for example, and the juxtaposition of the French and English are fraught with the sort of conflicts that are the life blood of the theatre. But until recently such moments in Canadian history have been ignored by Canadian playwrights. Instead we find that any subject that was volatile or had in it the stuff of drama was inevitably skirted as "controversial." A "Canadian" play was one in which you would find Indians acting essentially Shakespearean roles, or Gilbert and Sullivan on Parliament Hill. The characters were not real and it was presumably because their "realness" was assiduously avoided by the Canadian dramatist.[3]

Edwards's plea for "indigenous" dramatic content arises in a lament against the "imitative characteristics" of early Canadian drama, against Canadian dependence on British and American cultural models, and against a simultaneous—and slightly strange—tendency toward cultural isolationism.[4] The sense of absence that Edwards's comments signal is a dominant feature of Canadian dramatic criticism, one that was widely disseminated in the Massey Commission Report and reproduced from the 1960s–80s.[5] The widespread sense that Canada lacks a "real" history, cultural identity, or literary canon persists to this day: the question of what constitutes Canadian identity is one which is rehearsed and reproduced, so far without fail, in each Canadian drama or theatre course I teach and which, I suspect, is echoed across the country in both classrooms and theatres.

HISTORICAL DRAMAS AND THEIR DOUBLES

This cultural "vacuum"—to use Michael Tait's 1963 term—is, upon closer examination, remarkably full, if perhaps unevenly populated. Certain time periods—the 1880s and 90s, the 1920s and 30s, the 1970s—seem to have generated more historical drama than others. While this volume includes Charles Mair's 1886 play *Tecumseh*, similar histories are represented in Sarah Anne Curzon's *Laura Secord* (1887), John Hunter-Duvar's *De Roberval* (1888), and James Bovell Mackenzie's

3 Murray Edwards, *A Stage in Our Past: English-Language Theatre in Eastern Canada from the 1790's to 1914* (Toronto: U of Toronto P, 1968), 168.

4 Ibid., 165–67.

5 See Michael Tait, "Playwrights in a Vacuum," *Canadian Literature* 16 (1963): 5–18; Eugene Benson and L.W. Conolly, *English-Canadian Theatre* (Toronto: Oxford UP, 1987); Filewod, *Performing Canada*, 1–10; Alan Filewod, *Committing Theatre: Theatre Radicalism and Political Intervention* (Toronto: Between the Lines, 2011), 8–9.

Thayendanegea (1898). All four plays work through the relationship between an imagined and prototypical English-Canada and its "others": Americans, the British, the French, and Indigenous peoples. The next two plays in this anthology—Amy Redpath Roddick's *The Birth of Montreal* and Merrill Denison's *Alexander MacKenzie*—fall into the second time period; written contemporaneously with nationalist artistic upsurges such as the Little Theatre Movement and the socially progressive Workers' Theatre Movement, they could easily have been joined by plays such as Carroll Aikins's 1927 *The God of Gods*; Oscar Ryan, E. Cecil Smith, Frank Love, and Mildred Goldberg's *Eight Men Speak* (1933); or any of the other radio dramas in Denison's collection *Henry Hudson and Other Plays*. Historical subjects preoccupied many authors and playmakers in the 1970s as well: Sharon Pollock's *The Komagata Maru Incident* is one example of a single-authored historical play from this period; although documentary plays produced through collective creation methods, such as Theatre Passe Muraille's *1837: The Farmer's Revolt* (1976) and the Mummer's Troupe of Newfoundland's *Buchans* (1974), represent an alternative creation method they similarily focus on popular and populist histories.

Playwrights and practitioners also gravitated toward particular generic frames in representing Canadian history on stage. Although Edwards appears to advocate for some form of "realism" in Canadian drama, in general, dramatists representing historical events have tended to avoid strictly realist or naturalist conventions; Robertson Davies's *At My Heart's Core*, in this volume, is a clear exception to this rule. In the late nineteenth century, playwrights tended to use poetic drama to represent historical events, perhaps because the genre's literary, heightened rhetorical style and epic scope, not bound by Aristotelian unities, allowed for the range of history to come through. These plays, often characterized as "closet" drama, attempted to represent the fullness of events that playwrights imagined as nationally foundational. The tendency toward literary drama and toward textualization of history continues in Roddick's *The Birth of Montreal*, which, like its predecessors, stages events that encompass a long time period and a wide range of characters. It is also clear in Denison's radio plays, which relied exclusively on text and auditory effects to capture the scope of history. The literary dramas of the 1880s, with their broad historical reach, also anticipate epic theatre and Brecht's alienation effect. Such conventions, which we can observe in plays from the Workers' Theatre Movement, come into their own in the documentary and historical plays of the 1970s—the breaking of the fourth wall, the episodic rather than climactic structure, the use of metatheatrical or alienation techniques and framing devices, such as Pollock's Master of Ceremonies, all embody the principle of historicization for which Brecht advocated. The use of metatheatrical and other estrangement effects, such as diegesis rather than mimesis that marked the literary histories of the earlier period, also opens the door for postmodern critical assessments and deconstructions of history. In this volume, these techniques are exemplified by Lorena Gale's *Angélique*. The postmodern rejection of western, linear historiography is also demonstrated in Joseph A. Dandurand's *Please Do Not Touch the Indians*; the play's dramaturgy reflects Indigenous, specifically Stó:lō, worldviews in its multiple, simultaneous temporal structure.[6] Gale and Dandurand's plays could have been joined by many other examples of postmodern historical performance: Monique Mojica's *Princess Pocahontas and the Blue Spots* (1990); Daniel David Moses's *Almighty Voice and His Wife* (1990); and Damien Atkins, Paul Dunn, and Andrew Kushnir's *The Gay Heritage Project* (2018) immediately come to mind.

Historical drama always operates across the three temporal modes of past, present, and future. The past of historical drama appears, initially, straightforward: referring to the event(s) represented in a play, to the play's subject or themes. But when we approach historical drama written in a time not our own—reading Mair's *Tecumseh*, for example—we are confronted by at least two pasts: the past *in* the play, the War of 1812 in the case of *Tecumseh*; and the past that wrote the play, that is, Mair's present moment of writing, which is in our past. Both the present and future in historical drama are also always doubled: the present temporality includes the moment at which the author is writing and all the moments at which the play is received by readers or audience members; the future includes the playwright's imagined future, in which the play is received by readers and audience members; and the reader or audience member's futures, which the play—particularly in the case of socially or politically engaged drama—will shape. The complex temporal structures at work, which determine both production and reception of historical drama, raise critical historical, phenomenological, and affective questions. First, how does historical drama relate the past to the present? Why do authors pick particular past moments to represent and what do these choices, and the specific representational choices that follow, tell us about the moment at which authors were writing? Second, how do we, as readers or spectators, experience the past through historical drama, particularly through plays not of our own time? Third, why are drama and theatre effective modes of engaging with the past (or why do we imagine that they are)? What affective labour does historical drama perform? What affective connections does historical drama forge between past(s), present(s), and future(s)?

6 See Keith Thor Carlson, *The Power of Place, the Problem of Time: Aboriginal Identity and Historical Consciousness in the Cauldron of Colonialism* (Toronto: U of Toronto P, 2010).

INTER(IN)ANIMATING DRAMA

The play between pasts, presents, and futures in the creation and reception of historical drama might be characterized as what Rebecca Schneider, drawing on Fred Moten, drawing on John Donne, terms inter(in)animation: the "constant (re)turn of, to, from, and between states in animation."[7] Laura Levin extends and explains Schneider's term in relation to Elizabeth Freeman's concept of "temporal drag":

> [T]emporal drag asks us to consider how the past is never really left behind, but is rather physically "dragged" into any future iteration. So our very bodies register on their very "surfaces the co-presence of several historically-specific events, movements, and collective pleasures" (Freeman 729). In that sense Schneider proposes that we think about the ways that times touch—how time can be felt as a sticky substance that materializes in the confluence of bodies, gestures, and experiences.[8]

Inter(in)animation, Levin continues, allows us to "work against binaries of animate and inanimate, life and death, which are always at play in constructions of time."[9] In relation to Schneider's discussion of Abu Ghraib photographs, Levin comments, "In reframing photos not as events that *took place* but rather as events that *take place* in our hands, as we look at them, we see the political stakes of undoing media specificity. This stresses our own complicity in looking, in '*misrecognizing the past as past*' (162)."[10] Historical drama, similarly, not only captures events that took place (the events represented and the event of the author's writing), but also takes place each time it is encountered, by readers and audiences.

Greg Dening makes similar points to Schneider and Levin, but frames them within a broader discussion of the relationship between knowledge of the past and its representations in the present. "Histories, transformations of the past into expressions, clothe, constitute, *are* a present social reality," Dening remarks. He continues:

---

7 Rebecca Schneider, *Performing Remains: Art and War in Times of Theatrical Reenactment* (New York: Routledge, 2011), 7.

8 Roberta Barker, Heather Davis-Fisch, Kirsty Johnston, Laura Levin, Marlis Schweitzer, and Kim Solga, "Canadian Performance Genealogies: A Roundtable," *Theatre Research in Canada* 35.1 (2014): 93.

9 Ibid.

10 Ibid., 94.

> Histories always have this *double entendre*. They refer to a past in making a present. The knowledge of the past that re-presents the past in story or account makes the structures of the present—such as class or identity—in the expressing . . . Histories are fictions—something made of the past—but fictions whose forms are metonymies of the present. Histories are metaphors of the past: they translate sets of events into sets of symbols. But histories are also metonymies of the present: the present has existence in and through their expression. The present—social reality, the structures of our living—has being through representations of the past in coded public forms. We read or hear histories in this double way. We know in them both a present and a past.[11]

Not only can we only know the past through the present—and the present through how it relates to the past—Dening suggests that we can also only know the past through its textualizations. The past, Dening carefully points out, is not inherently logical despite our "confidence that the past itself is ordered in itself in such a way that we can make a narrative of it."[12] Histories are our way of knowing the past in the present, and it is only through textualizing the past that we can know it: "Histories" Dening writes, "are the texted past."[13]

Histories are relics marked by a bi-linear relationship to past and future: Dening identifies relics as "cultural artifacts of the moments that produce them, but they also become cultural artifacts of all the moments that give them permanence." Relics, he continues, "come directly from the past but they are reconstituted in their meanings by all the cultural systems that give them meaning. They gain meaning out of every social moment they survive."[14] Because they are deliberately selected and preserved for an imagined future, Dening's relics are much like the photographs Schneider describes or the plays anthologized here—not only artifacts of something that took place but also objects that take place repeatedly, in a range of present moments.

11 Greg Dening, *Performances* (Chicago: U of Chicago P, 1996), 37–38.

12 Ibid., 41.

13 Ibid., 42.

14 Ibid., 43.

EXPERIENCING RE-PRESENTATION

Framing historical drama's historicity in this way allows us to recognize it as a present social reality for authors, readers, and spectators; as a textualization that attempts to order an inherently disorderly past; as a relic from the past that is reconstituted and made meaningful in various presents; as, fundamentally, an inter(in)animation. This recognition raises phenomenological questions: how do we, as readers or spectators, experience historical drama and, through historical drama, experience the past?

In her essay "Performative Time," Tracy C. Davis distinguishes between two temporalities at work in performance: theatrical time and performative time. Theatrical time, according to Davis, is the time of the theatrical event—the represented time, whether it is "unified" in an Aristotelian sense or not—in contrast to the "real" time within which a spectator experiences life: "In the recognition of a play's commencement, duration, and end we do not so much suspend ordinary rules of elapsing clock-based time but augment them with another set of principles: I call this theatrical time, which weathers shifts in our awareness of true durational and represented time." "The concept of theatrical time," Davis continues, "describes the bidimensional and often dual-chronic experience of play attendance, rather than the ontology of performance alone."[15] Although theatrical time disrupts spectators' normal lived experience of time, it generally remains linear or multi-linear. Performative time, in contrast, does not refer to a suspension in the flow of normal time, but "allows for nonlinearity, or nonseriality, as a factor in perception as well as the teleology of time's asynchronicity, as a factor in perception . . . overturning a straightforward concept of temporal succession . . . [P]erformative time participates promiscuously in the past yet is ongoing: it has a fulcrum in the present yet receives appreciable force from both past and future."[16] Inter(in)animation and historical representation take place, I suggest, in performative time.

In watching or reading historical drama, the two registers of theatrical and performative time come together; phenomenologically speaking, we experience both times and must work to balance or shift between temporal modes. To return to the example of watching—or imagining watching—Charles Mair's *Tecumseh*, we witness years of events unfold during a present time span of a few hours; this is our experience of theatrical time. We also, however, experience shifts in the very

15 Tracy C. Davis, "Performative Time," in *Representing the Past: Essays in the Historiography of Performance*, Charlotte Canning and Thomas Postlewait, eds. (Iowa City: U of Iowa P, 2010), 147.

16 Ibid., 149.

linearity of time as the full range of moments that impact our understanding of the theatrical events come to consciousness, even when they are not represented on stage. In the case of *Tecumseh*, these could include: knowing that Mair was writing his play as Métis leader Louis Riel was on trial and awaiting execution, the Canadian government's implementation of a range of genocidal policies, our knowledge (or lack of knowledge) of the present reality experienced by Indigenous peoples in Canada, our own personal and familial relationships, and our prior encounters with the play or similar dramas. Davis describes how spectators experience these ephemeral, non-serial moments: "The phenomenological recurrence of memory, laminated by spectators onto subsequent performances, bridges productions of a play, interpretations of a character, and events at a site. Though the demonstrable record of performance may be ephemeral, performative ghosting (or haunting) splits the difference between ephemerality as perishable and ephemerality as transitive."[17] Our experience of reading drama or watching theatre is always, as Ric Knowles argues throughout *Reading the Material Theatre*, influenced by extra-theatrical realities; however, this experience is heightened when theatre represents "real" history.

FEELING TIME

Our experience of historical drama is, fundamentally, an affective one; although historical drama and performance allow us to think critically about the past, they do this through bodies both textually imagined and represented on stage, through sensual language, through sensation. Historical drama is effective because it is affective. This may, as Dening argues, be characteristic not only of historical drama but of historiography more generally: "Historiography I take to be those sensual, emotional, mindful, bodily, spiritual processes by which peoples collectively or personally read the signs of that surrounding metaphoric presence of the past and know that they truly belong to that past and that past truly belongs to them. Historiography, in my understanding, is a common, everyday phenomenon, not something belonging to Theory and Method classes."[18] A quick survey of theatre history demonstrates, furthermore, that theatre has been understood, specifically, as an effective pedagogical practice: we see this in examples ranging from classical Sanskrit drama to medieval English mystery plays to theatre for young audiences

17 Ibid., 154–55.

18 Greg Dening, "Respectfulness as a Performance Art: Way Finding," *Postcolonial Studies* 11.2 (2008): 145.

today. As a tangible, embodied, sensual medium, theatre is particularly suitable for not only teaching audiences "facts" about the past but also forging connections between past events and present spectators through compelling structures of feeling.

Historical drama, because it represents the past by creating transferable, textualized relics of it, is fundamentally concerned with questions of loss. As Dening points out: "The past itself is evanescent: it has existence only in histories."[19] Writing historical drama is an act of recuperation, of saving from loss. David Eng and David Kazanjian clearly outline the relationship between loss, remains, and history: "as soon as the question 'What is lost?' is posed, it invariably slips into the question 'What remains?' That is, loss is inseparable from what remains, for what is lost is only known by what remains of it, by how these remains are produced, read, and sustained."[20] Loss provokes a number of affective responses: nostalgia, mourning, surrogation, melancholia. These responses to loss are palpable in the plays included here and go far to explain why such plays continue to appeal to us: historical drama holds out the promise of recapturing and re-engaging with something lost in the past.

Contextualizing this point in relation to national identity, Filewod premises that both Canadian nationhood and Canadian theatre are "founded on fantasies of absent authenticity," suggesting a sense of vague but real loss at the core of Canadian drama.[21] Filewod's comment suggests a fundamental melancholia at the core of Canadian drama. Melancholia arises from the loss of a loved object and occurs when the lost object eludes consciousness, when one knows one has lost *something* but does not know what, exactly, has been lost.[22] One might argue, following Filewod, that Canadian drama, and Canadian historical drama specifically, responds to this sense of melancholic loss in a very particular way: arising from a sense of always-absent authenticity, Canadian historical drama attempts to fill this imagined void by putting forward experiences and events that exemplify "authentic" Canadian historical experience.

Understanding Canadian historical drama as fundamentally concerned with loss and considering one corollary of this—that we are drawn to historical drama because it promises to redress our senses of loss—does not have to be a

19 Dening, *Performances*, (Chicago: U of Chicago P, 1996), 42.

20 David Eng and David Kazanjian, eds., *Loss: The Politics of Mourning* (Berkeley: U of California P, 2003), 2.

21 Filewod, *Performing* (Kamloops, BC: UC of the Cariboo P, 2002), 1.

22 Sigmund Freud, "Mourning and Melancholia," in *The Standard Edition of the Complete Psychological Works of Sigmund Freud*, Vol. 14 (London: Hogarth, 1966), 237–58.

gloomy or paralyzing prospect, particularly when our dual sense of emotional desire for and actual alienation from an imagined past leads to critical reflection. Rosemarie K. Bank argues that our critical distance from the past has the potential to generate social change and even activism:

> The trick in staging the past, as Brecht knew, is how to realize the critical alienation that makes the familiar seem strange and the strange familiar. "Similarity" and "difference," "one" and "many" haunt American cultural history and bedevil its study—what is included, what is left out, what is developed, what suggested, and over all the twin specters of journeying either to the already discovered country, to a familiar, same, and safe place, or, like Walter Benjamin's storm-blown angel, to the land of history as wreckage in need of a fix.[23]

Bank specifically points out that considering the experiences of those who were historically marginalized—workers, non-whites, women—creates critical space to "change the rules as well as the players, that is, to reconceive what we think history is and how it operates as well as who or what it is 'about.'"[24] Theatre, and historical drama in particular, has the potential to generate hope and change. In her introduction to Lorena Gale's *Angélique*, Naila Keleta-Mae makes precisely this point: "When there is no clear delineation between then and now, theatre has the potential to intervene in the lives of its spectators, readers, and practitioners and unmoor them from the constraints of the past. It is precisely in these moments that theatre can inspire us to work and hope, in measured and pragmatic ways, for a more just future." This volume includes relatively contemporary plays explicitly concerned with social change—Gale's *Angélique*, Dandurand's *Please Do Not Touch the Indians*, and Pollock's *The Komagata Maru Incident*—and historical examples of historical drama, relics of their writers' engagement with the past in their own presents. Taken together, the works here can be read as a series of injunctions to readers and audiences, both in the present and in the future, as a series of calls for emotional and political engagement.

23 Rosemarie K. Bank, *Theatre Culture in America, 1825–1860* (Cambridge: Cambridge UP, 1997), 8.

24 Ibid., 165.

TECUMSEH

CHARLES MAIR

MANLINESS, PATHOS, AND "THE BRAVE OF YORE": CHARLES MAIR'S *TECUMSEH*

ROBERTA BARKER

Near the climax of Charles Mair's 1886 verse drama *Tecumseh*, the great Shawnee leader is faced with the ruin of his hopes. Though he has successfully united the tribes of the Western Confederacy to fight for their treaty rights, his efforts to regain ancestral Indigenous lands have been frustrated at every turn. His brother, the conniving Prophet, has betrayed him. He and his followers have joined the British against the Americans in the War of 1812, but his British friend and comrade, General Isaac Brock, has been killed at the Battle of Queenston Heights and replaced by the cowardly General Proctor, who commands retreat. Incensed, Tecumseh reminds Proctor that in past wars, the "British father" has repeatedly asked the Chiefs of America's First Nations to fight for him, promising that if they did so their stolen lands would be restored. "We have not shrunk from battle," declares the Shawnee warrior, "We have fought, / And many of our people have been slain! / Our promise is redeemed! But what of his?" Though disgusted by the mendacity of the settlers and the spinelessness of Proctor, Tecumseh remains determined to uphold his side of the bargain:

> But, brother, if you will not fight, you hold
> The arms our father furnished for our use.
> Give these to us, and you may go in peace.
> My people are in our Great Spirit's care!
> We are determined to defend our lands.
> Or, if He wills it, strew them with our bones.

Though Proctor is unimpressed by this appeal, others present are deeply moved. As Colonel Baby, a veteran soldier, cries, "Why, this is manliness, and pathos, too!"

Manliness and pathos are twin pillars of Mair's dramaturgy in *Tecumseh*, and indeed of the conception of Canada and its history that the play sets out to perform. A passionate nationalist, Mair (1838–1927) was one of the founding members of a group that dubbed itself Canada First. In the years immediately following Confederation, he and his comrades worked earnestly for the country's political and cultural advancement. As one member of the group, George Denison, wrote to Mair in 1868, they believed that Canadians—far from feeling themselves inferior to the English—should be "confident that we have a finer country, a more intellectual, chivalrous, high-spirited people."[1] To these young nationalists, Canadians epitomized Victorian notions of manliness, which celebrated "physical and moral strength" as well as "ideas of chivalry and gentlemanliness."[2]

As Mair matured, he increasingly came to associate the ideal of manliness not only with Canada's Anglo-Saxon settlers but also with its First Peoples, and especially with the Indigenous warriors who had fought alongside the British in the Seven Years' War, the American Revolutionary War, and the War of 1812. As a journalist and a government agent, he was a committed and vocal advocate of colonial settlement of the West; he often clashed with the Indigenous leaders of his own era, and had an especially fraught relationship with Louis Riel, whom he described as a "horrible villain."[3] But for the warriors of old he reserved only the deepest enthusiasm. In the "Prologue to *Tecumseh*," published in his 1868 volume *Dreamland and Other Poems*, he lauded them as "bold," "lofty," and "fierce."[4] Theirs were "th'heroic hours" of the continent: a lost age of nobility.[5] For lost, Mair believed, it was: the wild landscapes of Canada were still "imbued / With old traditions, but the brave of yore, / Who gave them meaning, tread

1 Cited in Norman Shrive, *Charles Mair: Literary Nationalist* (Toronto: U of Toronto P, 1965), 32.

2 Norman Vance, *The Sinews of the Spirit: The Ideal of Christian Manliness in Victorian Literature and Religious Thought* (Cambridge: Cambridge UP, 1985), 10.

3 Cited in Shrive, 176. Riel clearly returned this animosity, for during the Red River Rebellion of 1869 he imprisoned Mair, then working as paymaster for the construction of Fort Garry Road, and condemned him to death: a fate Mair narrowly escaped (see Shrive, 97–98).

4 Charles Mair, "Prologue to *Tecumseh*," in *Dreamland and Other Poems* (London: S. Low, 1868), 107.

5 Ibid., 106.

the paths no more."[6] The memories of vanished Indigenous heroes, he wrote, "haunt adown the wid'ning years, / Still teazing us from quiet into tears."[7] Their tremendous affective capital could make strong men weep. They had manliness, but pathos, too; they were lofty, but they were ghosts.

For Mair, the historical Tecumseh (1768-1813) epitomized this vision. His hard-fought but ultimately unsuccessful struggle to regain his people's ancestral lands exemplified pathos, while his alliance with Isaac Brock in the War of 1812 allowed the poet to stage the decisive contributions of two icons of manliness to the conflict he saw as the "turning point of our Canadian fortunes." When he wrote and published the "Prologue to *Tecumseh*" in the 1860s, Mair was already dreaming of a full-length verse drama in which the Shawnee chief would play a leading role; but he finally completed the play only in December 1885, shortly after the execution of Louis Riel. Preoccupied by the punishment of his old adversary, Mair wrote to a friend that he could not "get down to work on *Tecumseh*" until after "that hanging" was accomplished.[8] Heather Davis-Fisch has vividly imagined Mair at his desk in the autumn of 1885, "unable to adequately transmute his feelings" about Riel's impending demise "in order to complete the play that would frame Tecumseh's death as a tragedy that laid the groundwork for the birth of Canada."[9] When he finally completed his *magnum opus*, Mair's Canadian peers praised it as a manly work; "his utterance," wrote Charles G.D. Roberts in the *Halifax Critic*, "is such as fits the lips of a son of this land of splendid heritage and heroic stock—it is forceful, straightforward, and virile."[10] As Davis-Fisch writes, however, the play is also steeped in the unsettling pathos of Mair's "melancholic engagements" with Tecumseh and Riel, with Canada's heroic past and its uncertain future.[11]

These twin strains of manliness and pathos, virility and melancholia, come down to *Tecumseh* from the theatrical genres that influenced it, and shape all aspects of its dramatic form. As Alan Filewod has argued, Mair conceived his play not as a simple representation of the past but as a deliberate mobilization

6 Ibid.

7 Ibid.

8 Cited in Shrive, 177.

9 Heather Davis-Fisch, "Complicated Feelings: *Tecumseh* as Literary Land Claim," in *Theatres of Affect*, Erin Hurley, ed. (Toronto: Playwrights Canada, 2014), 132–33.

10 Charles G.D. Roberts, "The Poetic Outlook in Canada," *The Halifax Critic* (Halifax), June 1887 (Jubilee Issue), 10.

11 Davis-Fisch, 133.

of it, "a call to arms for the imagined stage" of the Canadian nation he desired.[12] Striving to create a nationalistic verse drama in the mold of *Henry V*, Mair drew upon both "the grandiose melodrama of his day, with its Shakespearean inflections" and "the traditions of rhetorical pageantry."[13] Especially in its fourth act, which celebrates the unimpeachably British imperial hero Isaac Brock, the play features a sequence of patriotic speeches and exemplary tableaux designed to confirm the "genius, political tact, and inspirational presence" of the manly Englishman.[14] In its portrayal of Tecumseh himself, it fits snugly into the genre of the heroic Indian tragedy, which was vastly popular on the nineteenth-century American stage.[15] Like John Augustus Stone's hit play *Metamora: Or, the Last of the Wampanoags* (1829) and its many imitators, *Tecumseh* frames its Indigenous hero as an exemplar of manliness: a warrior "of perfect parts" and a "worthy champion of his race."

Still, pathos remains an inextricable part of the equation. By the 1880s, Canada had long since established a fondness for gallant-yet-vulnerable heroes like General James Wolfe, whose martial triumphs were shadowed by their own impending doom.[16] Mair's Tecumseh fits this model to a tee. Like Metamora and so many other Indigenous characters on the nineteenth-century stage, he is destined from the first for failure and death; he is the "iconic Vanishing Indian," his fate exemplifying that of his people as it appeared to the settlers who first feared, then displaced, and finally wept for them.[17] Tecumseh's niece, Iena, who initially seems likely to make an intercultural marriage with the Romantic poet Lefroy, falls victim to the same fatality, sacrificing herself (like so many nineteenth-century heroines from Hugo's Éponine to Dumas's Marguerite Gautier) to save her lover. The tragic Indian must perish so that the white man may live. Yet the white man, too, is left hollowed out by the process of colonization. Brock dies, Proctor flees, and the Indigenized European Lefroy—clasping the dead

12 Alan Filewod, *Performing Canada: The Nation Enacted in the Imagined Theatre* (Kamloops: UC of the Cariboo P, 2002), 26.

13 Alan Filewod, "National Dramas: Canadian Monumental Drama and the Investiture of History," *Modern Drama* 38.1 (1995): 74.

14 Ibid., 77.

15 See Gordon M. Sayre, *The Indian Chief as Tragic Hero: Native Resistance and the Literatures of America from Montezuma to Tecumseh* (Chapel Hill: U of North Carolina P, 2005).

16 See Roberta Barker, "The Gallant Invalid: The Stage Consumptive and the Making of a Canadian Myth," *Theatre Research in Canada* 35.1 (2014): 69–88.

17 Katia Grubisic, "'Savage Nations Roam O'er Native Wilds': Charles Mair and the Ecological Indian," *Studies in Canadian Literature* 30.1 (2005): 61.

Iena in his arms—seems less the heir to Tecumseh's greatness than its mourner. He exits the play numbly, half Othello, half Lear: "My object's gone, and I am but a shell, / A husk, an empty case, or anything / That may be kicked about the world." Written for an imagined national theatre that would never quite materialize, Mair's play remained unperformed and was eventually dismissed by his biographer Norman Shrive as a work whose "ardent nationalism and sentimental melodrama" precluded artistic greatness.[18] Vanity of vanities; all is vanity.

Why, then, should we still read this closet drama from a bygone era, this Indian tragedy whose imperialist enthusiasms and worship of the "Noble Savage" may now seem not only antiquated, but actively repugnant? As most of its recent critics have observed, Mair's drama vividly performs the complications and contradictions of Romantic Euro-North American understandings of Indigenous identity. With his hymns to the woods and the trees, Mair's Tecumseh is the "ecological Indian" whose "environmental stewardship is presented as an example to the colonizing Europeans."[19] Disdainful of the American rabble, which Mair portrays as both comically crass and chillingly keen on genocidal violence, Tecumseh becomes an early emblem of Canada's self-construction as a modest, idealistic nation that defines itself in opposition to American ambition and greed.[20] He is also the lost leader: an Indigenous King Arthur spirited away to an "unknown grave," who knows more about the past and future of Canada than its colonizers can ever understand. In the play's haunting last lines, the American Harrison eulogizes Tecumseh by declaring that "Thou, master and strong spirit of the woods, / . . . / Couldst tell us now what hath been and shall be!" Tecumseh's body vanishes, denying his mourners closure and creating "an ongoing affective engagement, rather than a closed relationship, with the past."[21] Ecological warrior, quintessential Canadian, victim, prophet: for better and for worse, the conceptions of the Indigenous subject articulated by Mair still shape settlers' perceptions today.

Perhaps *Tecumseh*'s greatest legacy for later performances of Canadian history, however, lies in the indictment of colonialism so powerfully articulated by its Indigenous characters even as the pageant playing out around them lauds the Empire's glories. Iena dissects the mechanisms of genocide for her English lover, describing how some of her people are

18 Shrive, 177.

19 Grubisic, 61.

20 Glenn Willmott, "Canadian *Ressentiment*," *New Literary History* 32.1 (2001): 138.

21 Davis-Fisch, 149.

weaned away
And wedded to rough-handed pioneers[.] [. . .]
Some by outlandish fevers die, and some—
Caught in the white man's toils and vices mean—
Court death, and find it in the trader's cup.
And all are driven from their heritage[.]

Surely, it was passages like this—as well as her entry into battle, dressed in boy's clothing and ready to fight with her bow—that inspired E. Pauline Johnson (Tekahionwake) to praise Iena as a "happy inspiration" and a blessed relief from the "fawn-eyed, unnatural, maidenly idiots" that passed for "redskin girls" in other Indian dramas.[22] Like her uncle, Iena possesses both pathos and manly courage, and uses both to advocate for her people in the face of threatened extermination.

As for Tecumseh, he goes into his final battle sharply aware of the contrast between the privilege of his erstwhile British allies and his own situation:

What matters it
To those who fled, and left us, if they flee?
They can join palms, make peace, draw treaties up.
And son and father, reconciled again,
Will clap their hands, and glory in their race
Which hath despoiled our own. [. . .]
Oh, warriors, think of all, and strike like men
Whose homes are in their hands, whose souls are free.
The voice that calls you now will call no more[.]

Tecumseh pictures himself as the vanishing Indian, his voice passing from the world even as he speaks, while the British and American colonizers—their national differences erased by their racial hegemony—clap their hands in triumph. Still, his vision of "men / Whose homes are in their hands, whose souls are free" echoes forward in time. It haunts the final lines in which Harrison (after waffling about his support for Indigenous treaty rights) wistfully asks the voice of the dead "Yearner o'er Wyandot and Cherokee" to "tell us now what hath been and shall be!" This is the dramaturgy of empire: manly, pathetic, and riddled with contradictions. Even as it celebrates the march forward into

22 Cited in Shrive, 191.

the future, *Tecumseh* stages an uneasy recognition that the past is never, after all, quite dead.

When the white men first set foot on our shores, they were hungry; they had no places on which to spread their blankets or to kindle their fires. They were feeble; they could do nothing for themselves. Our fathers commiserated their distress, and shared freely with them whatever the Great Spirit had given to his red children.

—from Tecumseh's speech to the Osages

CHARACTERS

Indians

Tecumseh: Chief of the Shawanoes
The Prophet: Brother of Tecumseh
Tarhay: a chief in love with Iena
Stayeta: Chief of the Wyandots
Miami, Delaware, Kickapoo, and Dahcota Chiefs
Warriors, Braves, Josakeeds, and Runners
Mamatee: Wife of Tecumseh
Iena: Niece of Tecumseh
Weetamore, Winona, and other Indian maidens

Americans

General Harrison: Governor of Indiana Territory
General Hull
Colonel Cass
Barron: an Indian Agent
Twang, Slaugh, Gerkin, and Bloat: rough citizens of Vincennes
Five Councillors of Indiana Territory, Officers, Soldiers, Volunteers, Orderlies, and Scouts

British and Canadians

General Brock: Administrator of the Government of Upper Canada
Colonel/General Proctor
Glegg: Aide-de-camp to General Brock
Macdonell: Aide-de-camp to General Brock
Nichol: Colonel of Canadian volunteers
Baby: Colonel of Canadian volunteers
Elliott: Colonel of Canadian volunteers
McKee: Captain of Canadian volunteers
Robinson: Captain of Canadian volunteers
Lefroy: a poet-artist, enamoured of Indian life, and in love with Iena
Two Old Men of York, U.E. Loyalists, and other Citizens, Alien Settlers, Officers, Soldiers, Volunteers, Orderlies, and Messengers

ACT I

SCENE FIRST—THE FOREST NEAR THE PROPHET'S TOWN ON THE TIPPECANOE.

Enter the PROPHET.

PROPHET: Twelve moons have wasted, and no tidings still!
Tecumseh must have perished! Joy has tears
As well as grief, and mine will freely flow—
Sembling our women's piteous privilege—
Whilst dry ambition ambles to its ends.
My schemes have swelled to greatness, and my name
Has flown so far upon the wings of fear
That nations tremble at its utterance.
Our braves abhor, yet stand in awe of me.
Who ferret witchcraft out, commune with Heaven,
And ope or shut the gloomy doors of death.
All feelings and all seasons suit ambition!
Yet my vindictive nature hath a craft,
In action slow, which matches mother-earth's:
First seed-time—then the harvest of revenge.
Who works for power, and not the good of men,
Would rather win by fear than lose by love.
Not so Tecumseh—rushing to his ends.
And followed by men's love—whose very foes
Trust him the most. Rash fool! Him do I dread,
And his imperious spirit. Twelve infant moons

Have swung in silver cradles o'er these woods,
And still no tidings of his enterprise,
Which—all too deep and wide—has swallowed him.
And left me here unrivalled and alone.

Enter an INDIAN RUNNER.

There is a message in your eyes—what now?

RUNNER: Your brother, great Tecumseh, has returned,
And rests himself a moment ere he comes
To counsel with you here.

Exit RUNNER.

PROPHET: He has returned!
So then the growing current of my power
Must fall again into the stately stream
Of his great purpose. But a moment past
I stood upon ambition's height, and now
My brother comes to break my greatness up,
And merge it in his own. I know his thoughts—
That I am but a helper to his ends;
And, were there not a whirlpool in my soul
Of hatred which would fain ingulf our foes,
I would engage my cunning and my craft
'Gainst his simplicity, and win the lead.
But, hist, he comes! I must assume the role
By which I pander to his purposes.

Enter TECUMSEH.

TECUMSEH: Who is this standing in the darkened robes?

PROPHET: The Prophet! Olliwayshilla, who probes
The spirit-world, and holds within his ken
Life's secrets and the fateful deeds of men.
The "One-Eyed!" Brother to the Shooting Star—

TECUMSEH: With heart of wax, and hands not made for war.

PROPHET: Would that my hands were equal to my hate!
Then would strange vengeance traffic on the earth;
For I should treat our foes to what they crave—
Our fruitful soil—yea, ram it down their throats,
And choke them with the very dirt they love.

'Tis you, Tecumseh! You are here at last,
And welcome as the strong heat-bearing Spring.
Which opens up the pathways of revenge.
What tidings from afar?

TECUMSEH: Good tidings thence!
I have not seen the Wyandots, but all
The distant nations will unite with us
To spurn the fraudful treaties of Fort Wayne.
From Talapoosa to the Harricanaw
I have aroused them from their lethargy.
From the hot gulf up to those confines rude,
Where Summer's sides are pierced with icicles,
They stand upon my call. What tidings here?

PROPHET: No brand has struck to bark our enterprise
Which grows on every side. The Prophet's robe.
That I assumed when old Pengasega died—
With full accord and countenance from you—
Fits a strong shoulder ampler far than his;
And all our people follow me in fear.

TECUMSEH: Would that they followed you in love! Proceed!
My ears are open to my brother's tongue.

PROPHET: I have myself, and by swift messengers.
Proclaimed to all the nations far and near,
I am the Open-Door, and have the power
To lead them back to life. The sacred fire
Must burn forever in the red man's lodge.
Else will that life go out. All earthly goods
By the Great Spirit meant for common use
Must so be held. Red shall not marry white.
To lop our parent stems; and never more
Must vile, habitual cups of deadliness
Distort their noble natures, and unseat
The purpose of their souls. They must return
To ancient customs; live on game and maize;
Clothe them with skins, and love both wife and child.
Nor lift a hand in wrath against their race.

TECUMSEH: These are wise counsels which are noised afar,
And many nations have adopted them
And made them law.

PROPHET: These counsels were your own!
Good in themselves, they are too weak to sway
Our fickle race. I've much improved on them
Since the Great Spirit took me by the hand.

TECUMSEH: Improved! and how? Your mission was to lead
Our erring people back to ancient ways—
Too long o'ergrown—not bloody sacrifice.
They tell me that the prisoners you have ta'en—
Not captives in fair fight, but wanderers
Bewildered in our woods, or such as till
Outlying fields, caught from the peaceful plough—
You cruelly have tortured at the stake.
Nor this the worst! In order to augment
Your gloomy sway you craftily have played
Upon the zeal and frenzy of our tribes.
And, in my absence, hatched a monstrous charge
Of sorcery amongst them, which hath spared
Nor feeble age nor sex. Such horrid deeds
Recoil on us! Old Shataronra's grave
Sends up its ghost, and Tetaboxti's hairs—
White with sad years and counsel—singed by you!
In dreams and nightmares, float on every breeze.
Ambition's madness might stop short of this.
And shall if I have life.

PROPHET: The Spirit Great
Hath urged me, and still urges me to all.
He puts his hand to mine and leads me on.
Do you not hear him whisper even now—
"Thou art the Prophet?" All our followers
Behold in me a greater than yourself.
And worship me, and venture where I lead.

TECUMSEH: Your fancy is the common slip of fools.
Who count the lesser greater being near.
Dupe of your own imposture and designs,
I cannot bind your thoughts! but what you do

Henceforth must be my subject; so take heed,
And stand within my sanction lest you fall.

PROPHET: You are Tecumseh—else you should choke for this!

Crosses the stage and pauses.

Stay! Let me think! I must not break with him—
'Tis premature. I know his tender part.
And I shall touch it.

Recrosses the stage.

Brother, let me ask,
Do you remember how our father fell?

TECUMSEH: Who can forget Kanawha's bloody fray?
He died for home in battle with the whites.

PROPHET: And you remember, too, that boyish morn
When all our braves were absent on the chase—
That morn when you and I half-dreaming lay
In summer grass, but woke to deadly pain
Of loud-blown bugles ringing through the air.
They came!—a rush of chargers from the woods.
With tramplings, cursings, shoutings manifold.
And headlong onset, fierce with brandished swords,
Of frontier troopers eager for the fight.
Scarce could a lynx have screened itself from sight,
So sudden the attack—yet, trembling there.
We crouched unseen, and saw our little town
Stormed, with vile slaughter of small babe and crone.
And palsied grandsire—you remember it?

TECUMSEH: Remember it! Alas, the echoing
Of that wild havoc lingers in my brain!
O wretched age, and injured motherhood.
And hapless maiden-wreck!

PROPHET: Yet this has been
Our endless history, and it is this
Which crams my very veins with cruelty.
My pulses bound to see those devils fall
Brained to the temples, and their women cast
As offal to the wolf.

TECUMSEH: Their crimes are great—
Our wrongs unspeakable. But spare our own!
These gloomy sacrifices sap our strength;
And henceforth from your wizard scrutinies
I charge you to forbear. But who's the white
You hold as captive?

PROPHET: He is called Lefroy—
A captive, but too free to come and go.
Our warriors struck his trail by chance, and found
His tent close by the Wabash, where he lay
With sprained ankle, foodless and alone.
He had a book of pictures with him there
Of Long-Knife forts, encampments and their chiefs—
Most recognizable; so, reasoning thence,
Our warriors took him for a daring spy.
And brought him here, and tied him to the stake.
Then he declared he was a Saganash—
No Long-Knife he! but one who loved our race,
And would adopt our ways—with honeyed words.
Couched in sweet voice, and such appealing eyes,
That Iena, our niece—who listened near—
Believing, rushed, and cut him from the tree.
I hate his smiles, soft ways, and smooth-paced tread.
And would, ere now, have killed him but for her;
For ever since, unmindful of her race.
She has upheld him, and our women think
That he has won her heart.

TECUMSEH: But not her hand!
This cannot be, and I must see to it:
Red shall not marry white—such is our law.
But graver matters are upon the wing.
Which I must open to you. Know you, then.
The nation that has doomed our Council-Fires—
Splashed with our bloods— will on its Father turn,
Once more, whose lion-paws, stretched o'er the sea,
Will sheathe their nails in its unnatural sides.
Till blood will flow, as free as pitch in spring,
To gum the chafed seams of our sinking bark.

This opportunity, well nursed, will give
A respite to our wrongs, and heal our wounds;
And all our nations, knit by me and ranged
In headship with our Saganash allies,
Will turn the mortal issue 'gainst our foes,
And wall our threatened frontiers with their slain.
But till that ripened moment, not a sheaf
Of arrows should be wasted, not a brave
Should perish aimlessly, nor discord reign
Amongst our tribes, nor jealousy distrain
The large effects of valour. We must now
Pack all our energies. Our eyes and ears
No more must idle with the hour, but work
As carriers to the brain, where we shall store,
As in an arsenal, deep schemes of war!

A noise and shouting without.

But who is this?

Enter BARRON *accompanied and half-dragged by warriors. The* PROPHET *goes forward to meet him.*

BARRON: I crave protection as a messenger
And agent sent by General Harrison
Your rude, unruly braves, against my wish,
Have dragged me here as if I were a spy.

PROPHET: What else! Why come you here if not a spy?
Brouillette came, and Dubois, who were spies—
Now you are here. Look on it! There's your grave!

Pointing to the ground at BARRON*'s feet.*

TECUMSEH: *(joining them)* Nay, let him be! This
man is not a spy.

(to BARRON*)* Give me your message!

BARRON: The Governor of Indiana sends
This letter to you, in the which he says
(reading letter) "You are an enemy to the Seventeen Fires.
I have been told that you intend to lift
The hatchet 'gainst your father, the great Chief,
Whose goodness, being greater than his fear

Or anger at your folly, still would stretch
His bounty to his children who repent,
And ask of him forgiveness for the past.
Small harm is done which may not be repaired,
And friendship's broken chain may be renewed;
But this is in your doing, and depends
Upon the choice you make. Two roads
Are lying now before you: one is large,
Open and pleasant, leading unto peace.
Your own security and happiness;
The other—narrow, crooked and constrained—
Most surely leads to misery and death.
Be not deceived! All your united force
Is but as chaff before the Seventeen Fires.
Your warriors are brave, but so are ours;
Whilst ours are countless as the forest leaves,
Or grains of sand upon the Wabash shores.
Rely not on the English to protect you!
They are not able to protect themselves.
They will not war with us, for, if they do,
Ere many moons have passed our battle flag
Shall wave o'er all the forts of Canada.
What reason have you to complain of us?
What have we taken? or what treaties maimed?
You tell us we have robbed you of your lands—
Bought them from nameless braves and village chiefs
Who had no right to sell. Prove that to us.
And they will be restored. I have full power
To treat with you. Bring your complaint to me.
And I, in honour, pledge your safe return."

TECUMSEH: Is this it all?

BARRON: Yes, all. I have commands
To bear your answer back without delay.

PROPHET: This is our answer, then, to Harrison:
Go tell that bearded liar we shall go
With forces which will pledge our own return!

TECUMSEH: What shall my answer be?

PROPHET: Why, like my own—
There is no answer save that we shall go.

TECUMSEH: *(to BARRON)* I fear that our complaint lies all too deep
For your Chiefs' curing. The Great Spirit gave
The red men this wide continent as theirs,
And in the east another to the white;
But, not content at home, these crossed the sea.
And drove our fathers from their ancient seats.
Their sons in turn are driven to the Lakes,
And cannot farther go unless they drown.
Yet now you take upon yourselves to say
This tract is Kickapoo, this Delaware,
And this Miami; but your Chief should know
That all our lands are common to our race!
How can one nation sell the rights of all
Without consent of all? No! For my part
I am a Red Man, not a Shawanoe,
And here I mean to stay. Go to your Chief.
And tell him I shall meet him at Vincennes.

Exeunt all but TECUMSEH.

What is there in my nature so supine
That I must ever quarrel with revenge?
From vales and rivers which were once our own
The pale hounds who uproot our ancient graves
Come whining for our lands, with fawning tongues.
And schemes and subterfuge and subtleties.
O for a Pontiac to drive them back
And whoop them to their shuddering villages!
O for an age of valour like to his,
When freedom clothed herself with solitude.
And one in heart the scattered nations stood,
And one in hand. It comes! and mine shall be,
The lofty task to teach them to be free—
To knit the nations, bind them into one,
And end the task great Pontiac begun!

SCENE SECOND—ANOTHER PART OF THE FOREST.

Enter LEFROY, *carrying his rifle, and examining a knot of wildflowers.*

LEFROY: This region is as lavish of its flowers
As Heaven of its primrose blooms by night.
This is the Arum which within its root
Folds life and death; and this the Prince's Pine,
Fadeless as love and truth—the fairest form
That ever sun-shower washed with sudden rain.
This golden cradle is the Moccasin Flower,
Wherein the Indian hunter sees his hound;
And this dark chalice is the Pitcher-Plant,
Stored with the water of forgetfulness.
Whoever drinks of it, whose heart is pure,
Will sleep for aye 'neath foodful asphodel.
And dream of endless love. I need it not!
I am awake, and yet I dream of love.
It is the hour of meeting, when the sun
Takes level glances at these mighty woods,
And Iena has never failed till now
To meet me here! What keeps her? Can it be
The Prophet? Ah, that villain has a thought.
Undreamt of by his simple followers,
Dark in his soul as midnight! If—but no—
He fears her though he hates!
What shall I do?
Rehearse to listening woods, or ask these oaks
What thoughts they have, what knowledge of the past?
They dwarf me with their greatness, but shall come
A meaner and a mightier than they.
And cut them down. Yet rather would I dwell
With them, with wildness and its stealthy forms—
Yea, rather with wild men, wild beasts and birds,
Than in the sordid town that here may rise.
For here I am a part of Nature's self.
And not divorced from her like men who plod
The weary streets of care in search of gain.
And here I feel the friendship of the earth:
Not the soft cloying tenderness of hand

Which fain would satiate the hungry soul
With household honeycombs and parloured sweets,
But the strong friendship of primeval things—
The rugged kindness of a giant heart,
And love that lasts.
I have a poem made
Which doth concern earth's injured majesty—
Be audience, ye still untroubled stems!

(recites) There was a time on this fair continent
When all things throve in spacious peacefulness.
The prosperous forests unmolested stood,
For where the stalwart oak grew there it lived
Long ages, and then died among its kind.
The hoary pines—those ancients of the earth—
Brimful of legends of the early world,
Stood thick on their own mountains unsubdued.
And all things else illumined by the sun,
Inland or by the lifted wave, had rest.
The passionate or calm pageants of the skies
No artist drew; but in the auburn west
Innumerable faces of fair cloud
Vanished in silent darkness with the day.
The prairie realm—vast ocean's paraphrase—
Rich in wild grasses numberless, and flowers
Unnamed save in mute Nature's inventory,
No civilized barbarian trenched for gain.
And all that flowed was sweet and uncorrupt.
The rivers and their tributary streams,
Undammed, wound on forever, and gave up
Their lonely torrents to weird gulfs of sea,
And ocean wastes unshadowed by a sail.
And all the wild life of this western world
Knew not the fear of man; yet in those woods,
And by those plenteous streams and mighty lakes,
And on stupendous steppes of peerless plain.
And in the rocky gloom of canyons deep.
Screened by the stony ribs of mountains hoar
Which steeped their snowy peaks in purging cloud,
And down the continent where tropic suns

Warmed to her very heart the mother earth,
And in the congeal'd north where silence self
Ached with intensity of stubborn frost,
There lived a soul more wild than barbarous;
A tameless soul—the sunburnt savage free—
Free, and untainted by the greed of gain:
Great Nature's man content with Nature's food.

But hark! I hear her footsteps in the leaves—
And so my poem ends.

Enter IENA, *downcast.*

My love! my love!
What! Iena in tears! Your looks, like clouds,
Overspread my joy which, but a moment past.
Rose like the sun to high meridian.
Ah, how is this? She trembles, and she starts.
And looks with wavering eyes through oozing tears.
As she would fly from me. Why do you weep?

IENA: I weep, for I have come to say—farewell.

LEFROY: Farewell! I have fared well in love till now;
For you are mine, and I am yours, so say
Farewell, farewell, a thousand times farewell.

IENA: How many meanings has the word? since yours
Is full of joy, but mine, alas, of pain.
The pale-face and the Shawanoe must part.

LEFROY: Must part? Yes, part—we parted yesterday—
And shall today—some dream disturbs my love.

IENA: Oh, that realities were dreams! 'Tis not
A dream that parts us, but a stern command.
Tecumseh has proclaimed it as his law—
Red shall not marry white; so must you leave;
And therefore I have come to say farewell.

LEFROY: That word is barbed, and like an arrow aimed.
The maid who saved my life would mar it too!

IENA: Speak not of that! Your life's in danger now.
Tecumseh has returned, and—knowing all—

Has built a barrier betwixt our loves.
More rigid than a palisade of oak.

LEFROY: What means he? And what barrier is this?

IENA: The barrier is the welfare of our race—
Wherefore his law—"Red shall not marry white."
His noble nature halts at cruelty,
So fear him not! But in the Prophet's hand,
Dark, dangerous and bloody, there is death,
And, sheltered by Tecumseh's own decree.
He who misprizes you, and hates, will strike—
Then go at once! Alas for Iena,
Who loves her race too well to break its law.

LEFROY: I love you better than I love my race;
And could I mass my fondness for my friends,
Augment it with my love of noble brutes,
Tap every spring of reverence and respect.
And all affections bright and beautiful—
Still would my love for you outweigh them all.

IENA: Speak not of love! Speak of the Long-Knife's hate!
Oh, it is pitiful to creep in fear
O'er lands where once our fathers stept in pride!
The Long Knife strengthens, whilst our race decays,
And falls before him as our forests fall.
First comes his pioneer, the bee, and soon
The mast which plumped the wild deer fats his swine.
His cattle pasture where the bison fed;
His flowers, his very weeds, displace our own—
Aggressive as himself. All, all thrust back!
Destruction follows us, and swift decay.
Oh, I have lain for hours upon the grass.
And gazed into the tenderest blue of Heaven—
Cleansed as with dew, so limpid, pure and sweet—
All flecked with silver packs of standing cloud
Most beautiful! But watch them narrowly!
Those clouds will sheer small fleeces from their sides,
Which, melting in our sight as in a dream.
Will vanish all like phantoms in the sky.
So melts our heedless race! Some weaned away,

And wedded to rough-handed pioneers,
Who, fierce as wolves in hatred of our kind,
Yet from their shrill and acid women turn.
Prizing our maidens for their gentleness.
Some by outlandish fevers die, and some—
Caught in the white man's toils and vices mean—
Court death, and find it in the trader's cup.
And all are driven from their heritage,
Far from our fathers' seats and sepulchres.
And girdled with the growing glooms of war;
Resting a moment here, a moment there.
Whilst ever through our plains and forest realms
Bursts the pale spoiler, armed, with eager quest.
And ruinous lust of land. I think of all—
And own Tecumseh right. 'Tis he alone
Can stem this tide of sorrows dark and deep;
So must I bend my feeble will to his,
And, for my people's welfare, banish love.

LEFROY: Nay, for your people's welfare keep your love!
My heart is true: I know that braggart nation.
Whose sordid instincts, cold and pitiless.
Would cut you off, and drown your Council Fires.
I would defend you, therefore keep me here!
My love is yours alone, my hand I give,
With this good weapon in it, to your race.

IENA: Oh, heaven help a weak untutored maid,
Whose head is warring 'gainst a heart that tells,
With every throb, I love you. Leave me! Fly!

LEFROY: I kneel to you—it is my leave-taking.
So, bid me fly again, and break my heart!

IENA sings.

IENA: Fly far from me,
Even as the daylight flies,
And leave me in the darkness of my pain!
Some earlier love will come to thee again,
And sweet new moons will rise,
And smile on it and thee.

Fly far from me,
    Even whilst the daylight wastes—
Ere thy lips bum me in a last caress;
Ere fancy quickens, and my longings press,
    And my weak spirit hastes
For shelter unto thee!

Fly far from me,
    Even whilst the daylight pales—
So shall we never, never meet again!
Fly! for my senses swim—Oh, Love! Oh, Pain!—
    Help! for my spirit fails—
I cannot fly from thee!

IENA sinks into LEFROY's arms.

LEFROY: No, Iena! You cannot fly from me—
My heart is in your breast, and yours in mine;
Therefore our love—

Enter TECUMSEH, followed by MAMATEE.

TECUMSEH: False girl! Is this your promise?
Would that I had a pale-face for a niece—
Not one so faithless to her pledge! You owe
All duty and affection to your race,
Whose interest—the sum of our desires—
Traversed by alien love, drops to the ground.

IENA: Tecumseh ne'er was cruel until now.
Call not love alien which includes our race—
Love for our people, pity for their wrongs!
He loves our race because his heart is here—
And mine is in his breast. Oh, ask him there.
And he will tell you—

LEFROY: Iena, let me speak!
Tecumseh, we as strangers have become
Strangely familiar through sheer circumstance.
Which often breeds affection or disdain,
Yet, lighting but the surface of the man
Shows not his heart. I know not what you think
And care not for your favour or your love,
Save as desert may crown me. Your decree,

"Red shall not marry white," is arbitrary,
And off the base of nature; for if they
Should marry not, then neither should they love.
Yet Iena loves me, and I love her.
Be merciful! I ask not Iena
To leave her race; I rather would engage
These willing arms in her defence and yours.
Heap obligation up, conditions stern—
But send not your cold "Nay" athwart our lives.

IENA: Be merciful! Oh, uncle, pity us!

TECUMSEH: My pity, Iena, goes with reproach,
Blunting the edge of anger; yet my will
Is fixed, and the command to be obeyed—
This stranger must depart—you to your lodge!

MAMATEE: Tecumseh, I am in the background here.
As ever I have been in your affection.
For I have ne'er known what good women prize—
Earth's greatest boon to them—a husband's love.

TECUMSEH: My nation has my love, in which you share,
With special service rendered to yourself;
So that your cabin flows with mouffles sweet,
And hips of wapiti and bedded robes.
Teach me my duty further if you will!
My love is wide, and broods upon my race.

MAMATEE: The back is clad—the heart, alas! goes bare.
Oh, I would rather shiver in the snow—
My heart downed softly with Tecumseh's love—
Than sleep unprized in warmest couch of fur.
I know your love is wide, and, for that I
Share but a millionth part of it, and feel
Its meagreness, I plead most eagerly
For this poor white, whose heart is full of love,
And gives it all to her.

TECUMSEH: It cannot be!
You know not what you ask. 'Tis 'gainst our law.
Which, breached, would let our untamed people through.

LEFROY: I care not for your cruel law! The heart
Has statutes of its own which make for love.

TECUMSEH: You'd cross me too! This child's play of the heart.
Which sterner duty has repressed in me,
Makes even captives bold. *(aside)* I like his courage!

MAMATEE: If duty makes Tecumseh's heart grow cold,
Then shame on it! and greater shame on him
Who ever yet showed mercy to his foes,
Yet, turning from his own, in pity's spite
Denies it to a girl. See, here I kneel!

IENA: And I! O uncle, frown not on our love!

TECUMSEH: By the Great Spirit this is over much!
My heart is made for pity, not for war.
Since women's tears unman me. Have your will!
I shall respect your love, *(to LEFROY)* your safety too.
I go at once to sound the Wyandots
Concerning some false treaties with the whites.
The Prophet hates you, therefore come with me.

The PROPHET rushes in with a band of BRAVES.

PROPHET: She's here! Take hold of her and bear her off!

TECUMSEH: Beware! Lay not a finger on the girl!

The BRAVES fall back.

PROPHET: There is no law Tecumseh will not break.
When women weep, and pale-face spies deceive.

MAMATEE: Ah, wretch! not all our people's groans could wring
A single tear from out your murderous eye.

PROPHET: *(lifting his axe)* This is my captive, and his life is mine!

IENA: *(rushing to LEFROY)* Save him! Save him!

TECUMSEH interferes.

End of Act I.

ACT II

SCENE FIRST—BEFORE THE PROPHET'S TOWN.

Enter TECUMSEH *and* LEFROY.

TECUMSEH: No guard or outlook here! This is most strange.
Chance reigns where prudence sleeps.

Enter a BRAVE.

Here comes a brave
With frenzy in his face. Where is the Prophet?

BRAVE: He fasts alone within the medicine lodge,
And talks to our Great Spirit. All our braves,
Huddling in fear, stand motionless without,
Thrilled by strange sounds, and voices not of earth.

TECUMSEH: How long has it been thus?

BRAVE: Four nights have passed
And none have seen his face; but all have heard
His dreadful tongue, in incantations deep.
Fetch horrors up—vile beings flashed from hell.
Who fought as devils fight, until the lodge
Shook to its base with struggling, and the earth
Quaked as, with magic strength, he flung them down.
These strove with him for mastery of our fate;
But, being foiled, Yohewa has appeared,
And, in the darkness of our sacred lodge,
Communes with him.

TECUMSEH: Our Spirit great and good!
He comes not here for nought. What has he promised?

BRAVE: Much! for henceforth we are invulnerable.
The bullets of the Long-Knives will rebound.
Like petty hailstones, from our naked breasts;
And, in the misty morns of our attack,
Strange lights will shine on them to guide our aim,
Whilst clouds of gloom will screen us from their sight.

TECUMSEH: The Prophet is a wise interpreter,
And all his words, by valour backed, will stand;
For valour is the weapon of the soul,
More dreaded by our vaunting enemies
Than the plumed arrow, or the screaming ball.
What wizardry and witchcraft has he found
Conspiring 'gainst our people's good?

BRAVE: Why, none!
Wizard and witch are weeded out, he says;
Not one is left to do us hurt.

TECUMSEH: *(aside)* 'Tis well!
My brother has the eyeball of the horse.
And swerves from danger. *(to BRAVE)* Bid our warriors come!
I wait them here.

Exit BRAVE.

The Prophet soon will follow.

LEFROY: Now opportunity attend my heart,
Which waits for Iena! True love's behest,
Outrunning war's, will bring her to my arms
Ere cease the braves from gasping wonderment.

TECUMSEH: First look on service ere you look on love;
You shall not see her here.

LEFROY: My promises
Are sureties of my service—

TECUMSEH: But your deeds.
Accomplishments; our people count on deeds.
Be patient! Look upon our warriors
Roped round with scars and cicatrized wounds.

Inflicted in deep trial of their spirit.
Their skewered sides are proofs of manly souls.
Which, had one groan escaped from agony.
Would all have sunk beneath our women's heels,
Unfit for earth or Heaven. So try your heart,
And let endurance swallow all love's sighs.
Yoke up your valour with our people's cause,
And I, who love your nation, which is just,
When deeds deserve it, will adopt you here,
By ancient custom of our race, and join
Iena's hand to yours.

LEFROY: Your own hand first
In pledge of this!

TECUMSEH: It ever goes with truth!

LEFROY: Now come some wind of chance and show me her
But for one heavenly moment! as when leaves
Are blown aside in summer, and we see
The nested oriole.

Enter chiefs and warriors. The warriors cluster around TECUMSEH, *shouting and discharging their pieces.*

TECUMSEH: My chiefs and braves!

MIAMI CHIEF: Fall back! Fall back! Ye press too close on him.

TECUMSEH: My friends! our joy is like to meeting streams.
Which draw into a deep and prouder bed.

Shouts from the warriors.

DELAWARE CHIEF: Silence, ye braves! let great
Tecumseh speak!

The warriors fall back.

TECUMSEH: Comrades, and faithful warriors of our race!
Ye who defeated Harmar and St. Clair,
And made their hosts a winter's feast for wolves!
I call on you to follow me again,
Not now for war, but as forearmed for fight.
As ever in the past so is it still:
Our sacred treaties are infringed and torn;

Laughed out of sanctity, and spurned away;
Used by the Long-Knife's slave to light his fire.
Or turned to kites by thoughtless boys, whose wrists
Anchor their fathers' lies in front of Heaven.
And now we're asked to Council at Vincennes;
To bend to lawless ravage of our lands,
To treacherous bargains, contracts false, wherein
One side is bound, the other loose as air!
Where are those villains of our race and blood
Who signed the treaties that unseat us here;
That rob us of rich plains and forests wide;
And which, consented to, will drive us hence
To stage our lodges in the Northern Lakes,
In penalties of hunger worse than death?
Where are they? that we may confront them now
With your wronged sires, your mothers, wives, and babes,
And, wringing from their false and slavish lips
Confession of their baseness, brand with shame
The traitor hands which sign us to our graves.

MIAMI CHIEF: Some are age-bent and blind, and others sprawl.
And stagger in the Long-Knife's villages;
And some are dead, and some have fled away,
And some are lurking in the forest here.
Sneaking, like dogs, until resentment cools.

KICKAPOO CHIEF: We all disclaim their treaties. Should they come.
Forced from their lairs by hunger, to our doors.
Swift punishment will light upon their heads.

TECUMSEH: Put yokes upon them! let their mouths be bound!
For they are swine who root with champing jaws
Their fathers' fields, and swallow their own offspring.

Enter the PROPHET *in his robe—his face discoloured.*

Welcome, my brother, from the lodge of dreams!
Hail to thee, sagest among men—great heir
Of all the wisdom of Pengasega!

PROPHET: *(aside)* This pale-face here again! this hateful snake,
Who crawls between our people and their laws!

(to TECUMSEH*)* Your greeting, brother, takes the chill from mine,
When last we parted you were not so kind.

TECUMSEH: The Prophet's wisdom covers all. He knows
Why Nature varies in her handiwork,
Moulding one man from snow, the next from fire—

PROPHET: Which temper is your own, and blazes up,
In winds of passion like a burning pine.

TECUMSEH: 'Twill blaze no more unless to scorch our foes.
My brother, there's my hand—for I am grieved
That aught befell to shake our proper love.
Our purpose is too high, and full of danger;
We have too vast a quarrel on our hands
To waste our breath on this.

Steps forward and offers his hand.

PROPHET: My hand to yours.

SEVERAL CHIEFS: Tecumseh and the Prophet are rejoined!

TECUMSEH: Now, but one petty cloud distains our sky.
My brother, this man loves our people well.

Pointing to LEFROY.

LEFROY: I know he hates me, yet I hope to win
My way into his heart.

PROPHET: There—take my hand!
(aside) I must dissemble. Would this palm were poison!
(to TECUMSEH*)* What of the Wyandots? And yet I know!
I have been up among the clouds, and down
Into the entrails of the earth, and seen
The dwelling place of devils. All my dreams
Are from above, and therefore favour us.

TECUMSEH: With one accord the Wyandots disclaim
The treaties of Fort Wayne, and burn with rage.
Their tryst is here, and some will go with me
To Council at Vincennes. Where's Winnemac?

MIAMI CHIEF: That recreant has joined our enemies,
And with the peace-pipe sits beside their fire.
And whiffs away our lives.

KICKAPOO CHIEF: The Deaf-Chief, too,
With head awry, who cannot hear us speak
Though thunder shouted for us from the skies,
Yet hears the Long-Knives whisper at Vincennes;
And, when they jest upon our miseries.
Grips his old leathern sides, and coughs with laughter.

DELAWARE CHIEF: And old Kanaukwa—famed when we were young—
Has hid his axe, and washed his honours off.

TECUMSEH: 'Tis honour he has parted with, not honours;
Good deeds are ne'er forespent, nor wiped away.
I know these men; they've lost their followers.
And, grasping at the shadow of command.
Where sway and custom once had realty.
By times, and turn about, follow each other.
They count for nought—but Winnemac is true.
Though over-politic; he will not leave us.

PROPHET: Those wizened snakes must be destroyed at once!

TECUMSEH: Have mercy, brother—those poor men are old.

PROPHET: Nay, I shall tease them till they sting themselves;
Their rusty fangs are doubly dangerous.

TECUMSEH: What warriors are ready for Vincennes?

WARRIORS: All! All are ready.
Tecumseh leads us on—we follow him.

TECUMSEH: Four hundred warriors will go with me,
All armed, yet only for security
Against the deep designs of Harrison
For 'tis my purpose still to temporize.
Not lightly break with him till once again
I scour the far emplacements of our tribes.
Then shall we close at once on all our foes.
They claim our lands, but we shall take their lives;
Drive out their thievish souls, and spread their bones
To bleach upon the misty Alleghanies;
Or make death's treaty with them on the spot,
And sign our bloody marks upon their crowns

For lack of schooling—ceding but enough
Of all the lands they covet for their graves.

MIAMI CHIEF: Tecumseh's tongue is housed in wisdom's cheeks;
His valour and his prudence march together.

DELAWARE CHIEF: 'Tis wise to draw the distant nations on.
This scheme will so extend the Long-Knife force,
In lines defensive stretching to the sea,
Their bands will be but morsels for our braves.

PROPHET: How long must this bold project take to ripen?
Time marches with the foe, and his surveyors
Already smudge our forests with their fires.
It frets my blood and makes my bowels turn
To see those devils blaze our ancient oaks,
Cry "Right!" and drive their rascal pickets down.
Why not make war on them at once?

TECUMSEH: Not now!
Time will make room for weightier affairs.
Be this the disposition for the hour:
Our warriors from Vincennes will all return,
Save twenty—the companions of my journey—
And this brave white, who longs to share our toil,
And win his love by deeds in our defence.
You, brother, shall remain to guard our town,
Our wives, our children, all that's dear to us—
Receive each fresh accession to our strength;
And from the hidden world, which you inspect,
Draw a divine instruction for their souls.
Go, now, ye noble chiefs and warriors!
Make preparation—I'll be with you soon.
Tomorrow we shall make the Wabash boil,
And beat its current, racing to Vincennes.

Exeunt all but TECUMSEH and the PROPHET.

PROPHET: I shall return unto our sacred lodge,
And there invoke the Spirit of the Wind
To follow you, and blow good tidings back.

TECUMSEH: Our strait is such we need the help of Heaven.
Use all your wisdom, brother, but—beware!

Pluck not our enterprise while it is green,
And breed no quarrel here till I return.
Avoid it as you would the rattling snake;
And, when you hear the sound of danger, shrink.
And face it not, unless with belts of peace.
White wampum, not the dark, till we can strike
With certain aim. Can I depend on you?

PROPHET: Trust you in fire to burn, or cold to freeze?
So may you trust in me. The heavy charge
Which you have laid upon my shoulders now
Would weigh the very soul of rashness down.

Exit the PROPHET.

TECUMSEH: I think I can depend on him—I must!
Yet do I know his crafty nature well—
His hatred of our foes, his love of self.
And wide ambition. What is mortal man?
Who can divine this creature that doth take
Some colour from all others? Nor shall I
Push cold conclusions 'gainst my brother's sum
Of what is good—so let dependence rest!

Exit.

SCENE SECOND—VINCENNES, A STREET.

Enter GERKIN, SLAUGH, *and* TWANG.

GERKIN: Ain't it about time Barron was back, Jedge?

TWANG: I reckon so. Our Guvner takes a crazy sight more pains than I would to sweeten that ragin' devil Tecumseh's temper. I'd sweeten it with sugar o' lead if I had my way.

SLAUGH: It's a reekin' shame—dang me if it ain't. And that two-faced one-eyed brother o' his, the Prophet—I'll be darned if folks don't say that the Shakers in them 'ere parts claims him for a disciple!

TWANG: Them Shakers is a queer lot. They dance jest like wild Injuns, and thinks we orter be kind to the red rascals, and use them honestly.

GERKIN: Wall! That's what our Guvner ses too. But I reckon he's shammin' a bit. Twixt you and me, he's on the make like the rest o' us. Think o' bein' kind to a red devil that would lift your har ten minutes arter! And as for honesty—I say "set 'em up" every time, and then rob 'em. That's the way to clar them out o' the kentry. Whisky's better 'n gunpowder, and costs less than fightin' 'em in the long run.

Enter Citizen BLOAT.

TWANG: That's so! Hello, Major, what's up? You look kind o' riled today.

BLOAT: Wall, Jedge, I do feel right mad—have you heerd the news?

TWANG: No! Has old Sledge bust you at the kyards again?

BLOAT: Old Sledge be darned! I had jest clar'd him out o' continentals—fifty to the shillin'—at his own game, when in ript Roudi—the Eyetalian that knifed the Muskoe Injun for peekin' through his bar-room winder last spring—jest down from Fort Knox. You know the chap, General; you was on his jury.

SLAUGH: I reckon I do! The Court was agin him, but we acquitted him afore the Chief Justice finished his charge, and gave him a vote o' thanks to boot. There's a heap o' furriners creepin' inter these parts—poor downtrodden cusses from Europe—and, if they're all like Roudi, they'll do—a'most as hendy with the knife as our own people. But what's up?

BLOAT: Roudi saw Barron at Fort Knox, restin' thar on his way back from the Prophet's town, and he sez that red assassin Tecumseh's a-cumin' down with four hundred o' his painted devils to convarse with our Guvner. They're all armed, he sez, and will be here afore mid-day.

SLAUGH: Wall! our Guvner notified him to come—he's only gettin' what he axed for. There'll be a deal o' loose har flitterin' about the streets afore night, I reckon. Harrison's a heap too soft with them red roosters; he hain't got cheek enough.

GERKIN: I've heerd say the Guvner, and the Chief Justice too, thinks a sight o' this tearin' red devil. They say he's a great man. They say, too, that our treaty Injuns air badly used—that they shouldn't be meddled with on their resarves, and should hev skoolin'.

BLOAT: Skoolin'! That gits me! Dogoned if I wouldn't lam them jest one thing—what them regler officers up to the Fort larns their dogs—"to drap to shot," only in a different kind o' way like; and, as for their resarves, I say, give our farmers a chance—let them locate!

TWANG: That's so, Major! What arthly use air they—plouterin' about their little bits o' fields, with their little bits o' cabins, and livin' half the time on mush-rats? I say, let them move out, and give reliable citizens a chance.

SLAUGH: Wall, I reckon our Guvner's kind's about played out. They call themselves the old stock—the clean pea—the rale gentlemen o' the Revolooshun. But, gentlemen, ain't we the Revolooshun? Jest wait till the live citizens o' these United States and Territories gits a chance, and we'll show them gentry what a free people, with our institooshuns, kin do. There'll be no more talk o' skoolin' for Injuns, you bet! I'd give them Kernel Crunch's billet.

GERKIN: What was that, General?

SLAUGH: Why, they say he killed a hull family o' redskins, and stuck 'em up as scar'-crows in his wheat-fields. Gentlemen, there's nothin' like original idees!

TWANG: That war an original idee! The Kernel orter hev tuk out a patent. I think I've heerd o' Crunch. Warn't he with Kernel Crawford, o' the melish', at one time?

SLAUGH: Whar?

TWANG: Why over to the Muskingum. You've heerd o' them Delaware Moravians over to the Muskingum, surely?

SLAUGH: Oh, them convarted chaps! but I a'most forgit the carcumstance.

TWANG: Wall, them red devils had a nice resarve thar— as yieldin' a bit o' sile as one could strike this side o' the Alleghanies. They was all convarted by the Moravians, and pertended to be as quiet and peaceable as the Shakers hereabout. But Kernel Crawford—who knew good sile when he sot his eyes on it—diskivered that them prayin' chaps had helped a war-party from the North with provisions—or thort they did, which was the same thing. So—one fine Sunday—he surrounds their church with his melish'—when the Injuns was all a-prayin'—and walks in himself, jest for a minute or two, and prays a bit so as not to skeer them too soon, and then walks out, and locks the door. The Kernel then cutely—my heart kind o' warms to that man—put a squad o' melish' at each winder with their bayonets pinted, and sot fire to the Church, and charred up the hull kit, preacher and all! The heft o' them was burnt; but some that warn't thar skinned out o' the kentry, and got lands from the British up to the Thames River in Canady, and founded what they call the Moravian Town thar; and thar they is still—fur them Britishers kind o' pampers the Injuns, so they may git at our scalps.

SLAUGH: I reckon we'll hev a tussle with them gentry afore long. But for Noo England we'd a hed it afore now; but them Noo Englanders kind o' curries to the Britishers. A war would spile their shippin', and so they're agin it. But we hain't got no ships to spile in this western kentry, and so I reckon we'll pitch in.

GERKIN: We'd better get out of this Injun fry-pan fust, old hoss! I could lick my own weight in wild-cats, but this ruck o' Injuns is jest a little too hefty.

BLOAT: Maybe they want to come to skool, and start store and sich!

GERKIN: Gentlemen, I mean to send my lady down stream, and I reckon you'd better do the same with your 'uns—jest for safety like. My time's limited—will you liquor?

ALL: You bet!

BLOAT: *(meditatively)* Skoolin'! Wall, I'll be darned!

Exeunt.

SCENE THIRD—THE SAME. A ROOM IN GENERAL HARRISON'S HOUSE.

Enter General HARRISON, *and some officers of the American Army.*

HARRISON: What savage handiwork keeps Barron back?

Enter BARRON.

Ah, here he comes, his looks interpreting
Mischief and failure! It is as I feared.
What answer do you bring?

BARRON: Tecumseh comes
To council, with four hundred men at back,
To which, with all persuasion, I objected—
As that it would alarm our citizens.
Whose hasty temper, by suspicion edged.
Might break in broils of quarrel with his braves;
But, sir, it was in vain—so be prepared!
Your Council records may be writ in blood.

HARRISON: Will he attack us, think you?

BARRON: No, not now.
His present thought is to intimidate.
But, lest some rash and foul-mouthed citizen
Should spur his passion to the run, fore-arm!

HARRISON: Tut! Arms are scarce as soldiers in our town.
And I am sick of requisitioning.
Nay, we must trust to something else than arms.

Tecumseh is a savage but in name—
Let's trust to him! What says he of our treaties?

BARRON: Oh, he discharges them as heavy loads,
Which, borne by red men only, break their backs.
All lands, he says, are common to his race;
Not to be sold but by consent of all.

HARRISON: Absurd! This proposition would prevent
All purchase and all progress. No, indeed;
We cannot tie our hands with such conditions.
What of the Prophet? Comes he with the rest?

BARRON: The Prophet stays behind.

HARRISON: He is a foil
Used by Tecumseh to augment his greatness;
And, by good husbandry of incantation,
And gloomy charms by night, this Prophet works
So shrewdly on their braves that every man,
Inflamed by auguries of victory,
Would rush on death.

FIRST OFFICER: Why, General, I heard
He over-trumpt you once and won the trick.

HARRISON: How so?

FIRST OFFICER: Well, once, before his braves, 'tis said.
You dared him to a trial of his spells.
Which challenge he accepted, having heard
From white men of a coming sun-eclipse.
Then, shrewdly noting day and hour, he called
Boldly his followers round him, and declared
That he would hide the sun. They stood and gazed.
And, when the moon's colossal shadow fell,
They crouched upon the ground, and worshipped him.

HARRISON: He caught me there, and mischief came of it.
Oh, he is deep. How different those brothers!
One dipt in craft, the dye of cruelty.
The other frank and open as the day.

Enter an ORDERLY.

ORDERLY: Tecumseh and his braves have reached the landing!

Excitement. All rise hastily.

HARRISON: This room is smaller than our audience:
Take seats and benches to the portico—
There we shall treat with him.

Exeunt all but General HARRISON.

Could I but strain
My charge this chief might be my trusty friend.
Yet I am but my nation's servitor;
Gold is the king who overrides the right,
And turns our people from the simple ways
And fair ideal of their fathers' lives.

Exit.

SCENE FOURTH—THE SAME. THE PORTICO OF GENERAL HARRISON'S HOUSE. AN OPEN GROVE AT A LITTLE DISTANCE IN FRONT.

Curtain rises and discovers General HARRISON, *army officers, and citizens of various quality, including* TWANG, SLAUGH, GERKIN, *and* BLOAT, *seated in the portico. A sergeant and guard of soldiers nearby.*

Enter TECUMSEH *and his followers with* LEFROY *in Indian dress. They all stop at the grove.*

HARRISON: Why halts he there?
Go tell him he is welcome to our house.

An ORDERLY *goes down with message.*

FIRST OFFICER: How grave and decorous they look—"the mien
Of pensive people born in ancient woods."
But look at him! Look at Tecumseh there—
How simple in attire! that eagle plume
Sole ornament, and emblem of his spirit.
And yet, far scanned, there's something in his face
That likes us not. Would we were out of this!

HARRISON: Yes; even at a distance I can see
His eyes distilling anger. 'Tis no sign
Of treachery, which ever drapes with smiles

The most perfidious purpose. Our poor strength
Would fail at once should he break out on us;
But let us hope 'tis yet a war of wits
Where firmness may enact the part of force.

ORDERLY returns.

What answer do you bring?

ORDERLY: Tecumseh says:
"Houses are built for whites—the red man's house,
Leaf-roofed, and walled with living oak, is there—

Pointing to the grove.

Let our white brother meet us in it!"

SECOND OFFICER: Oh!
White brother! So he levels to your height,
And strips your office of its dignity.

THIRD OFFICER: 'Tis plain he cares not for your dignity,
And touchingly reminds us of our tenets.
Our nation spurns the outward shows of state,
And ceremony dies for lack of service.
Pomp is discrowned, and throned regality
Dissolved away in our new land and laws.
Man is the Presence here!

FIRST OFFICER: Well, for my part,
I like not that one in particular.

Pointing toward TECUMSEH.

THIRD OFFICER: No more do I! I wish I were a crab,
And had its courtly fashion of advancing.

HARRISON: Best yield to him, the rather that he now
Invites our confidence. His heavy force
Scants good opinion somewhat, yet I know
There's honour, aye, and kindness in this Chief.

Rising.

THIRD OFFICER: Yes, faith, he loves us all, and means to keep
Locks of our hair for memory. Here goes!

All rise.

Servants and soldiers carry chairs and benches to the grove followed by General HARRISON *and others, who seat themselves—*TECUMSEH *and his followers still stand in the lower part of the grove.*

HARRISON: We have not met to bury our respect,
Or mar our plea with lack of courtesy.
The Great Chief knows it is his father's wish
That he should sit by him.

TECUMSEH: My father's wish!
My father is the sun; the earth my mother,

Pointing to each in turn.

And on her mighty bosom I shall rest.

TECUMSEH *and his followers seat themselves on the grass.*

HARRISON: *(rising)* I asked Tecumseh to confer with me,
Not in war's hue, but for the ends of peace.
Our own intent—witness our presence here,
Unarmed save those few muskets and our swords.
How comes it, then, that he descends on us
With this o'erbearing and untimely strength?
Tecumseh's virtues are the theme of all;
Wisdom and courage, frankness and good faith—
To speak of these things is to think of him!
Yet, as one theft makes men suspect the thief—
Be all his life else spent in honesty—
So does one breach of faithfulness in man
Wound all his after deeds. There is a pause
In some men's goodness like the barren time
Of those sweet trees which yield each second year,
Wherein what seems a niggardness in nature
Is but good husbandry for future gifts.
But this tree bears, and bears most treacherous fruit!
Here is a gross infringement of all laws
That shelter men in council, where should sit
No disproportioned force save that of reason—
Our strong dependence still, and argument,
Of better consequence than that of arms.
If great Tecumseh should give ear to it.

TECUMSEH: *(rising)* You called upon Tecumseh and he came!
You sent your messenger, asked us to bring
Our wide complaint to you—and it is here!

Pointing to his followers.

Why is our brother angry at our force,
Since every man but represents a wrong?
Nay I rather should our force be multiplied!
Fill up your streets and overflow your fields,
And crowd upon the earth for standing room;
Still would our wrongs outweigh our witnesses,
And scant recital for the lack of tongues.
I know your reason, and its bitter heart.
Its form of justice, clad with promises—
The cloaks of death! That reason was the snare
Which tripped our ancestors in days of yore—
Who knew not falsehood and so feared it not:
Men who mistook your fathers' vows for truth,
And took them, cold and hungry, to their hearts,
Filled them with food, and shared with them their homes.
With such return as might make baseness blush.
What tree e'er bore such treacherous fruit as this?
But let it pass! let wrongs die with the wronged!
The red man's memory is full of graves.
But wrongs live with the living, who are here—
Inheritors of all our fathers' sighs,
And tears, and garments wringing wet with blood.
The injuries which you have done to us
Cry out for remedy, or wide revenge.
Restore the forests you have robbed us of—
Our stolen homes and vales of plenteous corn!
Give back the boundaries, which are our lives,
Ere the axe rise! aught else is reasonless.

HARRISON: Tecumseh's passion is a dangerous flood
Which sweeps away his judgment. Let him lift
His threatened axe to hit defenceless heads!
It cannot mar the body of our right,
Nor graze the even justice of our claim:
These still would live, uncancelled by our death.

Let reason rule us, in whose sober light
We read those treaties which offend him thus:
What nation was the first established here,
Settled for centuries, with title sound?
You know that people, the Miami, well.
Long ere the white man tripped his anchors cold.
To cast them by the glowing western isles.
They lived upon these lands in peace, and none
Dared cavil at their claim. We bought from them,
For such equivalent to largess joined,
That every man was hampered with our goods.
And stumbled on profusion. But give ear!
Jealous lest aught might fail of honesty—
Lest one lean interest or poor shade of right
Should point at us—we made the Kickapoo
And Delaware the sharer of our gifts,
And stretched the arms of bounty over heads
Which held but by Miami sufferance.
But, you! whence came you? and what rights have you?
The Shawanoes are interlopers here—
Witness their name! mere wanderers from the South!
Spurned thence by angry Creek and Yamasee—
Now here to stir up strife, and tempt the tribes
To break the seals of faith. I am surprised
That they should be so led, and more than grieved
Tecumseh has such ingrates at his back.

TECUMSEH: Call you those ingrates who but claim their own,
And owe you nothing but revenge? Those men
Are here to answer and confront your lies.

Turning to his followers.

Miami, Delaware, and Kickapoo!
Ye are alleged as signers of those deeds—
Those dark and treble treacheries of Fort Wayne.
Ye chiefs, whose cheeks are tanned with battle-smoke.
Stand forward, then, and answer if you did it!

KICKAPOO CHIEF: *(rising)* Not I! I disavow them!
They were made

By village chiefs whose vanity overcame
Their judgment, and their duty to our race.

DELAWARE CHIEF: *(rising)* And I reject the treaties in the name
Of all our noted braves and warriors.
They have no weight save with the palsied heads
Which dote on friendly compacts in the past.

MIAMI CHIEF: *(rising)* And I renounce them also.
They were signed
By sottish braves—the Long-Knife's tavern chiefs—
Who sell their honour like a pack of fur,
Make favour with the pale-face for his fee,
And caper with the hatchet for his sport.
I am a chief by right of blood, and fling
Your false and flimsy treaties in your face.
I am my nation's head, and own but one
As greater than myself, and he is here!

Pointing to TECUMSEH.

TECUMSEH: You have your answer, and from those whose rights
Stand in your own admission. But from me—
The Shawanoe—the interloper here—
Take the full draught of meaning, and wash down
Their dry and bitter truths. Yes! from the South
My people came—fall'n from their wide estate
Where Altamaha's uncongealing springs
Kept a perpetual summer in their sight,
Sweet with magnolia blooms, and dropping balm,
And scented breath of orange and of pine.
And from the East the hunted Delawares came.
Flushed from their coverts and their native streams;
Your old allies, men ever true to you.
Who, resting after long and weary flight,
Are by your bands shot sitting on the ground.

HARRISON: Those men got ample payment for their land,
Full recompense, and just equivalent.

TECUMSEH: They flew from death to light upon it here!
And many a tribe comes pouring from the East,
Smitten with fire—their outraged women, maimed,

Screaming in horror o'er their murdered babes,
Whose sinless souls, slashed out by white men's swords,
Whimper in Heaven for revenge. O God!
'Tis thus the pale-face prays, then cries "Amen";—
He clamours, and his Maker answers him,
Whilst our Great Spirit sleeps! Oh, no, no, no—
He does not sleep! He will avenge our wrongs!
That Christ the white men murdered, and thought dead—
Who, if He died for mankind, died for us—
He is alive, and looks from Heaven on this!
Oh, we have seen your baseness and your guile;
Our eyes are opened and we know your ways!
No longer shall you hoax us with your pleas.
Or with the serpent's cunning wake distrust,
Range tribe 'gainst tribe—then shoot the remnant down.
And in the red man's empty cabin grin.
And shake with laughter o'er his desolate hearth.
No, we are one! the red men all are one
In colour as in love, in lands and fate!

HARRISON: Still, with the voice of wrath Tecumseh speaks,
And not with reason's tongue.

TECUMSEH: Oh, keep your reason!
It is a thief which steals away our lands.
Your reason is our deadly foe, and writes
The jeering epitaphs for our poor graves.
It is the lying maker of your books.
Wherein our people's vengeance is set down,
But not a word of crimes which led to it.
These are hushed up and hid, whilst all our deeds,
Even in self-defence, are marked as wrongs
Heaped on your blameless heads.
But to the point!
Just as our brother's Seventeen Council Fires
Unite for self-protection, so do we.
How can you blame us, since your own example
Is but our model and fair precedent?
The Long-Knife's craft has kept our tribes apart,
Nourished dissensions, raised distinctions up,

Forced us to injuries which, soon as done,
Are made your vile pretexts for bloody war.
But this is past. Our nations now are one—
Ready to rise in their imbanded strength.
You promised to restore our ravaged lands
On proof that they are ours—that proof is here.
And by the tongues of truth has answered you.
Redeem your sacred pledges, and no more
Our "leaden birds" will sing amongst your corn;
But love will shine on you, and startled peace
Will come again, and build by every hearth.
Refuse—and we shall strike you to the ground!
Pour flame and slaughter on your confines wide,
Till the charred earth, up to the cope of Heaven,
Reeks with the smoke of smouldering villages,
And steam of awful fires half quenched with blood.

TWANG: Did you ever hear the like? If I hed my shootin'-iron, darn me if I wouldn't draw a bead on that barkin' savaee. The hungry devil gits under-holts on our Guvner every time.

SLAUGH: You bet! I reckon he'd better put a lump o' bacon in his mouth to keep his bilin' sap o' passion down.

BLOAT: That's mor'n I'd do. This is jest what we git for allowin' the skulkin' devils to live. I'd vittle 'em on lead pills if I was Guvner.

TWANG: That's so! Our civilizashun is jest this—we know what's what. If I hed my way—

HARRISON: Silence, you fools! If you provoke him here your blood be on your heads.

GERKIN: Right you air, Guvner! We'll close our dampers.

TECUMSEH: My brother's ears have heard. Where is his tongue?

HARRISON: My honest ears ache in default of reason.
Tecumseh is reputed wise, yet now
His fuming passions from his judgment fly.
Like roving steeds which gallop from the catch,
And kick the air, wasting in wantonness
More strength than in submission. His threats fall
On fearless ears. Knows he not of our force,

Which in the East swarms like mosquitoes here?
Our great Kentucky and Virginia fires?
Our mounted men and soldier-citizens?
These all have stings—let him beware of them!

TECUMSEH: Who does not know your vaunting citizens!
Well drilled in fraud and disciplined in crime;
But in aught else—as honour, justice, truth—
A rabble, and a base disordered herd.
We know them; and our nations, knit in one,
Will challenge them, should this, our last appeal.
Fall on unheeding ears. My brother, hearken!
East of Ohio you possess our lands.
Thrice greater than your needs, but west of it
We claim them all; then, let us make its flood
A common frontier, and a sacred stream
Of which our nations both may drink in peace.

HARRISON: Absurd! The treaties of Fort Wayne must stand.
Your village chiefs are heads of civil rule.
Whose powers you seek to centre in yourself.
Or 'vest in warriors whose trade is blood.
We bought from those, and from your peaceful men—
Your wiser brothers—who had faith in us.

TECUMSEH: Poor, ruined brothers, weaned from honest lives!

HARRISON: They knew our wisdom, and preferred to sell
Their cabins, fields, and wilds of unused lands
For rich reserves and ripe annuities.
As for your nations being one like ours—
'Tis false—else would they speak one common tongue.
Nay, more! your own traditions trace you here—
Widespread in lapse of ages through the land—
From o'er the mighty ocean of the West.
What better title have you than ourselves,
Who came from o'er the ocean of the East,
And meet with you on free and common ground?
Be reasonable, and let wisdom's words
Displace your passion, and give judgment vent.
Think more of bounty, and talk less of rights—
Our hands are full of gifts, our hearts of love.

TECUMSEH: My brother's love is like the trader's warmth—
O'er with the purchase. Oh, unhappy lives—
Our gifts which go for yours! Once we were strong.
Once all this mighty continent was ours,
And the Great Spirit made it for our use.
He knew no boundaries, so had we peace
In the vast shelter of His handiwork.
And, happy here, we cared not whence we came.
We brought no evils thence—no treasured hate,
No greed of gold, no quarrels over God;
And so our broils, to narrow issues joined,
Were soon composed, and touched the ground of peace.
Our very ailments, rising from the earth,
And not from any foul abuse in us,
Drew back, and let age ripen to death's hand.
Thus flowed our lives until your people came,
Till from the East our matchless misery came!
Since then our tale is crowded with your crimes,
With broken faith, with plunder of reserves—
The sacred remnants of our wide domain—
With tamp'rings, and delirious feasts of fire,
The fruit of your thrice-cursed stills of death,
Which make our good men bad, our bad men worse,
Ay! blind them till they grope in open day,
And stumble into miserable graves.
Oh, it is piteous, for none will hear!
There is no hand to help, no heart to feel,
No tongue to plead for us in all your land.
But every hand aims death, and every heart.
Ulcered with hate, resents our presence here;
And every tongue cries for our children's land
To expiate their crime of being born.
Oh, we have ever yielded in the past,
But we shall yield no more! Those plains are ours!
Those forests are our birth-right and our home!
Let not the Long-Knife build one cabin there—
Or fire from it will spread to every roof,
To compass you, and light your souls to death!

HARRISON: Dreams he of closing up our empty plains?
Our mighty forests waiting for the axe?
Our mountain steeps engrailed with iron and gold?
There's no asylumed madness like to this!
Mankind shall have its wide possession here;
And these rough assets of a virgin world
Stand for its coming, and await its hand.
The poor of every land shall come to this,
Heart-full of sorrows, and shall lay them down.

LEFROY: *(springing to his feet)* The poor! What care your rich thieves for the poor?
Those graspers hate the poor, from whom they spring,
More deeply than they hate this injured race.
Much have they taken from it—let them now
Take this prediction, with the red man's curse!
The time will come when that dread power—the Poor—
Whom, in their greed and pride of wealth, they spurn—
Will rise on them, and tear them from their seats;
Drag all their vulgar splendours down, and pluck
Their shallow women from their lawless beds,
Yea, seize their puling and unhealthy babes.
And fling them as foul pavement to the streets.
In all the dreaming of the Universe
There is no darker vision of despairs!

FIRST OFFICER: What man is this? 'Tis not an Indian.

HARRISON: Madman, you rave!—you know not what you say.

TECUMSEH: Master of guile, this axe should speak for him!

Drawing his hatchet as if to hurl it at HARRISON.

SECOND OFFICER: This man means mischief! Quick!
Bring up the guard!

General HARRISON and officers draw their swords. The warriors spring to their feet and cluster about TECUMSEH, their eyes fixed intently upon HARRISON, who stands unmoved. TWANG and his friends disappear. The soldiers rush forward and take aim, but are ordered not to fire.

End of Act II.

ACT III

SCENE FIRST—VINCENNES. A COUNCIL CHAMBER IN GENERAL HARRISON'S HOUSE.

Enter HARRISON *and five councillors.*

HARRISON: Here are despatches from the President,
As well as letters from my trusted friends,
Whose tenor made me summon you to Council.

Places papers on table.

FIRST COUNCILLOR: Why break good news so gently? Is it true
War is declared 'gainst England?

HARRISON: Would it were!
That war is still deferred. Our news is draft,
And void of spirit, since New England turns
A fresh cheek to the slap of Britain's palm.
Great God! I am amazed at such supineness.
Our trade prohibited, our men impressed,
Our flag insulted—still her people bend,
Amidst the ticking of their wooden clocks.
Bemused o'er small inventions. Out upon't!
Such tame submission yokes not with my spirit,
And sends my southern blood into my cheeks,
As proxy for New England's sense of shame.

SECOND COUNCILLOR: We all see, save New England, what to do;
But she has eyes for her one interest—

A war might sink it. So the way to war
Puzzles imagining.

HARRISON: There is a way
Which lies athwart the President's command.
The reinforcements asked for from Monroe
Are here at last, but with this strict injunction,
They must not be employed save in defence,
Or in a forced attack.

Taking up a letter.

Now, here is news,
Fresh from the South, of bold Tecumseh's work:
The Creeks and Seminoles have conjoined.
Which means a general union of the tribes,
And ravage of our Southern settlements.
Tecumseh's master hand is seen in this,
And these fresh tidings tally with his threats
Before he left Vincennes.

THIRD COUNCILLOR: You had a close
Encounter with him here.

HARRISON: Not over close.
Nor dangerous—I saw he would not strike.
His thoughts outran his threats, and looked beyond
To wider fields and trials of our strength.

FOURTH COUNCILLOR: Our tree is now too bulky for his axe.

HARRISON: Don't underrate his power! But for our States
This man would found an empire to surpass
Old Mexico's renown, or rich Peru.
Allied with England, he is to be feared
More than all other men.

FIRST COUNCILLOR: You had some talk
In private, ere he vanished to the South?

HARRISON: Mere words, yet ominous. Could we restore
Our purchases, and make a treaty line,
All might be well; but who would stand to it?

SECOND COUNCILLOR: It is not to be thought of.

OTHER COUNCILLORS: No, no, no.

HARRISON: In further parley at the river's edge,
Scenting a coming war, he clapped his hands,
And said the English whooped his people on,
As if his braves were hounds to spring at us;
Compared our nation to a whelming flood.
And called his scheme a dam to keep it back—
Then proffered the old terms; whereat I urged
A peaceful mission to the President.
But, by apt questions, gleaning my opinion,
Ere I was ware, of such a bootless trip,
He drew his manly figure up, then smiled,
And said our President might drink his wine
In safety in his distant town, whilst we—
Over the mountains here—should fight it out;
Then entering his bark, well manned with braves,
Bade me let matters rest till he returned
From his far mission to the distant tribes,
Waved an adieu, and in a trice was gone.

SECOND COUNCILLOR: Your news is but an earnest of his work.

FOURTH COUNCILLOR: This Chief's despatch should be our own example.
Let matters rest, forsooth, till he can set
Our frontier in a blaze! Such cheap advice
Pulls with the President's, not mine.

HARRISON: Nor mine!
The sum of my advice is to attack
The Prophet ere Tecumseh can return.

FIFTH COUNCILLOR: But what about the breach of your instructions?

HARRISON: If we succeed we need not fear the breach—
In the same space we give and heal the wound.

Enter a messenger, who hands letters to HARRISON.

Thank you, Missouri and good Illinois—
Your governors are built of western clay.
Howard and Edwards both incline with me,
And urge attack upon the Prophet's force.

This is the nucleus of Tecumseh's strength—
His bold scheme's very heart. Let's cut it out!

FIRST COUNCILLOR: Yes! yes! and every other part will fail.

SECOND COUNCILLOR: Let us prepare to go at once!

THIRD COUNCILLOR: Agreed.

FOURTH COUNCILLOR: I vote for it.

FIFTH COUNCILLOR: But should the Prophet win?

FOURTH COUNCILLOR: Why, then, the Prophet, not Tecumseh, kills us—
Which has the keener axe?

FIRST COUNCILLOR: Breech-clouted dogs!
Let us attack them, and, with thongs of fire,
Whip their red bodies to a deeper red.

HARRISON: This feeling bodes success, and with success
Comes war with England; for a well-won fight
Will rouse a martial spirit in the land
To emulate our deeds on higher ground.
Now hasten to your duties and prepare!
Bronzed autumn comes, when copper-coloured oaks
Drop miserly their stiff leaves to the earth;
And ere the winter's snow doth silver them,
Our triumph must be wrought

Exeunt.

SCENE SECOND—TECUMSEH'S CABIN IN THE PROPHET'S TOWN.

Enter IENA *and* MAMATEE, *agitated.*

IENA: My heart is sad, and I am faint with fear.
My friend, my more than mother, go again—
Plead with the Prophet for a single day!
Perchance within his gloomy heart will stir
Some sudden pulse of pity for a girl.

MAMATEE: Alas, my Iena, it is in vain!
He swore by Manitou this very morn.
That thou shouldst wed the chief, Tarhay, tonight.

IENA: Nay, try once more, oh, Mamatee, once more!
I had a dream, and heard the gusty breeze
Hurtle from out a sea of hissing pines.
Then dwindle into voices, faint and sweet.
Which cried—we come! It was my love and yours I
They spoke to me—I know that they are near,
And waft their love to us upon the wind.

MAMATEE: Some dreams are merely fancies in our sleep;
I'll make another trial, but I feel
Your only safety is in instant flight.

IENA: Flight! Where and how—beset by enemies?
My fear sits like the partridge in the tree,
And cannot fly whilst these dogs bark at me.

Exeunt.

SCENE THIRD—AN ELEVATED PLATEAU, DOTTED WITH HEAVY OAKS, WEST OF THE PROPHET'S TOWN.

Enter three of HARRISON's staff officers.

FIRST OFFICER: Well, here's the end of all our northward marching!

SECOND OFFICER: A peaceful end, if we can trust those chiefs
Who parleyed with us lately.

THIRD OFFICER: Yes, for if
They mean to fight, why point us to a spot
At once so strong and pleasant for our camp?

FIRST OFFICER: Report it so unto our General.

Exit THIRD OFFICER.

'Tis worth our long march through the forest wild
To view these silent plains! The Prophet's town,
Sequestered yonder like a hermitage.
Disturbs not cither's vast of solitude.
But rather gives, like graveyard visitors.
To deepest loneliness a deeper awe.

Re-enter THIRD OFFICER.

THIRD OFFICER: I need not go, for Harrison is here.

Enter HARRISON, *his force following.*

FIRST OFFICER: Methinks you like the place; some thanks we owe
Unto the Prophet's chiefs for good advice.

HARRISON: *(looking around keenly)* These noble oaks, the streamlet to our rear,
This rank wild grass—wood, water, and soft beds!
The soldier's luxuries are here together.

FIRST OFFICER: Note, too, the place overlooks the springy plain
Which lies betwixt us and the Prophet's town.
I think, sir, 'tis a very fitting place.

HARRISON: A fitting place if white men were our foes;
But to the red it gives a clear advantage.
Sleep like the weasel here, if you are wise!

FIRST OFFICER: Why, sir, their chiefs, so menacing at first,
Became quite friendly at the last. They fear
A battle, and will treat on any terms.
The Prophet's tide of strength will ebb away,
And leave his stranded bark upon the mire.

HARRISON: 'Tis the mixed craft of old dissembling Nature!
If I could look upon her smallest web.
And see in it but crossed and harmless hairs.
Then might I trust the Prophet's knotted seine.
I did not like the manner of those chiefs
Who spoke so fairly. What but highest greatness
Plucks hatred from its seat, and in its stead
Plants friendship in an instant? This our camp
Is badly placed; each coulee and ravine
Is dangerous cover for approach by night;
And all the circuit of the spongy plain
A treacherous bog to mire our cavalry.
They who directed us so warmly here
Had other than our comfort in their eye.

SECOND OFFICER: Fear you a night-attack, sir?

HARRISON: Fear it! No!
I but anticipate, and shall prepare.
'Tis sunset, and too late for better choice,

Else were the Prophet welcome to his ground.
Pitch tents and draw our baggage to the centre;
Girdle the camp with lynx-eyed sentinels;
Detail strong guards of choice and wakeful men
As pickets in advance of all our lines;
Place mounted riflemen on both our flanks;
Our cavalry take post in front and rear,
But still within the lines of infantry,
Which, struck at any point, must hold the ground
Until relieved. Cover your rifle pans—
The thick clouds threaten rain. I look to you
To fill these simple orders to the letter.
But stay! Let all our campfires burn
Till, if attacked, we form—then drown them out.
The darkness falls—make disposition straight;
Then, all who can, to sleep upon their arms.
I fear me, ere night yields to morning pale.
The warriors' yell will sound our wild reveille.

Exeunt.

SCENE FOURTH—TECUMSEH'S CABIN.

Enter IENA.

IENA: 'Tis night, and Mamatee is absent still!
Why should this sorrow weigh upon my heart,
And other lonely things on earth have rest?
Oh, could I be with them! The lily shone
All day upon the stream, and now it sleeps
Under the wave in peace—in cradle soft
Which sorrow soon may fashion for my grave.
Ye shadows which do creep into my thoughts—
Ye curtains of despair! what is my fault,
That ye should hide the happy earth from me?
Once I had joy of it, when tender Spring,
Mother of beauty, hid me in her leaves;
When Summer led me by the shores of song
And forests and far-sounding cataracts
Melted my soul with music. I have heard

The rough chill harpings of dismantled woods.
When Fall had stripped them, and have felt a joy
Deeper than ear could lend unto the heart;
And when the Winter from his mountains wild
Looked down on death, and, in the frosty sky,
The very stars seemed hung with icicles,
Then came a sense of beauty calm and cold,
That weaned me from myself, yet knit me still
With kindred bonds to Nature. All is past,
And he who won from me such love for him,
And he, my valiant uncle and my friend,
Come not to lift the cloud that drapes my soul.
And shield me from the fiendish Prophet's power.

Enter MAMATEE.

Give me his answer in his very words!

MAMATEE: There is a black storm raging in his mind—
His eye darts lightning like the angry cloud
Which hangs in woven darkness o'er the earth.
Brief is his answer—you must go to him.
The Long-Knife's campfires gleam among the oaks
Which dot yon western hill. A thousand men
Are sleeping there cajoled to fatal dreams
By promises the Prophet breaks tonight.
Hark! 'tis the war-song!

IENA: Dares the Prophet now.
Betray Tecumseh's trust, and break his faith?

MAMATEE: He dares do anything will feed ambition.
His dancing braves are frenzied by his tongue,
Which prophesies revenge and victory.
Before the break of day he will surprise
The Long-Knife's camp, and hang our people's fate
Upon a single onset.

IENA: Should he fail?

MAMATEE: Then all will fail;—Tecumseh's scheme will fail.

IENA: It shall not! Let us go to him at once!

MAMATEE: And risk your life?

IENA: Risk hovers everywhere
When night and man combine for darksome deeds.
I'll go to him, and argue on my knees—
Yea, yield my hand—would I could give my heart!
To stay his purpose and this act of ruin.

MAMATEE: He is not in the mood for argument.
Rash girl! they die who would oppose him now.

IENA: Such death were sweet as life—I go! But, first—
Great Spirit! I commit my soul to Thee.

Kneels.

SCENE FIFTH—AN OPEN SPACE IN THE FOREST NEAR THE PROPHET'S TOWN. A FIRE OF BILLETS BURNING. WAR-CRIES ARE HEARD FROM THE TOWN.

Enter the PROPHET.

PROPHET: My spells do work apace! Shout yourselves hoarse,
Ye howling ministers by whom I climb!
For this I've wrought until my weary tongue,
Blistered with incantation, flags in speech,
And half declines its office. Every brave.
Inflamed by charms and oracles, is now
A vengeful serpent, who will glide ere morn
To sting the Long-Knife's sleeping camp to death.
Why should I hesitate? My promises!
My duty to Tecumseh! What are these
Compared with duty here? Where I perceive
A near advantage, there my duty lies;
Consideration strong which over weighs
All other reason. Here is Harrison—
Trepanned to dangerous lodgment for the night—
Each deep ravine which grooves the prairie's breast
A channel of approach; each winding creek
A screen for creeping death. Revenge is sick
To think of such advantage flung aside.
For what? To let Tecumseh's greatness grow,

Who gathers his rich harvest of renown
Out of the very fields that I have sown!
By Manitou, I will endure no more!
Nor, in the rising flood of our affairs,
Fish like an osprey for this eagle longer.
But, soft!
It is the midnight hour when comes
Tarhay to claim his bride, *(calls)* Tarhay! Tarhay!

Enter TARHAY *with several braves.*

TARHAY: Tarhay is here!

PROPHET: The Long-Knives die tonight.
The spirits which do minister to me
Have breathed this utterance within my ear.
You know my sacred office cuts me off
From the immediate leadership in fight.
My nobler work is in the spirit-world,
And thence come promises which make us strong.
Near to the foe I'll keep the Magic Bowl,
Whilst you, Tarhay, shall lead our warriors on.

TARHAY: I'll lead them; they are wild with eagerness.
But fill my cold and empty cabin first
With light and heat! You know I love your niece.
And have the promise of her hand tonight.

PROPHET: She shall be yours!

(to the braves) Go bring her here at once—
But, look! Fulfillment of my promise comes
In her own person.

Enter IENA *and* MAMATEE.

Welcome, my sweet niece!
You have forestalled my message by these braves,
And come unbidden to your wedding place.

IENA: Uncle! you know my heart is far away—

PROPHET: But still your hand is here! this little hand!

Pulling her forward.

IENA: Dare you enforce a weak and helpless girl,
Who thought to move you by her misery?
Stand back! I have a message for you too.
What means the war-like song, the dance of braves,
And bustle in our town?

PROPHET: It means that we
Attack the foe tonight.

IENA: And risk our all?
O that Tecumseh knew! his soul would rush
In arms to intercept you. What! break faith,
And on the hazard of a doubtful strife
Stake his great enterprise and all our lives!
The dying curses of a ruined race
Will wither up your wicked heart for this!

PROPHET: False girl! your heart is with our foes;
Your hand I mean to turn to better use.

IENA: Oh, could it turn you from your mad intent
How freely would I give it! Drop this scheme,
Dismiss your frenzied warriors to their beds;
And, if contented with my hand, Tarhay
Can have it here.

TARHAY: I love you, Iena!

IENA: Then must you love what I do! Love our race!
'Tis this love nerves Tecumseh to unite
Its scattered tribes—his fruit of noble toil,
Which you would snatch unripened from his hand
And feed to sour ambition. Touch it not—
Oh, touch it not, Tarhay! and though my heart
Breaks for it, I am yours.

PROPHET: His anyway.
Or I am not the Prophet!

TARHAY: For my part
I have no leaning to this rash attempt,
Since Iena consents to be my wife.

PROPHET: Shall I be thwarted by a yearning fool!
(aside) This soft, sleek girl, to outward seeming good,

I know to be a very fiend beneath—
Whose sly affections centre on herself,
And feed the gliding snake within her heart.

TARHAY: I cannot think her so—

MAMATEE: She is not so!
There is the snake that creeps among our race,
Whose venomed fangs would bite into our lives,
And poison all our hopes.

PROPHET: She is the head—
The very neck of danger to me here,
Which I must break at once! *(aside)* Tarhay—attend!
I can see dreadful visions in the air;
I can dream awful dreams of life and fate;
I can bring darkness on the heavy earth;
I can fetch shadows from our fathers' graves.
And spectres from the sepulchres of hell.
Who dares dispute with me disputes with death!
Dost hear, Tarhay?

TARHAY and braves cower before the PROPHET.

TARHAY: I hear, and will obey.
Spare me! Spare me!

PROPHET: As for this foolish girl,
The hand she offers you on one condition,
I give to you upon a better one;
And, since she has no mind to give her heart—
Which, rest assured, is in her body still—
There,—take it at my hands!

Flings IENA violently toward TARHAY, into whose arms she falls, fainting, and is then borne away by MAMATEE.

(to TARHAY) Go bring the braves to view the Mystic Torch
And belt of Sacred Beans grown from my flesh—
One touch of it makes them invulnerable—
Then creep, like stealthy panthers, on the foe!

Exeunt.

SCENE SIXTH—MORNING. THE FIELD OF TIPPECANOE AFTER THE BATTLE. THE GROUND STREWN WITH DEAD SOLDIERS AND WARRIORS.

Enter HARRISON, the officers and soldiers, and BARRON.

HARRISON: A costly triumph, reckoned by our slain!
Look how some lie still clenched with savages
In all-embracing death, their bloody hands
Glued in each other's hair! Make burial straight
Of all alike in deep and common graves:
Their quarrel now is ended.

FIRST OFFICER: I have heard
The red man fears our steel—'twas not so here!
From the first shots, which drove our pickets in,
Till daylight dawned, they rushed upon our lines,
And flung themselves upon our bayonet points
In frenzied recklessness of bravery.

BARRON: They trusted in the Prophet's rites and spells,
Which promised them immunity from death.
All night he sat on yon safe eminence,
Howling his songs of war and mystery,
Then fled, at dawn, in fear of his own braves.

Enter an AIDE.

HARRISON: What tidings bring you from the Prophet's town?

AIDE: The wretched women with their children flee
To distant forests for concealment. In
Their village is no living thing save mice
Which scampered as we ope'd each cabin door.
Their pots still simmered on the vacant hearths,
Standing in dusty silence and desertion.
Naught else we saw, save that their granaries
Were crammed with needful corn.

HARRISON: Go bring it all—
Then burn their village down!

Exit AIDE.

SECOND OFFICER: This victory
Will shake Tecumseh's project to the base.
Were I the Prophet I should drown myself
Rather than meet him.

BARRON: We have news of him—
Our scouts report him near in heavy force.

HARRISON: 'Twill melt, or draw across the British line,
And wait for war. But double the night watch,
Lest he should strike, and give an instant care
To all our wounded men: tomorrow's sun
Must light us on our backward march for home.
Thence Rumour's tongue will spread so proud a story
New England will grow envious of our glory;
And, greedy for renown so long abhorred.
Will on old England draw the tardy sword!

Exeunt.

SCENE SEVENTH—THE RUINS OF THE PROPHET'S TOWN.

Enter the PROPHET, *who gloomily surveys the place.*

PROPHET: Our people scattered, and our town in ashes!
To think these hands could work such madness here—
This envious head devise this misery!
Tecumseh, had not my ambition drawn
Such sharp and fell destruction on our race.
You might have smiled at me! for I have matched
My cunning 'gainst your wisdom, and have dragged
Myself and all into a sea of ruin.

Enter TECUMSEH.

TECUMSEH: Devil! I have discovered you at last!
You sum of treacheries, whose wolfish fangs
Have torn our people's flesh—you shall not live!

The PROPHET *retreats, facing and followed by* TECUMSEH.

PROPHET: Nay—strike me not! I can explain it all!
It was a woman touched the Magic Bowl,
And broke the brooding spell.

TECUMSEH: Impostor! Slave!
Why should I spare you?

Lifts his hand as if to strike.

PROPHET: Stay, stay, touch me not!
One mother bore us in the self-same hour.

TECUMSEH: Then good and evil came to light together.
Go to the corn-dance, change your name to villain!
Away! Your presence tempts my soul to mischief.

Exit the PROPHET.

Would that I were a woman, and could weep,
And slake hot rage with tears! O spiteful fortune.
To lure me to the limit of my dreams.
Then turn and crowd the ruin of my toil
Into the narrow compass of a night.
My brother's deep disgrace—myself the scorn
Of envious harriers and thieves of fame.
Oh, I could bear it all! But to behold
Our ruined people hunted to their graves—
To see the Long-Knife triumph in their shame—
This is the burning shaft, the poisoned wound
That rankles in my soul! But why despair?
All is not lost—the English are our friends.
My spirit rises—Manhood, bear me up!
I'll haste to Maiden, join my force to theirs,
And fall with double fury on our foes.
Farewell, ye plains and forests, but rejoice!
Ye yet shall echo to Tecumseh's voice.

Enter LEFROY.

LEFROY: What tidings have you gleaned of Iena?

TECUMSEH: My brother meant to wed her to Tarhay—
The chief who led his warriors to ruin;
But, in the gloom and tumult of the night,
She fled into the forest all alone!

LEFROY: Alone! In the wide forest all alone!
Angels are with her now, for she is dead.

TECUMSEH: You know her to be skilful with the bow.
'Tis certain she would strike for some great lake—
Erie or Michigan. At the Detroit
Are people of our nation, and perchance
She fled for shelter there. I go at once
To join the British force.

Exit TECUMSEH.

LEFROY: But yesterday
I climbed to Heaven upon the shining stairs
Of love and hope, and here am quite cast down.
My little flower amidst a weedy world.
Where art thou now? In deepest forest shade?
Or onward, where the sumac stands arrayed
In autumn splendour, its alluring form
Fruited, yet odious with the hidden worm?
Or, farther, by some still sequestered lake.
Loon-haunted, where the sinewy panthers slake
Their noon-day thirst, and never voice is heard.
Joyous of singing waters, breeze or bird,
Save their wild wailings. *(A halloo without.)* 'Tis Tecumseh calls!
Oh, Iena! If dead, where'er thou art—
Thy saddest grave will be this ruined heart!

Exit.

End of Act III.

ACT IV

Enter CHORUS.

CHORUS: War is declared, unnatural and wild,
By Revolution's calculating sons!
So leave the home of mercenary minds,
And wing with me, in your uplifted thoughts.
Away to our unyielding Canada!
There to behold the Genius of the Land,
Beneath her singing pine and sugared tree,
Companioned with the lion. Loyalty.

SCENE FIRST—A ROOM IN FORT GEORGE.

Enter General BROCK *reading a dispatch from Montreal.*

BROCK: Prudent and politic Sir George Prevost!
Hull's threatened ravage of our western coast
Hath more breviloquence than your despatch.
Storms are not stilled by reasoning with air,
Nor fires quenched by a syrup of sweet words.
So to the wars. Diplomacy, for now
Our trust is in our arms and arguments
Delivered only from the cannon's mouth!

Rings. Enter an ORDERLY.

ORDERLY: Your Exc'llency?

BROCK: Bid Colonel Proctor come!

Exit ORDERLY.

Now might the head of grey Experience
Shake o'er the problems that surround us here.
I am no stranger to the brunt of war,
But all the odds so lean against our side
That valour's self might tremble for the issue.
Could England stretch its full assisting hand
Then might I smile though velvet-footed Time
Struck all his claws at once into our flesh;
But England, noble England, fights for life,
Couching the knightly lance for liberty
'Gainst a new dragon that a-frights the world.
And, now, how many noisome elements
Would plant their greed athwart this country's good!
How many demagogues bewray its cause!
How many aliens urge it to surrender!
Our present good must match their present ill.
And, on our frontiers, boldest deeds in war
Dismay the foe, and strip the loins of faction.

Enter Colonel PROCTOR.

Time waits not our conveniency; I trust
Your preparations have no further needs.

PROCTOR: All is in readiness, and I can leave
For Amherstburg at once.

BROCK: Then tarry not.
For time is precious to us now as powder.
You understand my wishes and commands?

PROCTOR: I know them and shall match them with obedience.

BROCK: Rest not within the limit of instructions
If you can better them, for they should bind
The feeble only; able men enlarge
And shape them to their needs. Much must be done
That lies in your discretion. At Detroit
Hull vaunts his strength, and meditates invasion,
And loyalty, unarmed, defenceless, bare.

May let this boaster light upon our shores
Without one manly motion of resistance.
So whilst I open Parliament at York,
Close it again, and knit our volunteers,
Be yours the task to head invasion off.
Act boldly, but discreetly, and so draw
Our interest to the balance, that affairs
May hang in something like an even scale,
Till I can join you with a fitting force.
And batter this old Hull until he sinks.
So fare-you-well—success attend your mission!

PROCTOR: Farewell, sir! I shall do my best in this.
And put my judgment to a prudent use
In furtherance of all.

Exit PROCTOR.

BROCK: Prudent he will be—'tis a vice in him.
For in the qualities of every mind
There's one o'ergrows, and prudence in this man
Tops all the rest. 'Twill suit our present needs.
But, boldness, go with me! for, if I know
My nature well, I shall do something soon
Whose consequence will make the nation cheer,
Or hiss me to my grave.

Re-enter ORDERLY.

ORDERLY: Your Excellency,
Some settlers wait without.

BROCK: Whence do they come?

Enter Colonel MACDONELL.

ORDERLY: From the raw clearings of Lake Erie, sir.

BROCK: Go bring them here at once.

Exit ORDERLY.

The very men
Who meanly shirk their service to the Crown!
A breach of duty to be remedied;
For disaffection like an ulcer spreads

Until the caustic ointment of the law,
Sternly applied, eats up and stays corruption.

Enter deputation of yankee settlers.

Good morrow, worthy friends; I trust you bear
Good hopes in loyal hearts for Canada.

FIRST SETTLER: That kind o' crop's a failure in our county.
General, we came to talk about this war
With the United States. It ain't quite fair
To call out settlers from the other side.

BROCK: From it yet on it too! Why came you thence?
Is land so scarce in the United States?
Are there no empty townships, wilds or wastes
In all their borders but you must encroach
On ours? And, being here, how dare you make
Your dwelling-places harbours of sedition,
And furrow British soil with alien ploughs
To feed our enemies? There is not scope,
Not room enough in all this wilderness
For men so base.

SECOND SETTLER: Why, General, we thought
You wanted settlers here.

BROCK: Settlers indeed!
But with the soldier's courage to defend
The land of their adoption. This attack
On Canada is foul and unprovoked;
The hearts are vile, the hands are traitorous.
That will not help to hurl invasion back.
Beware the lariat of the law! 'Tis thrown
With aim so true in Canada it brings
Sedition to the ground at every cast.

FIRST SETTLER: Well, General, we're not your British sort.
But if we were we know that Canada
Is naught compared with the United States.
We have no faith in her, but much in them.

BROCK: You have no faith! Then take a creed from me!
For I believe in Britain's Empire, and
In Canada, its true and loyal son.

Who yet shall rise to greatness, and shall stand
At England's shoulder helping her to guard
True liberty throughout a faithless world.
Here is a creed for arsenals and camps,
For hearts and heads that seek their country's good;
So, go at once, and meditate on it!
I have no time to parley with you now—
But think on this as well! that traitors, spies,
And aliens who refuse to take up arms,
Forfeit their holdings, and must leave this land,
Or dangle nearer Heaven than they wish.
So to your homes, and ponder your condition.

Exeunt settlers ruefully.

This foreign element will hamper us.
Its alien spirit ever longs for change.
And union with the States.

MACDONELL: O fear it not,
Nor magnify the girth of noisy men!
Their name is faction, and their numbers few.
While everywhere encompassing them stands
The silent element that doth! not change;
That points with steady finger to the Crown—
True as the needle to the viewless pole.
And stable as its star!

BROCK: I know it well.
And trust to it alone for earnestness.
Accordant counsels, loyalty and faith.
But give me these—and let the Yankees come!
With our poor handful of inhabitants
We can defend our forest wilderness,
And spurn the bold invader from our shores.

Re-enter ORDERLY.

ORDERLY: Your boat is ready, sir!

BROCK: Man it at once—
I shall forthwith to York.

Exeunt.

SCENE SECOND—YORK, THE CAPITAL OF UPPER CANADA. THE SPACE IN FRONT OF OLD GOVERNMENT HOUSE.

Enter two U.E. loyalists, separately.

FIRST U.E. LOYALIST: Well met, my friend! A stirrer like myself.

SECOND U.E. LOYALIST: Yes, affairs make me so. Such stirring times
Since Brock returned and opened Parliament!
Read you his speech?

FIRST U.E. LOYALIST: That from the Throne?

SECOND U.E. LOYALIST: Ay, that!

FIRST U.E. LOYALIST: You need not ask, since 'tis on every tongue,
Unstaled by repetition. I affirm
Words never showered upon more fruitful soil
To nourish valour's growth.

SECOND U.E. LOYALIST: That final phrase—
Oh, it struck home: a sentence to be framed
And hung in every honourable heart
For daily meditation.

"We are engaged in an awful and eventful contest. By unanimity and despatch in our councils, and by vigour in our operations, we may teach the enemy this lesson, that a country defended by free men, enthusiastically devoted to the cause of their king and constitution, can never be conquered."

FIRST U.E. LOYALIST: That reaches far; a text to fortify
Imperial doctrine and Canadian rights.
Sedition skulks, and feels its blood a-cold,
Since first it fell upon the public ear.

SECOND U.E. LOYALIST: There is a magic in this soldier's tongue.
Oh, language is a common instrument;
But when a master touches it—what sounds!

FIRST U.E. LOYALIST: What sounds indeed! But Brock can use his sword
Still better than his tongue. Our state affairs,
Conned and digested by his eager mind,
Draw into form, and even now his voice
Cries, Forward! To the Front!

SECOND U.E. LOYALIST: Look—here he comes!

FIRST U.E. LOYALIST: There's matter in the wind; let's draw-a-near.

Enter General BROCK, *accompanied by* MACDONELL, NICHOL, ROBINSON, *and other Canadian officers and friends conversing.*

BROCK: 'Tis true our Province faces heavy odds:
Of regulars but fifteen hundred men
To guard a frontier of a thousand miles;
Of volunteers what aidance we can draw
From seventy thousand widely scattered souls.
A meagre showing 'gainst the enemy's
If numbers be the test. But odds lie not
In numbers only, but in spirit too—
Witness the might of England's little isle!
And what made England great will keep her so—
The free soul and the valour of her sons;
And what exalts her will sustain you now
If you contain her courage and her faith.
So not the odds so much are to be feared
As private disaffection, treachery—
Those openers of the door to enemies—
And the poor crouching spirit that gives way
Ere it is forced to yield.

ROBINSON: No fear of that!

BROCK: I trust there is not: yet I speak of it
As what is to be feared more than the odds.
For like to forests are communities—
Fair at a distance, entering you find
The rubbish and the underbrush of states.
'Tis ever the mean soul that counts the odds,
And, where you find this spirit, pluck it up—
'Tis full of mischief.

MACDONELL: It is almost dead.
England's vast war, our weakness, and the eagle
Whetting his beak at Sandwich, with one claw
Already in our side, put thought to steep
In cold conjecture for a time, and gave
A text to alien tongues. But, since you came,

Depression turns to smiling, and men see
That dangers well opposed may be subdued
Which, shunned, would overwhelm us.

BROCK: Hold to this!
For since the storm has struck us we must face it.
What is our present count of volunteers?

NICHOL: More than you called for have assembled, sir—
The flower of York and Lincoln.

BROCK: Some will go
To guard our frontier at Niagara,
Which must be strengthened even at the cost
Of York itself. The rest to the Detroit,
Where, with Tecumseh's force, our regulars.
And Kent and Essex loyal volunteers,
We'll give this Hull a taste of steel so cold
His teeth will chatter at it, and his scheme
Of easy conquest vanish into air.

Enter a company of militia with their officers, unarmed. They salute, march across the stage, and make their exit.

What men are those? Their faces are familiar.

ROBINSON: Some farmers whom you furloughed at Fort George,
To tend their fields, which still they leave half reaped
To meet invasion.

BROCK: I remember it!
The jarring needs of harvest-time and war,
Twixt whose necessities grave hazards lay.

ROBINSON: They only thought to save their children's bread,
And then return to battle with light hearts.
For, though their hard necessities over-poised
Their duty for the moment, they are men
Who draw their pith from loyal roots, their sires.
Dug up by revolution, and cast out
To hovel in the bitter wilderness.
And wring, with many a tussle, from the wolf
Those very fields which cry for harvesters.

BROCK: Oh, I observed them closely at Fort George—
Red-hot for action in their summer-sleeves.
And others drilling in their naked feet—
Our poor equipment (which disgraced us there)
Too scanty to go round. See they get arms,
An ample outfit and good quarters too.

NICHOL: They shall be well provided for in all.

Enter Colonels BABY[1] and ELLIOTT.

BROCK: Good morning both; what news from home, Baby?

BABY: None, none, your Excellency—whereat we fear
This Hull is in our rear at Amherstburg.

BROCK: Not yet; what I unsealed last night reports
Tecumseh to have foiled the enemy
In two encounters at the Canard bridge.
A noble fellow, as I hear, humane.
Lofty and bold, and rooted in our cause.

BABY: I know him well; a chief of matchless force.
If Mackinaw should fall—that triple key
To inland seas and teeming wilderness—
The bravest in the West will flock to him.

BROCK: 'Twere well he had an inkling of affairs.
My letter says he chafes at my delay—
Not mine, but thine, thou dull and fatuous House—
Which, in a period that whips delay,
When men should spur themselves and flash in action,
Let'st idly leak the unpurchasable hours
From our scant measure of most precious time!

BABY: 'Tis true, your Excellency, some cankered minds
Have been a daily hindrance in our House.
No measure so essential, bill so fair,
But they would foul it by some cunning clause,
Wrenching the needed statute from its aim
By sly injection of their false opinion.
But this you cannot charge to us whose hearts
Are faithful to our trust; nor yet delay;

1 Pronounced Baw-bée.

For, Excellency, you hurry on so fast
That other men wheeze after, out of breath,
And haste itself, disparaged, lags behind.

BROCK: Friends, pardon me, you stand not in reproof.
But haste, the evil of the age in peace,
Is war's auxiliary, confederate
With Time himself in urgent great affairs.
So must we match it with the flying hours!
I shall prorogue this tardy Parliament,
And promptly head our forces for Detroit.
Meanwhile, I wish you, in advance of us.
To speed unto your homes. Spread everywhere
Throughout the West broad tidings of our coming,
Which, by the counter currents of reaction.
Will tell against our foes and for our friends.
As for the rest, such loyal men as you
Need not our counsel; so, good journey both!

BABY: We shall not spare our transport or ourselves.

Enter a travel-stained MESSENGER.

ELLIOTT: Goodbye.

BABY: Tarry a moment, Elliott!
Here comes a messenger—let's have his news.

MESSENGER: It is his Excellency whom I seek.
I come, sir, with despatches from the West.

BROCK: Tidings, I trust, to strengthen all our hopes.

MESSENGER: News of grave interest, this not the worst.

Handing a letter to General BROCK.

BROCK: No, by my soul, for Mackinaw is ours!
That vaunted fort, whose gallant capture frees
Our red allies. This is important news!
What of Detroit?

MESSENGER: Things vary little there.
Hull's soldiers scour our helpless settlements.
Our aliens join them, but the loyal mass—
Sullen, yet overawed—longs for relief.

BROCK: I hope to better this anon. You, sirs,
(to his aides) Come with me; here is matter to despatch
At once to Montreal. *(to BABY and ELLIOTT)* Farewell, my friends.

BABY: We feel now what will follow this, farewell!

Exeunt BABY, ELLIOTT, and MESSENGER.

BROCK: Now, gentlemen, prepare against our needs,
That no neglect may check us at the start.
Or mar our swift advance. And, for our cause.
As we believe it just in sight of God,
So should it triumph in the sight of man.
Whose generous temper, at the first, assigns
Right to the weaker side, yet coldly draws
Damning conclusions from its failure. Now
Betake you to your tasks with double zeal;
And, meanwhile, let our joyful tidings spread!

Exeunt.

SCENE THIRD—THE SAME.

Enter two old men of York, separately.

FIRST OLD MAN: Good morrow, friend! a fair and fitting time
To take our airing, and to say farewell.
'Tis here, I think, we bid our friends God-speed,
A waftage, peradventure, to their graves.

SECOND OLD MAN: 'Tis a good cause they die for, if they fall.
By this grey pate, if I were young again,
I would no better journey. Young again!
This hubbub sets old pulses on the bound
As I were in my teens.

Enter a CITIZEN.

What news afoot?

CITIZEN: Why everyone's afoot and coming here.
York's citizens are turned to warriors,
And gentle hearts beat high for Canada!
For, as you pass, on every hand you see.
Through the neglected openings of each house—

Through doorways, windows—our Canadian maids
Strained by their parting lovers to their breasts;
And loyal matrons busy round their lords,
Buckling their arms on, or, with tearful eyes,
Kissing them to the war!

FIRST OLD MAN: The volunteers
Will pass this way?

CITIZEN: Yes, to the beach, and there
Embark for Burlington, whence they will march
To Long Point, taking open boats again
To plough the shallow Erie's treacherous flood.
Such leaky craft as farmers market with:
Rare bottoms, one sou-wester-driven wave
Would heave against Lake Erie's wall of shore.
And dash to fragments. 'Tis an awful hazard—
A danger which in apprehension lies.
Yet palpable unto the spirit's touch
As earth to finger.

FIRST OLD MAN: Let us hope a calm
Mav lull this fretful and ill-tempered lake
Whilst they ascend.

Military music is heard.

CITIZEN: Hark! here our soldiers come.

Enter General BROCK, with his aides, MACDONELL and GLEGG, NICHOL, and other officers, followed by the volunteers in companies. A concourse of citizens.

MACDONELL: Our fellows show the mark of training, sir,
And many, well-in-hand, yet full of fire,
Are burning for distinction.

BROCK: This is good:
Love of distinction is the fruitful soil
From which brave actions spring; and, superposed
On love of country, these strike deeper root,
And grow to greater greatness. Cry a halt—
A word here—then away!

Flourish. The volunteers halt, form line, and order arms.

Ye men of Canada!
Subjects with me of that Imperial Power
Whose liberties are marching round the earth:
I need not urge you now to follow me,
Though what befalls will try your stubborn faith
In the fierce fire and crucible of war.
I need not urge you, who have heard the voice
Of loyalty, and answered to its call.
Who has not read the insults of the foe—
The manifesto of his purposed crimes?
That foe, whose poison-plant, false liberty.
Runs o'er his body politic and kills
Whilst seeming to adorn it, fronts us now!
Threats our poor Province to annihilate.
And should he find the red men by our side—
Poor injured souls, who but defend their own—
Calls black Extermination from its hell
To stalk abroad, and stench your land with slaughter.
These are our weighty arguments for war.
Wherein armed Justice will enclasp her sword.
And sheath it in her bitter adversary;
Wherein we'll turn our bayonet points to pens.
And write in blood:—*Here lies the poor invader*;
Or be ourselves struck down by hailing death;
Made stepping stones for foes to walk upon—
The lifeless gangways to our country's ruin.
For now we look not with the eye of fear;
We reck not if this strange mechanic frame
Stop in an instant in the shock of war.
Our death may build into our country's life,
And failing this, 'twere better still to die
Than live the breathing spoils of infamy.
Then forward for our cause and Canada!
Forward for Britain's Empire—peerless arch
Of Freedom's raising, whose majestic span
Is axis to the world! On, on, my friends!
The task our country sets must we perform—
Wring peace from war, or perish in its storm!

Excitement and leave-taking. The volunteers break into column and sing:

"O hark to the voice from the lips of the free!
O hark to the cry from the lakes to the sea!
Arm! arm! the invader is wasting our coasts,
And tainting the air of our land with his hosts.
Arise! then, arise! let us rally and form,
And rush like the torrent, and sweep like the storm.
On the foes of our King, of our country adored,
Of the flag that was lost, but in exile restored!

And whose was the flag? and whose was the soil?
And whose was the exile, the suffering, the toil?
Our Fathers'! who carved in the forest a name.
And left us rich heirs of their freedom and fame.
Oh, dear to our hearts is that flag, and the land
Our Fathers bequeathed—'tis the work of their hand!
And the soil they redeemed from the woods with renown
The might of their sons will defend for the Crown!

Our hearts are as one, and our spirits are free.
From clime unto clime, and from sea unto sea!
And chaos may come to the States that annoy,
But our Empire united what foe can destroy?
Then away! to the front! march! comrades away!
In the lists of each hour crowd the work of a day!
We will follow our leader to fields far and nigh,
And for Canada fight, and for Canada die!"

Exeunt with military music.

SCENE FOURTH—FORT DETROIT. THE AMERICAN CAMP.

Enter General HULL, *Colonel* CASS, *and other officers.*

CASS: Come, General, we must insist on reasons!
Your order to withdraw from Canada
Will blow to mutiny, and put to shame
That proclamation which I wrote for you.
Wherein 'tis proudly said, "We are prepared
To look down opposition, our strong force
But vanguard of a mightier still to come"

And men have been attracted to our cause
Who now will curse us for this breach of faith.
Consider, sir, again!

HULL: I am not bound
To tack my reasons to my orders; this
Is my full warrant and authority—

Pointing to his instructions.

Yet, I have ample grounds for what I do.

CASS: What are they, then?

HULL: First, that this proclamation
Meets not with due response, wins to our side
The thief and refugee, not honest men.
These plainly rally round their government.

FIRST OFFICER: Why, yes; there's something lacking in this people,
If we must conquer them to set them free.

HULL: Ay, and our large force must be larger still
If we would change these Provinces to States.
Then, Colonel Proctor's intercepted letter—
Bidding the captor of Fort Mackinaw
Send but five thousand warriors from the West,
Which, be it artifice or not, yet points
To great and serious danger. Add to this
Brock's rumoured coming with his volunteers.
All burning to avenge their fathers' wrongs.
And our great foe, Tecumseh, fired o'er his;
These are the reasons; grave enough, I think,
Which urge me to withdraw from Canada,
And wait for further force; so, go at once.
And help our soldiers to recross the river.

CASS: But I see

HULL: No "buts"! You have my orders.

CASS: No solid reason here, naught but a group
Of flimsy apprehensions

HULL: Go at once!
Who kicks at judgment, lacks it.

CASS: I

HULL: No more!
I want not wrangling but obedience here.

Exeunt CASS *and other officers, incensed.*

Would I had ne'er accepted this command!
Old men are out of favour with the time.
And youthful folly scoffs at hoary age.
There's not a man who executes my orders
With a becoming grace; not one but sulks,
And puffs his disapproval with a frown.
And what am I? A man whom Washington
Nodded approval of, and wrote it too!
Yet here, in judgment and discretion both,
Ripe to the dropping, scorned and ridiculed.
Oh, Jefferson, what mischief have you wrought—
Confounding Nature's order, setting fools
To prank themselves, and sit in wisdom's seat
By right divine, out-Heroding a King's!
But I shall keep straight on—pursue my course.
Responsible and with authority.
Though boasters gird at me, and braggarts frown.

Exit.

SCENE FIFTH—SANDWICH, ON THE DETROIT. A ROOM IN THE BABY MANSION.

Enter General BROCK, *Colonels* PROCTOR, GLEGG, BABY, MACDONELL, NICHOL, ELLIOTT, *and other officers.*

BABY: Welcome! thrice welcome!
Brave Brock, to Sandwich and this loyal roof!
Thank God, your oars, those weary levers bent
In many a wave, have been unshipped at last;
And, now, methinks those lads who stemmed the flood
Would boldly face the fire.

BROCK: I never led
Men of more cheerful and courageous heart,
But for whose pluck foul weather and short seas,

'Twere truth to say, had made an end of us.
Another trial will, I think, approve
The manly strain this Canada hath bred.

PROCTOR: 'Tis pity that must be denied them now.
Since all our enemies have left our shores.

BROCK: No, by my soul, it shall not be denied!
Our foe's withdrawal hath a magnet's power
And pulls my spirit clean into his fort.
But I have asked you to confer on this.
What keeps Tecumseh?

ELLIOTT: 'Tis his friend, Lefroy,
Who now rejoins him, after bootless quest
Of Iena, Tecumseh's niece.

BROCK: Lefroy!
I had a gentle playmate of that name
In Guernsey, long ago.

BABY: It may be he.
I know him, and, discoursing our affairs.
Have heard him speak of you, but in a strain
Peculiar to the past.

BROCK: He had in youth
All goods belonging to the human heart,
But fell away to Revolution's side—
Impulsive ever, and o'er prompt to see
In kings but tyrants, and in laws but chains.
I have not seen or heard of him for years.

BABY: The very man!

BROCK: 'Tis strange to find him here!

ELLIOTT: He calls the red men freedom's last survival;
Says truth is only found in Nature's growth—
Her first intention, ere false knowledge rose
To frame distinctions, and exhaust the world.

BROCK: Few find like him the substance of their dreams.
But, Elliott, let us seek Tecumseh now.
Stay, friends, till we return.

Exeunt BROCK *and* ELLIOTT.

GLEGG: How odd to find
An old friend in this fashion!

PROCTOR: Humph! a fool
Who dotes on forest tramps and savages.
Why, at the best, they are the worst of men;
And this Tecumseh has so strained my temper,
So over-stept my wishes, thrid my orders,
That I would sooner ask the devil's aid
Than such as his.

NICHOL: Why, Brock is charmed with him!
And, as you saw, at Amherstburg he put
Most stress upon opinion when he spoke.

MACDONELL: Already they've determined on assault.

PROCTOR: Then most unwisely so! There are no bounds
To this chiefs rashness, and our General seems
Swayed by it too, or rashness hath a twin.

NICHOL: Well, rashness is the wind of enterprise,
And blows its banners out. But here they come
Who dig beneath their rashness for their reasons.

Re-enter General BROCK *and Colonel* ELLIOTT, *accompanied by* TECUMSEH, *conversing.*

TECUMSEH: We have been much abused! and have abused
Our fell destroyers too—making our wrongs
The gauge of our revenge. And, still forced back
From the first justice and the native right,
Ever revenge hath sway. This we would void,
And, by a common boundary, prevent.
So, granting that a portion of our own
Is still our own, then let that portion be
Confirmed by sacred treaty to our tribes.
This is my sum of asking—you have ears!

BROCK: Nay, then, Tecumseh, speak of it no more!
My promise is a pledge, and from a man
Who never turned his back on friend or foe.
The timely service you have done our cause.

Rating not what's to come, would warrant it.
So, if I live, possess your soul of this—
No treaty for a peace, if we prevail,
Will bear a seal that doth not guard your rights.
Here, take my sash, and wear it for my sake—
Tecumseh can esteem a soldier's gift.

TECUMSEH: Thanks, thanks, my brother, I have faith in you;
My life is at your service!

BROCK: Gentlemen,
Have you considered my proposal well
Touching the capture of Detroit by storm?
What say you. Colonel Proctor?

PROCTOR: I object!
'Tis true, the enemy has left our shores.
But what a sorry argument is this!
For his withdrawal, which some sanguine men.
Jumping all other motives, charge to fear.
Prudence, more deeply searching, lays to craft.
Why should a foe, who far outnumbers us.
Retreat o'er this great river, save to lure
Our poor force after him? And, having crossed—
Our weakness seen, and all retreat cut off—
What would ensue but absolute surrender,
Or sheer destruction? 'Tis too hazardous!
Discretion balks at such a mad design.

BROCK: What say the rest?

FIRST OFFICER: I fear 'tis indiscreet

SECOND OFFICER: 'Twould be imprudent with our scanty force.

BROCK: What say you, Nichol, to my foolish scheme?

NICHOL: I think it feasible and prudent too.
Hull's letters, captured by Tecumseh, prove
His soldiers mutinous, himself despondent.
And dearly Rumour loves the wilderness,
Which gives a thousand echoes to a tongue
That ever swells and magnifies our strength.
And in this flux we take him, on the hinge

Of two uncertainties—his force and ours.
So, weighed, objections fall; and our attempt.
Losing its grain of rashness, takes its rise
In clearest judgment, whose effect will nerve
All Canada to perish, ere she yield.

BROCK: My very thoughts! What says Tecumseh now?

TECUMSEH: I say attack the fort! This very night
I'll cross my braves, if you decide on this.

BROCK: Then say no more! Glegg, take a flag of truce.
And bear to Hull this summons to surrender.
Tell him Tecumseh and his force are here—
A host of warriors brooding on their wrongs,
Who, should resistance flush them to revenge.
Would burst from my control like wind-borne fire.
And match on earth the miseries of hell.
But, should he yield, his safety is assured.
Tell him Tecumseh's word is pledged to this.
Who, though his temperate will in peace is law.
Yet casts a loose rein to enforced rage.
Add what your fancy dictates; but the stress
Place most on what I speak of—this he fears,
And these same fears, well wrought upon by you,
May prove good workers for us yet.

GLEGG: I go,
And shall acquit myself as best I can.

Exit GLEGG.

BROCK: Tecumseh, wonder not at such a message!
The guilty conscience of your foes is judge
Of their deserts, and hence 'twill be believed.
The answer may be "nay," so to our work—
Which perfected, we shall confer again.
Then cross at break of morn.

Exeunt all but TECUMSEH.

TECUMSEH: This is a man!
And our Great Father, waking from his sleep.
Has sent him to our aid. Master of Life,

Endue my warriors with double strength!
May the wedged helve be faithful to the axe,
The arrow fail not, and the flint be firm!
That our great vengeance, like the whirlwind fell.
May cleave through thickets of our enemies
A broad path to our ravaged lands again.

Exit.

SCENE SIXTH—MOONLIGHT. THE BANK OF THE DETROIT RIVER, NEAR THE BABY MANSION.

Enter Captain ROBINSON.

ROBINSON: I thought to find my brother here—poor boy.
The day's hard labour woos him to his rest.
How sweet the night! how beautiful the place!
Who would not love thee, good old Sandwich town!
Abode of silence and sweet summer dreams—
Let speculation pass, nor progress touch
Thy silvan homes with hard, unhallowed hand!
The light wind whispers, and the air is rich
With vapours which exhale into the night;
And, round me here, this village in the leaves
Darkling doth slumber. How those giant pears
Loom with uplifted and high-ancient heads.
Like forest trees! A hundred years ago
They, like their owner, had their roots in France—
In fruitful Normandy—but here refuse,
Unlike, to multiply, as if their spirits
Grieved in their alien home. The village sleeps.
So should I seek that hospitable roof
Of thine, thou good old loyalist, Baby!
Thy mansion is a shrine, whereto shall come
On pilgrimages, in the distant days.
The strong and generous youths of Canada,
And, musing there in rich imaginings.
Restore the balance and the beaver-pack
To the wide hall; see forms of savagery.
Vanished for ages, and the stately shades

Of great Tecumseh and high-hearted Brock.
So shall they profit, drinking of the past,
And, drinking loyally, enlarge the faith
Which love of country breeds in noble minds.
But now to sleep—good night unto the world!

Exit.

Enter IENA, *in distress.*

IENA: Oh, have I eaten of the spirit-plant!
My head swims, and my senses are confused.
And all grows dark around me. Where am I?
Alas! I know naught save of wanderings.
And this poor bosom's weight. What pang is here.
Which all my pressing cannot ease away?
Poor heart! poor heart! Oh, I have travelled far.
And in the forest's brooding place, or where
Night-shrouded surges beat on lonely shores.
Have sickened with my deep, dread, formless fears;
But, never have I felt what now I feel!
Great Spirit, hear me! help me!—this is death!

Staggers and swoons behind some shrubbery.

Enter General BROCK *and* LEFROY.

BROCK: You may be right, Lefroy! but, for my part,
I stand by old tradition and the past.
My father's God is wise enough for me,
And wise enough this grey world's wisest men.

LEFROY: I tell you, Brock,
The world is wiser than its wisest men,
And shall outlive the wisdom of its gods,
Made after man's own liking. The crippled throne
No longer shelters the uneasy king.
And outworn sceptres and imperial crowns
Now grow fantastic as an idiot's dream.
These perish with the kingly pastime, war,
And war's blind tool, the monster. Ignorance!
Both hateful in themselves, but this the worst.
One tyrant will remain—one impious fiend
Whose name is Gold—our earliest, latest foe!

Him must the earth destroy, ere man can rise.
Rightly self-made, to his high destiny,
Purged of his grossest faults; humane and kind;
Co-equal with his fellows, and as free.

BROCK: Lefroy, such thoughts, let loose, would wreck the world.
The kingly function is the soul of state,
The crown the emblem of authority.
And loyalty the symbol of all faith.
Omitting these, man's government decays—
His family falls into revolt and ruin.
But let us drop this bootless argument,
And tell me more of those unrivalled wastes
You and Tecumseh visited.

LEFROY: We left
The silent forest, and, day after day,
Great prairies swept beyond our aching sight
Into the measureless West; uncharted realms.
Voiceless and calm, save when tempestuous wind
Rolled the rank herbage into billows vast,
And rushing tides which never found a shore.
And tender clouds, and veils of morning mist,
Cast flying shadows, chased by flying light,
Into interminable wildernesses.
Flushed with fresh blooms, deep perfumed by the rose,
And murmurous with flower-fed bird and bee.
The deep-grooved bison-paths like furrows lay.
Turned by the cloven hoofs of thundering herds
Primeval, and still travelled as of yore.
And gloomy valleys opened at our feet—
Shagged with dusk cypresses and hoary pine;
And sunless gorges, rummaged by the wolf,
Which through long reaches of the prairie wound,
Then melted slowly into upland vales.
Lingering, far-stretched amongst the spreading hills.

BROCK: What charming solitudes! And life was there!

LEFROY: Yes, life was there! inexplicable life,
Still wasted by inexorable death.
There had the stately stag his battle-field—

Dying for mastery among his hinds.
There vainly sprung the affrighted antelope.
Beset by glittering eyes and hurrying feet.
The dancing grouse, at their insensate sport.
Heard not the stealthy footstep of the fox;
The gopher on his little earthwork stood.
With folded arms, unconscious of the fate
That wheeled in narrowing circles overhead;
And the poor mouse, on heedless nibbling bent,
Marked not the silent coiling of the snake.
At length we heard a deep and solemn sound—
Erupted moanings of the troubled earth
Trembling beneath innumerable feet.
A growing uproar blending in our ears,
With noise tumultuous as ocean's surge.
Of bellowings, fierce breath and battle shock.
And ardour of unconquerable herds.
A multitude whose trampling shook the plains,
With discord of harsh sound and rumblings deep,
As if the swift revolving earth had struck,
And from some adamantine peak recoiled,
Jarring. At length we topped a high-browed hill—
The last and loftiest of a file of such—
And, lo! before us lay the tameless stock,
Slow wending to the northward like a cloud!
A multitude in motion, dark and dense—
Far as the eye could reach, and farther still,
In countless myriads stretched for many a league.

BROCK: You fire me with the picture! What a scene!

LEFROY: Nation on nation was invillaged there,
Skirting the flanks of that imbanded host;
With chieftains of strange speech and port of war.
Who, battle-armed, in weather-brawny bulk.
Roamed fierce and free in huge and wild content.
These gave Tecumseh greetings fair and kind.
Knowing the purpose havened in his soul.
And he, too, joined the chase as few men dare;
For I have seen him, leaping from his horse;

Mount a careering bull in foaming flight.
Urge it to fury o'er its burden strange,
Yet cling tenacious, with a grip of steel.
Then, by a knife-plunge, fetch it to its knees
In mid-career, and pangs of speedy death.

BROCK: You rave, Lefroy! or saw this in a dream.

LEFROY: No, no; 'tis true—I saw him do it, Brock!
Then would he seek the old, and with his spoils
Restore them to the bounty of their youth.
Cheering the crippled lodge with plenteous feasts.
And warmth of glossy robes, as soft as down.
Till withered cheeks ran o'er with feeble smiles,
And tongues, long silent, babbled of their prime.

BROCK: This warrior's fabric is of perfect parts!
A worthy champion of his race—he heaps
Such giant obligations on our heads
As will outweigh repayment. It is late.
And rest must preface war's hot work tomorrow.
Else would I talk till morn. How still the night!
Here Peace has let her silvery tresses down.
And falls asleep beside the lapping wave.
Wilt go with me?

LEFROY: Nay, I shall stay awhile.

BROCK: You know my quarters and the countersign—
Good night, Lefroy!

LEFROY: Good night, good night, good friend!

Exit BROCK.

Give me the open sleep, whose bed is earth,
With airy ceiling pinned by golden stars,
Or vaultage more confined, plastered with clouds!
Your log-roofed barrack-sleep, 'twixt drum and drum.
Suits men who dream of death, and not of love.
Love cannot die, nor its exhausted life,
Exhaling like a breath into the air.
Blend with the universe again. It lives.
Knit to its soul forever. Iena!

Dead in the forest wild-dearth cannot claim
Aught but her own from thee. Sleep on! sleep on!

IENA: *(reviving)* What place is this?

LEFROY: Who's there? What voice is that?

IENA: Where am I now?

LEFROY: I'll follow up that sound!
A desperate hope now ventures in my heart!

IENA: Help me, kind Spirit!

LEFROY: I could pick that voice
From out a choir of angels! Iena!

Finds her behind the shrubbery.

'Tis she! 'tis she! Speak to me, Iena—
No earthly power can mar your life again.
For I am here to shield it with my own.

IENA: Lefroy!

LEFROY: Yes, he!

IENA: My friends! found, found at last!

LEFROY: Found, found, my love! I swear it on your lips.
And seal love's contract there! Again—again—
Ah, me! all earthly pleasure is a toil
Compared with one long look upon your face.

IENA: Oh, take me to my friends! A faintness came
Upon me, and no farther could I go.

LEFROY: What spirit led you here?

IENA: My little bark
Is yonder by the shore—but take me hence!
For I am worn and weak with wandering.

LEFROY: Come with me then.

Enter the PROPHET, who stalks gloomily over the stage—scowling at IENA and LEFROY as he passes out.

IENA: The Prophet! I am lost!

LEFROY: This monster here! But he is powerless now.
Fear him not, Iena! Tecumseh's wrath
Burns 'gainst him still—he dare not do thee hurt.

IENA: Must I endure forever this fiend's hate?
He stabbed me with his eye—

LEFROY: Oh, horrible!
Let us but meet again, and I shall send
His curst soul out of this accursed world!

Exeunt.

SCENE SEVENTH—THE HIGHWAY THROUGH THE FOREST LEADING TO FORT DETROIT. THE FORT IN THE DISTANCE; CANNON AND GUNNERS AT THE GATE.

Enter TECUMSEH, STAYETA, and other chiefs and warriors.

TECUMSEH: There is the Long-Knives's fort, within whose walls
We lose our lives or find our lands today.
Fight for that little space—'tis wide domain!
That small enclosure shuts us from our homes.
There are the victors in the Prophet's strife—
Within that fort they lie—those bloody men
Who burnt your town to light their triumph up.
And drove your women to the withered woods
To shudder through the cold slow-creeping night,
And help their infants to out-howl the wolf.
Oh, the base Long-Knife grows to head, not heart—
A pitiless and murdering minister
To his desires! But let us now be strong,
And, if we conquer, merciful as strong!
Swoop like the eagles on their prey, but turn
In victory your taste to that of doves;
For ever it has been reproach to us
That we have stained our deeds with cruelty,
And dyed our axes in our captives' blood.
So, here, retort not on a vanquished foe,
But teach him lessons in humanity.

Now let the big heart, swelling in each breast,
Strain every rib for lodgment! Warriors!
Bend to your sacred task, and follow me.

STAYETA: Lead on! We follow you!

KICKAPOO CHIEF: Advance, ye braves!

TECUMSEH: Stay! make a circuit in the open woods—
Cross, and recross, and double on the path—
So shall the Long- Knives overcount our strength.
Do this, Stayeta, whilst I meet my friend—
My brave white brother, and confer with him.

Enter General BROCK, PROCTOR, NICHOL, MACDONELL, *and other officers and forces, on the highway.*

TECUMSEH *goes down to meet them.*

BROCK: Now by God's providence we face Detroit,
Either to sleep within its walls tonight
Or in deep beds dug by exulting foes.
Go, Nichol, make a swift reconnaissance—
We'll follow on.

NICHOL: I shall, but ere I go
I do entreat you. General, take the rear;
Those guns are shrewdly placed without the gate—
One raking fire might rob us of your life,
And, this lost, all is lost!

BROCK: Well meant, my friend!
But I am here to lead, not follow, men
Whose confidence has come with me thus far!
Go, Nichol, to your task!

Exit NICHOL. TECUMSEH *advances.*

Tecumseh, hail!
Brave chieftain, you have made your promise good.

TECUMSEH: My brother stands to his! and I but wait
His orders to advance—my warriors
Are ripe for the assault.

BROCK: Deploy them, then,
Upon our landward flank, and skirt the woods,
Whilst we advance in column to attack.

TECUMSEH rejoins his warriors.

Signal our batteries on the farther shore
To play upon the Fort! Be steady, friends—
Be steady! Now upon your country turn
Your multiplying thoughts, and strike for Her!
Strike for your distant and inviolate homes.
Perfumed with holy prayer at this hour!
Strike! with your fathers' virtue in your veins
You must prevail—on, on, to the attack!

BROCK and forces advance towards the fort. A heavy cannonading from the British batteries. Re-enter NICHOL hastily.

NICHOL: Stay, General! I saw a flag of truce
Cross from the Fort to the Canadian shore.

BROCK: Halt! There's another from yon bastion flung;
And, see! another waves adown the road—
Borne by an officer! What think you, Nichol?

NICHOL: Your threats are conquerors! The Fort is ours!

GLEGG: Yes, look I the gunners have been all withdrawn
Who manned the cannon at yon western gate.

PROCTOR: So many men to yield without a blow!
Why, this is wonderful! It cannot be!

BROCK: Say, rather, should not be, and yet it is!
'Tis plainly written oh this captain's face.

OFFICER with flag of truce approaches.

OFFICER: This letter from our General contains
Proposals to capitulate—pray send
An officer to ratify the terms.

General BROCK reads letter.

BROCK: You have a wise and politic commander!

OFFICER: Our General, knowing your superior force—

NICHOL: *(aside)* Oh, this is good! 'tis barely half his own!

OFFICER: And, noting your demand of yesterday,
With clearer judgment, doth accede to it.
To bar effusion of much precious blood
By reasonable treaty of surrender.

BROCK: Why, this is excellent, and rare discretion!

OFFICER: He fears your Indians could not be restrained.
Our women's prayers—red visions of the knife—
We know not what—have melted his stout heart,
And brought him to this pass.

BROCK: Ay, ay, how good!
Great judgment and humanity combined.
Glegg and Macdonell, go at once and sign
Those happy stipulations which restore
Fair Michigan to empire and the crown.

Exeunt GLEGG, MACDONELL, *and* OFFICER *with flag.*

We shall await our officers' return—
But now prepare to occupy the Fort!
With colours flying we shall enter it,
And martial music, as befits the scene.
No Sunday ever saw a finer sight—
Three cheers for Canada and England's right!

Shouts and congratulations from the soldiery.

SCENE EIGHTH—FORT DETROIT. A TUMULT OF AMERICAN SOLDIERS AND CITIZENS.

Enter General HULL *and one of his officers, accompanied by* BROCK*'s aides,* GLEGG *and* MACDONELL.

HULL: Here is the paper! Tell your General
Divine humanity, which bath in me
A deeper root than fear of him, thus yields:
A sheer compunction lest the savage axe
Should drink too deeply in confused revenge.

GLEGG: Depend upon it, we shall tell him so,
And shall away at once.

Exeunt GLEGG *and* MACDONELL.

HULL: 'Tis well I lived
To stop this bloody work! Deferment played
Into the hands of death.

OFFICER: Oh, sir, I think
That what begins in honour so should end—
First deeds, not stained, but dusted by the last;
For thus the long day of a useful life
Seems burnished by its close.

HULL: My friend, had all
Been trusty as the men of your command!
But—I am great in silence and shall speak
No more of this! What's done is for the best.

Retiring.

OFFICER: A bleached and doting relic of stale time!
His best is bad for us.

A squad of volunteer militia insultingly surround the general, hooting and groaning.

FIRST VOLUNTEER: Hull! hold the fort!

SECOND VOLUNTEER: Resist! We'll back you up!

HULL: Insolent ruffians!
Some men are here in whose sincerity
And courage I have perfect faith—but you!—
Untaught, unmannerly, and mutinous—
Your muddy hearts would squirm within your ribs
If I but gave the order to resist!
You would command me! You who never learned
The simple first note of obedience!
Stand off, nor let me! I regard you not.
Fine Volunteers are you, who mutinied
O'er such privations as true soldiers laugh at!
Fine Volunteers! whom we were forced to coax
And almost drag upon the forest march.
Oh, if I had a thousand more of men,
A thousand less of things—which is your name—
I would defend this Fort, and keep it too.
Stand off, and let me pass!

Exit.

FIRST VOLUNTEER: The General
Talks well, boys, when he's mad!

Enter an OFFICER.

OFFICER: Fall in! Fall in!
Here come the British troops—the Fort's surrendered!

Enter General BROCK *and forces, with colours flying and military music. The American soldiers sullenly ground arms, and march out of the fort.*

BROCK: This is a happy end! You, Nichol, make—
With Proctor—rough lists of our spoils of war,
Then join with us in grateful prayers to Heaven.

Exeunt NICHOL *and* PROCTOR.

Enter TECUMSEH *and* STAYETA *(the latter wearing* BROCK*'s sash) with other chiefs and warriors, and* LEFROY.

TECUMSEH: My valiant brother is the rising sun—
Our foes the night, which disappears before him!
Our people thank him, and their hearts are his!

BROCK: Why, here is misdirection! For their thanks—
They fall to you, Tecumseh, more than me!
And, lest what lies in justice should too long
Stand in expectancy—till thanks seem cold—
Take mine, Tecumseh! for your services
Have won, with us, the honours of the day,
And you shall share its spoils.

TECUMSEH: Freedom I prize.
And my poor people's welfare, more than spoils!
No longer will they wander in the dark;
The path is open, and the sky is clear.
We thank you for it all!

BROCK: Nay, then, our thanks
We'll interchange—take mine, as I take thine!
But how is this? Is friendship's gift unused?
Where is my brother's sash?—

TECUMSEH: That gift I deemed
Conferred on me as on a warrior,

And, when I saw a worthier than myself,
I could not wear it. 'Tis Stayeta's now—
He keeps it till he finds a worthier still.

BROCK: Noble Tecumseh! thou art still the best!
Men envy their own merit in another—
Grudging e'en what's superfluous to themselves—
But thou, great valour's integer, wouldst share
Its very recompense with all the world!
Here are my pistols—take them from a friend—
Nay—take them! Would I had a richer gift!

LEFROY: This is a noble friendship.

BROCK: Ah, Lefroy!
What think you now of war?

LEFROY: If this war shield
Nature's most intimate and injured men,
I shall revoke my words and call it blest.

Re-enter General HULL.

HULL: You asked not for my sword—but here it is!
I wielded it in honour in my youth.
And now to yield it, tarnished, in old age,
Vexes me to the soul.

BROCK: Then keep it, sir!

HULL: Trenton and Saratoga speak for me!
(aside) I little thought that I should have to knead.
In my grey years, this lumpy world again.
But, when my locks were brown, my heart aflame
For liberty, believe me, sir, this sword
Did much to baffle your imperious King!

BROCK: That stands not in dispute, so keep the sword!
'Tis strange that those who fought for liberty
Should seek to wrench it from their fellowmen.
Impute not guilty war to Kings alone.
Since 'tis the pastime of Republics, too!
Yours has its dreams of glory, conquest, spoil—
Else should we not be here. But, General,
Wilt dine with us? We shall discuss this matter!

HULL: Nay, let me to my house; I cannot eat.

BROCK: Sir, as you will—but, prithee, be prepared!
I sail in six days for Niagara,
And you for Montreal.

HULL: Till then, adieu!

Exit General HULL.

TECUMSEH: Why should my brother leave Detroit so soon?

BROCK: Our foes are massing at Niagara,
And I must meet them; Colonel Proctor stays
In this command.

TECUMSEH: I know him very well.
My brother's friend says "Go!" but you say "Come!"

BROCK: *(aside)* How am I straitened for good officers!
(to TECUMSEH*)* Friend Proctor's prudence may be useful here.

TECUMSEH: I do misgive me o'er my brother's friend.

Re-enter NICHOL *and* PROCTOR.

NICHOL: Large stores, munitions, public properties;
A rare account of needed stands of arms;
A brig of war, and military chest—
These are the spoils of bloodless victory.

Handing General BROCK *a list.*

BROCK: Nought is much prized that is not won with blood!

GLEGG: And yet I would old England's victories
Were all as bloodless, ample, and complete.

MACDONELL: Oh, 'tis a victory fitly gained this day;
Great turning point of our Canadian fortunes!
This day forever should red-lettered stand
In all the calendars of our loved land!

Exeunt.

End of Act IV.

ACT V

Enter CHORUS.

CHORUS: O Canada!
Bright youth among the greybeards of the earth,
Dark days have come upon thee! Brock is slain—
That spirit glorious who fired thy soul,
And led thee to renown and victory.
Alas! the rare advantages he won,
By weak successors (equals in command,
But, oh, of what inferior mould in greatness!)
Have been let slip unto the winds, thy hopes
By an untimely armistice destroyed,
Those fleets he would have captured from the foe,
But for a hateful truce on him enjoined.
Were, in a fataler still, equipped, and loosed
To lord it o'er thee on the lakes. One bore
Destruction to thy upper Capital—
The other meets thy poorly furnished hulls
On Erie's bosom, and with hosts of men
And weight of armament doth bear them down.
O lamentable hour, which paves the way
To sad remaining scenes—a coward's part,
And the last pulse-beat of a hero's heart.

Exit.

SCENE FIRST—THE INDIAN COUNCIL HOUSE, AMHERSTBURG.

Enter BABY *and* ELLIOTT.

BABY: Now, Elliott, what think you keeps our fleet?
We heard the crash of battle yesterday.
And still no tidings come.

ELLIOTT: I fear the worst.

BABY: I fear it, too! Worse still to think this worst
Owes to sheer folly—to an armistice
Astutely urged, and too politely granted.
Some chance politenesses obstruct themselves,
Like meeting men who shuffle in the street,
Each striving to give way; but this, of Sheaffe's,
Was of the stately kind! He stood aside;
Bowed, hat in hand, and let the foe pass by
To build his navy up.

ELLIOTT: Well, we have here
A fool who beats Sheaffe's folly at the game,
But for whose slackness we might still record
Some gains on land, 'gainst losses on the lake.

BABY: You speak of Proctor; hum! a prudent man.
Who loves his life, and will maintain his love.
'Tis a safe temper.

ELLIOTT: Ay, for peace, not war.
But what a damper to our volunteers!
They left their customable, proper toil
To ought, not for a wage, but for their freedom—
A thing to be achieved by instant ways.
Though they run blood. Thus, if they won and lived.
The sooner to their homes; and, if they died—
Fair end: their lives went for their country's good.
But how, by bootless and lame leadership,
Has Proctor soured the temper of our men;
Cooling them to contempt, till, in a pique,
He straight disarms, then sends them to their homes!

BABY: Unheard-of folly! All this is a text
From which I often preach unto myself.

ELLIOTT: Would that by preaching we could mend the matter!
Even Tecumseh he insults, whose cause
Lies close to ours; and, saving him and us,
(Whose aid he would dispense with if he dared,)
What force is left him but his regulars.
Whose sickly frames and broken confidence
Would scarcely face the effigies of foes!

BABY: True! true! it breeds fear but to think of it.

ELLIOTT: Then hear him prate about the charge he bears
Upon his individual shoulders—his!
Oh, it is galling! while he boasts withal
What he would do were things fortuitous,
And in a fairer plight; and this fudged stuff
Goes down with some. But, not to spin it out,
We know that, at Sandusky, Harrison
(Who is as good a substitute for Hull
As ours a poor one for immortal Brock)
Waits transport to invade us in large force.
So—lest our General means to beat retreat,
Or ruinously yield—'tis time to stir.

BABY: What can we do? We are not in command.

ELLIOTT: Force him who is to face our enemies—
First calling back our volunteers.

BABY: Force him.
Who would not face yourself, to face five thousand!
Why, Elliott, we might as well expect
Light from a cave, as leadership from him.

Enter MCKEE.

What news, McKee?

MCKEE: It could not well be worse.
Our fleet is captured, and the General
Has issued orders to retreat.

BABY: Ay, ay;
We had already lost our fleet in thought.

Which ofttimes pre-digests calamities.
But this retreat—how looks Tecumseh at it?

MCKEE: I never saw him in so strange a temper—
Calm on the surface, but convulsed beneath,
Just poising on the edge of whirling rage.
He now harangues his chiefs and warriors.
And has demanded conference with Proctor,
Wherein I look for deep outbursts of wrath.
For Proctor, fearing him, pretends our fleet
Is absent for repairs—a foolish lie.
Which yet will deepen what it but prorogues.

BABY: We must compose this threatened broil, McKee;
Dissension now would ruin everything.

MCKEE: Tecumseh thinks there's ruin in retreat.
Proctor can't thumb his temper to the point,
Nor rove him through his plans.

BABY: Well, certainly,
Had we but power and time enough to mass
Our people's strength 'twould be the nobler part
To risk a battle here. But, pshaw! this counts
In mere conjecture as to what might be
Had we command; for Proctor will retreat!
He feels endangered in a special sense.
The savage massacre of prisoners
At Old Miami and at Raisin River
Has made him hated by the enemy.
Who, right or wrong, put all the blame on him,
And this he knows.

Enter General PROCTOR.

MCKEE: Would Brock were still alive!

PROCTOR: Pardon my overhearing ears!—what then?

MCKEE: *(turning sharply)* Then we should fight!
Some bold, some daring plan,
Would still forefend retreat.

PROCTOR: Some strange exploit!
Some headlong rashness which would find you graves.

'Twas prologue to his own; a fault in him
I would not emulate.

ELLIOTT: A fault in him!
His death was of the parcel of the man.
In him example, striving to excel
The precept, made him reckless of his life.
'Twas thus he lost it: his main force behind—
With but a handful, taken by surprise.
Rather than flee he charged! and, with the words,
"Push on, my brave York Volunteers!" he fell.
Oh, such a fall atoned for such a fault;
For by that fall he lashed his followers
Up to a sure and terrible revenge.
It was a fearful victory! Our foes,
Flying from death to death, sprang o'er the cliffs
And precipices of Niagara,
And, on the rocks, or in the swirling flood.
Made expiation of their foul invasion.
Let this dwell in our minds! and let not death.
Or, rather, fear of death, repel us now.
Nor turn us to a base retreat from it.

PROCTOR: Let wisdom dwell, too, in our minds, I urge.
Bethink you: Harrison is on the wing—
Thousands to hundreds is his argument!
Our fleet is captured; our supplies are scant;
And winter may be scented in the air.
We must retreat, since men must eat or die;
So, winding up these threads of sense, prepare!
Lest time desert our opportunity.

BABY: What will Tecumseh say to this?

PROCTOR: That dog,
Who barks at all I do, must come with us.
And guard our rear—else were his absence best.

MCKEE: Should he refuse?

PROCTOR: Then tell him we retire
But further east to make a desperate stand.
'Tis well to say it lest he cross my plans.

As for his prate, not all the forest's combs
Could sweeten such a tongue.

BABY: I think you lack
The fair idea of this chief; his mind
Has greatness in it—but here comes the man:
Confer with him yourself!

Enter TECUMSEH and a concourse of chiefs and warriors.

PROCTOR: Nay, I must go,
And push our preparations—

TECUMSEH: *(confronting PROCTOR)* Stay, my friend!

PROCTOR: I cannot stay; speak to him, gentlemen.

Going.

TECUMSEH: *(touching his hatchet)* I am Tecumseh.
You are Proctor—stay!

PROCTOR: *(aside)* What means this madman? He is insolent.

TECUMSEH: Brother! My people are before you now!
In the last war, the British father gave
Our chiefs the hatchet, and they fought for him;
But in that bloody strife the Long-Knife laid
The King upon his back; whereat he took
Our foes, without our knowledge, by the hand.
Again the Long-Knife warred upon the King;
Again our father handed us the axe,
With promise that our lands would be restored.
We have not shrunk from battle. We have fought,
And many of our people have been slain!
Our promise is redeemed! but what of his?
Oft have we heard you, boasting of him, say
He never would withdraw from British ground.
Yet, neither asking nor advising us,
We mark you now preparing to retreat—
Afraid to even see his enemies!
My brother, you are like a lusty dog
Which proudly curls its tail upon its back,
But, when affrighted, whips it 'tween its legs,
And runs for life! Why should you meanly flee?

The Long-Knives have not yet defeated us
By land, nor is it certain that your ships
Are captured on the lake; but, even so.
First fight, and, if defeated, then retreat!
But, brother, if you will not fight, you hold
The arms our father furnished for our use.
Give these to us, and you may go in peace.
My people are in our Great Spirit's care!
We are determined to defend our lands.
Or, if He wills it, strew them with our bones.

BABY: Why, this is manliness, and pathos, too!

PROCTOR: We must retreat. We cannot spare the arms
You now demand of us.

TECUMSEH: Not spare them, brother?
Do I hear aright?

PROCTOR: We cannot spare them.

TECUMSEH: By Manitou, you shall! Those arms are ours.
I would not quarrel lightly with my friend,
Nor cut the bands which bind me to his cause
Upon a small occasion; but those arms,
Useless to him, are precious life to us,
And we shall have them.

PROCTOR: Yes, if you retreat!
We cannot spare them else.

TECUMSEH: And why retreat?
The timid woman and the child will stand
And struggle when assaulted by their kind;
Nay, hares resist, and gnats and flies will fight.
One thing alone runs from its sort in fear,
And thou art it!

PROCTOR: The wildest talk in sleep
Out-measures this in sense. We must retreat!

TECUMSEH: Must! must! Oh, could my kindred spirit, Brock,
But live again—be here—would he retreat?
Yours his command—but why should I compare
The king-bird with the crow? Brave Brock retreat!

Oh, when that badger was abroad, dogs hid
And gave the lie to nature! Here we stay.
Give us the arms, and we shall act like him.
Whilst you make off in peace.

PROCTOR: This man would breed
A deadly quarrel—prudence bear me through!
(aside) I mean to give those arms, but for a use
More wise than you would put them to. Retreat
Is but to find some vantage in the woods—
Some footing for defence; so, come with us;
I would not ask you else.

TECUMSEH: Seek your own kind!
Go boom in festering swales, or, like a frog.
Croak your dull night-song in the standing pool—
Your voice is not a man's.

PROCTOR: This chief is fevered.
Explain the why and wherefore of retreat.
Then let him come with us or stay; I care not.

Going.

TECUMSEH: Ha! There are cares my brother never cared for;
Duties to which he never paid his duty;
Sacred agreements, oaths and covenants
Which he would break like twigs. Coward and liar!
There's something here that whispers to my hand

Drawing his hatchet.

To set you free from all.

BABY, ELLIOTT, and MCKEE interpose.

ELLIOTT: Tecumseh, hold!

BABY: This is unworthy of you. Be a man!

TECUMSEH: A man! Oh, if to honour words by deeds;
To look on truth as on the healthful air.
Without which I should suffocate and die!
To love my injured people, and oppose
My constant spirit 'gainst tumultuous wrongs—
If this is lack of manhood mark me down.

But to be over-reached and thrown aside—
Our mighty sacrifices and our service
Rated as nothing in this coward's plans—
It rends my soul. Back! I shall chop his own
From out its frame, and send the mould of lies
Down to his people's hell! Away!

MCKEE: No! no!

ELLIOTT: Stay, be advised by us!

PROCTOR retires.

BABY: Do nothing rash!
We are your friends—you know us to be true.
And we, like you, despise this General.
Fear bares the coward's heart. The gaudy acts
Whereby unsoundness shores its credit up
Are at its touch exposed. 'Tis so with him—
And thus far we are with you. But retreat
Hath a discreetness too. This Harrison,
Once landed (for our long and liberal shores
We cannot well defend), might circle us.
And, with overwhelming numbers, hem us in.
But, by retreat, we have the choice of place.
And Harrison you know the man—will follow.
The forest will befriend us—we can stand
Where'er we please, and shall whene'er you please.

TECUMSEH: So! Proctor's promises deceive you, too!

BABY: Nay, 'tis my promise, and you know the stuff
My word is built on. Deal with me, Tecumseh,
As you had dealt with Proctor, if I lie.

TECUMSEH: My friend, your reason breaks a spirit's wing
That ne'er touched ground before. Oh, I grow weak—
Cast from my thoughts, and banished from my dream!
The plumed hope droops—fate's shadow covers it;
And dim forebodings peer into my soul.
I am not what I was—there—there—I'll go!

BABY: I hope to see you smile at this ere long.

Exeunt.

SCENE SECOND—A WOOD NEAR AMHERSTBURG. TECUMSEH'S CAMP. A VISTA TO THE EAST, THE SUN'S UPPER RIM JUST RISING ABOVE THE HORIZON.

Enter warriors and Josakeeds. The warriors extend their weapons toward the sun. The Josakeeds advance, facing it.

FIRST JOSAKEED: He comes! Yohewah! the Great Spirit, comes
Up from his realm— the place of Breaking Light!
Hush, nations! Worship, in your souls, the King,
Above all Spirits! Master of our lives!
I-ge-zis! He that treads upon the sky,
And makes the light!

SECOND JOSAKEED: He comes! he comes! he comes!
The ever-dying, ever-living One!
He hears us, and he speaks thus to mine ears!
I wipe once more the darkness from the earth;
I look into the forest, and it sings—
The leaves exult; the waters swim with joy.
I look upon the nations, and their souls
Strengthen with courage to resist their foes.
I will restore them to their fathers' lands;
I will pour laughter on the earth, like rain,
And fill the forest with its ancient food.
Corn will be plenteous in the fields as dust,
And fruits, moved to their joy, on every bough
Will glow and gleam like ardent fire and gold.

THIRD JOSAKEED: O mighty Spirit! Guardian of our Breath!
We see thy body, and yet see thee not.
The spirits in our forms, which no man sees,
Breathe forth to thee, for they are born of thee.
Hear us, thy children, and protect our lives!
Our warriors retreat—it is thy will!
Declare the way—the fateful time to stand!
Then, if in battle they decline in death,
Take them, O master, to thy Mighty Heart—
Thy glorious Ground and Shining Place of Souls!

Yohewa! Master of Breath! Yohewa!
Hear us! Hear us!

ALL: Master of Breath—hear us!

Exeunt.

SCENE THIRD—THE SAME.

A girl's voice singing without, then enter IENA, WINONA, WEETAMORE, *and other Indian maidens—some at quill-work, others embroidering.*

IENA: There is within my heart, I know not why,
An apprehension I ne'er felt before.

WINONA: The night-sun set in cloud, and curling mists
Hid the plumed star from sight. Mayhap, those signs
Bode danger to our loves. Sing, Weetamore—
Your tender voice will charm away our fears.

IENA: Nay, sing no more in strains so sorrowful!
Why is it all our people's songs are sad?

A bird's note is heard.

WINONA: I know not why; no more than yon poor bird
Knows why it mourns.

IENA: It is the wood pewee,
That haunts the deepest forest. 'Tis the bird
Yohewa gave to solitude for voice—
The lonely heart within the lonely heart!
Why comes this feathered sadness from its wilds.
To thrill us with its pain?

Enter MAMATEE.

O Mamatee!

MAMATEE: Alas, alas, the Long-Knife's big canoes
Are on the lake, and sweeping to our shores!
Fort Maiden burns; our warriors retreat;
And we, poor souls! must fly to densest woods,
And wait till they return?

IENA: Till they return—
Ah! when shall they return?

Enter LEFROY.

Here comes my love,
With parting in his eyes.

LEFROY: You speak the word!
But, if we part, we part to meet again.
And, thus, to leave you for love's sake makes sweet
The bitter word, and will uphold my heart.
Tecumseh is already gone—farewell.

IENA: Farewell, and we shall meet again—here? where?
Yes, yes, I know—there's something tells me where.
Farewell! my love will follow you on wings
High-flighted as the swan's—my soul! my soul!

LEFROY *places* IENA *in* MAMATEE*'s arms.*

LEFROY: In loving arms I place this precious charge.
Oh, cherish her! for she is dear to me
As is the Intercessor to your race.

Exit LEFROY.

IENA: Now let me go—see—I am well again!
An impulse rises from the seat of dreams—
Love's apprehension may be cured by love.
Winona, will you help me?

WINONA: Sister, how?

IENA: Your brother, Chaska, is a slender youth,
With features softly fashioned. 'Tis a boy
Some say resembles me; and like me, too,
His gentle form contains a venturous soul.
You make a young brave's suit for him, I think.

WINONA: Yes, for his huskenaw; you call it that—
We have another name. Look, this completes it!

Holding up an ornamented moccasin.

'Tis from the self-piece cut, and quill'd all o'er—
Your gathered edges show not half so well.

IENA: Oh, if you love me, let me have this dress.

WINONA: With all my heart: but tell me, Iena,
What means this strange request?

IENA: Come to your lodge!
I there shall tell you all I have in mind.

Exeunt IENA *and* WINONA.

MAMATEE: The girl conceives some folly. To my cares!
O weary woman, thine the weary work!

Exit MAMATEE.

FIRST MAIDEN: Iena asked, and I do marvel why,
Our songs are all so sad. We forest maids
Should sing as lightly as our forest leaves.
'Tis strange!

WEETAMORE: You are too happy-young to think
'Tis else than strange. Now I shall answer you
Ere Iena can come to chide the strain.

WEETAMORE *sings.*

"Who would not be a forest-maid,
  And ever spend at ease
The flowery season in the shade
  Of sighing summer's sweetest trees?
But who would be a forest-maid,
  Beset by foes and fears?
To see in every flash a blade,
  To start at every sound she hears!

We flit—we fly—no home have we,
  And terror is the tale!
A fate is whispered by the tree—
  A doom is uttered by the gale.
Short season of delight have we.
  But that of pain is long;
And, so, 'tis sorrow, and not glee.
  That gives the burden to our song."

Re-enter IENA, *dressed as a young Indian brave.*

IENA: Now for my bow! my quiver! here it is!
This quiver slung, I'm ready for the field.

FIRST MAIDEN: Why, this is Iena!

IENA: Yes, Iena.
But, sisters, lock this secret in your hearts.
Love's Spirit whispered in a dream—*"Go, shield*
Your lover in the fight!"

SECOND MAIDEN: A dream, a dream!

THIRD MAIDEN: A sacred dream!

ALL: We promise to be true.

The maidens join hands and move in a circle round IENA, *chanting:*

Spirit of Love! Spirit of Love!
  That in Great Nature's heart doth dwell:
Spirit of Love! Spirit of Love!
  Go with our sister—shield her well!

Exeunt.

SCENE FOURTH—THE RUINS OF FORT MALDEN AT AMHERSTBURG.

Enter General HARRISON *and other American officers.*

HARRISON: All gone! all gone! Naught here but smoking ruins!
Now would I give this Province for one man,
Were that man only Proctor. Perfidy!
Thy manager has fled; and we are balked
In our just vengeance.

FIRST OFFICER: Let us follow him!
There are no ties 'twixt mercy and this man
That we should spare him.

HARRISON: No, his ruthless axe,
Stayed only by Tecumseh's noble rage,
Has lit upon too many helpless heads.
Their blood cries, "After him!" and with our force
We can overwhelm his if we overtake him.

SECOND OFFICER: 'Tis strange Tecumseh hugs his flying fortunes!

THIRD OFFICER: Think you he is gone?

HARRISON: No doubt of it, else would he face us here.

SECOND OFFICER: Had he remained we might perchance have made
Our peace with him, and ended this long feud.

HARRISON: Made peace with him! There is no peace on earth
For him, save in it. We are what we are;
And if some miracle will work a change
In us, then shall we find him, as we would,
Contented but with peace. This much I say,
Knowing the man—but this is not the point!
'Tis Proctor, not Tecumseh, we discuss,
And Proctor we must capture if we can.

Enter a SCOUT.

What tidings have you gathered?

SCOUT: Proctor's force
Is making for the Heights of Burlington.
'Tis said Tecumseh made him pledge his word
To stand, and fight at the Moravian Town,
Should we pursue.

HARRISON: Will hounds pursue the hare?
'Tis boot-and-saddle, and quick marches now,
If we would catch the foe.

Exeunt.

SCENE FIFTH—THE HIGHWAY THROUGH THE FOREST ON THE RIVER THAMES, NEAR THE MORAVIAN TOWN.

Enter TECUMSEH *and his chiefs, General* PROCTOR, *Colonel* BABY *and other officers, and Proctor's* ORDERLY.

TECUMSEH: I'll go no further.

PROCTOR: A little further—
Toward the heights—'twere well!

TECUMSEH: No, not a step.
Were they the Alleghanies! Here we stand!
The enemy draws near, and we must fight.

PROCTOR: Well, here we stand—here shall I lay my bones,
If so God wills it. Ha—I like the spot!
A river to protect us on our left;
Swamps to the north, and forest everywhere.
What a gigantic panoply of woods!
Why here are maples scarce three men could girth
With their encircling arms. What trees!

TECUMSEH: Yes, yes—
Would they were soldiers, brother; they are strong,
And, being rooted to their place, would ne'er
Give way as we have done. But to affairs—

PROCTOR: Ay, to the proper ordering of our force.
Do you direct! What think you now is best?

TECUMSEH: Two swamps are here o'ergrown with swollen trunks
Of black and moss-hung ash. Their underbrush,
Thick-set, and tangled with the blistering vine,
No cavalry can pass. Between them lies
A neck of open woods and turfy soil.
Where I shall plant my braves; but this straight path—
This highway by the river—is your ground.
Here place your cannon, and await attack,
Whilst I oppose it there.

Enter a SCOUT.

SCOUT: Make ready, sirs!
The enemy approaches—we can hear
His trumpet-calls resounding through the woods.

Exit SCOUT.

PROCTOR: Then, briefly, my opinion sides with yours.
The trial hour is come—farewell, my friend!
We two shall stand or fall upon this field,
And fame it to all time.

TECUMSEH: Keep a stout heart,
I pray you, brother; all will thus be well.

Exeunt TECUMSEH *and his chiefs.*

BABY: I think this disposition excellent.

PROCTOR: It is, it is. Now let us fight it out!
There are occasions when the spirit mounts,
Uplifted by what threats it; this is one.
Go, gentlemen, and marshal up our force—
I shall await you here. Stay you with me,
(to his ORDERLY*)* I have instructions for you.

Exeunt all but PROCTOR *and his* ORDERLY.

Come hither!
We may be beaten here—

ORDERLY: I think we shall.

PROCTOR: What right have you to think?

ORDERLY: You said it, sir.

PROCTOR: I said we may— *(aside)* tut! this is less than prudent.
Go, put my fleetest horses to my carriage;
Have others ready-saddled in our rear,
And, with some trusty fellows, stay by them—
They may be useful in emergency.

Exit ORDERLY.

If there are seasons in the soul of man,
As in the year, it is my bleakest now.
How many rail at me, and call me coward.
Because with prudent outlook I foresee
What can be done and what cannot be done!
One must endure! though to be misconceived,
To find one's actions and one's qualities
Framed in misapprehension; to be deemed
The thing that one is not, might well offend.
But that which guides my life enables me
To bear against the rub of false opinion;
So, prudence, miscalled cowardice by those
Who count their rashness virtue, tend me still!
Tecumseh foolishly resolves to die—
For who, against such odds, can hope to live?
And, if there be a virtue in mere death.
Then is he welcome to his grave and all
The honour and the glory death can give.

But those who have some business still on earth—
Something to do that cannot else be done—
Look on this matter with a different eye.
It is our trumpet call; my soldiers come.
In the adieu to death the quick resolve
Must spur calm judgment on to execution.

Exit.

SCENE SIXTH—TECUMSEH'S PART OF THE FIELD.

Enter TECUMSEH.

TECUMSEH: This is our summer—when the painted wilds,
Like pictures in a dream, enchant the sight.
The forest bursts in glory like a flame!
Its leaves are sparks; its mystic breath the haze
Which blends in purple incense with the air.
The Spirit of the Woods has decked his home,
And put his wonders like a garment on,
To flash, and glow, and dull, and fade, and die.
Oh, let not manhood fade within my soul!
And thou, pale doubt, that hast distracted me—
Ye forecasts that would drag my spirit down—
Hence and forever flee! Ye have no place.
No business in this breast. My field is here!
Here must my people's cause be lifted up,
Or sink to rise no more.

Exit.

Enter three American scouts, looking cautiously about them.

FIRST SCOUT: This is their spot.

SECOND SCOUT: I see them coming. Look! away—away—

Exeunt.

Firings and other sounds of conflict are heard from PROCTOR*'s part of the field, and then suddenly stop.*

Re-enter TECUMSEH, *with* STAYETA *and his other chiefs and warriors.*

STAYETA: The noise of battle rose, and then it ceased
Almost upon beginning. This is strange.

TECUMSEH: It is; ah, Proctor, how my soul mistrusts thee!
Go, some of you, see what this silence means—
But stay—here comes a witness of the fight.

Enter LEFROY, *out of breath and excited.*

LEFROY: The line was broken by a charge of horse,
And, in the British quarter, all is lost.

TECUMSEH: And Proctor—he who meant to leave his bones,
If so God willed it—

LEFROY: Willed it otherwise!
Upon the instant of attack he fled;
And, seeing this, the line gave way at once.

TECUMSEH: 'Twas this I feared. He loves his wretched life
Too well to leave his vile bones anywhere.
Dastard and coward! Oh, the heavens should crack,
And dart their lightning down upon this slave!
How come such creatures 'mongst the breed of men
To make their nation blush?

LEFROY: I cannot tell.
Like sulphur in rain-channels after storms.
Or little frogs, one marvels how they come.
But some fought well; Baby, among the rest.
Who now is prisoner. Myself was saved
Most strangely by a boy—a youthful brave,
Whose arrows helped me in a dangerous spot.
I never saw so sweet a lad before.
His face! I started when I saw it first—
It seemed so like to Iena's! Think you.
Could she be here?

TECUMSEH: Impossible!

DAHCOTA CHIEF: No, no.
'Twas Chaska, of our nation; one who longs
For plumes before his time. He has been seen,
Yet is so active that we cannot catch him.

LEFROY: Ah, then, 'twas he! This way he ran before me.
Round the rough angle of the lower swamp,
Then darted into it. I followed fast.
And sought, but could not find him—he was gone.

A flourish of trumpets without, sounding the advance of the American force.

STAYETA: Hark! Now the Long-Knives come!

TECUMSEH: Yes, now they come.
Courage! Warriors, courage! Let our deeds
Take colour from the scene. Now must we fight
Like men; not run like slaves. What matters it
To those who fled, and left us, if they flee?
They can join palms, make peace, draw treaties up.
And son and father, reconciled again,
Will clap their hands, and glory in their race
Which hath despoiled our own. For us, no peace
Save what our axes gain, or, in our graves.
Therefore—as men fore-doomed to war or death—
Let valour make excuse that we shall live.
And, breathing vengeance, shake our spoilers so
That they will reel in terror to the East,
From whence they came, and cry—"The West is yours!"
Oh, warriors, think of all, and strike like men
Whose homes are in their hands, whose souls are free.
The voice that calls you now will call no more.
For something whispers to this fearless heart—
Here must I fight, and for my people die!

DELAWARE CHIEF: Then shall we fight and die with you like men.

DAHCOTA CHIEF: Or live to see you Chief of all our race.

A flourish without, then enter the American forces. A fierce hand-to-hand conflict begins.

TECUMSEH: Our foes are turning! Strike them! Beat them back!

STAYETA: Pursue! pursue!

The American troops retreat fighting. Exeunt omnes.

Enter IENA, *from behind.*

IENA: I hear, yet cannot see,
The dreadful fray! My arrows all are spent.
There are a thousand in my quivered heart
Could I but match them to this useless bow.
What shall I do? Ah, this is our own tree!
It will protect me whilst I wait the end.

Retires behind a large sugar maple.

Re-enter a small band of braves, driven back by soldiers, who chase them out and then return.

FIRST SOLDIER: Ha, ha, those redskins fled like hunted wolves!
Away, and start another pack!

Exeunt forward.

IENA: *(looking out)* Alas!
Our people 'gin to flee—I fear—I fear.
Here comes my love! Oh, for one arrow more!

Enter LEFROY *and an American* OFFICER *fighting with swords. In the struggle they draw abreast of* IENA*'s tree, and pause.*

OFFICER: You are a white man.

LEFROY: I am a white man.

OFFICER: And what a soulless one are you who leave
Your place in civil, good society
To herd with savages; from one extreme
Falling away unto the basest side—
The furthest from the humanized world.

LEFROY: Nay, I deny it! Further, I would say,
My genius leans, like Nature, to all sides.
Can love them all at once, and live with all.

OFFICER: So! so! you are a poet, painter, what?
Well, that is nothing; I must try and kill you.

They fight again, and LEFROY *disarms the* OFFICER.

LEFROY: Now might I kill you if I had the heart.
Be prisoner instead; I cannot kill
A man thus, in cold blood.

Re-enter two soldiers.

OFFICER: 'Tis more than kind.

FIRST SOLDIER: Why, that's our captain there, disarmed—let fly!
My carbine is unloaded.

Second soldier aims at LEFROY. IENA, *with a cry, leaps from her shelter and intercepts the shot.*

LEFROY: Who is this?
Not Chaska! Oh, no, no—'tis Iena!
I see her now, who could not see my love—
Love clear and incorruptible as glass.
Love that had dared a monster, wilds and floods—
Dare fire, and draw the bow that shielded me.
Speak to me, Iena! No voice—she's dead!

OFFICER: This is the strangest chapter of my life—
Soldiers, stand off, and rest upon your arms.

LEFROY: Silent forever! Oh, my girl! my girl!
Those rich eyes melt; those lips are sun-warm still—
They look like life, yet have no semblant voice.
Millions of creatures throng, and multitudes
Of heartless beings flaunt upon the earth:
There's room enough for them; but thou, dull Fate—
Thou cold and partial tender of life's field.
That pluck'st the flower, and leav'st the weed to thrive—
Thou hadst not room for her! Oh, I must seek
A way out of the rack—I need not live.

OFFICER: The world grows less familiar every hour:—
Is that a girl?

LEFROY: Yes, yes, but she is dead—
And love is left upon the earth to starve.
My object's gone, and I am but a shell,
A husk, an empty case, or anything
That may be kicked about the world.

Exit LEFROY, *carrying* IENA.

OFFICER: I see!
I have a tear or two behind these eyes,
And they are coming. If he need a friend
I know of one.

SECOND SOLDIER: Now, dang me, who'd 'a thought
That was a girl!

OFFICER: *(turning aside)* What strange and selfless paths
Do skirt the world's hard highway! I have seen
What gives me sight. The tide of battle rolls
Back, and our people win, as win they must:
But, now, methinks, I'll strive with different heart.
Come, soldiers, let's away and join the fight.

Exeunt through a by-entrance.

Re-enter TECUMSEH'S *warriors driven back, and then re-enter* TECUMSEH, STAYETA, *and other chiefs.*

TECUMSEH: Has death died out, that no one now can die?
Or are you driven back by fear of it?
Oh, slaves or men, determine which you are!

Re-enter the American troops, in pursuit.

STAYETA: Tecumseh calls! On, warriors, strike them down!

TECUMSEH *and his warriors, by a fierce onslaught, again drive their opponents back. The fight continues without—then re-enter* TECUMSEH *mortally wounded.*

TECUMSEH: Great Spirit, hadst thou spared me but one hour—
Yet thy behest rules all.

Re-enter DELAWARE CHIEF, *also wounded.*

DELAWARE CHIEF: What! wounded too?

TECUMSEH: Yes, I am shot. Recall some warriors
To bear my body hence. Give no alarm.
Lest our poor braves lose courage; but make haste—
I have not long to live. Yet hear my words
Bury me in the deep and densest forest,
And let no white man know where I am laid.
Promise this ere you go.

DELAWARE CHIEF: I promise it.
Alas, alas, our bravest and our best!

Exit DELAWARE CHIEF.

TECUMSEH: The hour is come! these weary hands and feet
Draw to the grave. Oh, I have loved my life,

Not for my own but for my people's cause.
Who now will knit them? who will lead them on?
Lost! lost! lost! The pale destroyer triumphs!
I see my people flee—I hear their shrieks—
And none to shield or save! My axe! my axe—
Ha—it is here! No, no—the power is past.
Mighty Spirit, shelter—save—my people!

Dies.

SCENE SEVENTH—ANOTHER PART OF THE FIELD.

Enter General HARRISON *and other American officers and Colonel* BABY, *a prisoner.*

HARRISON: You were too brave a man, Baby, to swell
The craven Proctor's flight of followers.

BABY: Speak not of him! I mourn the death of one—
A soldier—and a savage if you will—
Able and honourable, valiant, pure.
As ever graced the annals of the earth.

HARRISON: You mean Tecumseh; search is made for him.
I hope to give him fitting burial.

BABY: Oh, sir, he loved his people! They are men
Much hated by the small and greedy mind—
The mind that is not gentle, and that jeers
And laughs at all forlorn and broken fortune.
And some there be who coldly pass them by
As creatures ruled by appetite, not law;
Yet, though to such they seem but human beasts,
They are to those who know, or study them,
A world of wonders! I entreat you, sir.
To make right use of your authority.
And shield them if you can.

HARRISON: I shall, I shall.
Right feeling tends this way, though 'tis a course
Not to be smoothly steered.

Enter a party of soldiers.

FIRST SOLDIER: Tecumseh's body
Cannot be found; 'twas borne away and buried
By faithful friends who would not name the place.
If they were tortured.

FIRST OFFICER: He is well content
Without our honours. This man's race hath lost
A lofty spirit.

SECOND OFFICER: All will mourn for him!
No need had he of schools or learned books—
His soul, his mentor, his keen lion-looks
Pierced to the heart of things. Nor needed he
Counsels of strength and goodness. To be free
Required no teacher, no historic page.
No large examples sought from age to age.
For such things were himself, and, as his breath.
Instinctive, pleaders 'gainst the fears of death.

HARRISON: Sleep well, Tecumseh, in thy unknown grave,
Thou mighty savage, resolute and brave!
Thou, master and strong spirit of the woods.
Unsheltered traveller in sad solitudes,
Yearner o'er Wyandot and Cherokee,
Couldst tell us now what hath been and shall be!

Exeunt.

The end.

THE BIRTH OF MONTREAL

A CHRONICLE PLAY

AMY REDPATH RODDICK

REIMAGINING A LOST HISTORY IN AMY REDPATH RODDICK'S *THE BIRTH OF MONTREAL*

MARLENE MENDONÇA

Amy Redpath Roddick, the author of over a dozen books of drama and poetry, is one of many playwrights whose recovered work has gained recognition for its contribution to women's drama in Canada.[1] Plays written by women at the turn of the century often explored the political, economic, and cultural changes that occurred during the period in which they were written. Typically these plays were didactic or political, and written according to unpopular generic conventions, such as those of the closet drama.[2] While some of these recovered plays are recognized for their contribution to Canada's theatrical archive, an absence of critical consideration or wide anthologization of women's dramatic work during this period continues.

One of the first English plays to be written in Canada, according to Craig Walker, was a closet drama in 1766.[3] The closet drama was at times referred to as

1 "Canadian Early Women Writers: Amy Redpath Roddick," Simon Fraser University Digital Library, accessed 25 October 2016, http://digital.lib.sfu.ca. Redpath's works include: *The Flag and Other Poems* (1918); *The Armistice, and Other Poems* (1919); *The Seekers: An Indian Mystery Play* (1920); *The Birth of Montreal: A Chronicle Play* (1921); *The Romance of a Princess: A Comedy, and Other Poems* (1922); *In a Venetian Garden, St. Ursula: Two Plays* (1926); *From Montreal Elsewhere* (1929); *I Travel to the Poet's Mart* (1936); *Tharbis: A Poetic Drama* (1937); *The Tomahawk: A Playlet, and Other Poems* (1938); *The Iroquois Enjoy a Perfect Day, A Chance Meeting, and Other Poems* (1939); *England's Oldest Colony* (1940); and *Waiting's Wedding, and Other Poems* (1941).

2 Kym Bird, *Redressing the Past: The Politics of Early English-Canadian Women's Drama, 1880–1920* (Montreal: McGill-Queen's UP 2004), 5.

3 Craig Walker, "Canadian Drama and the Nationalist Impulse," in *The Oxford Handbook of Canadian Literature*, Cynthia Sugars, ed. (New York: Oxford UP, 2016). According to Walker, George Cocking's *The Conquest of Canada; or, the Siege of Quebec* was written as a closet drama in 1766. Although the text is lost, it "introduced the two

poetic or verse drama because of its stylistic and rhetorical elements. Critics note how its dramaturgical structure was dominated by "the literary element," making these primarily literary texts with little performative potential.[4] Alan Filewod highlights the "pompous verse," and "bombastic patriotism" as qualities specific to the closet drama.[5] Its "lengthy, [and] often stodgy verse lines,"[6] and its lack of dramatic action and juicy plot lines make it difficult to stage. The reason closet dramas "seem so untheatrical and naive today," Filewod suggests, is "precisely because they were deliberately written against the popular taste; they were written for an imagined theatre that did not exist."[7] These characteristics appear in Roddick's four-act play, which takes place over a twenty-year time span, beginning in the living room of Monsieur and Madame de La Dauversière in La Fleche, France, in the year 1639 and ending in 1660 with the establishment of New France in Canada. *The Birth of Montreal* defies verisimilitude and Aristotle's unity of time, which—according to critics of closet dramas—were crucial in staging plays effectively.

This historical play, like many early Canadian plays, used historical events to help shape national identity. Both Charles Mair's *Tecumseh* (1886) and Sarah Ann Curzon's *Laura Secord: The Heroine of 1812* (1887) employed the conventions of closet dramas to provide a glimpse "back to the most significant direct experience of violence in what was then still-living Canadian memory."[8] *The Birth of Montreal* functions in much the same way as these earlier plays, using an event from the past to address the political and cultural turmoil that continued to haunt the city.

Playwrights who wrote in this genre were generally affiliated with upper-class society, of which Roddick was a member. Roddick was born on 16 May 1868, and was the granddaughter of the founder of Redpath Sugar. She lived at 1065 Sherbrooke Street in Montreal's affluent Square Mile, a gated community

---

major traditions that characterize early English-Canadian drama: poetic drama and satire," 371.

4 Om Prakash Mathur, "The Closet Drama of the Romantic Revival," quoted in Catherine B. Burroughs, *Closet Stages: Joanna Baillie and the Theatre Theory of British Romantic Women Writers* (Philadelphia: U of Pennsylvania P 1997), 16.

5 Alan Filewod, "Named in Passing: Deregimenting Canadian Theatre History," in *Writing and Rewriting National Theatre Histories*, S. E. Wilmer, ed. (Iowa City: U of Iowa P, 2004), 112.

6 Karen Raber, *Dramatic Difference: Gender, Class, and Genre in Early Modern Closet Drama* (Newark, NJ: U of Delware P 2001), 18.

7 Alan Filewod, 112. Filewod suggests, "The literariness and lack of theatrical sophistication in these texts were markers of cultural authenticity" and of a refusal to be part of New York City's theatre scene.

8 Walker, 371.

that was home to some of the wealthiest families in Canada. At the age of thirty-eight, she married Sir Thomas Roddick (1846–1923), one of Canada's most esteemed surgeons and the eventual Dean of Medicine at McGill University. Her economic and social status allowed her the luxury of writing as an occupation. Theatre historian Kym Bird reveals Roddick's strong commitment to various arts and women's groups, including the Women's Canadian Club, the Montreal Art Association, and the Canadian Authors Association; she was also an honorary member of the McGill Alumni.[9] She was active in her literary and cultural contributions, receiving a gold medal from the Schroeder Foundation of St. Louis for her literary achievement in 1948.[10]

Roddick's extensive corpus of poetry generally explores the natural landscape of Canada, with some of her plays—including *The Seekers: An Indian Mystery Play* (1920), *The Tomahawk: A Playlet* (1938), and *The Iroquois Enjoy a Perfect Day* (1939)—paying homage to the First Nations of Canada. In 1939, she was initiated into the Bear Clan of the Iroquois at Kahnawake in recognition of her plays about First Nations culture and history.[11] She was named an honorary Kahnawake princess for her commitment to, and genuine interest in, helping the Kahnawake, including her paying for the restoration of a longhouse.[12] When *The Birth of Montreal* was published in 1921, the Indigenous population in Canada had been silenced and "firmly marginalized."[13] Roddick's life experience and interests would have revealed this reality to her, and the play demonstrates her interest in thematizing this social concern.

The Birth of Montreal testifies to a historical moment that altered the lives of many Canadians. This pivotal moment in history shaped Canada's cultural identity; in the words of the play's Madame de la Peltrie, a devout Christian: "To think my hands have helped / To plant this seed. That future generations / Will hold these things in memory." The importance of looking back in order to understand how history shapes our present and future is one of Roddick's chief concerns. The cross that is planted on Mount Royal in the play's second act to

9 Kym Bird, "Blood On The Sheets: Lesbian History and Identity in the Life and Theatre of Amy Redpath Roddick," (Paper presented at Q2Q: A Symposium on Queer Theatre and Performance in Canada, SFU Woodward's Goldcorp Centre for the Arts, 2016), 4.

10 "Canadian Early Women Writers: Amy Redpath Roddick," Simon Fraser University Digital Library.

11 "Canadian Early Women Writers: Amy Redpath Roddick," Simon Fraser University Digital Library.

12 Bird, "Blood", 4.

13 Marianna Valverde, *The Age of Light, Soap, and Water: Moral Reform in English Canada, 1885–1925* (Toronto: U of Toronto P, 2008), 15.

symbolize the victory of the French still remains today as a physical remnant of the events that occurred during the seventeenth century, a reminder of the political turmoil and violence that accompanied the founding of the city.

In exploring the effects of colonization on the First Nations near Montreal, *The Birth of Montreal* foregrounds what Roddick perceived as problems with the values and ideologies of her own time. Between 1857 and 1921, Canada imposed a series of acts that were intended to "civilize" First Nations. The Gradual Civilization Act (1857), the Civilization and Enfranchisement Act (1859), and the Indian Act (1876) each increased the government's authority over decision-making and governance, land claims, and who could identify as an Indian.[14] These legislative acts positioned the First Nations as a group incapable of making decisions independently. By the late nineteenth century, the residential school system had been established in a further attempt to "civilize" First Nations, based on the racist belief that Indigenous cultures were "backward, further ensuring that they needed to be civilized."[15]

The Birth of Montreal criticizes the colonization of Montreal and settlers' contradictory attempts to civilize these nations by instigating wars to attain their land and strip their people of their identities. In Act II, Mademoiselle Mance, one of the founders of Montreal and a nurse who established the city's first hospital, discusses the arrival of the French in Ville Marie with Jeanne, an Indigenous woman who was born as Meadow Rose but changed her name upon her conversion to Christianity. Mlle. Mance states, "How still and beautiful the day that brought / Fulfillment. Peace on earth—and peace endureth!" This statement is later contrasted with the underlying brutality caused by colonization, which left "a bitter legacy of lost traditions and broken families for First Nations People."[16] Writing against the backdrop of the implementation of the residential school system, Roddick was aware of the severity of racism against the First Nations in Canada. Jeanne's response to Mlle. Mance's romantic depiction of her arrival can be read as an analogy for the treatment of First Nations. She says: "Marraine! 'twas I who caught the fireflies, trapped / Them carefully within the stoppered phial. / The shiny insects flickered, glad to serve / The Holy Sacrament." Just as the fireflies were "trapped" and forced to "serve / The Holy Sacrament," so were the First Nations in Canada.

---

14 *Indigenous and Northern Affairs Canada*, Government of Canada, accessed 12 October 2016, www.aadnc-aadnc.gc.ca.

15 Daniel Coleman, *White Civility: The Literary Project of English Canada* (Toronto: U of Toronto P, 2006), 12.

16 Alan McMillan and Eldon Yellowhorn, *First Peoples In Canada* (Vancouver: Douglas & MacIntyre, 2009), 334.

In further establishing the mistreatment of the First Nations, the third act explores the broken and complicated relationship between Jeanne and her family that follows her conversion to Christianity. She asks that they too convert in order for their relationship to be repaired. In her refusal to accept their offerings, she says:

> What choice have I,
> Till you have earned a Frenchman's name? Return
> Next spring, learn Christian truth; beneath the guns
> Of Ville Marie some fallow land awaits
> Our toil, and there I'll watch expectantly!

Her father, Chehteh, tells Jeanne that she has been "bewitched" to "Forget your people," an accusation that infers how residential schools isolated children from their families, traditions, values, and cultures. In this way, *The Birth of Montreal* highlights the systemic racism that existed at the time of the nation's founding and continued to shape the lives of First Nations in Roddick's present day. It exposes the idea that civility, an attempt to create "justice and equality," has been maintained through "uncivil violence and unfair exclusion."[17] The final stage directions ask that the "*audience and* COLONISTS *unite in singing 'O Canada.'*" This final moment implicitly challenges readers and the imagined audience to reflect on the values and history that have shaped the country.

As such, *The Birth of Montreal* is a complicated text that attempts to unveil a lost and forgotten history. The complexity of this closet drama is reflected in the ambiguity of the characters' motives. While on the one hand, the play interrogates the act of colonization and highlights its detrimental effects, on the other, it situates its characters within a framework that affords them questionable agency. What emerges above all else is an argument that the birth of a nation is as much a political process as it is a theatrical one.

17 Coleman, 20.

CHARACTERS

Marinette: an Attendant
Madame de La Dauversiere
Monsieur de La Dauversiere
The Baron de Fancamp
Jeanne: a Huron Convert
Mademoiselle Jeanne Mance
Monsieur de Maisonneuve
Madame de la Peltrie
Chehteh: Huron Chief
Anontaha: Huron Chief
Mitiwemeg: Algonquin Chief
Jesuit Father
Pierre Laimery
Jean Robelin
Adam Dollard: Sieur des Ormeaux
Sister Marguerite Bourgeois
Colonists

ACT I
THE VISION.

SCENE I

The living room of a house in La Fleche, France, late in the autumn of the year 1639, showing the owners to be in moderate circumstances. MARINETTE *draws the curtains and lights the candles.* MADAME *de La Dauversiere, sitting on the sofa, impatiently turns over the pages of a book, then throws it from her and sighs.*

MARINETTE: Madame is restless?

MADAME: Restless scarce describes
Anxiety. No peace by day or night
Since first, through visionings, your Master found
His destiny, an island wilderness,
Encompassed by fierce scalping savages.
Of nothing else he speaks but Montreal,
Montreal.

MARINETTE: Where is this Montreal?

MADAME: In Canada.

MARINETTE: Ah, Canada, that sounds
Familiar.

MADAME: More familiar than I wish.
Would that Jacques Cartier had been satisfied
With this old France, nor risk discoveries
Beyond the sea; would that the Jesuits
Had been content with silent venturings,

Nor scatter broadcast skillful narratives,
Inflaming souls till life that's everyday
Grows dull, till visions come and voices speak.

MARINETTE: This trip to Paris may divert.

MADAME: Small chance,
I fear, his letters sound too jubilant,
Though nought but messages of love. All else
Is secret, pending his return.—What ails
The clock? It ticks incessantly, but stays
The same.

MARINETTE: Madame herself might hasten it,
Did she confide in one who honestly
Has served through children's ailments, worryings
And much derangement.

MADAME: 'Tis true, upheavals mark
This house, whose Master smiles serenely, talks
Of peace— *(sobbing)* of peace in heathen lands!

MARINETTE: *(sitting down)* Monsieur
Has changed?

MADAME: He feels himself inspired to build
A sacred city, he whose means suffice
But ill for family support; who has
No influence, a tax-receiver.

MARINETTE: Like
St. Matthew!

MADAME: Yes, that's how the Baron speaks,
Encouraging, as ardent now himself,
Until a fancied hospital has stretched,
And in their minds a city now exists,
Whose buildings all are placed, environments
Well known—four years to raise with fertile dreams,
How long with stones?

MARINETTE: Four years since first Monsieur
Returned from Mass, his face so shining-bright,
A halo glowed, I thought.

MADAME: 'Tis past belief,
This mission then received, and yet at times
His fervour quells my doubt; an enterprise
Thus shadowy and yet such confidence;
To found a new religious Order, he,
A married man, a laic; then to build
A hospital where serve these nursing-nuns,
St. Joseph honouring, in Montreal,
A forest-isle; their patients, savages,
Immodest, fierce and liable to outbursts
On slightest provocation, brandishing
Great axes, sharpened stones! He thinks our young
French girls invincible—to cope with frost,
And snow that's mountain-high, convert such men,
Some cannibals, to Christian gentleness.

MARINETTE: And such God's will?

MADAME: So says Monsieur, the voice
Then heard, how often since! celestial—come
The Father Confessor now admits, reward
For penitence and flesh that's nightly scourged.
The whip you've seen of iron chains, but not
The belt that sharply pricks twelve hundred wounds.
Poor man, I grieve this body roughly used;
But still his spirit soars, the single gift
He asks of God is Faith—assuredly
Already his.

A pause, followed by the sound of loud knocking.

They come! they come!

She springs up. Exit MARINETTE. *Enter Monsieur de La* DAUVERSIERE *and the Baron* DE FANCAMP. *The former kisses his wife on either cheek, the latter kisses her hand.*

Like boys
Released from school you laugh, not thus tired men
Discouraged from rash venturing.

DAUVERSIERE *hands his wife a wallet.*

DAUVERSIERE: See here,
My wife, one hundred louis, precious coins!
Now hold and weigh them lovingly, then tell
Some day your children's children once within
Your grasp the egg whence came the roofs and towers
Of Ville Marie in Montreal.

MADAME weighs the wallet in her hand.

MADAME: 'Tis light
For so much worth!

DAUVERSIERE: Our flooding Loire was once
A trickling brook; how many rivers flush
Its course! *(taking back wallet)* What streams of gold will weight this purse!

Enter MARINETTE with a tray of light refreshments for the travellers, who find chairs near the table. MADAME de La Dauversiere reposes on the sofa.

Ah, Marinette, such dainty fare! To break
My fast you scheme! and unashamed, you smile.

MARINETTE: I would Monsieur showed kindness to himself.

DAUVERSIERE: Too kind at times; the watchful Enemy
A frailty oft detects.

Exit MARINETTE. Monsieur de La DAUVERSIERE eats sparingly, the Baron DE FANCAMP more heartily.

DE FANCAMP: These cakes are nice,
Madame. A privilege to share this home!
And now, this most stupendous task!

MADAME: *(wearily)* For all
Our sakes a humbler one would better suit;
But anxious I to hear the news, you thirst
To tell.

DE FANCAMP: Success beyond our fondest hope,
But where, amid such wealth of circumstance,
Shall we begin?

DAUVERSIERE: With Satan's harsh assault,
His stroke was darkness. Indecisions, doubts
Arose. Three times, irresolute, we turned;
Three times, with dragging effort, drove ourselves

To fresh belief. The fallen Angel feared
This wedge we sought within his boundaries,
Foresaw his vast dominions jeopardized,
So strained to weaken us, by fell design;
Till Heav'n vouchsafed anew her surety.

DE FANCAMP: Yes,
That sense of dull despair, that sickly sense
That falsifies and dims, has ever been
The Evil One's most cruel dart. With loss
Of confidence, how ask our friends for help
In this prodigious work; we saw their heads
Low-drooped to hide the pity felt for crazed
Imaginings.

MADAME: *(sarcastically)* So I should think!

DAUVERSIERE: But, wife,
How, chartless, knew I then each bay and dent
Of that fair isle, called Montreal, its length
And varied breadth, the streams meandering,
The fertile plain and densely wooded slopes,
That thrice-crowned mount, suggesting Trinity.

MADAME: Our house lacks much, but books are plentiful.

DAUVERSIERE: Most lose their knowledge; mine's exact, and hark!
How verified!

After a pause, he rises, his face flushed with excitement.

But first, in ecstasy
Most glorious, my soul relieved of gloom,
Hell's Potentate o'erthrown—

MADAME: At least that once!

DAUVERSIERE: The vision, then revealed, has hardened me
Against his sharpest pricks. 'Twas at Notre-Dame;
Before the Blessed Virgin's altar, where
I knelt, imploring fervently, this grace
Was granted me. Those transports roused by Mass,
Within the sombre edifice, effaced
All thought of self; in rapturous amaze
I clearly saw that august Family,

He bows his head.

Jesus, Mary, Joseph. Thrice our Lord,
The Christ-child, radiant, distinctly spoke:
  Where find a faithful servant?
  Where find a faithful servant?
  Where find a faithful servant?
Then softly touching me, His Mother said!
"Behold! my Son, this faithful servant," O,
What bliss ineffable! He gazed on me
And smiled: "Henceforth my faithful servant! I
Have need of you: fear nought; I give my strength
And wisdom; where your Guardian Angel points,
There lies the path; its goal is tangible;
My grace suffices!" I saw his hand outstretched,
A ring was gently tendered; it bore these words:
"Jesus, Mary, Joseph," graven.

MADAME: *(visibly moved)* Almost
I see—

DAUVERSIERE: Some day, in Montreal, my nuns
Will wear such token.—Where stood the Holy Group
Now shadowed forth great churches, godly schools,
Infirmaries as erstwhile seen; and then,
In long procession, eager faces passed,
Each stamped in memory forever, each
A glad co-worker in salvation's scheme!

MADAME: In spite of self, your ardour seizes me,
Yet 'tis but visions, visions!

DE FANCAMP: Nay, Madame,
This apparition's proved: the gold you've seen,
Who gave, in priestly garb, walked first. My friend
Described him perfectly, for since, we've met,
And in God's time, his reverent array
Of followers will too declare themselves.

DAUVERSIERE: At Muedon, summoned by the Chancellor.

MADAME: So you remembered earth's affairs, what then?

DAUVERSIERE: Within the castle-gallery a form
Approached, a moment's startled pause—I touched
Who lead that dream-cortege, his face and vestments.
Then clasped, as ancient friends, in dear embrace,
We volleyed welcomes forth; no episode
In either life unknown. 'Twas like St. Paul,
The Hermit, meeting first St. Anthony,
St. Francis greeting first St. Dominic!
"I wish to share in God's design," he said,
With meek simplicity, then handed me
This gold.

MADAME: Enthusiasts are plentiful!
Yet few, thus credulous, distribute coin.

DAUVERSIERE: Like mine, his evidence was heaven-sent,
He heard my voices, dreamt my dreams! a priest,
Named Olier, a torch to light the Gentiles!
For three long hours we walked the castle-grounds
And as we strolled, the town of Ville Marie,
In Montreal, became a certainty.

DE FANCAMP: Astonishing! Next day their schemes were shared
With me. The great on earth, who have their times
Of lofty exaltation, never know
That gladness, bathed with tears and lit with smiles,
Wherewith the Holy Spirit seals the bonds
Of those who league in hallowed enterprise—
Three great Communities were planned, three heads
On earth, these two dear friends of mine and one,
A maid of Troyes, through Heaven's prompting known;
The Priests to consecrate their lives to Christ;
The Nursing-nuns to Joseph, those who teach
To Mary—Ville Marie, through faith, assured
The Holy Family's safe-guarding!

DAUVERSIERE: Yes,
We three associates—

DE FANCAMP: The mystic three
Affirming!

DAUVERSIERE: Felt no need to hesitate.
Idealists are oft more practical,
My wife; than those whose round of drudgery
Remains unlit by starry promises.
We ordered twenty tons of carefully
Assorted foods, utensils, tools, all sent
Next spring to Canada, awaiting there
Our future colony.

MADAME: 'Twill drain that purse!

DE FANCAMP: My fortune first of streams to swell its size!
Warm hearts expectantly now beat in France
Whose wealth will flow as mine. With confidence
Unshakable our shoulders are set to plough,
Although, in Montreal, we have acquired
No rights, nor will an absent Master speak
Of sale; although who finds a foothold there
Must face the tomahawk of Iroquois.

MADAME: Not I alone; but others, those with sense,
Will call this scheme, foolhardy, rash; across
A wreck-strewn ocean lies that land, ice-locked,
Surprised by constant butcheries; expense
That's infinite!—despising trade, though furs
Might reimburse; such strained philanthropy,
If needful, well, the King should undertake.

DAUVERSIERE: *(exultantly)* Ay wife, a King's work!—
We, His servitors,

MADAME: O, think of those young, clinging hands, that search
Their future through a father's care? For self,
For comfort, I'll not beg; but see, I kneel
For them!

MADAME kneels imploringly.

DE FANCAMP: If she were right, what then?

DAUVERSIERE: The Tempter
Triumphant! Through paternal instincts now
He works.

MADAME: Forget this madness, born of dreams.

DAUVERSIERE: Ay, dreams, but living dreams, nought now I fear.
An earthly king who builds a structure rare
And beautiful, protects its burnished grace
And guards the skilled contrivers. How, but think
The King, Omnipotent, will blow the winds
To fill our sails—see, wife, that vision there!

A vision appears of the future City of Montreal. Enter MARINETTE. *All stand with clasped hands in deep amazement.*

ACT II
THE CROSS.

SCENE I

The storeroom of the Fort of Ville Marie in Montreal, near midnight, Christmas, in the year 1642. MADEMOISELLE MANCE *and* JEANNE *are putting away some utensils after the festivities.*

JEANNE: Rest, Meadow Rose, I'll pile these things for you.

MADEMOISELLE MANCE sits down, somewhat wearily.

MADEMOISELLE MANCE: Why call me that?

JEANNE: Was I not christened, Jeanne,
Your name? 'Tis fair exchange to give you mine,
Marraine, and Meadow Rose becomes you well.
Its sweetness thrives where rocks are thickest strewn,
No passerby's refused a smooth-stemmed bud.
But why these sighs on Little Jesus's day?

MADEMOISELLE MANCE: This Christmas, though a wondrous novelty
For you, my Jeanne, incites remembrance. France
Has grown most dear tonight,—a prison once
It seemed, such chains of argument, convention,
And tender ties that must be harshly broken;
But God sustained.—We smile, the past is past,
'Tis Christmas night in Ville Marie! We watch
Our dream's unfoldment, here, in Montreal.

JEANNE: With thunder-words the big guns spoke the news
That Jesus, born in Bethlehem, had come

To Hochelay. 'Twas fine the noise they roared
To celebrate the day. The Black Robes said
That demons mourned; but Guardian Angels marked
The tale in Paradise. I know mine laughed,
And I'll be good to keep him thus rejoiced.

MADEMOISELLE MANCE: Most constant watchfulness or vain's your boast.

JEANNE: When eyes are sparkled with festivity,
The slumber-sprite is vexed. Though late, let me
Sit here *(sits on the floor, leaning against MADEMOISELLE MANCE)* and think of midnight mass, the lights
That starred through spice of trailing evergreen,
The little manger, God-Papoose, strange beasts,
And sweet-faced Squaw, the solemn songs and then
Today, the games as played in France—and much
To eat!

MADEMOISELLE MANCE: Poor Jeanne, that boast is seldom heard.

JEANNE: For meat and drink your smile's enough, to work
With you, 'tis happy play. In Silery
I learnt French-talk, but none soft-voiced as you,
And most I loved you when, last shad-fish moon,
Arriving here, you plucked a trillium, held
It so, admiringly, and seemed to breathe
A song from it, the way my people do.
You kissed it then before 'twas pressed asleep,
'Mid blessed words, in this Novena.

She draws the book from MADEMOISELLE MANCE's pocket. MADEMOISELLE MANCE stretches for the book and opens it where the flower lies.

MADEMOISELLE MANCE: Ay!
Fit emblem of our great adventure, thou,
Fair-omened flower, thrice-bladed Truth, that hymnest
The Holy Family's response to earth,
Reminder now of that auspicious day,
When, skirting first these shores all blossom-strewn,
We sighted, near a stream, the visioned spot,
Where Ville Marie should spring in praise of God.

Enter Monsieur de MAISONNEUVE.

JEANNE: *(rising)* "Were every tree an Iroquois, I still
Would found a colony in Montreal,
My honour, as my duty, calls me forth."

MAISONNEUVE: So little Jeanne remembers well my words
And thus she flatters!—Still a forfeit's owed,
Each sought to entertain; but you, when asked
A story, wriggled like a frightened dog.
Then slipped away.

He sits on a packing case.

JEANNE: My people fear these tales.
When winter's grasp is loosed and Manitou's
Awake. It thaws tonight.

MAISONNEUVE: A Christian fear
These idle tales! we'll have one now, then prayer
And bed!

JEANNE: *(unwillingly)* This comes from ancient times; may be
'Tis safe.—Long moons ago a great Chief's eye
Flushed red with shooting pain. Enraged he tore
It out, replaced it with a hummingbird's,
That scarcely filled the cavity and so
Was lost. A turtle's vision next was tried,
But worse confusion followed, now he groped
Through lonesome veils of mist. Perplexed and dazed
He had but sense to fling that eye afar;
Then chose a fish-hawk's keener sight, alas!
What fresh alarm! This eye so glancing-quick
The lake and river bottoms jumped to view,
The smallest minnow could be plainly traced
As spawning salmon; O such dread abyss
That opened 'neath his frail canoe! Aghast,
He even glimpsed the Lizard of the Pond
Whose bulging-awfulness demanded prey;
But just in time the wicked eye slipped out.
What noise is that?

MAISONNEUVE: The wind, 'tis rough outside.

JEANNE: Still quiv'ring, he essayed a dog's, and now
Success! both eyes well matched, the dog and man
See things alike.

Enter MADAME DE LA PELTRIE.

MADAME DE LA PELTRIE: The river is rising fast, Monsieur.

JEANNE: I said 'twas ill to mention names.
My people know that spirits take offence.
Such tales are only told when frost strikes deep,
And Winter gives his shivering consent.

MADAME DE LA PELTRIE: 'Tis Satan's work. St. Lawrence basin's broad,
Small need to wash the shore; and yet, they say,
The flood's most dang'rous high.

MAISONNEUVE: A winter-freshet,
We hope it spreads enough to drown such fears.

Exit Monsieur de MAISONNEUVE.

JEANNE: Much else will drown but not their fears.

MADEMOISELLE MANCE: Come, Jeanne,
Repeat those words that Father Vimont used
When first God's praise was heard in Montreal,
Then speak no more of fears.

JEANNE: Marraine, I tremble

MADEMOISELLE MANCE: Sit here, you foolish girl.—This settlement's
A grain of mustard; but 'tis thrown by hands,
So pious, so inspired by living faith,
How doubt that Heaven has great and fair designs.
This feeble grain will branch and multiply;
Its wondrous growth will some day shadow far!

MADAME DE LA PELTRIE: O Mademoiselle! to think my hands have helped
To plant this seed. That future generations
Will hold these things in memory.

MADEMOISELLE MANCE: Of that
I've little thought! God's work suffices.

MADAME DE LA PELTRIE: O
That day when first we gained this hallowed spot,
Our hearts aglow with thankfulness, when first

Our Captain sprang ashore, we following;
All sank in prayer, tears and laughter mixed.
And hymns and canticles, each sang aloud
A joyous gratitude, none knew what words
Were used,—they mingled with the trill and chirp
Of forest birds, a melody of hope!
And there, 'mid opening leaves, they raised the altar
That we, O Mademoiselle, were privileged
To drape befitting that august occasion.

MADEMOISELLE MANCE: How still and beautiful the day that brought
Fulfillment. Peace on earth—and peace endureth!

JEANNE: Marraine! 'twas I who caught the fireflies, trapped
Them carefully within the stoppered phial.
The shiny insects flickered, glad to serve
The Holy Sacrament.

MADAME DE LA PELTRIE: A happy thought,
Our oil forgotten:—flame endowed with life,
Those tiny, clustered tapers, suiting well
Their lodgment; our cathedral bricked with sward
And foliage, its roof the firmament,
Where friends invisible gave comfort, strength,

Enter Monsieur de MAISONNEUVE.

While gentle, lapping waters spoke of those
In France, who prayed and worked with us.

MAISONNEUVE: In truth
These waters are not gentle now, Madame,
Your fears were just.

JEANNE: *(starting up)* My warning dropped unheeded.
Ville Marie's in sorry plight!

MADEMOISELLE MANCE: Hush, Jeanne,
Think you God's promises are worthless? Has he
Not proved through signs and wonders? Who first conceived
This colony showed me a sketch, and there,
Most plainly featured: chapel, living-house
And fort as now established; shielded well
By river, stream and tangled wood. Next year

A hospital and so a city's growth. *(reflectively)*
Why doubt such revelation, justified
Thus far.—In La Rochelle, renewed by Mass,
I met that saintly man, who welcomed me
To fellowship with arms outstretched. Untold
He knew my name and inward longings, how
Despite a sickly frame and friends averse,
I craved to bear Christ's burden in the wilds
Of Canada. *(addressing MAISONNEUVE)* He then extolled your worth,
Monsieur! Your followers, God-fearing folk;
But men at best need woman's care; so I,
Though vowed to maidenhood, was drawn to pledge
My services; most truly gratified
That others of my sex have found this road
To Heaven—that I have sweet companionship!
What search you there, Monsieur?

MAISONNEUVE draws some paper from a box.

MAISONNEUVE: A scrap of paper,
Ah, here's your quill. To show the Fathers, I
Would write some words. *(writing)* O God, if such thy glory,
Thrust back these floods; if not, we humbly pray,
Make known some proper place, where we may serve
And worship Thee.

MADAME DE LA PELTRIE: There's danger, then?

MAISONNEUVE: Most real!
To stay the troublous tide, I'd plant a cross,
Attaching first these lines, if favour be
Accorded, I would raise another, a greater,
A lasting cross upon Mount Royal's brow.
Acknowledging God's clemency. I seek
The Fathers to consult with them, will then
Announce our project, begging fervent prayer.

MADEMOISELLE MANCE: No righteous prayer goes amiss, but still
My faith assures that Ville Marie has dug
Her roots.

Exeunt Monsieur de MAISONNEUVE and the ladies, who throw cloaks over their shoulders. JEANNE opens a door in the centre of the stage and peeps out.

JEANNE: A blustrous night!—and menacing!
The Water-Demon spits his wrath and claws
The earth with dripping hands. The Frenchman's prayer
Lacks strength. Offended Spirits scarce will heed
The Stranger's tongue; but I, who worked this mischief,
Have medicine to cure, or Ville Marie
Will be destroyed, and how my friends will grieve.

She drops off her dress and is seen in an undergarment of linen, stained with butternut juice. She unbinds her hair and shakes it loose, then takes a pistol from the shelf.

French prayer helps much in certain ills; their Devil's
Discouraged by soft words; but ours is bold!—

She fires the pistol through the central doorway.

That awful noise should frighten him; O how
The waters swish!

She takes in her arms a small white dog that has been awakened by the noise and recites with movements to suit the words.

Great Lizard of the Pond,
  Thy waters creep,
Great Lizard of the Pond,
  Thy waters sweep,
Great Lizard of the Pond,
  Thy waters leap!
Leap! Leap!—Leap!—Leap!

Great Lizard of the Pond,
  My gift, O keep! *(She throws the dog far outside.)*
Great Lizard of the Pond,
  Drink deep, drink deep,
Great Lizard of the Pond,
  Fall fast asleep,
Sleep, sleep,—sleep, sleep,
Sleep, sleep,—sleep, slee—

Enter MADEMOISELLE MANCE *and Monsieur de* MAISONNEUVE.

MADEMOISELLE MANCE: Jeanne, Jeanne! who fired that gun? What mummery!
And this immodest dress!

MAISONNEUVE: That scarce would shame
A titled dame in France; but ill becomes
An honest Indian girl.

JEANNE: *(speaking very low)* Hush, hush, I thought
To fright the demon, then to charm asleep.

MAISONNEUVE: *(addressing MADEMOISELLE MANCE)* Mademoiselle, such fall from grace reproves
Your pride! But yesterday, I heard you boast
This convert's piety!

Monsieur de MAISONNEUVE exits.

MADEMOISELLE MANCE: O Jeanne, you shame
My prayers.

JEANNE: No, no, Marraine.

She runs to MADEMOISELLE MANCE and pets her hand, then pointing.

But see my gift's
Refused, the Demon's still unpacified!

The dog creeps back. MADEMOISELLE MANCE takes a towel and rubs the shivering animal. After a time she looks at JEANNE, who pulls a small bag from her bodice.

MADEMOISELLE MANCE: The dog is drenched, poor beast! What nonsense now?

JEANNE: My medicine! an owlet's feathered horn!
When dawned my fourteenth summer, as our custom,
I sought the distant solitude; there fasting
Some fourteen suns, an owl's beak pricked my brain,
Its yellow eyes stared mine awake—the owl's
My manitou and I am wise beyond
Most Indian girls. My medicine but needs
An offering, some puffed tobacco smoke;
To exorcise, some magic words.

MADEMOISELLE MANCE: Then drop
That senseless thing, and beg forgiveness.

JEANNE: My wisdom! nay, disastrous thought!

MADEMOISELLE MANCE: *(pointing outside)* Look! look!
They raise the Cross as all now sink in prayer,
Quick, throw that evil charm; ah, there it goes!
Let savage wisdom bend to Christian grace.

Kneel here with me, this blanket wrapped around,
So may God's mercy flush and warm your soul,
Resentment fades as supplication stirs
The heart, and self is merged in reverence.

Voices from outside.

When rock with wood was smitten,
 Clear waters gurgled forth,
The Faith, that led through deserts,
 Has tamed this frigid North.

Though here the waters gather,
 Tempestuous and bold,
Let wood now save and shelter,
 As Noah's arc of old.

O tree of sweet salvation,
 That stills the soul's unrest,
Whence hung a precious burden,
 The Word made manifest.

O teach our flesh to suffer,
 If such thy message be,
Uphold us though and strengthen;
 God save our Colony!

Enter MADAME DE LA PELTRIE *and Monsieur de* MAISONNEUVE.

MAISONNEUVE: O heavy thought! So soon to be demolished,
The fruit of anxious prayer! of stern endeavour!
Our long months' work is vanity.—God's will
Be done!

MADAME DE LA PELTRIE: 'Tis fierce without, the skies submerge
A land sufficient soaked, and winds now whet
Like tidal waves, the flood's incoming rush,
Small use to move our goods, where refuge them?

MAISONNEUVE: The boxed munitions might be saved, at least
An effort made.

Monsieur de MAISONNEUVE *exits.*

MADAME DE LA PELTRIE: *(lifting some packages)* These parcels raised, why stand
Deploring, arms unbusied?

MADEMOISELLE MANCE: Something, not
Of self, persuades no flood will damp this place;
God's purpose here has been so oft revealed.

MADAME DE LA PELTRIE: *(turning)* What splashes there? 'tis like a fountain playing
In France, a Sabbath melody; nay now
A fierce cascade that tears an Alpine slope
With torrent snows!

JEANNE: The waters overcharge
And swell the moat.

MADAME DE LA PELTRIE: O, Mary, save us now!

MADEMOISELLE MANCE: Beyond this threshold not one drop will pass,
As Abraham was purified, so God
Perfects our faith through dire extremities.

MADAME DE LA PELTRIE: God grant, you utter truth, but see the flood
Ascends as though alive with steady purpose—
Malevolence, pit-brewed by that fell Power
Whose favourite preserves we seek to wrest,

Stooping with JEANNE over the threshold.

My hand is wet with spatterings, 'tis-time
To plan our flight.

MADEMOISELLE MANCE: And leave the Tempter here
Victorious! his challenge undisputed!

JEANNE: Marraine, but one hand-length to climb.

MADEMOISELLE MANCE: But one
Hand-length—and then, no more.

Enter Montreal's first COLONISTS, singing.

COLONISTS: Ville Marie, conceived by vision,
  Born of prayer and sacrifice;
Privileged to nurse thy glory,
  Shall we haggle at the price?

Symbol of earth's resurrection,
  Phoenix sprung renewed from fire,
Red and golden plumage shining,
  Thus the town of long desire.

Jesus, Mary, Joseph, help us
    In this hour of awful need,
Jerusalem to sing your praises,
    Watch, preserve its stainless seed.

The COLONISTS start moving the heavy cases.

MADAME DE LA PELTRIE: The water now has touched the threshold, see
It slowly levels, soon will overpour,
While we stay thus transfixed.

MADEMOISELLE MANCE: It will not pass!

MADAME DE LA PELTRIE: The brink is reached! O God, have mercy.

MADEMOISELLE MANCE: Ay,
He has. The trembling water comes no further.
By saving Faith confounded, lo, it slinks
Away.

JEANNE: 'Tis true! the flood retires!

MADAME DE LA PELTRIE: Now, God
Be praised!

COLONISTS: Ville Marie! conceived by vision,
    Born of prayer and sacrifice,
Wardened by the God of Ages,
    Rise and live, a Paradise!

SCENE II

The summit of Mount Royal, Epiphany, in the year 1643, twelve days after the great flood. Fresh fallen snow sparkles in the morning sunshine.

Enter JEANNE from left.

JEANNE: Toward straight-limbed pine the shadow backward creeps
To mark the time and place—And there he comes
With two besides—Ho! Granddad, ho! I wait.

Enter from right CHEHTEH, ANONTAHA, and MITIWEMEG on snowshoes, in winter travelling garb, each pulling a loaded toboggan, the fruit of the chase.

CHEHTEH: Ho! Meadow Rose. You fail us not. As plump
As some teased porcupine; *(patting JEANNE)* though not so prickly.
The strangers do not grudge their food—

JEANNE: Their store
Is low; but scantiness they share.

CHEHTEH: A virtue
Peculiar to all people then, that they
Of dog-like countenance should practise it.
But come you empty-handed? You, who boast
The owlet's knack of pilfering.

JEANNE: I bring
The news you asked and nought besides. To learn
The White-man's ways, to find his purpose here,
That was the cruel task you set, to flatter,
To fawn—to steal his secrets and his goods.
His secret, open as the day, I share
With you; his goods are bound with friendship's cord.
French squaws I ever loved, their Braves were most
Repugnant though, with bristled faces, shrugs,
And noisy bursts of laughter; now I love
Them too, a maid may walk among the roughest,
Nor blush at covert jest.

CHEHTEH: Come, Meadow Rose,
This young man's mother grows infirm, a wife
He seeks. Plant not the seed of jealousy.

ANONTAHA: This necklace, strung with finest purple shells,
Will plead.

He hands JEANNE a string of beads.

JEANNE: They're perfect-matched!—but take it.

ANONTAHA: You
Refuse my offering!

JEANNE: What choice have I,
Till you have earned a Frenchman's name? Return
Next spring, learn Christian truth; beneath the guns
Of Ville Marie some fallow land awaits
Our toil, and there I'll watch expectantly!

CHEHTEH: Those black-robed wizards have bewitched, to so
Forget your people.

JEANNE: Truth, I've learnt, a charm
That heals the wounded heart, with quiet thoughts,
To sift the stranger's prompting I was bid.
What inner motive forced this settlement,
How could this feeble effort hope to stem
The Iroquois, who have so oft rebuked
Our Huron Pride, what selfish end induced
Such danger! well, 'twas friendliness and love.

CHEHTEH: Then what was prophesied has come to pass,
And Hochelay endures!—But whence that sound? *(looking toward the left downwards)*
The French attempt snake-dancing, so, what droll,
What languid coils! the hill fatigues and such
A burden that poor wretch is shouldering;
Two weighty, crosswise beams! some punishment!

JEANNE: Why, that's their Chief, great Maisonneuve, whom all
Obey and reverence!

CHEHTEH: To show his prowess?
A Brave's defiance then?

JEANNE: In gratitude
That cross is humbly carried, here 'twill loud
Proclaim the White-man's Manitou's supreme!

CHEHTEH: Whist! Silence, girl! The depths have ears, though locked
By frost. 'Tis most unsafe to stay. Our spirits
Are not of stuff to brook such arrogance.

JEANNE: Fear nought, unless, in pride, derisive words
You speak. Before the Frenchman's Manitou
Our mighty stream has cringed and fled, though roused
Through thaw to deluge-strength. Great batt'ring waves
Attacked, they scorned the sacrificial dance
And filched my medicine; but dared not pass
The little Jesus's dwelling place—O much
Instruction's needed!—Hark! long moons ago,
The Black Robes say, wise kings presented gold,
Sweet perfumed smokes and you, three powerful chiefs
Who trailed thus far for stolen goods, this day
Will leave rich gifts behind.

Distant singing now grown louder. Enter left procession of COLONISTS, *led by Monsieur de* MAISONNEUVE *carrying a heavy cross, closely followed by the* JESUIT FATHER, MADEMOISELLE MANCE, *and* MADAME DE LA PELTRIE.

COLONISTS: Mystic gifts the Magi bring,
Incense breathes eternity,
Gold announces Christ, the King,
Myrrh assumes mortality.

Priceless gifts the Babe bestows,
Perfect faith for incense rare,
harity, for gold, o'erflows,
Truth and hope for myrrh's despair.

Lowly bend the Magi now,
Neath the cross, with staff and bowl,
Earthly rank they disavow,
Crowns of martyrdom their goal!

Monsieur de MAISONNEUVE *staggers.* MADEMOISELLE MANCE *and some of the* COLONISTS *hasten to help him. At the back others arrange the pedestal for the cross and raise the altar, superintended by the* JESUIT FATHER *and* MADAME DE LA PELTRIE.

MADEMOISELLE MANCE: Relieve Monsieur, he sinks exhausted, O
If we had brought some covering, a shawl
At least. I blame myself! 'Tis most unwise
To lie exposed when moist from such a strain.
Why Jeanne, a timely thought!

JEANNE *hands* MADEMOISELLE MANCE *a fur rug taken from her grandfather's toboggan.*

JEANNE: A bear-skin rug.
My granddad begs the great French chief to accept.

MADEMOISELLE MANCE: *(covering Monsieur de* MAISONNEUVE*)* Whence come these men?

JEANNE: From Eastern lands with gifts.
When we descend, before the lighted crib
They'll kneel, presenting them; three mighty Chiefs.

CHEHTEH: East and West and North and South, my people
Are scatterlings! though once in Hochelay
They lived content, in Hochelay, whose ruins

Now peep where beavers dammed a purling brook.
That work remains, the beavers still are housed—
But what of ancient Hochelay, whose pride
The poets sang? In tales alone we trace
Those stubborn palisades and lodges stored
With grain above—beneath wide chambers whence
Arose the sounds of hived-humanity,
Joking sounds, but querulous they grew,
"Prosperity had robbed our simple ways,"
Sighed Grandfather, dwelling oft on days long fled,
His childhood passed in luxury, his youth
And age in hopeless wandering. A prophet
Had warned of coming doom; but who, when food
Is plentiful, gives ear to caution's voice?
And Hochelay was passing proud, a town
Of feast and dance and song, a meeting place
For joyous villages that straggled far; *(pointing)*
Some perched where rise those pleasant hills that vary
The grace of plain and sky as travels the sight
Across our mighty stream. Yes, Hochelay
Was proud and strong,—today dust-mounds but scratch
A grassy wilderness, so marks the hand
Of Fate!

JESUIT FATHER: *(coming forward)* God's spirit has moved, the savages
Vacate this land, that Ville Marie may rise
To sing his praise, extend his boundaries!

MAISONNEUVE: And yet 'tis sad, a past so blotted out,
What force has wrought such harm?

CHEHTEH: A maiden was
The seeming cause; but under-drifts forewarned
Approaching tragedy. Two powerful tribes,
When giants roamed, subdued this neighbourhood,
Enjoyed the mellow breeze and fruitful soil,
Grew stout, pretentious, loved display, abjured
Instructive tales; the impure jest was caught
And thrown, from nothingness dissensions spread.
A forest, bathed with sunshine, is easily
The prey of some chance spark.—A Huron maid

Ensnared a Seneca, his father spurned
The girl, whose beauty soon avengers found;
A murdered chief in pomp of burial!
Sufficed no presents now. A death-grip locked
Two mighty tribes, whose beggared sons deplore
The affluence their fathers tossed aside.

MAISONNEUVE: A second Troy! whose reprimand creates
Forebodings;—but our Ville Marie's secured
By prayer!

JESUIT FATHER: *(addressing* CHEHTEH*)* Beyond most savages your thought.

CHEHTEH: Among my ancestors I boast a Prophet;
His silver tongue spilled music. Of Hochelay
Prostrate he sang; above its crumbled ruins
Another race should habit, and then another.

JESUIT FATHER: Farms tilled by Indians, in happy clusters,
We hope to further; receiving light and truth
From Ville Marie. Each race acknowledging
The Lys of France!

CHEHTEH: Your words are wasted breath,
The tomahawk of Iroquois is still
Unburied. The evil spirit has long been roused,
And unafraid he walks, for good has vanished.

MAISONNEUVE: Nay, good has armoured us to fight and win,
And I'm first Soldier of the Cross, as those
Who faced the Saracen in Palestine.
This morning's ordinance has opened vistas
Elate with sacrifice! A lad. I poured
O'er tales of chivalry, undreaming I
Should hear our church repeat those words: "Dieu vult."

JESUIT FATHER: None worthier!

MAISONNEUVE: Would that were so! As I,
Toiled upward, weighted with Salvation's standard,
I seemed to gently float, so light the burden!
While surged within my brain the Church's promise:
"Lord, we pray your clemency, deliver
From peril, always safeguard this your servant,

Who following your word, in your employ,
Desires to bear his cross, to fight your foes,
To fortify your chosen people."

MADEMOISELLE MANCE: Monsieur
Is nathless much fatigued.

MAISONNEUVE: 'Twill pass. How came
I though to make such speech, my inward thought
Discovering! Excitement jerks the lid
From cold reserve—like caldron-steam, needs vent.
This day has crowned my life! *(after a pause)* I had forgot
These friends, most fit their presence here to witness
From off this Royal Mount, Christ's kingdom far
Proclaimed!

CHEHTEH: Your thought's obscure, but this I glean
The White-man's Manitou now triumphs here.
His power, the future; not the present, proves!—
If signs and omens give consent, when suns
Are highest this shall he our meeting place;
With others of our tribe we'll come; we'll hear
Your wisdom, weigh its meaning, sift the truth,
Embrace—or disagree. Till then *(glancing at the altar)*
Who would
Suppose? A feast, in winter time, without
A fire!

MAISONNEUVE: *(rising)* Ay, God's Feast!

CHEHTEH, ANONTAHA, and MITIWEMEG walk over and examine the altar. The cross is raised.

COLONISTS: *(facing the cross)* Hail the Saviour! Hail the Cross!
  Banner stained with Victory!
Law and Truth restored through less,
  Glory won through Calvary:

Hail to thee, Salvation's sign!
  Wood protecting, wood august,
Hail the soul's eternal shrine,
  Star of peace and perfect trust!

ACT III
THE COMBAT.

SCENE I

The common room of the Fort of Ville Marie, the morning of the thirtieth of March, in the year 1644. A dog's bark without gives teaming of an Iroquois ambuscade. Monsieur de MAISONNEUVE, PIERRE *Laimery, and* JEAN *Robelin replace some accoutrements they have just taken down.* JEANNE *is dusting.*

MAISONNEUVE: Those skulking devils back! What lives were lost?
If our Pilotte forgot her watchful guard,
Her warning yelp bids us remain within,
Our work is sadly handicapped.

PIERRE: Monsieur,
There is a remedy; let us attack
The teasing foe, so strike that he will shun
This neighbourhood as we his presence now.

MAISONNEUVE: Invite disaster! How can we, a handful,
Pursue the Iroquois, whose tactics serve
The forest glade while ours, the open field.
If, yielding to your ardour, we embark
On enterprise thus perilous; how soon,
Think you, before some ambuscade entraps,
A score of bristling savages, 'gainst each
Of us. A little patience! When God inspires
More friends to cross the sea, sufficient blows
We'll risk! Today we'll build as Heav'n sees fit,
Nor tempt discomfiture through foolish prompting.

The courage, born of youth, needs discipline,
Till time wakes sacrifice from vain bravado.

MAISONNEUVE exits.

PIERRE: Our governor, in Holland, was reputed,
If less abstemious, belike Dutch courage!
For here his prudence points to cowardice.

JEAN: Unsoldier-like he shunned companionship,
'Tis rumoured, strung hymn-tunes upon his lute,
Preserving thus a strict integrity,
'Mid libertines and heretics; most worthy,
But savouring of over vigilance.

PIERRE: There barks Pilotte encouraging her pups,
Our leader tamely whiles the time.

JEANNE: He works
As any five of you!

PIERRE: Ay, works! that's tame
Enough! Those yapping pups excite my blood.
One goodly thrust to teach the Iroquois
Our ships brought men from France, nor prisoned rats.

JEAN: Hush! his step! No petty spy who treads
Thus noisily.

Enter Monsieur de MAISONNEUVE.

MAISONNEUVE: The Fathers need your help,
To place some chapel-pictures. Bestir yourselves.

PIERRE: Monsieur, Pilotte's incessant bark has stirred
Full measure. 'Tis troublesome to give our minds
To aught but taunting savages! Let us
Account for some—at least.

MAISONNEUVE: My child, the time
Has not arrived, suppose, through happy chance,
One hundred of our enemy dispatched,
What consequence? a droplet 'mid such hordes.
How different with us, a half-score dead—
Our colony would be reduced to grim
Despair—the dregs of brave adventure! In troth

We must preserve our strength else would I be
Much blamed. The daily task should satisfy.

MAISONNEUVE exits.

PIERRE: A chicken heart in virtue's livery!
And he's our Governor! Each time that bays
The dog, proclaiming hidden foes, let us
So gibe, a dunce would find our meaning—shamed
He'll lead us forth or—threats may influence.

JEAN: Mutiny has not a pretty sound,
And yet those brave companions unavenged!
Can we stay reconciled? Have we not motive
To force an issue—or slip the curb?

JEANNE: Their fate
You relish! I dropped some tears for them; but never
A flower I'll strew when our three lonely graves
Shrink from some newly garnered bones. That end's
Too fair! Your flesh may tempt the Iroquois,
Absorbing thus your bravery!

JEAN: Beshrew
The girl! suggesting baneful chance!

PIERRE: Our mates
Were trapped, were unprepared; but we, full-armed,
Another tale!

JEAN: Pray God, the telling soon!

Exeunt PIERRE Laimery and JEAN Robelin. JEANNE stands in thought. Enter MADEMOISELLE MANCE.

MADEMOISELLE MANCE: The Fathers wait, why Jeanne those men have vanished

JEANNE: *(placing a chair)* Sit here, Marraine, those men are scarcely angels;
I fail to trace their lifting wings, hell yawns
For them.

MADEMOISELLE MANCE: —Your meaning, Jeanne? 'Tis best explained,
Or else repented.

JEANNE: They call us savages,
But which of us defies his Chief? nor man,
Nor beast. Our friends, the beasts, each vaunt a master;

The Hares, a mighty Hare, each tribe its leader,
And all comply submissively. The Pale-face
Against his Sagamore low-mutters.

MADEMOISELLE MANCE: I
Have feared; and yet how reconcile such qualms
With quiet faith that breathes from Ville Marie.
Suspicions voiced oft prove the cause of ill,
Repressed by silent prayer, they melt away.

JEANNE: Mosquitoes buzz before they sting, suspicions
Unnoticed, worse may follow.

MADEMOISELLE MANCE: You hint our men—

Enter Monsieur de MAISONNEUVE.

JEANNE: Disloyal! yes, the Chief shall know, Monsieur,
They brand you coward!

MAISONNEUVE: *(calmly)* Well, a grave affront,
And yet since Noah's day 'tis ever thus,
Age censures youth and youth denounces age—

JEANNE: You plan a slow revenge, 'tis better so
Than sudden burst of passion.

MAISONNEUVE: *(addressing MADEMOISELLE MANCE)* Jeanne forgets
Herself; despite your teaching, Mademoiselle,
She is a pagan still, though overbold,
As some spoilt child in Christian lands—e'en so,
This question interests us. A soreness, come
These last few months, has led to grievous words
That fester soon, unless some treatment be
Discovered. Like the Church, when Peter preached
And Mary walked remembering, we thought
Our settlement—one soul, one common life;
Command, obedience distinguished scarce,
So fervent all in godly exercise.
But now authority's endangered, swift
The change—and swift the cure.—We'll hazard flesh
Than risk dissensions. Hark! the dog is barking,
This time, a trumpet-blast!

JEANNE: Monsieur, 'tis death,

MADEMOISELLE MANCE: Maybe 'tis life!

MAISONNEUVE: That God approve my choice!

Enter PIERRE *Laimery,* JEAN *Robelin, and some of the* COLONISTS.

PIERRE: Monsieur, the foe still flouts us scathless. We
Aloof, indifferent! *(sneeringly)* or terror stricken!

MAISONNEUVE: Your snowshoes, guns, accoutrements! prepare
To march! the Iroquois will gladly test
Your courage. Let the muster-bell peal forth
Our news; for Montreal we fight, this day,
We fight, pray God, we win!

Exit JEANNE.

The COLONISTS *hesitate, then start preparing.*

JEAN: *(holding up a snowshoe)* But see, Monsieur,
My snowshoe's warped.

PIERRE: And mine's mislaid, the snow
Begins to honeycomb, a month's delay
Would better serve, we must mature our plans.
This sudden rush—

MAISONNEUVE: Monsieur d'Ailleboust will guard
The Fort, take charge if I should be detained.
These fellows, trained by Dutch intriguers, are sure
Of aim, yet we'll account for some. Quick, arm
Yourselves. Remember, we're not on church parade;
More solemn work. We'll ask God's blessing; then,
Who knows?

The muster-bell is heard tolling.

SCENE II

Same as Scene I, some three hours later. Everything is tidy, showing JEANNE'S *work; she turns as* MADEMOISELLE MANCE *enters. The latter carries a pile of old linen, which she places on the table; drawing a chair, she begins to tear bandages.*

MADEMOISELLE MANCE: The room reflects your care, my Jeanne.

JEANNE: Marraine's,
As calm as some flag-bordered pool, while I,

A frenzied torrent, dash uncertainly *(sobbing)*
If none return, what then?

She throws herself on a chair beside MADEMOISELLE MANCE, *who hands her some linen.*

MADEMOISELLE MANCE: Here, take this linen,
Hold it carefully; now tear some strips,
Then roll in even bandages, the hand
Pressed so *(showing how)* that's better, yes, that's right,
Now think
Of when last year, as those crusading knights
Admired in picture books, our Governor,
With all the Church's solemn-pomp, was made
Protector of the Cross—the Cross in turn
Protects! It beacons from our mountain's brow,
It bruits, our settlement is more than some
Pale, faded leaf the winds may toss aside.

JEANNE: But thirty men against stupendous odds!
I would not lose a single one; nor Pierre;
Nor Jean, who stirred this hornet's nest, a sting
For punishment's enough.

MADEMOISELLE MANCE: Their lips might move,
The Devil spoke; chagrined, his subtle brain
Devised this scheme to fend his property,
Such strings of friendly savages baptised,
Requiting our sincerity—to soil
The font he scatters dust, he sows dissensions.

JEANNE: But he, the man I've loved, whose gift I've spurned,
Until it comes from Christian hands, is truly
Sincere; he says for food and guns some take
French names; but he's not thus convinced, so I,
A Huron woman, remain unwed.

MADEMOISELLE MANCE: A child
Yon seem; a dainty, woodland nymph portrayed
In old mythologies.

JEANNE: Marraine's astute,
Through books and prayers, a child in aught besides—

This is not rudeness—her heart has never beat
Like mine! and she's my mother's age.

MADEMOISELLE MANCE: 'Tis true
My heart is nun-like, still with human love
I sympathize. The Holy Family
Acknowledges the Man as head, the Woman
The greater one, the Babe supreme! When God
Has stayed this scourge of Iroquois, fair homes
Will sanctify a gladdened Montreal;
May marriage bells oft peal their happy tunes!

JEANNE: Marraine, I hear mine echo now! but faint
Like tinkling whispers, angel-sounds may be.

A bell is faintly heard, then louder.

Nay, hark! the bells are real, vicious rumbles
Of dread alarm, our doom is sealed. The foe's
Advancing fast, has overwhelmed our Braves!
Marraine, I grieve your fate! *(listening)* Why, now, 'tis joy
That volumes forth, the noisy joy of men
Returned, victorious.

JEANNE exits.

MADEMOISELLE MANCE: Thank God, they're safe.

Stooping, she picks up some linen JEANNE has dropped, then calmly continues her work. After a time, enter JEANNE.

JEANNE: Not victory, but rout, such wild disorder!
Unrecognized these flying men that fear
Had winged! "The enemy!" our sentry called.
Imprudently one fired the cannon, 'twas trained
That way; but God was merciful! the shot
Missed fire, the charge was poor, else holocaust
For Ville Marie. And Jean came first, brave Jean,
Outrunning Pierre like him whom Jesus loved.
St. Jean! forgive the thought! a laggard else!

MADEMOISELLE MANCE: Our Governor?

JEANNE: No wary caribou,
But fierce bull-moose which horns the foe, while seek
Their yard the scattering herd.

Enter JEAN *Robelin and* PIERRE *Laimery, breathless and disordered.*

We welcome Jean,
Brave Jean and Pierre, dishevelled, but—with legs
That run!

JEAN: Your right to jeer I'll not dispute,
Some water though, a dizziness!

He lies on a bench.

JEANNE: *(fetching a mug of water)* My gibes
Lose point, when modesty's the target. I'm
Disarmed—if not the Iroquois.

MADEMOISELLE MANCE: *(feeling* JEAN's *pulse)* Cease jesting,
Have all escaped uninjured? Where's your Captain?

JEAN: Jean Mattemal and Pierre Bigot lie dead.
The better Jean and Pierre than we. Our Captain,
This day acclaims his valour, may the Saints
Protect!

Enter JESUIT FATHER.

JESUIT FATHER: *(addressing* MADEMOISELLE MANCE*)* A sad affair! Guillaume Lebout
Is sinking fast. Nay stay, the ladies, late
From France, suffice to help our worthy surgeon,
Your tender care and knowledge, he requests
For wounds less serious, will send such here
Where space is not so precious. Jeanne returns
With salves and lotions.

Exeunt JESUIT FATHER *and* JEANNE.

PIERRE, *who has been leaning against the mill, takes a step forward.*

MADEMOISELLE MANCE: Quick, this chair, you stumble,
Your sleeve is dripping blood.

Helping PIERRE *to a chair, she takes off his coat and turns up the sleeve of his shirt.*

A nasty wound!
I'll raise your arm; 'twill stay the flow. Would Jeanne
Were back!

She holds up PIERRE*'s arm.*

PIERRE: As we approached the woods, a silence—
Forebodings rose, unasked; our Chief, though marched
As on parade, we following. Scarce twigs
Were snapped and brushed ere bullets whizzed as from
An unknown source. "To shelter!" cried Monsieur,
Now forest trees each branched a gleaming gun,
Well hid, who pressed the trigger; Shields God plants
For French as Savages! We laughed! the fire
Was hot and heavy. Then a shriek of pain,
A friend lay dead; another; ammunition
Was running low; but thirty we against
That whooping crew, two hundred, haply more.
A slow retreat was grimly ordered, facing
From time to time the Iroquois. A nightmare,
That wooded waste, ere reached the beaten track,
Like infantry that flees from cavalry,
Our snowshoes dropped or ill attached we sank
Each step, while lightly skimmed the enemy.
How gained, God only knows, the road we drag
Those cumbrous logs, whose weight we've oft complained—
But never more. The ground was firm, we sprinted,
Nor looked behind, each man for self; the Saints
Be praised! were lost to sight those hideous
Befeathered, painted beasts.

Enter JEANNE, *with remedies, which she places on a table. She holds* PIERRE*'s arm while* MADEMOISELLE MANCE *attends to the wound.*

JEANNE: Less frightened some,
They raised and helped the wounded,—he, who made
This possible, attracting to himself,
Has not returned. Mourn, Hochelay, your Chief!
A sacrifice! Mourn Hochelay!

MADEMOISELLE MANCE: *(applying remedies)* My tears
Will flow when I have viewed his lifeless flesh,
Your supposition's false, God tells me so.

JEANNE: Alive or dead his body will be seen
No more through loving eyes. Alas, our chief!

A vaunted captive! tortured, burnt, then eaten
By vengeful Iroquois.

MADEMOISELLE MANCE: Hush, girl, repeat
Some Aves now,—but hark! what noise disturbs?

Shouting without, heard faintly, then louder.

JEANNE: *(listening)* A funeral dirge—how now! what!
Vivat, vivat!
Our Governor, the dead arise! *(pausing)* His tread!
Vivat, vivat!

Enter Monsieur de MAISONNEUVE, followed by cheering COLONISTS.

MADEMOISELLE MANCE: *(raising her arms)* Returned, uninjured, safe,
Our Soldier of the Cross!

PIERRE: The bravest man
In Canada! we voice our reverence.
Vivat! Vivat!

MAISONNEUVE: *(sitting down)* Somewhat tired, my children,

MADEMOISELLE MANCE runs toward him.

Attend your wounded, Mademoiselle.

JEANNE: *(feeling him)* Monsieur
Is real? He's not a ghost-transparency,
Through which my hand can lightly glide.

JEAN: But how,
Mon Dieu! have you escaped, a single man
Against such frightful odds?

MAISONNEUVE: A miracle!
Humbleness permits the tale,—not prowess,
'Twas Heavenly intervention. You, my men,
Deserted me; but God stood by! A slow
Retreat I ordered, fast methinks your flight;
Like rabbits, panic-struck, that fetch their warren,
A sudden vanishing. I faced the foe,
An easy mark; but they now recognized
The Governor of Ville Marie, a prize
To clutch alive, a victim capable
Of suffering, a worthy spectacle

For village feasts. Their chief should boast this capture,
To him alone such honour! Suddenly
He stooped and sprang at me, my pistol missed
Its fire. In fury, towering now, I felt
His breath above, his arms encircled me.
A shot, my second pistol spoilt his triumph,
Unblinking, dead, he fell. And I was free,
The sky and earth were mine! A moment's pause,
Then like my trusty friends, the rabbits here,
I scurried home, though why allowed, beyond
My power to guess.

JEANNE: To aid our Governor,
They feared a sudden sortie. Their duty, then,
Was plain. The Chief's dead body must receive
Their care, be rescued, avoiding thus all chance
Of ravishment by stranger hands, a trophy
To gloat upon, dishonouring the name
Of Iroquois. Such shame must be prevented,
In carrying away the sad remains,
You, Monsieur, have been forgotten.

MAISONNEUVE: You've solved
Our riddle, Jeanne. Forgotten!—by friends and foes.
Alike.

PIERRE: Monsieur, as long as Montreal
Endures, this combat's writ in memory!

JEAN: Monsieur, we yield you homage.

ACT IV
FULFILLMENT.

SCENE I

The street of Ville Marie, near the Parish Church, early in April of the year 1660. The COLONISTS *collect after their day's work. Among them Adam* DOLLARD, *who sits on a bench at the back oblivious to his surroundings,* PIERRE *Laimery,* JEAN *Robelin,* JEANNE, *and* ANONTAHA. *A fiddler, playing a solemn air, suddenly changes to dance music.*

JEAN: In France, 'twas last I heard that tune. My feet
Were younger then; they're scarce disabled yet.

PIERRE: A dance to welcome spring, so suddenly
'Tis come.

JEAN: Sweet June forgets the calendar
Has waked two months ahead.

He offers his hand to a woman.

We'll take some turns
To keep the laughing damsel here. Aha!

A few couples take a turn in an old country dance, then stop as the vesper bell rings. Exeunt PIERRE *Laimery,* JEAN *Robelin, and* COLONISTS *through the church door. Enter Monsieur de* MAISONNEUVE *and* MADEMOISELLE MANCE.

JEANNE: Such jauntiness in Ville Marie! A flash
Proceeds the storm. *(turning to* ANONTAHA*)* Monsieur awaits, unfold
Your tale. *(addressing* MADEMOISELLE MANCE*)* Stay, Mademoiselle, my husband speaks.

ANONTAHA: These last few moons, a cloud of fear has dimmed
The hopes of thinking men, the cloud approaches,
Its thunder stirs. I've heard the gathering
Of warriors, their heavy tread resounds;
The French are hardened 'gainst the skirmishers'
Light step; calamity advances now.
In concord march Five Nations, armed with fire
And malice, purposing the White-man's doom.
Eight hundred Iroquois at Roche Fondue,
A vanguard, more are mustering. Your strength
Is man's opposed to Fate; your hour has come.

MADEMOISELLE MANCE: "Jesus, Mary, Joseph," are writ within
The corner-stone of our dear parish church;
Three Communities, acknowledging,
Now walk the streets of Ville Marie. The tree
Has branched as visioned once. Its roots are true.

ANONTAHA: Five Nations raise the tomahawk, what trunk
Withstands their blow?

MADEMOISELLE MANCE: The wood of martyrdom,
The gate to Paradise.

MAISONNEUVE: *(addressing ANONTAHA)* Your news is surely
Of grave import, a creeping menace now
Reveals its cruel fangs. Prompt action is
The remedy, yet how repel this host?
I feel my age today, *(sitting on near bench)* still let me think.

MADEMOISELLE MANCE: Our dangers have been manifold since first,
In Montreal, the Holy Sacrament
Was raised, God's stepping stones, I think.—A score
Of men encamped that summer, eighteen years
Ago, and we few women, how easily
The prey of hostile tribes!—our fort was built,
Our strength increased, before discovery.
Our dangers have been many, our mercies too!
Divers times what fears have risen, more victims
To satisfy the Foe; but Ville Marie
Still testifies.

ANONTAHA: *(addressing Monsieur de MAISONNEUVE)* The wolf's quick, snapping bite,
You've parried oft, the bears' upstanding blow.
Beware! The tortoise now forgets his splash—
Three families, Five Nations, linked as one.

MADEMOISELLE MANCE: My youth grew stern 'mid massacre and pillage.
The Empire's soldiers ravished France; the tides
Of war beat round Nogent, a frontier town.
My Mother loved to talk of one Jeanne d'Arc;
Some sneered and called her witch; the world is thus,
Ofttimes, the beautiful's misunderstood.
My Mothers' face would flush with earnestness,
A maid of seventeen once saved our France,
God works through humble instruments.

JEANNE: My name
Is Jeanne, and yours, Marraine.

MADEMOISELLE MANCE: Her name we bear,
Her stalwart heart is his, who waits, impatience
Scarce bridling. *(addressing Adam DOLLARD)* Saviour of New France, why stay
You silent?

DOLLARD: *(coming forward)* So, my secret's guessed.

MAISONNEUVE: To raise
The voice has ever been a young man's folly,
He feels his growing weight, forgetting aught
But self, though selfishness is not your habit,
My son. Explain your thought, we catch at straws,

DOLLARD: When this attack was rumoured, sixteen youths,
And I, engaged to sell our lives, our all,
That Ville Marie might live. We plan a quick
Advance to catch the napping foe; our aim
Thermopylae! our fairest hope!

MAISONNEUVE: A brave
Resolve! Too brave, alas! too hazardous!
We'll first consult the older men, take counsel.

DOLLARD: I've talked with Major Closse and Charles Le Moyne.
"The ground must be prepared and seeded, then

We'll lead you forth. Our duty's here; postpone
This enterprise," they say. Where is the use
Of ploughing, if none to harvest? Our time is now—
Or never.

MADEMOISELLE MANCE: The heart of youth is generous.
We greet Jeanne d'Arc of Canada!

DOLLARD: You flatter!
My past has been, alas! a young man's story,
A spotted page! pray God the future cleans
A smut or two; give me that chance, Monsieur.

MAISONNEUVE: Then search the Notary, the Priest, if bent
On sacrifice, few cares must dim such lustre.

DOLLARD: Before St. Joseph's altar we intend
A solemn vow, to ask no clemency,
Receive no quarter, fight till death absolves,
My soul at peace!

MAISONNEUVE: *(pointing to Church)* God's blessing waits, O Lord,
Have pity!

MAISONNEUVE exits through the door of the church.

ANONTAHA: *(addressing Adam DOLLARD)* Halt, Monsieur, the French, though brave,
Are poorly versed in ruse and forest craft;
A child's attempt! Take me as guide, some things
I understand!

DOLLARD: *(from Church steps)* Protectors, Ville Marie
Requires; not we! our little force is strong
Enough.

DOLLARD exits through the door of the church.

ANONTAHA: The Pale-face shares his benefits,
But hugs his perils niggardly.

JEANNE: So burns
His torch the brighter. Let its glory flash!
I keep my husband.

ANONTAHA: Long in memory,
I trust.

JEANNE: Disdained by that proud youth, you ask
Again?

ANONTAHA: I would, La Mouche, my nephew showed
Such bravery. With forty so-called warriors,
He seeks to catch some straggling Iroquois,
Nor thinks of such attack, yet begs my help.
The path is plainly blazed—I'll lead these men,
Awake the ancient Huron fire, the Pale-face
I'll reinforce, an allied victory!
But subterfuge—the French go forth alone,
We follow, meet when danger thickens, sure
Of welcome smiles.

JEANNE: My smile, tear-laden, bids
You stay. *(touching her necklace)* One necklace, see, and only one!
Most women boast their beaded conquests, string
On string, by divers hands presented. You
Alone have fondled me. O Frenchman's God,
Let others go, though not this Brave who claimed
Me wife but yestermorn.

ANONTAHA: Nay, Jeanne, twelve moons
Of happiness we've known, few boast as much.

JEANNE: Twelve moons of happiness, what winter frosts
For such short summer! Twelve moons of happiness!

ANONTAHA: You sob. Is't grief or joy or mingled weather?

JEANNE: Stay, stay with me! My love's a sickly thing;
Do you break through its cords.

ANONTAHA: Its cords are firm
And pure and true, through sacrifice their strength.
We're Christians, Jeanne; see, girl, you beckoned, yet
I stayed till Faith acquired my right to hold
You thus *(taking JEANNE in his arms)* through endless moons of happiness;
Our parting's brief, one kiss—farewell, my wife!

Breaking from his wife, he strides away. Exit.

JEANNE: *O Mary, how I suffer! (calling)* Husband! He
Has gone. Has never turned a backward glance.

She sinks on a bench, weeping bitterly.

SCENE II

Same as Scene I, nearly two months later. MADEMOISELLE MANCE *sits on a bench, reading some letters newly arrived from France.*

Enter Monsieur de MAISONNEUVE.

MAISONNEUVE: From La Fleche your news? Dauversiere?

MADEMOISELLE MANCE: Monsieur, he's dead!

MAISONNEUVE: A world in ashes, then!
These seventeen dear youths, d'Ailleboust, and now
Our founder! All, all are dead.—What rumours fly,
The certainty of things has lost its hold;
This seeming God-directed sacrifice
Has roused the foe to fury-pitch. The mill,
Our two redoubts, the hospital, the fort,
Our homes, what thought can strengthen them against
The vengeance gathering? The Church's prayers,
May be, if such God's will, interpreted
Aright. But read your news, I'll strive to follow—
My mind though jumps from this weak point to that.

MADEMOISELLE MANCE: 'Tis from the Baron, dated last November.
He writes while fresh impressed, no incident's
Too trivial, all precious jewels; still,
I'll skim his words to suit anxiety.

MAISONNEUVE: *(sitting down)* A man revived, you fancied?

MADEMOISELLE MANCE: Yes, last June,
As eighteen years ago, his cheering presence
Forced back the tears that welled for France. Between
Our ship and land the water broad'ned, the shore
Grew faint and fainter; that dear face ablaze
With righteous love, no exigence can dim,
No foolish doubt can conquer. Yes, his work,
Like Father Olier's, was finished; he

Had blessed his nursing daughters, waved farewell
Upheld, we sailed together; and here we stay,
Though stressed with poverty, though Iroquois
Disquiet us.

MAISONNEUVE: A pretty word: "disquiet,"
Beneath a threatened avalanche!—Proceed.

MADEMOISELLE MANCE: A short respite was lent God's Servant, thus
Enabling him to fill his mission, help
Secure his prophesies of Montreal.
He watched our ship that jammed the distance, then
He turned, and lo! his maladies assailed
Afresh! 'twas martyrdom! all slipped from him
But sense of suff'ring. His torments racked and gnawed
And fought for conquest—at last he weakened, was
Confined to bed, and there he lay some months,
A skeleton whose cov'ring formed a mass
Of putrid flesh; but draw the veil o'er man's
Corruption, brightly shone the Faith that nought
Could tarnish. His friends were lost, his reputation,
Misunderstood, involved in debt, yet dying
His wasted hands were meekly crossed, his face
Serene!

MAISONNEUVE: May God's great Servant intercede
This day for Ville Marie!

MADEMOISELLE MANCE: Assuredly,
His faith is ours! A story well explains
Our sainted founder. A blessing once was offered;
His then Confessor bade him choose the Grace
That sinneth not. "My Father," he replied,
"This life is but a striving toward perfection,
A looking upward, how expect to scale
The height ere Heav'n be reached; but Faith's a light
From which ill shadows flee, whose lantern man
May clasp."

Enter JEANNE, *carrying a basket laden with herbs and trailing greens.*

JEANNE: Hold! hold it high! Our Ville Marie
Has need, yet what care I for Ville Marie,
My husband's dead!

JEANNE bursts into tears.

MADEMOISELLE MANCE: Poor girl, your grief is young,
To envy him's permissible, not weep
A Christian's death.

JEANNE throws flowers from her basket.

JEANNE: Then let us strew the ground
With flowers! The Iroquois advance with gifts
Of torture, massacre; we offer scalps,
Securing Christian death though scarce, I think,
A Christian burial.

MAISONNEUVE: *(rising)* Unholy talk!

Monsieur de MAISONNEUVE exits. JEANNE picks flowers from the ground.

JEANNE: Poor flowers! why suffer for my sorrow. You
Were plucked to deck our Lady's altar. See!
Gay, dancing columbine, blood-red, and here's
A fallen star! I saw it flash the skies
Late yesternight, a token never touched
Before by human hands.

MADEMOISELLE MANCE: A dandelion!
Dear, homely weed that sings of peace and France,
What child has puffed the time of day, what wind
Has blown a filmy seed, what ship has borne
Such fragile freight, what destiny has called
You here? Prophetic weed! once rooted, none
Can stay your course. I see these meadows, dipped
With gold, surrounding happy Christian homes.
But Jeanne, your basket's filled with forest bloom.
Here's colic-root, a precious find! these sprigs
Of fresh young winter-green, so clean and glossy,
When steeped, no safer cure: and partridge-vine!
For rheums most efficacious; here's a bunch
Of leafing snake-root—kind, though nauseous draught.
Such herbs were mentioned in our prayers last night,
Today I handle them!—Forbidden risk,
To dare beyond the town's confine. O Jeanne,
What rash adventure!

JEANNE: Why, Marraine, I walked
Unnoticing; my husband's dead and fear
With happiness has flown! 'Tis dull this grief,
To gather flowers nor feel wee bursts of joy,
To brave the mountain-slopes, the thickest woods,
Nor dread a treach'rous tomahawk! 'Tis dull,
This grief and heavy, still, I sought precaution;
These herbs must be safe-guarded. Look, what's here,
A surer medicine than owlet's horn!

MADEMOISELLE MANCE draws from the basket a small wooden statue.

MADEMOISELLE MANCE: O Jeanne, there's breath within those parted lips,
Madonna, wonderful, with Infant Christ,
Who carved such charm and holiness? She smiles,
A miracle of tender, helpful love.

JEANNE: Anontaha! rest his soul! A King
From Eastern lands; this gift was fashioned moons
Ago. 'Twas when, with Mitiwemeg, friend
Till death, and my Granddad, he knelt adoring
Before the lighted crib in that dream-chapel,
Our first, then sweetly framed from birchen bark;
Wondering he glanced around; his eyes
Attracted by Our Lady's—long he gazed
Entranced, this statue speaks that memory.

MADEMOISELLE MANCE: And speaks the Sculptor's purity; but why
Was he so stubborn then, so proud, so primed
With argument, refusing till last year
The privilege of baptism; you, his sponsor!

JEANNE: Anontaha said: "The Frenchman's God
Is just; but Manitou's are plentiful,
Ours teach the truth." The Black Robe said: "Take good
From yours, a higher good from God Almighty."
Anontaha said: "Our wise old men
Exhort to righteousness; at festivals,
Amid the sacrificial dance and song,
Discourses point the way, their teaching's followed."
The Black Robe said: "'Tis good, our wisdom's better."
Anontaha said: "The beasts have souls."

The Black Robe harshly shook his head. Discouraged
My husband turned aside. The laws of Christ
Were not his stumbling block; but how desert
Our friends, the beasts, allies from dawn of time.
O weary moons of troubled thought! At length
The simple goodness shown by Montrealers,
Self-sacrifice, heroic deeds unsung,
Converted him whose ancestor, long since,
Was named the one good man of Hochelay,
Remembered still with pride—my husband's dead!

MADEMOISELLE MANCE: Poor Jeanne, glad Jeanne! A golden book records
Your husband's merit, strive to imitate
His worth!—Those herbs require attention though.
Their care should wake the mind from grief. They've come
In answer to our prayer. Herbs so gathered
In healing flesh, will heal a wounded heart.

Exit JEANNE; MADEMOISELLE MANCE turns to her letter. Enter Sister Marguerite BOURGEOIS.

SISTER BOURGEOIS: An ardent flame's extinguished, God's great Servant
Receives his crown, his exile's finished! This news
Has come from France, they say.

MADEMOISELLE MANCE: And our foundation
Has vanished, shipwrecked with our Founder's fortune.
Ah, well! Our Lady Poverty's a stern,
But wholesome Councillor.

SISTER BOURGEOIS: *(sitting down)* The sweetest friend!
I dread this talk, a vaster Montreal,
Some day a city sprung from Ville Marie.—
Few dream of that today, 'tis true; each house
Is barricaded. Our Huron scouts have been
Detained—

MADEMOISELLE MANCE: From martyrdom none shrink; but all
Must guard our mission-work, must watch its growth.
When God has stayed these threatening's, then let
Us build in humbleness, and trust the future.
A happy augury your stable-school;
The little lives unfold where Christ was born—

Within a manger. Indians and French
Are grouped together, one family! one hope!

SISTER BOURGEOIS: Another fear, if heretics, some day,
Should find an entrance here as in Quebec.

MADEMOISELLE MANCE: The Saints forbid; yet once in La Rochelle
I housed, unwittingly, with Huguenots.
Discovering my error, I spent the night
In frightened prayer; next day, I found safe lodging;
But since have thought my hostess kind, though pained
To note such fear of her; and that last voyage
To France, when hymns were sung by these protesters,
How I blenched; yet looking back, their faces
Were kind as hers, their conduct, too, was mild,
Reproachless, Dutch Calvinists in Orange Fort
Once saved the life of Father Jogues. He spoke
Of them with love, then why should we fear stain.
Let prayer suffice!

SISTER BOURGEOIS: And penitence!

MADEMOISELLE MANCE: What Saint's
Austerity surpasses yours, my Sister?
Your food, too hot, too cold, with cinders sprinkled;
Your lips, but once a day with water moistened;
Your mattress, board; a hurtful block for pillow;
Your sleep, but pause 'twixt all-night orisons,
And not content, the sorry inner-cap
That bristles pins! I shudder from the thought,
Though I have known the ecstasy of pain.

SISTER BOURGEOIS: Your suffering was past endurance!
Only
A miracle has cured that withered arm!
Your usefulness is still required.—Divulge
To none my secrets. O, if God were touched
To save one sinner through my feeble efforts,
These pin-points soft as cushioned-feathers.

Enter PIERRE *Laimery.*

PIERRE: 'Tis strange
To find you loit'ring here, who never waste

A moment's breath, Ah, letters! once their seals
I tore with hope, found bitterness within.
And now they cease to come. Who cares? Not I!
A petty thing man's grief, that years can wash
Away.—But these commands and countermands
Have so confused, I scarcely know which one
Was spoken last, or what's my latest errand;
The Hurons 'scaped tell different tales; but all
Assert the maddened foe's approaching. 'Twere well
You laid those letters by and screened yourselves,
Though what can shelter 'gainst these coming hordes?

Enter CHEHTEH.

CHEHTEH: Three kings from Eastern lands, and two have won
The Frenchman's crown! I bear glad tidings! Hail!
Your mighty slain!—Announce my presence, I,
Once Chehteh, Paul baptised. Let all assemble,
Your Chief esteems his old ally.

Exit PIERRE *Laimery.*

CHEHTEH *picks up the Madonna left by* JEANNE; *after examining it, he places it prominently on a post.*

That toy's
A subtle piece of work, the drapery,
And, ah, the smile! why 'tis the Manitou
Of Ville Marie! well may she smile this day!

Enter Monsieur de MAISONNEUVE *followed by some of the* COLONISTS, *others assemble later.*

MAISONNEUVE: Our trusty Paul, your open face bespeaks
A mind that's free from treachery, yet 'tis
Unwise to gather here; one word, your news?

CHEHTEH: —Great Chief, rejoice, though I, a Huron, weep,
Your tribe will prosper, multiply, while mine,
A craven remnant, slinks to earth.

MAISONNEUVE: Your news?

CHEHTEH: The Iroquois retreat with silent drums,
With vaunting songs unsung, with lagging steps.

MAISONNEUVE: Incredible! I fail to follow!—your speech
Is meaningless. *(noticing the Madonna)* Whence came that statue, there?
Madonna radiant; look, look! She smiles!
A miracle! You speak the truth, good Paul,
My words are blocked with gratitude. O God!
Accept our humble thanks. Heroic blood's
Not spilt in vain.

A pause, while all kneel in silent prayer.

Your story, Paul, how come
These hordes of Iroquois, embittered, stung
By Bollard's check, to turn from victory
Assured, their vengeance unappeased.

CHEHTEH: False tales
You've heard from Huron fugitives, deserters,
Ashamed of truth. Forget their names. One Brave,
Anontaha, wakes our ancient fame.
With forty warriors he met the Pale-face,
With Mitiwemeg, great Algonquin Chief
And his three followers. The Captain Dollard
Smiled welcome, called the Red man, brother. There,
Long Sault, where tossing waters steal the quiet
From forest-gloom, a blackened clearing glowed
With bright campfires; the kettles spluttered cheer
That helped to magnify a weak defence,
The little palisaded fort, half ruined.
Suspense was lulled by sweet hymn-tunes that pierced
The noisy, drumming rapids, caught the chant
Of mating birds and breathed the will to high
Exploit. Asudden two canoes approached
Above, our people fired; alas! some few
Escaped to carry tidings; soon there swarmed
Three hundred Iroquois, our Braves were pressed
Within that frail redoubt, their kettles spilt,
Dry-throated must they fight, dry-throated bear
Their wounds. My tribesmen failed the test. La Mouche
Grew restive, tempted by fair promises,
He leapt the barricade, surrendering,
By twos and threes the caitiff Hurons followed.

Anontaha stayed—forget the rest!
The four Algonquins too held high their heads.
The enemy were reinforced, eight hundred
Assailants, seasoned warriors all, and yet
That sturdy band of Montrealers, reeling
From sheer exhaustion, faced unflinchingly
Each maddened onset, till war-whoops turned to moans,
Till Iroquois were thinned by death, then swerved
And faltered.

MAISONNEUVE: Then? What then?

CHEHTEH: "Enough," some counselled;
But others said: "Eternally disgraced
Should we return, acknowledging defeat,
Eight hundred pitted 'gainst this paltry few."
The trial-faggots then were bunched and thrown,
A breathless pause—who stooped and gathered them,
Great Braves, afraid of cowardice, not death.
Behind their mighty shields these men advanced,
The heartened multitude, a cloud of strength,
Enveloping. Poor Montrealers! still
Undaunted! their loopholes flashed a constant fire
That mowed fell lanes; yet undeterred, o'er mounds
Of quiv'ring flesh, the Iroquois now climbed;
A breach was made; young Dollard crammed and plugged
A musketoon, he lit the fuse and far
He hurled, alas it failed the palisade,—
Confusion, wounds and death!—nor quarter asked,
Nor given, hand to hand the fighting, yells
Of victory; though triumph faded soon,
One victim faintly stirred, the rest had passed
Beyond all spite, all power to torture, yes,
Our Braves are dead; but hark! if seventeen
French striplings, four Algonquins, one great Huron,
Behind a tott'ry picket shelter, held
Thus long eight hundred Iroquois at hay,
How hope to capture Montreal, much less
Quebec!—Their squaws may weep sad losses, we

Rejoice! Our Ville Marie has stemmed the tide!
The White-man's Manitou is Chief of chiefs!

COLONISTS: Almighty God! our prayer is granted!
Saved to build thy citadel.
In Montreal, each stone that's carried,
Meekly borne, let none rebel!

Nor riches asked, nor earthly pleasures,
Christ once lived in Nazareth,
Let mortal flesh absorb His spirit,
Service wakes from living death!

The audience and COLONISTS *unite in singing "O Canada."*

ALEXANDER MACKENZIE

MERRILL DENISON

MAKING RADIO, MAKING HISTORY: MERRILL DENISON'S *ALEXANDER MACKENZIE*

KAILIN WRIGHT

Merrill Denison's *Alexander MacKenzie* (1931) gives historical weight to a fledgling medium (radio) and a nation (Canada).[1] In 1930, Austin Weir (the Canadian National Railway's, or CNR's, Director of Radio) commissioned Denison to write a series of radio plays in order to give credibility to a national radio network. *Alexander MacKenzie* is only one of Denison's twenty-five radio plays that make up the *Romance of Canada* series, which also includes dramas about Canadian historical figures such as Laura Secord and events such as the Battle of Seven Oaks. With the series, Denison became one of the first and most prominent Canadian radio dramatists of his time.

Early explorers, like Mackenzie,[2] were fitting subjects for the series when one considers that Weir and Denison were navigating new terrain in creating original programming to establish a new national radio network. Denison's radio plays, however, did more than secure a future for Canadian radio broadcasting; they also injected history into a new medium for a relatively new nation. In this way, *Alexander MacKenzie* at once contributes to the history of radio in Canada and dramatizes a moment in national history. In making radio, Denison was making history.

Although Denison's work helped define Canadian radio culture and represent national history, he was conflicted about his Canadian citizenship. Denison was born in Detroit, Michigan, in 1893 to a Canadian mother and an

1 Merrill Denison, *Alexander MacKenzie*, in *Henry Hudson and Other Plays: Six Plays for the Microphone from the "Romance of Canada" Series of Radio Broadcasts* (Toronto: Ryerson, 1931), 151–83.

2 Denison used the spelling "MacKenzie" when he wrote the play, and it is maintained within the play text reprinted here for historical posterity.

American father. His mother, Flora MacDonald Denison, was an anti-monarchist and travelled to the US to give birth because she did not want her child to be born under the British crown.[3] When Denison was six months old, his family returned to Ontario. Denison's Canadian and American citizenships define his biographies, as does his self-ascribed moniker "Mugwump," a colloquial term for "a politician who sits on a fence and faces two directions at once."[4] Denison's reluctance to be categorized as exclusively American or Canadian underpins any examination of his contributions to Canadian history or his role as a "Canadian" playwright.

Despite Denison's reluctant Canadian status, he defined a type of uniquely Canadian hero in early twentieth-century drama: the solemn backwoodsman, deft at navigating the bush. In 1910, Denison's mother purchased the Bon Echo Resort (now a provincial park) on Mazinaw Lake near Cloyne, Ontario, and used it as a retreat for artists. The resort and the backwoods people it often hosted were major inspirations for Denison's writings: it seems fitting that Denison went on to dramatize the histories of backwoodsmen such as Mackenzie and to celebrate the exploration of Canadian terrain.

Denison's career as a playwright began, as dubious legend would have it, with him being locked in a room. In 1920, Denison served as Art Director of Hart House Theatre when Roy Mitchell (Hart House's artistic director at the time) bolted the door of an office and would not let Denison out until he wrote a play. As Denison explains: "At the end of breakfast, the two scoundrels locked me in the director's room and said 'just put it down on paper. If you want to eat, remember that the faculty dining room closes at two.' Well, with no inhibitions and a deadline, I was able to accomplish the feat in about four and a quarter hours."[5] Denison put pen to paper and wrote *Brothers in Arms*, a satiric comedy about a couple in the backwoods of Canada, in which an urban major and a rural private debate war, values, and the economy.[6] *Brothers in Arms*, according to

---

3 Allana Lindgren, "Merrill Denison: The Political and Modernist Writer at 120," *Theatre Research in Canada* 34.2 (2013): 281–92. Flora MacDonald Denison was an influential, political Canadian in her own right; see Deborah Gorham, "Flora MacDonald Denison: Canadian Feminist," in *A Not Unreasonable Claim: Women and Reform in Canada, 1880s-1920s*, Linda Kealey, ed. (Toronto: Women's P, 1979), 47–70.

4 Alan Filewod, "American Mug, Canadian Wump: Merrill Denison and *Marsh Hay*," *Canadian Theatre Review* 89 (1996): 70.

5 Dick MacDonald, *Mugwump Canadian: The Merrill Denison Story* (Montreal: Content Publishing, 1973), 29.

6 Merrill Denison, "*Brothers in Arms*," in *The Unheroic North* (Toronto: McClelland & Stewart, 1923).

Denison, became one of the most frequently produced English plays in Canada, with over 1,500 productions by 1970.[7]

Denison's success as a playwright earned him the opportunity to pen the radio history plays that make up the *Romance of Canada* series. At the time, radio was a private enterprise whose programming was mostly made up of American broadcasts, but Weir wanted to change that and create a national public broadcasting corporation. "It was," as Allana Lindgren says, "a bold initiative when, in 1930, [Weir] commissioned Denison to write scripts for *Romance of Canada* [. . .] in honour of the CNR's sixteen station coast-to-coast radio network."[8] *Romance of Canada* would help Weir sell his nation-wide radio network to the federal government and establish the Canadian Radio Broadcasting Commission (CRBC) in 1932 and the Canadian Broadcasting Corporation (CBC) in 1936.[9]

Just as his radio plays told the history of early pioneers such as Mackenzie, Denison himself was, as one historic plaque puts it, "a pioneer in radio drama."[10] Radio (and with it radio drama) was a new medium in 1920s North America.[11] According to Mary Vipond, the first radio plays aired on Canadian radio stations in 1924.[12] Lindgren proclaims: "With few precedents to follow, Denison, Guthrie and their production team not only recreated scenes from Canadian history, but made radio history on a weekly basis."[13] In fact, the *Romance of Canada* series, as Vipond reminds us, "set high standards" and was "most certainly the exception" for radio programming in the 1920s and 30s, which focused

7 Filewod, 70–74.

8 Lindgren, 285.

9 Howard Fink, "Beyond Naturalism: Tyrone Guthrie's Radio Theatre and the Stage Production of Shakespeare," *Theatre Research in Canada* 2.1 (1981): 19–32.

10 This historic plaque commemorating "Merrill Denison" can be found in the county of Hastings, Tweed, Ontario.

11 There are many important histories of radio in Canada; see Frank W. Peers, *The Politics of Canadian Broadcasting, 1920–1951* (Toronto: U of Toronto P, 1969); Marc Raboy, *Missed Opportunities: The Story of Canada's Broadcasting Policy* (Kingston: McGill-Queens UP, 1990); Mary Vipond, *Listening In: The First Decade of Canadian Broadcasting, 1922–1932* (Kingston: McGill-Queen's UP, 1992); E. Austin Weir, *The Struggle for National Broadcasting in Canada* (Toronto: McClelland & Stewart, 1965).

12 Vipond, 96. Vipond reminds us not to focus exclusively on the history of CBC Radio, suggesting that for more information on early radio dramas in Canada, one might consider the professional CNRV Players who produced ninety-five radio plays between 1927 and 1931.

13 Lindgren, 285.

on musical entertainment.[14] Denison would go on to write articles about radio, such as "Why Isn't Radio Better?" (1934), "Editorial Policies of Broadcasting Companies" (1937), and "Freedom, Radio, and the FCC" (1939).[15] In becoming a strong advocate of the medium, Denison praised radio because it "appeal[ed] directly to the imagination unhampered by the objective limitations of the proscenium arch."[16]

If Denison was drawn to radio because it was "unhampered" by "objective limitations," he seems to have been similarly inspired by the fact that Mackenzie was not to be stopped by the Canadian landscape's limitations. *Alexander MacKenzie* was produced by Tyrone Guthrie and "broadcast by the Canadian National Railways from Station CNRM, Montreal, over a chain of thirteen Canadian National and three associated stations" on 23 April 1931.[17] That same year, *Alexander MacKenzie* was published in Denison's *Henry Hudson and Other Plays*, the first anthology of Canadian radio drama.[18] The play tells the story of how Mackenzie (1764-1820) discovered an overland passage from Canada's Peace River to the Pacific and was the first European to cross North America north of Mexico.[19] Despite the fact that Mackenzie's voyage predates Canadian Confederation, Denison's script emphasizes Mackenzie's contribution to "Canada" and how the Canadian Pacific coast may have been claimed by another nation if it had not been for Mackenzie's perseverance.

Alexander MacKenzie emphasizes the sheer courage needed to cross Canada—a feat further underscored by the Canadian National Railway. Denison's dramatization of Canadian discovery complements the fact that radio listeners were often on the railway and crossing the very terrain Mackenzie

---

14 Vipond, 97.

15 Merrill Denison, "Why Isn't Radio Better?" *Harper's Monthly Magazine* 168 (1934): 576–86; Merrill Denison, "Editorial Policies of Broadcasting Companies," *The Public Opinion Quarterly* I (1937): 64–82; Merrill Denison, "Freedom, Radio, and the FCC," *Harper's Monthly Magazine* 178 (1939): 629–40.

16 MacDonald, 101.

17 Guthrie produced *Romance of Canada*'s first season, while Rupert Caplan and Esmie Moonie produced the second season. Howard Fink, "English-Language Radio Drama," *The Canadian Encyclopedia* (Historica Canada, 2006).

18 Denison's *The Last Voyage of Henry Hudson* (January 1931) was the first play to air as part of the *Romance of Canada* series. Denison, *Henry Hudson and Other Plays.*

19 Mackenzie's expedition was historic in that he was the first European to reach the Pacific by land through what we now call Canada, but his passage was not usable as a trade route because it was too rough.

fought so hard to navigate. The play's introduction highlights the relationship between Mackenzie and train passengers as fellow travellers of Canada:

> Today world-famous trains roar through the canyons of the Rocky Mountains, speeding in luxurious comfort the travel of a nation, and yet, less than 150 years ago, white men first made the crossing to the Pacific ocean by land from Canada.
>
> The play attempts to convey something of the background of that significant journey, the reason for its undertaking, and the manner of man who accomplished it—Alexander MacKenzie—fur trader, explorer and statesman.

As Denison makes clear, the play not only advertises the heroics of past Canadians but also markets the "world-famous trains" on which the broadcast was aired. With *Alexander MacKenzie,* Denison at once promotes Canada, the train, and the potential of radio drama.

As the *Romance of Canada* series progresses, Howard Fink suggests that the plays demonstrate "a sense of freedom from the necessities of history and realistic accuracy" and "show a smoother flowing technique of alternating narrative and dialogue."[20] The script of *Alexander MacKenzie* demonstrates the early development of radio drama techniques such as the effective transitions from narrative to dialogue. Each scene begins with the narrator as an aural way of announcing a new setting without the visual cues of a physical set. At the start of the play, the narrator's opening description establishes that "the year is 1788" and fur traders are meeting on the "northwest shore of Lake Superior;" the opening speech transitions from the narrator's description of the voyageurs' journey to the voyageurs themselves, "*singing a song of the rivers*" and discussing their route to the Grand Portage.

After Mackenzie and his men arrive at the Grand Portage, Mackenzie convincingly argues for the value of exploration, both for the play's characters and for the real listeners. Denison portrays Mackenzie's men as loyal but also reveals the dangers of the expedition, which highlights the importance of Mackenzie's dedication to and confidence in his voyage. As the narrator explains, "it is only the seeming indifference of their leader [Mackenzie] to all obstacles and all hardships that keeps the party on its quest." In highlighting Mackenzie's leadership, Denison presents the exploration of the Pacific as ultimately the feat of one individual: Mackenzie. In the final scene, Mackenzie reaches the Pacific

20 Fink, 21.

and paints the following famous words on a rock: "Alexander MacKenzie, from Canada, by land, the twenty-second day of July, one thousand seven hundred and ninety-three;" as a voyageur in the play proclaims, "I think perhaps that that says quite a lot." The markings still stand today at the site of Sir Alexander Mackenzie Provincial Park.

With no curtain to fall and no stage bows, the narrator cues the listeners that they have reached "the end of the play," much like a train conductor might announce a final stop. The closing lines of the play declare Mackenzie's national importance as the figure that "blazed the trail that secured the Pacific Coast for Canada." With these final lines, Denison historicizes the very terrain that the Canadian National Railway and the radio listeners were crossing.

Although Denison was a celebrated Canadian playwright in his lifetime, he is relatively forgotten today. Alan Filewod laments: "Denison has been remembered mainly by a small group of academic theatre historians."[21] Lindgren similarly notes: "His embrace of Canadian subjects [. . .] set him apart from many of his contemporaries" but "despite his numerous accomplishments, Denison has arguably receded from our collective memory."[22] Denison has been celebrated as the first prominent Canadian radio dramatist,[23] and even as "Canada's greatest dramatist,"[24] yet his contributions to Canadian history, theatre, and radio warrant further attention. With *Alexander MacKenzie*, after all, Denison mythologizes Canada as a nation with its own unique history and heroics.

21 Filewod, 70.

22 Lindgren, 281.

23 Ibid.

24 W.S. Milne, "Merrill Denison," *The Canadian Forum* XIII.146 (1932): 64.

A play for the microphone by Merrill Denison. Produced under the direction of Tyrone Guthrie, and broadcast by the Canadian National Railways from Station CNRM, Montreal, over a chain of thirteen Canadian National and three associated stations, April 23rd, 1931.

Narrator: R.D.G Brown
MacKenzie: Alex Baird
Singer: Paul Valade
First Voyageur: L. Tourangeau
Second Voyageur: Leopold Fortin
Third Voyageur: C.J. Dupuis
First Partner: J. Macdougall Miller
Second Partner: R.A. Young
Third Partner: A.J. Black
MacTavish: Kendall McNeill
MacLeod: J. Macdougall Miller
Roderick: W. Mclean
MacKay: J. Scott Walker
Indian Chief: R.H. Roberts

Today, world-famous trains roar through the canyons of the Rocky Mountains, speeding in luxurious comfort the travel of a nation, and yet, less than 150 years ago, white men first made the crossing to the Pacific Ocean by land from Canada.

The play attempts to convey something of the background of that significant journey, the reasons for its undertaking, and the manner of man who accomplished it—Alexander MacKenzie—fur trader, explorer, and statesman.

CHARACTERS

Narrator
MacKenzie
Singer
First Voyageur
Second Voyageur
Third Voyageur
First Partner
Second Partner
Third Partner
MacTavish
MacLeod
Roderick
MacKay
Indian Chief

The play begins.

NARRATOR: The year is 1788. From the counting houses of Montreal and from the slopes of the Rockies, the canoe brigades of the Northwest Company are converging on the Grand Portage, the sheltered harbour on the northwest shore of Lake Superior, where the nabobs of Montreal arrive in July of each year to meet the wintering partners with the fur from the far-flung posts of the country-up-above.

Along the waterways from north and west they come—the voyageurs, lusty, strong, light-hearted, driving their fur-laden canoes toward the meeting place. Across the lakes, down the rivers, through the rapids, across the portages come the voyageurs, stopping only during the hours of darkness to gum the bark canoes and light their campfires.

A VOYAGEUR singing a song of the rivers.

FIRST VOYAGEUR: *(when song ceases)* Ho, Antoine. That was all right. Now, how about another song?

VOYAGEURS: Come on, Antoine!

SINGER: No! It is too late. What do you want to do? Sing the whole night through? Look at that moon. Where do you think you are? At Grand Portage?

FIRST VOYAGEUR: We soon will be, Antoine. Five days . . .

SINGER: Not if we stay up half the night, we won't.

VOYAGEURS: Don't be an old woman, Antoine. One more song and we'll call it a day.

SINGER: All right then. One more and then no more. Eh, Mr. MacKenzie? You'll make these bullyars of yours get some sleep, eh?

MACKENZIE: I'll be for bed myself, knowing what's before us on the morrow.

FIRST VOYAGEUR: Where do we sleep tomorrow night, Factor?

MACKENZIE: Below Lake la Claire.

VOYAGEURS: Ho! You're going to make us paddle, eh?

MACKENZIE: From now on this brigade moves as if old Joe Batiche himself was on its heels. I want to make the Grand Portage by Sunday.

SECOND VOYAGEUR: Don't worry, Factor. You'll sleep in the big house next Saturday night along with your friends from Montreal. I guess you won't be sorry, eh?

MACKENZIE: Then it means we're off by four, my lads, with eight portages and six discharges before we turn in tomorrow night.

FIRST VOYAGEUR: Huh! That's easy, Mr. MacKenzie. Six packs to a man and we'll have you beyond Lake la Claire by sunset! What say you, voyageurs?

VOYAGEURS: By gar, yes! The foot of Lake la Claire by sunset.

SECOND VOYAGEUR: We'll show them how the men of the north country can paddle.

VOYAGEURS: Hurrah! Come on, Antoine. That song!

The singer resumes.

MACKENZIE: Good night to you, men, and a good day's run tomorrow.

VOYAGEURS: Good night, good night, Mr. MacKenzie.

FIRST VOYAGEUR: How about a fire?

SECOND VOYAGEUR: Oh, that's all right. It is not cold. *(yawns)* The foot of Lake la Claire tomorrow night. Hm. I bet you, Baptiste, we are there before you.

FIRST VOYAGEUR: You think so, eh? *(laughs)* Make the stakes worthwhile and we will think about it. Hey, Antoine, where are my blankets?

SINGER: By joe, they must be where you left them unless they have walked off by themselves.

General laughter.

FIRST VOYAGEUR: I left them by the bow of this canoe. Hey, who's got my blankets?

VOYAGEUR: They ran away, Baptiste.

FIRST VOYAGEUR: That's you making the big joke, eh, François? Let's see what you got there. Ho, ho! So that's where my blankets went, huh? Here, give me those. Now, move over there. Give me some room under that canoe.

THIRD VOYAGEUR: Hey, stop that kicking, Baptiste. Who do you think you are? Old Marquis MacTavish? There's room for all of us.

SECOND VOYAGEUR: Ho, Baptiste! What stakes do you want?

FIRST VOYAGEUR: Oh, I don't know. Let's find out in the morning. *(yawns)* That will be time enough. Good night! Good night, my friends.

VOYAGEURS: Good night, Baptiste. Good night, Pierre.

The sleepy murmurs of the camp are followed by the distant plaintive cry of a loon.

———

NARRATOR: Across the nine-mile portage to the north, in from the wild expanse of Lake Superior come the voyageurs, until three thousand men are gathered at the Grand Portage for the annual parliament of the fur trade. Here on the shore of a small, sheltered bay, is to be seen the most colourful pageant in all America. Here are Indians from the Peace, half-breeds from the Smoky, clerks from the Athabasca, interpreters from the Saskatchewan, guides from the Missouri, voyageurs from the Assiniboia; men who have been buried in the lonely wilderness a twelve-month, come to join in the great celebration of the year. Here are the wintering partners, lords of solitudes larger than the kings in Europe rule, and here are the princes of the trade, the senior partners from Montreal.

By night the Grand Portage gives itself over to prodigious revelry. Night after night the lords of the lakes and forests sit down to feasts prepared by chefs brought from Montreal, and presided over by old Simon MacTavish, the Marquis of the fur trade. The long tables are loaded down with the weight of game from the woods, fish from the lakes and luxuries brought from Montreal. Over beakers of wine and bumpers of rum the squared rafters of the great banqueting hall ring with the old Scottish songs once sung in the feudal castles of the Highlands.

The sounds of a hilarious party, across which are heard snatches of song, and the voices of separate revellers.

A VOICE: Hey!

SECOND VOICE: Sit down, Billy, afore you fall down.

FIRST VOICE: Stop your clacking, Finlay. I'm going to give 'em a toast. Hey! To the Lords of the Lakes and Rivers.

ALL: Hurrah!

MACTAVISH: Get on your feet, MacKenzie, man, and give them an answer to it.

SECOND VOICE: To Alex MacKenzie, the chieftain frae Athabasca, who's brought down 6,000 peltries.

ALL: Quiet! Shut up! MacKenzie's going to make a speech.

THIRD VOICE: Wait! Wait! My glass is empty.

FIRST VOICE: Give him the keg.

Quiet.

MACKENZIE: I'll not be responding to that toast for it's not my place. There's but one here you want to hear from, the laird himself, Simon MacTavish, the oldest of them all. Up, Mr. MacTavish, and let's have a word from you.

Prolonged cheers.

MACTAVISH: Partners all! 'Tis no time for speech-making with such food and drink before us and only till daylight to consume it.

Cheers.

I'll give you another toast instead. To the ancient spirit of the Northwest Company, and confound our rivals!

Cheers, and a voice takes up a Scotch drinking song. All join in the chorus with great lustiness. Two or three verses are sung, followed by general chatter, across which MACTAVISH and MACKENZIE are heard.

MacKenzie!

MACKENZIE: Mr. MacTavish?

MACTAVISH: The general council will convene at noon.

MACKENZIE: I hope I'm alive for it.

MACTAVISH: You'd better be alive for it, man.

MACKENZIE: Why is that?

MACTAVISH: We'll consider these proposals that you've come down to make.

MACKENZIE: Aye?

MACTAVISH: This dither about exploring that's upon your mind, man. You don't mean to tell me you've forgotten it.

MACKENZIE: No, no!

MACTAVISH: Then we'll discuss the matter in the morning and learn what the partners say. Mind you, I'm against it myself, MacKenzie, for I can see but little gain from it and large expenses, but you'll have your say at noon tomorrow.

MACKENZIE: Never worry, Mr. MacTavish, I'll be there, and if that's the case I'll be slipping off to bed now. Good night to you. Good night, Finlay.

ALL: Heigh, MacKenzie!
Where are you going?
Come back here!
You can still walk, man, sit down!

MACKENZIE: *(back)* Good night. I'm off to bed.

VOICE: MacKenzie!

MACTAVISH: Leave MacKenzie be, men. He's got a grand and useless scheme—he's come 1,900 miles, from Isle la Crosse, to unfold it to us—and I'm thinking he wants a clear head for it, even though it will do him little good. Come on, now. The night's young. All together.

MACTAVISH starts song and is joined by others.

———

NARRATOR: And by day grave deliberations are held in the council room; policies are decided; the campaign laid out for the coming year. At noon of the next day the partners gather behind locked doors in that same council room that served for last night's banquet. On one side of a long table are seated the wintering partners, stern, bearded men from the country-up-above; on the other side are the agents and the partners from Montreal. At the head of the table is MacTavish, the Marquis. Half-way down the wintering side is standing Alexander MacKenzie, addressing the gathering of the seniors of the fur trade.

MACKENZIE: And, gentlemen, through the Athabasca country flows this mighty river—as great as the St. Lawrence. Its source is in the Rocky Mountains, but where does it empty? That is the question that must be answered.

MACTAVISH: And why must it be answered at the expense of the Northwest Company, Mr. MacKenzie?

MACKENZIE: Why, Mr. MacTavish, the general utility of such a discovery is so universally acknowledged that it seems hardly necessary to justify the undertaking.

MACTAVISH: I am not taking exception to the general utility of such a venture. It's the particular utility I question. What are we of the Northwest Company to gain from it?

VOICE: The Hudson's Bay Company think they have a monopoly of everything. Let them monopolize the expense of exploration.

MACKENZIE: But what are these expenses that are talked about? There can be no great expense, gentlemen.

MACTAVISH: Before we come to them, let's find out more clearly what the gains are apt to be.

MACKENZIE: But, Mr. MacTavish, surely you can see . . .

MACTAVISH: Just a moment, please, MacKenzie, till I've had a word or two. I can see some things plainly enough. Now, for instance, I can see that it would be a fine thing to fill up some of the white spaces on the map of North America—extend the bounds of geographic science, Mr. MacKenzie is wont to call it—and I can see that it would be a grand opportunity for a restless, ambitious man of twenty-eight or thirty . . .

MACKENZIE: But Mr. MacTavish, my personal ambitions . . .

MACTAVISH: Please, MacKenzie, I have the floor. I say again this venture would be a grand opportunity for a restless, ambitious man, longing to escape from the wearisome, humdrum monotony of the fur post, to win for himself great personal renown, but is it a plan that offers any rewards for the partners which they do not now enjoy?

VOICE: A good trader stays at his post.

MACKENZIE: I must disagree with you there, sir. That has been the policy of the Hudson's Bay Company, but not of the Canadian fur trader, and we are of Canada, gentlemen. We belong not to the tradition of the Gentlemen Monopolists of Hudson's Bay who have sat on the seacoast for 120 years waiting for the furs to be brought to them, but to the tradition of Champlain, Pierre Raddisson, la Vérendrye. Men who built their posts upon this very spot, and thrust out from here to find new breeding grounds of the beaver. Where would the fur trade be today had it not been for the explorers? We of the Northwest and the French before us? It would be at an end, gentlemen.

Murmurs of approval.

Gentlemen, we must continue westward until we have found the last boundaries of this continent.

SECOND VOICE: I see this matter as MacKenzie does. The Russians have found the northwest corner of the continent in Unalaska. Hearne has been to the Arctic for the Hudson's Bay Company. In between may lie the Northwest Passage and MacKenzie's river may lead to it.

MACTAVISH: Will it lead to more furs? That's the question I want answered.

MACKENZIE: It must add new countries to the realms of British commerce, Mr. MacTavish.

THIRD VOICE: And if we do not undertake this exploration the Hudson's Bay Company certainly will.

SECOND VOICE: And if not they, then the Americans must soon grow curious of what lies west of them.

MACKENZIE: That is a most important point, Mr. MacTavish. The Spaniards claim the southern coast; the Russians that to the north. If Britain is to win what lies between, her claims will be strengthened greatly by an expedition from the interior.

VOICE: Perhaps we'd better have MacKenzie tell us what this is likely to cost us, Mr. MacTavish.

MACTAVISH: I can see no gain to be won whatever from this business. We are fur traders, gentlemen, interested alone in profits.

MACKENZIE: But, Mr. MacTavish, you don't accuse me of being insensible to profits? Consider what's to be won if we could gain a monopoly of trade on the Pacific Coast.

MACTAVISH: And further, gentlemen, the articles of agreement between us all set forth plainly that no partner shall engage in other pursuits than those of interest to the company.

SECOND VOICE: But Mr. MacKenzie's proposal would seem to be in the interests of the company, Simon.

MACTAVISH: That is what you must decide, my friends. I am against it. MacKenzie is young, he is restless, he wants to see what lies beyond the next range of hills. I don't blame him for that, but I say that it will do us little good. I've had my say. Now, MacKenzie, let's hear what this will cost us all.

Murmur.

MACKENZIE: But little, gentlemen. Here's what I plan. My cousin, Roderick MacKenzie, is now at the fort at Isle la Crosse, a short distance short of my own post, Fort Chipewyan. For all practical purposes the two forts can be combined. All I ask is that my cousin spend the winter with me at Chipewyan and that he bring the brigade down next summer instead of me. There will be no expenses, save for another clerk.

VOICE: Then we won't see you next summer, Alex?

MACKENZIE: Not if you're all agreed.

SECOND VOICE: It's little enough to hazard, I'm thinking. What do we stand to lose? MacKenzie's company next summer . . .

MACTAVISH: I'd not sorrow too greatly over that for the man'll not be the best of company if this wish is denied him now.

VOICE: Then we'd best have a formal motion . . .

MACTAVISH: There's no need for any formal motion. Are you all agreed that MacKenzie absents himself from his post next summer to conduct an exploration?

ALL: Aye, etc.

MACTAVISH: Then that is settled. MacKenzie will conduct an exploration in search of the Pacific, leaving his cousin, Roderick, in charge of his post at Chipewyan. *(fading)* And now let's take up some business that may make some money for us. There's the matter of the Hudson's Bay Company . . .

———

NARRATOR: A few days later, the parliament of the northwest breaks up, the canoes set out for the distant posts loaded to the gunwales with the goods for the winter's trading, and the Grand Portage sinks once again into its ten-months' quiet.

Back to his post goes MacKenzie, through the Lake of the Woods, up Lake Winnipeg, up the long reaches of the Saskatchewan, across the height of land to the Athabasca and down north to his own post at Chipewyan—1,900 miles by canoe.

Here he spends the winter with his cousin, Roderick MacKenzie, Cuthbert Grant, the plains ranger, who is later to become involved in the massacre at Seven Oaks;

Leroux, the hunter, and MacLeod, the clerk. In May Roderick is dispatched to the Grand Portage with the results of the winter's trading, and MacKenzie makes his final preparations to explore the Grand River of the North.

On the morning of June 3rd, 1789, three new birch-bark canoes are placed in the waters of Lake Athabasca in front of Fort Chipewyan. Two carry the India guide, English Chief—who accompanied Hearne to the Arctic—and his wives and sons. In the largest canoe are five Canadian voyageurs, two of them with wives who will sew and cook for the expedition. In groups upon the shore, the Indians from the fort encampment are watching stolidly.

The expedition is ready to push off. At the water's edge MacKenzie and MacLeod shake hands.

MACKENZIE: Well, Norman . . . we're all ready to set off on the grand adventure.

MACLEOD: And I wish I was going with you, Mr. MacKenzie. It's grand new sights you'll be seeing before you come back to the post.

MACKENZIE: You'll be of more service stopping here, Norman.

MACLEOD: I'll take good care of everything; you can put that worry from your mind.

MACKENZIE: Aye, for if anything went amiss while I'm gallivanting off to place new observations for longitude and latitude upon the maps, the partners would never forgive me. They're suspicious enough of the undertaking as it is.

MACLEOD: *(chuckling)* There's many of them will have a great shock when you return, maybe with the twenty-thousand pound prize for finding the Northwest Passage in your pocket book.

MACKENZIE: I'm not counting on it too greatly, Norman.

MACLEOD: No, but you can never tell, Mr. MacKenzie. Well . . .

MACKENZIE: Well, Norman. There's little left to do but say good-bye.

MACLEOD: Mr. MacKenzie, there's much I'd like to tell you, but I'm not much of a man for words at such a time. Good-bye, good luck, and God bless you.

MACKENZIE: Thank you, Norman. I know how you feel, for words are not easily come by when they're sought to express what's deep within us. Good-bye.

MACLEOD: Good-bye, sir.

MACKENZIE: If my cousin returns before I do tell him not to be worrying about my return. Who can tell? I might find my way to China and go round by England.

MACLEOD: Less likely things have happened. I'll tell Roderick you'll be here when you get back.

MACKENZIE: *(laughs)* Aye, that's a sensible message to leave for him. Good-bye, Norman. Hey! Antoine. Bring that canoe closer.

MACLEOD: Let me hold it for you.

MACKENZIE: Good. It's the last touch of gentility I'll know for many months. Good-bye again, Norman.

MACLEOD: Good-bye, good-bye ,sir, and good luck.

MACKENZIE: Shove off, Antoine!

VOYAGEUR: Hy! Now, all together! One, two, Marche!

MACLEOD: *(calling to those on shore)* Come on, give 'em a send-off.

There is great cheering and commotion as the expedition sets forth. These sounds fade, followed by the dip of the paddles.

———

NARRATOR: And so Alexander MacKenzie set forth into the north. One hundred and twenty days later, after travelling 3,000 miles along the great river that now bears his name, he returns to Fort Chipewyan. Here, outside the trading post, he talks over his trip with his cousin, Roderick MacKenzie.

RODERICK: *(fading in)* It was the tide, then, that told you you had reached the Arctic Ocean?

MACKENZIE: Aye, but I'd known for weeks that the river's course would never lead us to the Pacific.

RODERICK: And that was why you named the river The Disappointment?

MACKENZIE: Have you a better name for it, Rory?

RODERICK: I'm thinking, man, that they'll be calling it the MacKenzie.

MACKENZIE: They can call it what they will. To me it will recall nothing but a gigantic disappointment.

RODERICK: Are you cured, then, of exploring, Alec, and content to settle down as old MacTavish wants you to?

MACKENZIE: Do you mean, will I be satisfied with the life of a fur trader, Rory?

RODERICK: 'Tis what is expected of you, Alec. At the Grand Portage this summer, the Marquis had much to say about the nonsense of your undertaking

MACKENZIE: He called it nonsense, did he?

RODERICK: Nonsense was the kindest word he had for it.

MACKENZIE: MacTavish will see no good in anything there's no immediate profit from. But I tell you, Rory, that I am going overland to the Pacific if I reap no reward but my own satisfaction.

RODERICK: Your journey to the Arctic has not cooled your ardour then?

MACKENZIE: Cooled my ardour, Rory? Can you not see, man, that what was a desire has become an obsession? Five months ago I was anxious to learn where these waters emptied. Now I know. I've established that there can be no Northwest Passage. The dream of three centuries is ended, Rory. And by what? The Rockies! For forty days I had them on my left, sometimes so close that I could see them; sometimes three hundred miles away. Once, I thought we might pass them to the north where the river runs due west from Great Slave Lake for upwards of three hundred miles. And then our course swung north and I saw the mountains once again. Rory, I'm determined to cross that barrier and tie the plains to the Pacific.

RODERICK: You'd not be thinking of starting out at once?

MACKENZIE: No. First l want to push our posts as far up the Peace as may be. It will take a year at least . . .

RODERICK: And then?

MACKENZIE: And then? The arrangement between the partners comes to an end next year. It would be feckless of me not to appear with a sizable brigade of furs to prepare for its renewal and an increase in my shares.

RODERICK: Think you the partners will agree to another exploration?

MACKENZIE: And why not? This last expedition to the north may be but a spur to my ambition, but it has opened a wealth of new country for the Northwest Company. I saw one black fox upon the Arctic, Rory, that was worth a Chieftain's ransom.

RODERICK: Hm. And when they've signed for this new agreement, Alec? Will you set out that fall? For I suppose you intend to winter near the headwaters of the Peace?

MACKENZIE: Aye, that is my plan, Rory, but I've a mind to spend my year of leave in England first.

RODERICK: What, man? You'd seek the soft luxuries of London when the unknown's calling to you so strongly?

MACKENZIE: I'll not be seeking luxuries, Rory.

RODERICK: Would you go home for any other reason?

MACKENZIE: Aye. To study, man. To learn more of both astronomy and navigation.

RODERICK: Study navigation to cross the Rockies? *(laughs)* What is this joke you're coming at?

MACKENZIE: There's no joke about it, Roderick. There's no difference between uncharted seas and lands that are uncharted, and if my great voyage is to be of any value I must be able to make accurate observations for both latitude and longitude.

RODERICK: I thought you could make both now. You're forever gazing at the stars.

MACKENZIE: Latitude, now, I can make a pretty fair fist of, but as for longitude . . . Well, I'm fair ashamed of some of the reckonings I made this last voyage to the north . . .

RODERICK: Don't be so sad-mouthed about them, Alec. I'll wager they won't turn out so badly when others get around to check them.

MACKENZIE: I fear they will, but a year in London will give me the equipment that I'm lacking now, and when I start west again it will be with proper instruments and no longer as a skilful amateur, but as a trained professional.

RODERICK: And you've made your plans to go to all these pains, Alec, three or four years in advance?

MACKENZIE: Nothing worth a little was ever accomplished without forethought.

RODERICK: But is it on your mind to quit the fur trade altogether?

MACKENZIE: Not the fur trade, Rory, but the post of trader; for I think it unpardonable for anybody to remain in this country who can leave it.

RODERICK: Meaning?

MACKENZIE: That this is no life for a man of education or imagination. Three thousand miles from civilization, with nothing more to turn his mind to than barter with the Indians. No, I've a grander scheme ahead of me than vegetating here. Roderick, did you ever think what a union of the Hudson's Bay and Northwest Companies might accomplish?

RODERICK: No man nor firm could stand against it, Alec.

MACKENZIE: And if my adventure to the Pacific proves successful, such a united company could seek and win a monopoly of the trade on the Pacific!

RODERICK: Hm. Hm! You're powerfully long-sighted, Alec, man.

MACKENZIE: *(laughs)* Ah, there's more in this than old MacTavish dreams of. But more of this when I've done my nightly stint. Clear off the table, Rory, and let me get to work on my journal. Thanks. *(sighs)* I'd rather make the voyage again than write the story of it. Let me see now, how far did I get? Ah, yes. Here it is. Saturday, July 11, 1789. How does this sound, Rory? "I sat up all night to observe the sun while the men reposed until three-quarters after three, when we set sail . . ."

His voice fades away.

———

NARRATOR: The spring of 1792, three years later, finds the plans of the indomitable MacKenzie marching steadily toward fruition. Much that he outlined to his cousin Roderick at Chipewyan has come to pass. MacKenzie has built the Athabasca district into the most profitable of all the fur regions of the Northwest Company; he has signed a new agreement with the partners despite the growing jealousy of Simon MacTavish; he has spent a year in London, almost as a recluse, perfecting his knowledge of mathematics.

Now, in the month of April, 1792, we see him in a palisaded fort far up the Peace River where he has wintered to make ready for the Great Journey. Late in April spring comes with a rush and preparations at the post are speeded up. There are the winter's furs to be sent east to Chipewyan, and we hear MacKenzie and his second in command, MacKay, with some Canadians at work checking over bales of furs.

MACKENZIE: *(fading in)* Forty-two . . . twelve . . . eighteen . . . six . . . I've got those. Now, let me have the rest, MacKay.

MACKAY: Fifty-eight prize beavers, twenty-seven otters, eight wolves, thirty-six marten, and four bear.

MACKENZIE: Is that the lot?

MACKAY: Yes, sir, that's everything.

MACKENZIE: Charbonneau!

VOYAGEUR: Yes, Mr. MacKenzie.

MACKENZIE: You can start to work packing these furs now. How many canoe loads do you say we have?

VOYAGEUR: Oh, that's hard to say until they're packed, Mr. MacKenzie. There's a big load there, eh? Six, seven big canoes?

MACKENZIE: I thought about six. How's that, MacKay? Come in with two small canoes of goods and send out six large canoes of furs?

VOYAGEUR: There will be six big loads at least there.

MACKAY: It's a very satisfactory winter's work, I'm thinking, Mr. MacKenzie. A very satisfactory winter's work.

MACKENZIE: Good enough, MacKay. All right, Charbonneau. Get your crew together and start to work.

VOYAGEUR: Right after dinner, Mr. MacKenzie?

MACKENZIE: Umm, it *is* almost dinner time. All right, Charbonneau.

VOYAGEUR: Very good, Factor.

Door closes.

MACKENZIE: That's out of the way. The account books are closed. What shall we turn our minds on next?

MACKAY: Have you settled on the supplies we're going to take when we start west, sir? For if you have I might be getting them together.

MACKENZIE: The list is there on the table, MacKay, but I've been trying to prune it down still further.

MACKAY: What dead weight have you now?

MACKENZIE: As nearly as I can make out about 3,300 pounds. I want to bring it down to 3,000.

MACKAY: Three thousand pounds?

MACKENZIE: Including provisions, goods for presents, arms, ammunition, baggage and the equipage of ten of us.

MACKAY: And how big is that canoe you're building?

MACKENZIE: It's almost built, MacKay. I hope to see it finished by this afternoon. It's to be twenty-five feet long within, twenty-six inches hold and four feet nine inches beam.

MACKAY: A four fathom craft substantially. Ten men . . . say sixteen hundred pounds . . . 3,000 pounds of baggage . . . two tons. It's load enough! Mr. MacKenzie, and there'll be many a time when we'll wish we had but half of it.

MACKENZIE: MacKay, there'll be many a time when we'll wish that we had wings to fly upon before we've crossed the Rockies.

MACKAY: Aye, but for that we'd have need of being angels, and there's few of them among the fur trade. Have you decided on your crew?

MACKENZIE: Yes. Yourself . . .

MACKAY: Aye . . .

MACKENZIE: Six Canadians . . . Landry, Ducette, Beaulieux, Bisson, Courtois and Jacques Beauchamp. Landry and Ducette were with me to the Arctic . . .

MACKAY: They're all bonny men, as fine a lot as could be found anywhere in the north.

MACKENZIE: And then there'll be two Indians, hunters and interpreters, and my dog—he goes, too, MacKay.

MACKAY: Have you got the hunters?

MACKENZIE: No, but I expect to have them before the day is over. The old Beaver Chief has told me that he has two nephews. I'm going to palaver with him later in the day.

MACKAY: Then we've little more to do.

MACKENZIE: Nothing, once I have secured the guides, written my last despatches to the company and sent off the brigade to Chipewyan. Once those things are done, MacKay, we'll be on our way.

MACKAY: Aye, and it's a grand thought too. To be treading land where the feet of white men have never trod before. I'm proud to be among the company.

A stick beating against an iron pot is heard.

MACKENZIE: There goes dinner, MacKay. Let's have some food and give over thinking of the splendour of the journey until we're back from it.

Door opens.

Go along, man.

MACKAY: But still and all, sir, it's a magnificent opportunity whatever, and I . . .

Door closes.

———

NARRATOR: A day or two later the ice goes out with a mighty roar, and soon after the new canoe is launched. On the bank of the river the two Scotchmen and an old Indian chief are standing while they watch a group of voyageurs and Indians give the new boat its first trial.

Very faintly throughout the scene the men in the canoe are heard—shouting, calling and singing.

MACKENZIE: She handles well, MacKay.

MACKAY: There's no doubt whatever but she's a well-made craft, Mr. MacKenzie. See how sweetly she holds her headway.

MACKENZIE: She'll carry a big load.

MACKAY: She has need to, sir.

MACKENZIE: And yet she's so light that two men could carry her for miles without a rest. Landry and Ducette had her on their shoulders before you came down. Like a feather . . .

CHIEF: Umh! Your men have built a good canoe, white chief MacKenzie. Big. Strong. Light. But, it will never reach the Stinking Lake.

MACKENZIE: No, chief?

CHIEF: No, chief MacKenzie. The rapids are too fierce and the whirlpools are too many. There are great falls and rocks tumbling from the mountains. Your canoe will be crushed to pieces.

MACKENZIE: See, MacKay, how she handles with a load of fifteen men aboard her.

MACKAY: Aye, I'm noticing.

MACKENZIE: But, chief, your own people have been up the waters many sleeps.

CHIEF: Only beyond the first mountain to the borders of our enemies, the Carriers.

MACKENZIE: But you have told me of no obstruction on the way.

CHIEF: We did not go by water, white chief. We were hunting far back from the river. But I have heard from others. The rivers that flow down into the Stinking Lake are such that no boat built by man can float upon them.

MACKAY: Why do they call it Stinking Lake?

CHIEF: I do not know, but such is the only name my people know for it.

MACKENZIE: It is so named, MacKay, because it's salt and so unfit to drink. 'Tis the common name for it among all peoples inland who have heard legends but have never seen the sea.

CHIEF: The departure of my nephews makes my heart pain, Chief MacKenzie.

MACKENZIE: Now, chief, you have made your promise and you have received many gifts.

CHIEF: I am not seeking more presents. I say that I fear for my young men as they fear for themselves. Were they not to be with you, the white chief, I know not what I should do. But you have been kind to me and my people and my young men must follow you. I have spoken.

MACKENZIE: Then there'll be no more talking with them?

CHIEF: No. They are going with you.

MACKENZIE: You have spoken well, chief, for now we can be upon our way. MacKay, call those men in or they'll play out there half the afternoon.

MACKAY: *(calling)* Halloo! Halloo!

A faint answering shout is heard and the babble of the laughing paddlers coming closer.

CHIEF: It rides the water like a swan, but it is going where no swans dare go.

There is a loud shout, the sound of paddles hitting the gunwales in unison, and a sound of splashing as the men get out into the water.

MACKENZIE: Well, Ducette, how is she?

VOYAGEUR: By gar, she is just like one frightened deer, she goes so swift. She leaks a little bit, but we'll soon fix that. And I believe she'll hold three ton. *(ordering canoe-men)* All together, now, get her on shore. Ho! Run for it!

MACKENZIE: MacKay, are the fur canoes all ready?

MACKAY: All but the last-minute gumming, sir.

MACKENZIE: Then the brigade sets down east tomorrow. And on the next day . . . we will make our start.

VOYAGEUR: What's that you say, Mr. MacKenzie? We leave in two days more?

MACKENZIE: Yes, men, we leave in two days more.

VOYAGEUR: By joe then, my friends, we must have one good time tonight, eh?

An answering shout of agreement and laughter, which fades away.

———

NARRATOR: On May 9th the single canoe with ten men and one small dog aboard breasts the flood waters of the Peace and heads upstream.

Here is no broad, gently flowing stream down which to float at fifty miles a day as MacKenzie did on his own river, but a brawling turmoil of swift waters rushing down from the mighty slopes ahead. Here each mile must be battled for against the racing waters, for the current is too swift for paddling. Hour after hour the men throw their full strength against the poles, and when the frail craft rests motionless despite the combined efforts of them all, they plunge into the icy stream and struggle along the steep banks straining against the towing lines.

The silken rush of swift water is heard.

VOYAGEUR: *(under great physical stress)* Hold her!

SECOND VOYAGEUR: The poles will break for sure.

VOYAGEUR: Hold her. There is place there to the left, Mr. MacKenzie. Shall we try it?

MACKENZIE: I don't think that we can make it.

VOYAGEURS: Ho, we'll try.
Come on now. All together.
One more try. Now!

The crew are heard straining in unison.

SECOND VOYAGEUR: No, no, Ducette, it is no use.

VOYAGEUR: Hold her! Hold her then!

MACKAY: She'll not budge an inch, sir.

THIRD VOYAGEUR: Hold those poles, you men. Don't let her slip.

SECOND VOYAGEUR: Swing into the shore.

MACKENZIE: Yes, Ducette. We'll have to tow again.

VOYAGEUR: All right, you're boss. Ho, Landry! All right to let her go?

THIRD VOYAGEUR: Ease her off, Charlie.

SECOND VOYAGEUR: Not so fast there.

THIRD VOYAGEUR: All right now. All together on the left. Now!

MACKENZIE: Look out, we're shipping water.

VOYAGEUR: Four men out. Quick, quick. Grab her now. That's right.

THIRD VOYAGEUR: Swing her in behind that rock. That's right . . . yes, yes . . . go on . . .

SECOND VOYAGEUR: Look out you don't slip there, Mr. MacKenzie.

THIRD VOYAGEUR: Throw out those tow lines. Here you, grab hold.

MACKENZIE: Two men on the lines. Four men take one pack each. You two stay in the boat. Mr. MacKay, we'll go ahead with axes. All right men, lead off.

VOYAGEUR: All right, there Joe?

THIRD VOYAGEUR: All right, Charlie.

VOYAGEUR: Then both together. Pull, you bullyars, pull!

Their shouts die away.

———

NARRATOR: A week of ceaseless toil against the current, and the wide valley begins to narrow to a mountain gorge. Sheer walls of several hundred feet in height tower above the river and more than once stones thundering down from the heights above narrowly miss the canoe.

Two weeks and the Peace has narrowed to a raging flume between two high walls of rock a few hundred feet apart. For two days MacKenzie struggles onward, making but a mile or two a day and stopping every hour to repair the canoe with new bark and gum. At last an accident occurs, the stem is ripped from the canoe, and while repairs are being made two men are sent forward to see what lies ahead. It is almost dark, when they return to the camp fire on a spit of shingle around which MacKenzie and his men are sitting.

The song of the waters, much fainter than before. A distant halloo is heard.

MACKAY: There they are, sir, coming in now.

VOYAGEUR: There they are, see?

A shout of welcome from the camp.

MACKENZIE: There's someone with them.

MACKAY: They've picked up two Indians.

MACKENZIE: I hope they don't try and make our men desert.

MACKAY: They'll try, we need have no fear of that, but six inches of tobacco should fend them off. Will you look at Ducette's legs, sir. He must have gone through some foul country.

MACKENZIE: Hm. I see, MacKay.

The confused sounds of welcome is heard.

Well, Ducette, what have you found out and who are these Indians you brought back with you?

VOYAGEUR: They are two beaver hunters. We found them above the rapids.

THIRD VOYAGEUR: They both say the same. We must carry around this place.

MACKENZIE: What did you find out for yourselves?

VOYAGEUR: Oh, that's the truth all right. I don't think a fish could run those rapids. I never saw their like.

MACKENZIE: How far is it around them?

VOYAGEUR: That is not too easy to tell, the going is bad. I say about twelve miles. Joe says it is not more than ten.

THIRD VOYAGEUR: And we shall have to cut our own trail most of the way.

MACKENZIE: Is there no path made by the Indians?

VOYAGEUR: We found a trace of one in places.

THIRD VOYAGEUR: By joe, it was covered half the time by windfalls, and there has been a fire through there.

VOYAGEUR: Look here at my pants. Look at my moccasins. Hm! I shall need a new pair right away.

MACKENZIE: Then it means a carry, does it?

THIRD VOYAGEUR: There is nothing else for it, and we shall have to drag the canoe most of the way. It is too steep to carry it.

MACKENZIE: Hm! How long will it take us?

VOYAGEUR: Mr. MacKenzie, if we were above the rapids in three days we should be lucky.

THIRD VOYAGEUR: I think so, too.

MACKENZIE: And what's beyond? Do those Indians know that?

VOYAGEUR: Well, they seem to know to the headwaters of the Peace. They say seven sleeps from the beginning of the rapids we come to a forks . . .

MACKENZIE: Yes, the old chief said the same.

VOYAGEUR: And we must take the left. That is the one coming from the south.

THIRD VOYAGEUR: The faster of the two, they say.

MACKENZIE: Hm! Well, there's some rice with sugar on the fire, and Mr. MacKay has a regale for both of you.

VOYAGEUR: Mr. MacKenzie, Joe and I would like to say something.

MACKENZIE: Yes, Ducette?

VOYAGEUR: Mr. MacKenzie, we don't think we should go on.

Sullen murmur.

MACKENZIE: And why not?

VOYAGEUR: Because we shall all be killed, and even if we are not killed we will get nowhere.

THIRD VOYAGEUR: Each day was worse than the day that went before, M'sieur. Each of us owes his life to some miracle already.

SECOND VOYAGEUR: The canoe has almost been smashed to pieces.

VOYAGEUR: Even if we make this portage, how do we know what lies ahead? I think we should turn back.

A sullen murmur, quite extended.

MACKENZIE: Stop men! Are you not forgetting the boast of your breed? The boast of the north men? Are you frightened by a nine-mile walk because it's a little steep? And how will you be liking the tales that are told about the canoe-men that turned back when they met their first bad rapids? You'll be the joke of the year at the Grand Portage.

THIRD VOYAGEUR: Maybe, Mr. MacKenzie. But maybe some of us would rather be live jokes than dead heroes. I don't know.

Murmur of agreement.

MACKENZIE: Ducette! Landry! You were with me to the Arctic. Would you turn back now? I don't believe it. I'll not believe it of you!

VOYAGEUR: I don't want to turn back, Mr. MacKenzie, but this wild river is not like the river of the north.

THIRD VOYAGEUR: If it were ten times as bad I should not mind, but this river is one hundred times as bad. I think we should go back.

MACKENZIE: You do! Then let me tell you something of the meaning of this jaunt we're taking. Somewhere to the west lies the Pacific. Three countries now are preparing to lay claim to its coast. Spain, Russia, Britain; and the Americans will not be far behind. If we can win our way through to it and establish the claim to the intervening lands then it will become part of Canada. And the greater the difficulties, men, the greater will be the honour that you'll win. And whether you go on or not, I will go on if I have to go alone, and walk the entire distance. For six years I have planned this voyage and I not be turned back now.

VOYAGEUR: Well, we don't mean that we would leave you.

THIRD VOYAGEUR: No, no! We don't mean that, Mr. MacKenzie. If you go on we go with you. Eh, my friends? We'll not turn back and leave our leader to go on alone?

Murmur.

That is not the way the Northwesters do, eh?

VOYAGEUR: If the chief says, "go on," we'll follow whether we want to go or not.

MACKENZIE: I was not thinking you'd desert me, men. Now, get some food inside your bellies, and let's thank God there's no mosquitoes so that we can get a fair night's rest. Mr. MacKay, would you be good enough to bring those two Indians over here to me?

MACKAY: I will, sir, at once. *(calling, and his voice fades out)* Hey, you! Cancre! Tell those two new men that Mr. MacKenzie wants to speak to them . . .

———

NARRATOR: Two days' gruelling work sees them across the portage, and a week's steady poling through the main chain of the Rockies finds them at the forks of two rivers, one flowing from the north and west, one from the south and east. They have taken twenty-three days to travel two hundred and fifty miles.

Although all are agreed that the northern stream seems to be the one that they should take, MacKenzie remembers the explicit instructions of all the Indians he has met, and goes up the stream that flows to the east and south.

Ignoring the open grumbling of his men, MacKenzie turns up the Parsnip River. For seventeen days they see no Indians. It seems to all that they are on a wild goose chase. Even the leader becomes anxious. The discontent of the men grows greater as each day passes, and it is only the seeming indifference of their leader to all obstacles and all hardships that keeps the little party on its quest.

At last, one month after starting, they come across a tribe of Indians whose tongue none of them know. For two days MacKenzie questions them without success until he hears a word he thinks may mean "great river that flows to the sea."

A map is drawn with burnt charcoal on a piece of birchbark, and his hope is at once confirmed. The new-found Indians agree to guide him, and two days later MacKenzie crosses the great divide on a well-worn portage, eight hundred paces long.

But if the journey up the Peace was difficult and dangerous, the journey down the mountain current that falls toward the west is ten times more so. Ascending the stream, they could see danger before they came to it. Going downstream each quickening of the current may mean a cataract ahead, each new bend in the river's course may hide some menace that will dash them to their deaths.

On the thirteenth of June calamity befalls them. Before the crew realizes the danger, the canoe is in the grip of onrushing, foaming waters. The men work madly, but here no paddles can give the frail craft direction. Down, down it races, darting from side to side, like some tormented thing frantic to escape. A great boulder looms ahead. The foreman drops his long paddle square across the bow. The canoe veers off. It clears the rock by inches, but the stern swings in and crashes. Now, they are in the full sweep of the current. The foreman tries to stem the wild descent by seizing the branches of a tree. He is jerked ashore as if by a giant's hand.

The foreman gone, the bow now meets the same fate as the stern, and a number of large holes are broken in the bottom. The canoe is now a wreck, held afloat by the swiftness of the current. The crew jump overboard, and, clinging to her sides, are swept up on a great flat rock hundreds of feet below.

Now comes a new test of MacKenzie's genius for leadership. The canoe shattered, all the bullets sunk in the river, the men benumbed with the cold, all declare that nothing remains now but to go back.

MacKenzie listens to them patiently and raises no objections, appears, in fact, to agree with them, and says nothing until their clothes are dried, a hearty meal consumed and an extra-large measure of rum issued all around.

A little apart from the campfire, MacKay attempts to console his leader for the crashing blow to his ambitions.

The men's voices are heard faintly above the sound of the river.

VOYAGEUR: *(in the background)* There's some more stew in the pot. Who wants it?

VOYAGEURS: Not me. No, I had enough. No thanks. Who's got some dry tobacco?

MACKAY: *(dolefully)* Can I get you some more to eat, Mr. MacKenzie?

MACKENZIE: *(quite cheerfully)* No, thanks, MacKay. I've eaten enough to bloat an ox.

MACKAY: Mr. MacKenzie, it's beyond my comprehension how you can take this with such spirit.

MACKENZIE: Take what, MacKay?

MACKAY: This desperate blow to all our hopes, sir.

MACKENZIE: But we're all alive, MacKay. Even the dog came through without a scratch.

MACKAY: Aye, but I'm thinking more of the enforced need of turning back.

MACKENZIE: What makes you think we're turning back, MacKay?

MACKAY: What else is there to do, sir? The Indians, and the men have all agreed that there is no hope of going forward now. You have said the same yourself, sir.

MACKENZIE: No, no, MacKay. If you remember, I said nothing.

MACKAY: But you made no protest when the men were talking.

MACKENZIE: Do you think, MacKay, I'm such a fool as to argue with men when they're half frozen, their bellies empty and just saved from the brink of death?

MACKAY: But, Mr. MacKenzie, you're surely not believing that we can go on now? The canoe smashed to pieces . . . the bullets gone . . . It can't be done, man. You heard the crew, sir. They're in no mood to go another step.

MACKENZIE: They *were* in no mood, MacKay, to go another step. But now they're warm and dry and they've had both food and drink. I'm going on, MacKay, and my men are going with me.

MACKAY: Sir, you cannot make them do it. The heart's gone out of them and while I'll follow where you lead, I see no hope myself whatever. How can we travel? How can we kill food?

A hearty laugh is heard faintly from the voyageurs. A snatch of conversation—"ho, ho, she told you that, eh!"—and fragment of boastful song.

MACKENZIE: Hear that, MacKay? Does that sound like discouraged men who'll turn back before the task's accomplished?

Laughter is heard again.

MACKAY: I'm thinking, sir, it's the thought of going back that makes them sound so cheerful. They've reached the end of their endurance, sir, I know it.

MACKENZIE: We'll see, MacKay, whether you and I go alone or with them for company. I'll speak to them now.

The laughter of the men is heard again.

Men!

The chatter ceases.

We're all to be congratulated on being alive tonight.

Murmur.

And today's experience, dreadful though it was while we were in it, may be a lesson and a warning to us to proceed with more caution in the future.

Murmur.

Yes, I said *proceed,* because there has been some talk of turning back. I do not think you men mean that. You all knew, before you volunteered to come with me, of the difficulties and dangers we'd encounter. Honour is to be won by conquering disasters; disgrace if we do not attain the object of this expedition.

VOYAGEUR: That's all very well, Mr. MacKenzie, but how can we go on?

MACKENZIE: I'm coming to that part, Ducette. We need musket balls . . .

VOYAGEUR: Yes, but how are we to get them? Can you tell us that?

MACKENZIE: Is there any reason why we should not melt up the small shot that we have? . . .

THIRD VOYAGEUR: By joe, that's so now. Why did we not think of that?

SECOND VOYAGEUR: But we can melt up nothing that will fix that canoe. Find us a new canoe and there will be no question of our going on.

MACKENZIE: We can build a new canoe as soon as we come upon a grove of birch . . .

SECOND VOYAGEUR: Yes, but when will we come upon those birch trees, eh?

MACKENZIE: The Indians say three sleeps from here. But they say that one day's march there is enough bark to make good the damage. So, men, all your objections have been met. What do you say? Do you go on or not?

VOYAGEUR: Mr. MacKenzie, I will go on. Yes.

THIRD VOYAGEUR: *(fading)* And me, too, and as long as there's any way of going and we won't starve to death.

———

NARRATOR: Two days' work. The canoe is patched, and the party moves forward. Days of almost unbelievable toil follow until they come to a broad, gently flowing stream, which we know today as the Fraser.

For days they paddle down it, and it appears that the worst of their troubles are over, when MacKenzie learns from Indians that the big river flows far to the south and that no man has ever ventured down it in a boat.

There is a shorter way to the sea, the Indians say, across country. MacKenzie is now forced to turn back up the Fraser and face the prospect of an unknown journey across the mountains. Food is running short, but one hundred and fifty rounds of ammunition are left to him, and at this critical stage of the voyage the old canoe gives out, and a new one must be built.

Now the men are consulted, the perils that lie before them frankly explained, and MacKenzie asks whether they are prepared to go on or not. There is not one dissenting voice, and they turn upstream following the new guide they have secured.

The canoe is cached, pemmican buried against the return home, and the party sets out on foot, passing from tribe to tribe, until they reach the sea. Here, on the shores of the Pacific at a point between the present town of Prince Rupert and the northernmost tip of Vancouver Island, six weatherbeaten white men, clad in ragged garments, stand grouped about their leader who is bending over a large flat rock. Beside him stands MacKay holding in his hand a birchbark cone containing melted grease.

MACKENZIE: Have you got that mixed, MacKay?

MACKAY: I don't think it's red enough, but you can look.

MACKENZIE: Let me see. No, put in some more vermilion. Here's the package.

MACKAY: Do you think that it will last?

MACKENZIE: It should last some time for it's much the same pigment as the Indians here use upon their totem poles. I wish that we had time to carve the rock but with the threatening manner of these Indians it would be foolish. How is that paint now?

MACKAY: As good as it will ever be, I'm thinking.

MACKENZIE: Then hand it here. Thanks. Now . . . how does that look, MacKay?

MACKAY: It looks all right to me, sir.

MACKENZIE: There's no need of saying anymore is there?

MACKAY: It seems little enough, considering the effort it's cost to place it there.

MACKENZIE: *(laughs)* We should build a monument, I suppose, MacKay. Well . . . here goes. We'll see now what kind of a painter I would make.

There is a pause.

VOYAGEUR: *(quietly, as if he did not wish to disturb the man at work)* Landry, what is Mr. MacKenzie doing there, eh?

SECOND VOYAGEUR: Making some letters there on the rock with that red paint. Have you no eyes, Ducette? What do you think he's doing?

VOYAGEUR: I know, I know. But what does it say?

SECOND VOYAGEUR: Well . . . I . . . That's his name, there, see . . . I can read that much.

VOYAGEUR: Oh, you can read no more than I can. I'll find out from Mr. MacKay. *(a little louder, but still in a suppressed voice)* Mr. MacKay!

MACKAY: Eh, Ducette?

VOYAGEUR: What's that say there, that writing Mr. Macenzie is putting on that rock?

MACKAY: That? Oh, that's nothing much, Ducette. It just says—"Alexander MacKenzie, from Canada, by land, the twenty-second day of July, one thousand seven hundred and ninety-three."

VOYAGEUR: *(with a significant short laugh)* I don't know, Mr. MacKay, I think perhaps that that says quite a lot, eh Landry?

———

NARRATOR: That is the end of the play. And here we leave Alexander MacKenzie. On August 24th the party arrived back at the Fort. They had been gone one hundred and eight days, seventy-five days going and only thirty-three days coming back. Their whole journey, except at the very end, had been through country never seen before by white men, and, as on the Arctic voyage, there had been no loss of life.

MacKenzie had found the answer to his question and blazed the trail that secured the Pacific Coast for Canada.

AT MY HEART'S CORE

ROBERTSON DAVIES

ECHOES OF NATIONALISM: HISTORICIZING DEBATES ABOUT CANADIAN CULTURE IN ROBERTSON DAVIES'S *AT MY HEART'S CORE*

LINDSAY THISTLE

Canadians "are ignorant of the enrichment of life which can come through literature and the arts."[1]
—Robertson Davies

Robertson William Davies was born in Thamesville, Ontario, in 1913. Although Davies was a playwright, essayist, journalist, editor, professor, and even—briefly—actor, he is most widely known for his literature and achieved his greatest success as a novelist.[2] His awards and accomplishments are plenty: Companion of the Order of Canada, founding Master of the University of Toronto's Massey College, a member of the Board of Governors for the Stratford Festival, winner of the Governor General's Literary Award, and recipient of the Lorne Pierce medal from the Royal Society of Canada, to list a few standouts. Davies passed away in 1995, but remains a mythological figure in Canada through his opinionated proclamations about art, culture, and identity, and his impressive career spanning over half a century.

Davies studied at Queen's University in Kingston, Ontario, and at Balliol College at the University of Oxford in the 1930s. He returned to Canada in 1940 and became the editor of the *Peterborough Examiner* in 1942.[3] While running

1 Judith Skelton Grant, ed. *Robertson Davies Discoveries: Early Letters 1938–1975* (Toronto: McClelland & Stewart, 2002), 51.

2 Elspeth Cameron, "Robertson Davies," *The Canadian Encyclopedia*, revised by Daniel Baird April 3, 2015, accessed August 23, 2016, http://www.thecanadianencyclopedia.ca/en/article/robertson-davies/.

3 Ibid.

the newspaper, Davies looked to local history and wrote *At My Heart's Core*. The three-act dramatic comedy was first produced by the Peterborough Summer Theatre Company as part of Peterborough's 1950 Centennial celebrations.[4] In the years that followed, the play received mainly amateur productions in Edmonton; Toronto; Ottawa; London, Ontario; and Knowlton, Quebec. Despite Davies's precarious relationship with critics, it received primarily positive reviews and was "hailed as his finest [play] to date."[5]

At My Heart's Core takes place in 1837 at the end of the Upper Canada Rebellion, an uprising against British imperial power and specifically against the Family Compact, a powerful group of privileged British elitists who ran the colony. The rebels, led by William Lyon Mackenzie, fought for democratic reform, responsible government, greater autonomy from Britain, and less colonial control of their land and laws. The rebellion, however, was not only a protest against the policies of the established powers. Mackenzie and his followers also attempted to take control of the government and turn Upper Canada from a colony into an independent nation. After a short-lived march down Yonge St. in Toronto, the seven hundred or so poorly equipped rebels were defeated by loyal supporters of the British government. Although the Rebellion did not succeed, it planted the seed for three decades of national politics and debate, directly resulting in Lord Durham's 1838 Report,[6] the Act of Union that united Upper and Lower Canada as the Province of Canada in 1840, and of course, Canadian Confederation in 1867.[7]

The play dramatizes the historical figures of Frances Stewart, her husband Thomas Stewart, Edmund Cantwell, and sisters Catherine Parr Traill and Susanna Moodie. The action begins with Catherine and Susanna visiting Frances

---

4 Susan Stone-Blackburn, *Robertson Davies, Playwright: A search for the self on the Canadian stage* (Vancouver: UBC Press, 1985), 71.

5 Ibid, 91.

6 After the rebellion in Upper Canada and a similar but more violent rebellion in Lower Canada that same year, Lord Durham arrived from England to investigate the growing desire for independence from Britain. He concluded that before the relationship between the colonies and Britain could be mended, the divisions between Upper Canada (English) and Lower Canada (French) had to be resolved. Durham recommended that the two colonies be united into one. This would establish a strong English majority and, according to Durham, the smaller, much less cultured French minority would simply assimilate, creating a unified Canada.

7 Carol Wilton's *Popular Politics and Political Culture in Upper Canada 1800–1850* (Montreal: McGill-Queen's UP, 2000) provides a thorough look at the Upper Canada Rebellion, the historical events that followed, and their connections to the socio-political climate of Canada.

after hearing rumours of a soldier outside the Stewart home, but upon arrival they see the mysterious guest is only Honour Brady. Honour has just given birth and run away from her baby's much older father, Phelim, who almost immediately shows up drunk and angry to claim her and his child. Meanwhile, Edmund Cantwell, Frances's neighbour, arrives to speak with her husband Thomas, but upon seeing Phelim and hearing that Thomas is away, stays to protect the women. Edmund's interactions with Frances, Susanna, and Catherine make up the central action of the play, and it is through their interactions that Davies introduces his thematic concerns: debates about the value of art to a society and questions about Canadian cultural identity, both at the time of the Rebellion and when the play was written.

Herbert Lindenberger aptly argues that "historical plays are at least as much a comment on the playwright's own times as on the periods about which they are ostensibly written."[8] Historical plays use acute moments in the past to paradoxically draw attention to issues of "now"—the time and place at which the play was written, and following that, the where and when of the performance. Davies's choice of historical event, and his treatment of it, are especially telling. Both historical periods—1837 Upper Canada and 1950 Canada—were rich with discussions of nationalism.

In 1950, Canada was in the thick of debates surrounding the fostering, protection, and growth of national arts and culture, spurred by the Royal Commission on National Development in the Arts, Letters and Sciences established by Prime Minster Louis St. Laurent and chaired by Vincent Massey. This was a major period for questioning how Canada could sustain its own cultural industries, create opportunities for Canadian artists, and establish a culture distinct from the United States and Britain. Davies was a vocal participant in these debates, contributing "The State of Theatre in Canada," a dramatic dialogue featuring the fictional Lovewit and Trueman debating what should be done, to the published Massey Commission Report.

Davies wrote *At My Heart's Core* within this cultural climate, setting his play at a similar historical moment of nationalist reflection when local pioneers challenged imperial control. The events of 1837 marked the beginning of a decades-long period of national change; post-World War II Canada, Davies's play and contemporary writings might be viewed as the commencement of a similarly intensive era of national transformation. In both 1837 and 1950, ordinary Canadians, rather than mainly typical leaders and politicians, took action,

8 Herbert Lindenberger, *Historical Drama: The Relation of Literature and Reality* (Chicago: U of Chicago P, 1975), 5.

and the implications of their deeds on Canada's political and cultural landscapes were—at those moments—uncertain.

Audiences in 1950 could enter the world of the 1837 Rebellion and recognize, in the play's representation of national debates, many of the same uncertainties they faced. While a reader or spectator might first notice the play's domestic setting and its thematic focus on the value of art, the far-away Rebellion is always in the background. The Rebellion signifies questions of Canadian independence, representing an early push toward political and national sovereignty for Canada. By suggesting similarities between 1837 and 1950, Davies appears to argue that despite the political and national autonomy gained in the aftermath of the Rebellion, Canada in 1950 was, in many ways, no more independent as a country than in 1837, because it was still culturally dominated by others. Davies strongly advocates for the need to create a thriving national culture, in order to complete the process of Canadian independence.

Davies was a Canadian artist looking for opportunity, an advocate for the necessity of art and the value it can bring to society, and a strong believer in the need to improve and professionalize the arts in Canada. Despite this, the content of the play and his cultural advocacy around 1950 was complex in its nationalist orientation, cynically elitist rather than populist, and anglophilic. Davies idolized Britain's artistic tradition, and at points in his career, was very critical of Canada's. In a 1945 letter to a British film critic Davies wrote, "Canada does not actively dislike English films: it is just too dumb, as a usual thing, to understand anything which is not thoroughly familiar."[9] He constantly lamented the lack of professional opportunities and in a letter to Herbert Whittaker wrote, "The average Canadian amateur actor is a clod untroubled by a spark."[10]

Rather than finding a Canadian artistic tradition, or distinguishing Canada from its imperial power's influence, Davies thought that Canada should look to Britain as a model. The characters in the play reflect this privileging of British culture, and believe that the rebels fighting against the crown are inferior. Furthermore, Edmund and the ladies often reminisce about the rich culture of writers and artists they left behind when they settled in Upper Canada. The expression of these beliefs in the play draws attention to Davies's feeling that in 1950, despite all the gains in Canadian independence, the country had yet to overcome its lack of culture and art. In short, Davies very much saw Canada as a young colonial country with much to learn from Britain. He believed that Canada should strive to develop classical, philosophical, and intellectual art

9 Quoted in Skelton Grant, 23.

10 Ibid., 67.

rather than what he called, "the childishness of Hollywood" and American popular culture.[11] These views opened Davies to criticism for being an elitist (he even assumed an upper-class English accent). Lois Sherlow argues that as opportunities grew in Canada, his beliefs "cultivated an egotistical separateness from the new Canadian audience that developed with an emerging professional theatre that was making a break from the international canon."[12]

What is also interesting about *At My Heart's Core* is that despite setting it at a nationally significant moment, Davies does not focus the play on the Rebellion. In fact, Davies's decision to highlight the experiences of the female characters rather than the experiences of the men fighting in the Rebellion is notable and complex. At the beginning of the play, we see Catherine, Susanna, and Frances as three hard-working, intelligent, and accomplished women defending Honour and easily standing up to Phelim. The arrival of Edmund, however, complicates this depiction. Through emotional manipulation, Edmund raises doubts in the ladies' minds about the merit of their lives and their work as settlers, instead fostering indulgent daydreams of what might have been if they had stayed in Britain and Ireland. He reminds them of the luxuries they replaced with long days of hard work to survive and build homes in the woods. Paradoxically, although Cantwell is able to easily get a rise out of the women, he ultimately encourages them to not stand passively in support of their husbands, but to pursue their own desires and successes.

Davies is not the only Canadian playwright to dramatize the events of the 1837 Rebellion. Perhaps best known is Rick Salutin's *1837: The Farmers' Revolt*,[13] a collective creation first produced at Theatre Passe Muraille in 1973 that focuses almost exclusively on political issues, Canadian nationalism, and recounting the events of the Rebellion. *1837* presents the Rebellion differently from *At My Heart's Core*, as a moment of pride when average Canadians fought back against Britain's imperial control. There is also Anne Chislett's *Yankee Notions*,[14] which premiered in 1992 at the Blyth Festival and begins during the aftermath of the Rebellion when the lives of two rebels are at stake. In both plays, characters hold a negative opinion of the British and the Family Compact.

---

11 Ibid., 23.

12 Lois Sherlow, "Metadrama and Melodrama: Postmodern Elements in the Plays of Robertson Davies," in *Robertson Davies: A Mingling of Contrarieties*, Camille R. Bossière and Linda M. Morra, eds. (Ottawa: U of Ottawa P, 2003), 82.

13 Rick Salutin, *1837: The Farmers Revolt* (Toronto: J. Lorimer, 1976).

14 Anne Chislett, *Yankee Notions* (Toronto: Playwrights Canada, 1993).

Davies wrote *At My Heart's Core* to participate in pressing discussions of arts and culture in Canada during the 1950s, asserting the necessity of art to the individual, the community, and the nation. To make his argument convincing, Davies refers to a historical event addressing similar national concerns and merges it with the dramatic construction of his point of view. Plays about historical events of centuries past can be made new again because theatrical performance, as a live event, takes place in an ever-changing "now." How history is understood and how it is written are also performances of "now." We can only understand historical plays through today's eyes. To this end, the historical events of the play, and the events and context of the writing and performance, are fused together to create an act of historiography.

At My Heart's Core was first produced at the Niagara Falls Summer Theatre the week of August 22, 1950, and then moved to the Peterborough Summer Theatre on August 28. It was directed by Robertson Davies.

CHARACTERS

Mrs. Frances Stewart
Sally
Mrs. Catherine Parr Traill
Mrs. Susanna Moodie
Honour Brady
Phelim Brady
Mr. Edmund Cantwell
The Hon. Thomas Stewart, M.L.C., J.P.

SETTING

The action takes place at Auburn, the home of the Stewarts in Douro settlement, on a December day in 1837.

ACT I

The scene is Auburn, the homestead of the Honourable Thomas Alexander STEWART, *a Member of the Legislative Council, in the district of Douro in Upper Canada. The time is early in December, 1837.*

As we look at the stage most of it is filled by the house itself, which, standing at the audience's right, is open to us, like a doll's house. The room that we see is the best chamber; because this is the dwelling of settlers of some means and taste it is an attractive place. The logs which form the walls have been trimmed down to a flat, glowing wooden surface; the furniture is good, though plain, and is of mahogany and walnut; there are bookshelves filled with books, bound chiefly in leather, some maps, and two or three good engravings. In the lefthand wall, as we look from the audience, is a big fireplace with a wooden mantel, and over it hang guns and a few Indian trophies. On the mantel are some fossils, and on the walls are the skins of a few small animals, for MRS. STEWART *is a naturalist of uncommon ability. Also in the lefthand wall is a window and the door to the outside. A door to kitchen quarters is on the righthand side at the back. On the righthand wall is a bunk bed, with curtains to shut in the sleepers; there is also a curtain which can be drawn parallel with the fireplace wall to cut this room in two, so that the occupant of the bunk may have space to dress in privacy.*

On the left we are able to see the dooryard and a part of the forest which surrounds the house, so that we can see people approach, as others are busy inside. The trees are bare, but no snow has fallen.

The curtain rises on a bright December morning. Inside the house there are some signs of disorder; a basin stands on the table and there are one or two towels on the floor; a large kettle sits on the hearth. The door at the back opens and

MRS. STEWART and SALLY enter, carrying between them a large pioneer cradle, which they place near the bed.

Mrs. Frances STEWART is a woman of unusually pleasing and youthful appearance, plainly dressed. When she speaks it is apparent that she is Irish and also a lady "brought up," as her friend Maria Edgeworth said, "in all the refinements of high cultivation." In other words, a real lady and not a spurious one. If possible, let her have a beautiful voice.

SALLY is an Indian of indeterminate age, of pillowy figure. Her customary expression is a broad smile, and from time to time she giggles for no apparent reason. She wears a loose gown and moccasins, and has a few odds and ends of ill-chosen adornment.

MRS. STEWART: Sally, clear away, will you.

She goes to the bunk and tenderly lifts from it an infant, wrapped in a blanket.

You've chosen a very strange time to settle in Douro, young person. And a girl, too! Don't you know we have too many girls in Douro already? What use are girls, young person, will you tell me? Don't you know that we need men, to fight the rebels? Don't you know that we need men to defend us from the outrageous and bloodthirsty Indians, like Sally?

SALLY giggles hugely.

I'm really astonished at your impertinence, young person. Do you intend to take up an extensive piece of land? Pray oblige me by letting me inspect your settler's ticket.

She solemnly inspects a tiny hand.

Ah, as I thought; no ticket. Now what do you suppose the Honourable Thomas Alexander Stewart, M.L.C., J.P., will say to a very young settler with no ticket?

SALLY: Master, he laugh. He all time laugh.

She laughs, herself.

MRS. STEWART: Oh, Sally, I wish he were here to laugh at this minute.

SALLY: Master, he fine. He all time fine. Missus no fret.

MRS. STEWART: I am not fretting, Sally. I positively deny that I am fretting. Still, a rebellion is no laughing matter.

But SALLY laughs until she shakes all over.

Except to you, of course. Everything is a laughing matter to you. How your people acquired their reputation for impassiveness I shall never understand.

Now, young person, into the cradle with you. And do not presume to stir until I have had my breakfast.

SALLY: What you want?

MRS. STEWART: Bring me the loaf and I shall make toast. And tea—the ordinary tea.

SALLY goes to the kitchen. MRS. STEWART moves to the bed and gives a nurse's look at its occupant. Then she looks into the cradle, and tucks the infant a little more closely. SALLY returns with a settler's loaf—cottage loaf—from which she cuts a slice, and spearing it on a toasting fork, sits down to prepare her mistress' breakfast. MRS. STEWART sits in a chair, and seems disposed to sleep. It is at this point that MRS. MOODIE and MRS. TRAILL appear through the woods, walking briskly. Though MRS. MOODIE is a year younger than her sister, she is the dominant one, and there is a ladylike hint of the drill-sergeant in her demeanour. MRS. TRAILL is a gentle and abstracted person, whose characteristic expression is a charming but rather vague smile. They both wear large shawls and poke bonnets, and their dress is for use rather than style.

MRS. TRAILL: Frances has not yet been abroad, I perceive.

MRS. MOODIE: Sensible woman, to take her sleep when she can.

MRS. TRAILL: Perhaps she has had good news.

MRS. MOODIE: We shall soon know.

MRS. MOODIE knocks, and MRS. STEWART starts in her chair; she quickly gains possession of herself, and draws the curtain which shuts off the bedroom part of the chamber. Then she admits them.

MRS. STEWART: Oh my dears, how very early you are abroad. Have you had some news?

MRS. MOODIE: That is what we have come to ask you.

MRS. STEWART: No, nothing whatever.

MRS. MOODIE: Then it was only rumour after all.

MRS. STEWART: Even a new rumour might be better than nothing. What have you heard?

MRS. TRAILL: Very early this morning it came to our ears that a man in a red coat was seen at your door late last night. We thought that it might have been a messenger.

MRS. STEWART: What a curious story.

MRS. TRAILL: Then you have had no news?

MRS. STEWART: No, none at all.

MRS. MOODIE: A red coat would be very conspicuous in the forest. A strange thing to make a mistake about.

MRS. STEWART: At this time people have red coats on the brain.

MRS. MOODIE: The sight of a red coat would not trouble anyone whose loyalty was above question.

MRS. TRAILL: Then we have had our walk for nothing.

MRS. STEWART: Oh, please don't say that. You will have something to eat, won't you? You have not lost your journey when it gives me so much joy to see you. Pray sit down. You will take off your bonnets, will you not?

MRS. MOODIE: If I take off my bonnet, Frances, I warn you that I shall stay a long time.

MRS. STEWART: Nothing could please me better.

SALLY takes both bonnets and MRS. MOODIE's shawl to the kitchen quarters. They both wear caps under their bonnets.

MRS. TRAILL: But you have much to do. Are the children awake?

MRS. STEWART: I sent them to Peterborough, to the Reverend Mr. Taylor two days ago. He is so very kind, and I thought that if I had to make a sudden journey, or the house were to be upset for any reason, it would be better not to distress them.

MRS. TRAILL: I think that Peterborough must be full of settlers' children. Susanna and I sent ours there yesterday.

MRS. STEWART: We really cannot keep them in the forest. Not that there is likely to be any danger, of course, but if there should be, they are much better off where there are men to defend them.

MRS. MOODIE: I have no very great opinion of the Peterborough militia. The best have already gone to York to fight the rebels there, and many of those who remain are Methodists.

MRS. STEWART: But Susanna, I know several of them and they are most respectable persons.

MRS. MOODIE: Methodists are all very well, but they have a strong leaning toward rebellion.

MRS. STEWART: Yes, it is most vexing of them, but it cannot be helped now. Do sit down. See, Sally has made quite a lot of toast, and we can begin.

MRS. MOODIE: Breakfast will be very welcome. We have walked quite eight miles.

MRS. TRAILL: Oh, sister, we used to walk much greater distances in England and think nothing of it.

MRS. MOODIE: Very rarely before breakfast. I will make no secret of it; I am uncommonly sharp-set.

MRS. STEWART: How fortunate. I have excellent grape jelly.

MRS. MOODIE: I dote upon grape jelly.

MRS. STEWART: And we shall have real tea, for a treat.

MRS. MOODIE: None of your boilings of hemlock bark. How I detest that abominable apology for tea. I have almost taken to drinking whisky to avoid it.

MRS. TRAILL: Susanna dear, you would make a stranger think that you were quite greedy.

MRS. STEWART: As we are all females it is not necessary for Susanna to conceal the fact that she has an appetite.

MRS. MOODIE: I always have an appetite; I always have had one. Even when I was a romantic girl, and most in love, I never ceased to have an appetite. And now that I do a man's work, I believe I eat as much as a man.

MRS. STEWART: I feel certain that it is the exercise of your intellectual powers which makes you so hungry, my dear. Thomas says that two hours of work over his books make him hungrier than a day pulling stumps. Have some toast.

During this scene she is busy measuring tea from a caddy and infusing it, in making toast at the fire, and in attending to the wants of the others. SALLY *goes to the kitchen.*

MRS. TRAILL: I do not think it quite right to say that you work like a man, Susanna. We all do a great many things, of course, that we would not do at home, but we must not lose our sense of proportion.

MRS. MOODIE: Let me say, then, that I work like an English farmer. That is how the women work in Upper Canada. As for the men—they work as horses might be expected to work in England. Does that restore the proportion?

MRS. STEWART: Certainly one finds oneself doing things that would have been quite out of one's scope at home. You know, when I was a girl in Ireland, I used to turn quite faint at the sight of blood. Here I have bathed and bandaged I cannot guess how many wounds, not one of them caused by a quarrel, I am happy to say.

MRS. TRAILL: And I hope it may continue so, my dear. But if the rebellion should not be so easily put down as we hope, some of us may be wanted as nurses.

MRS. STEWART: Oh, we must trust that it will be a very short disturbance.

MRS. MOODIE: I am not hopeful of it. Those Methodists are uncommonly tenacious of a mistaken opinion.

MRS. STEWART: My dear Susanna, you seem determined that it is all the fault of the Methodists.

MRS. MOODIE: And I am right. When you say Methodist, you say Radical. They all think that the world can be improved by rebellion against authority. It can't.

MRS. STEWART: But Mackenzie leads the rebellion, and he is not a Methodist, I believe.

MRS. MOODIE: Mackenzie, I am perfectly convinced, is an atheist. But he knows how to get the Methodists to fight for him. They are opposed to authority and so is he.

MRS. TRAILL: You are familiar with Susanna's "Oath," Frances, are you not?

MRS. STEWART: No, but I have heard it spoken of. Would you be good enough to tell me about it, my dear?

MRS. MOODIE: Nothing would give me greater pleasure. It is merely a simple, rough thing that I threw off at white heat and dispatched at once to Montreal and to Toronto and to all the nearby papers. You must not expect any of the grace which critics have so kindly ascribed to my other things. It is called "The Oath of the Canadian Volunteers."

She rises, brushes crumbs from her bosom, takes a commanding position on the hearth and declaims, not without effect.

Huzza for England! May she claim
  Our fond devotion ever;
And by the glory of her name
Our brave forefathers' honest fame
  We swear—no foe shall sever
Her children from the parent's side;
  Though parted by the wave,
In weal or woe, whate'er betide,
  We swear to die, or save

Her honour from the rebel band
Whose crimes pollute our injured land!

MRS. STEWART: Oh how very stirring, my dear. Nothing about the Methodists yet?

MRS. TRAILL: The Methodists do not come into the poem, Frances.

MRS. MOODIE: I do not consider Methodists, even in a time of crisis, to be the stuff of which poetry is made. Was your query intended to be ironical, Frances?

MRS. STEWART: I am sorry. I should not have quizzed you, Susanna.

MRS. MOODIE: I shall not continue unless you wish it.

MRS. STEWART: Oh, pray continue. Let us have it all.

MRS. MOODIE: Then courage, loyal volunteers!
  God will defend the right;
That thought will banish slavish fears,
That blessed consciousness still cheers
  The soldier in the fight.
The stars for us will never burn,
  The stripes may frighten slaves,
The Briton's eye will proudly turn
  Where Britain's standard waves.
Beneath its folds, if Heaven requires
We'll die, as died of old our sires!

MRS. STEWART: Oh my dear, it is beautiful of course, but I wish that gloomy talk of dying didn't come in at the end of it.

MRS. MOODIE: That is merely poetic licence, my dear. If there is any dying to be done, it will be done by the rebels. Our husbands are, after all, professional soldiers, and officers. Where the danger is greatest, there they will be found, but not needlessly exposed.

MRS. TRAILL: Surely you are not concerned for Mr. Stewart? He is a civilian; how could he be in danger?

MRS. STEWART: I have not had your experience in these matters. You are soldiers' wives; you have learned not to be foolishly concerned. It would be such a very great misfortune if anything were to happen to Thomas.

During MRS. MOODIE*'s spirited recitation the sleeper in the bunk at the right has awakened; first a hand appears, feeling the curtains; then a pair of bare legs appear over the side, and a girl steps to the floor. She wears a short coarse shift, and her hair hangs loose. She is a little weak when first she stands, but gains* *strength; she looks with curiosity into the cradle, then at the chest of drawers and into the mirror over it; then, slowly, she pulls on a draggled skirt which she gets from the bed, and a soldier's scarlet coat, which is too big for her, though not farcically so. She squats by the cradle and examines the baby; she then begins to rock it, crooning softly, but enough to be heard by the women on the other side of the curtain.*

MRS. TRAILL: Did you say that all the children had gone into Peterborough, Frances?

MRS. STEWART: Yes, the day before yesterday. Why do you ask?

MRS. TRAILL: I am mistaken, of course, but I thought I heard a child's voice singing.

MRS. STEWART: I do not know how that could be, do you?

MRS. TRAILL: No, though I am not usually deceived. Indeed, I pride myself that my hearing is uncommonly good.

MRS. STEWART: Yes, my dear, I know that you do. More toast?

MRS. MOODIE: Yes. You really ought not to tease us in this way, Frances. The rebellion has made us all very edgy.

MRS. STEWART: And very curious?

MRS. MOODIE: No curiosity about it. Mine is an open nature; I detest mysteries—particularly other people's. We are aching to know who is behind that curtain.

MRS. TRAILL: Is it anyone we know?

MRS. STEWART: I don't think so. I don't know her myself. Wait a moment.

She goes through the curtain.

You are stirring! Is that really wise, my dear? Ought you not to lie down?

THE GIRL: Ah, sure, I'm fine.

MRS. STEWART: But do you not feel weak and ill? Are you not light-headed?

THE GIRL: No, I'm fine.

MRS. STEWART: But you must be hungry. You must have breakfast at once. And I may as well draw this curtain; it's no longer wanted.

She does so, and MRS. MOODIE *and* MRS. TRAILL*, who have been listening with keen interest, see the stranger.*

MRS. MOODIE: So there's your redcoat! Frances, how you love to torment us all!

MRS. TRAILL: Who is she?

MRS. STEWART: You know quite as much as I do. Who are you, my girl?

THE GIRL: Honour.

She curtsies.

MRS. STEWART: Honour who?

THE GIRL: Honour Brady, I'm thinking.

She curtsies again.

MRS. STEWART: I don't recall that name. Do you live hereabout?

HONOUR: A piece up the river.

MRS. MOODIE: Brady? Any connection of old Phelim Brady?

HONOUR: Ah, sure, that's himself.

MRS. STEWART: I know him; is he your father?

HONOUR: Well, in a queer kind of way you might say he was.

MRS. STEWART: And does he know about your child?

MRS. TRAILL: Child!

She darts across the room, quickly followed by MRS. MOODIE, and they gaze with interest into the cradle.

HONOUR: He does that.

MRS. STEWART: My poor girl! Was he very angry with you?

HONOUR: No; what way would he have a right to be angry?

MRS. STEWART: But you are unmarried?

HONOUR: Well, just at the present.

MRS. STEWART: But have you some hope that you may be married?

HONOUR: Ah, sure, just the minute herself's buried.

MRS. MOODIE: This is a remarkably fresh-appearing infant. When was it born?

MRS. STEWART: At four o'clock this morning in that bed.

MRS. MOODIE: That's as fresh as anyone could desire. And you were midwife, I presume.

MRS. STEWART: I was.

MRS. MOODIE: And I see you on your feet, Honour, and ready for anything. That's nimble, even for Douro.

MRS. STEWART: It was an easy birth, I must say.

HONOUR: Oh, I took my measures. I didn't want you to be destroyed with me screaming and roaring, so I drank a full pint of gin as soon as I felt me pains, and hurried here while I could still see out o' me eyes.

MRS. MOODIE: GIN!

MRS. TRAILL: GIN!

HONOUR: It's the best thing for a delivery there is. You never feel a qualm, and when the baby comes it'll sleep like Moses for half a day or so. It gives you a chance to get on your feet and start your milk, so.

MRS. TRAILL: I never cease to marvel at the infinite adaptability of Nature.

MRS. MOODIE: Nature never framed anything more indestructible than the Irish settler. Behold Nature's masterwork—in the ironmongery line!

HONOUR: Sure, you've no call to say that! Didn't the cholera take me father and mother in a single day? The Irish are terrible delicate.

MRS. STEWART: Did you not tell me that Brady was your father?

HONOUR: He brought me up since I was four.

MRS. STEWART: This is becoming very confused. Please tell me more about yourself, and perhaps I shall be able to help you. Now, Brady is your foster-father?

HONOUR: He is that.

MRS. STEWART: He knows that you are having a child?

HONOUR: He does that.

MRS. STEWART: And you say that he is not angry?

HONOUR: Little good it would do him to be angry.

MRS. STEWART: And is there any hope that the father of this child will marry you?

HONOUR: And isn't his own sainted wife after telling him he must?

MRS. STEWART: Oh dear! Please don't confuse me any more. Whose wife?

HONOUR: Old Phelim's wife. "Marry her," says she, "as soon as the breath has passed from me body."

MRS. STEWART: You mean that this is Brady's child?

HONOUR: You'd best sit quiet and let me explain. You're getting yourself all confused. Brady's wife took a creeping inflammation of the tubes of the head a year ago, and she knew her time was near. So she told himself that when she was gone he was to marry me, to have someone to look after him, you see. So he promised he would, and from time to time after that he sought my companionship as I was living handy in the house as I'd done from a child. And in time herself died—six weeks ago it was—and as soon as she's out of the way we'll be married surely.

MRS. STEWART: You mean, when a proper period of mourning is over?

HONOUR: I mean nothing of the kind. I mean that the priest that buries her will marry us that same day.

MRS. STEWART: Not buried!

HONOUR: Brady had a disagreement with the priest because he wasn't as close married to herself as he might have been. There's some ugly talk that she might have been a Protestant. But the Protestants'll have nothing to do with it, and the priest won't bury her at all. So Brady puts the corpse out on the roof the way the wolves won't get at it, and sits down to wait the whole lot of 'em out. He's a lucky old divil, for the frost has been strong ever since, and the priest is weakening. We'll be married by Christmas.

MRS. TRAILL: In all my time in the backwoods I do not think that I have ever heard a more horrible tale!

HONOUR: The horrible part has still to be told. Phelim didn't want me to come here last night. "Stay snug in your bed," says he. "What," says I, "and bring forth the child with herself that was like a mother to me above on the roof friz as stiff as a cedar log? Sure, I've a proper regard for the feelings of the dead if you have none," says I, "and I'll not affront her with such bold behaviour." So I lowered the gin down me gullet as I told you, and came straight here, for it's well known ma'am that you turn nobody from your door.

She curtsies to MRS. STEWART.

MRS. STEWART: Well Honour, I suppose that there is nothing for me to say except that the delicacy of your feelings does you credit.

HONOUR: Thank you, ma'am. Her that brought me up gave me a notion of what was owing to a corpse that Queen Victoria herself wouldn't better.

MRS. STEWART: And what do you propose to do now?

HONOUR: Sure I don't know. Would I do right to go back?

MRS. TRAILL: Oh no! You cannot take a child to a house where there is a body on the roof!

MRS. STEWART gives HONOUR a generous hunch of bread and a cup of tea.

MRS. MOODIE: Catherine, I advise you not to concern yourself in this matter unless you are ready to make yourself responsible for the child in some degree. And as you already have as many children of your own as you can manage that would be an extremely rash undertaking.

MRS. TRAILL: Susanna dear, sometimes you assume the tone almost of an elder sister. Pray permit me to decide on my own course of conduct.

MRS. MOODIE: I meant only to be kind, Catherine.

MRS. TRAILL: We must not allow kindness to make us peremptory and dictatorial, must we, dear? Let me hold the child.

She fetches the child from the cradle.

This is a bonny child, Honour, but you must shape its head a little. I shall show you what to do. You must hold the child on your lap like this, and roll its head very gently between your palms, thus.

MRS. MOODIE: Catherine, pray be cautious! You will addle the child's brains with your rolling and squeezing!

MRS. TRAILL: I have done this with many settlers' children, Honour, and they all have uncommonly pretty heads. I may say that I am quite famous for my skill in this respect. You must not be fearful. Do this for a few minutes two or three times each day. Now you do it.

HONOUR takes the child and begins a somewhat heavy-handed and rapid imitation of what MRS. TRAILL has done.

HONOUR: Is this the trick of it, ma'am?

MRS. MOODIE: O Gemini, Catherine, she's twisting its head like a doorknob! Stop, girl, before you are an unwitting infanticide!

HONOUR: Sure and what's that you're calling me, ma'am?

She gives the head a dreadful jerk in her anxiety.

MRS. TRAILL: Don't meddle, Susanna. You know nothing of children.

MRS. MOODIE: I know enough to keep free of your bone-twisting tricks.

MRS. STEWART rescues the baby from HONOUR.

MRS. STEWART: Please! I helped the child into the world, and I shrewdly suspect that I shall be the one who cares for it and its mother. We shall shape its head later, Catherine, when it is a little more secure on its neck.

She gives the child to MRS. TRAILL.

And Susanna, can I not persuade you to take a little more toast? I am sure you need it. And tea, as well? Honour, I wish that you would lie down again. I am sure that you feel perfectly well, but it would really oblige me greatly if you would rest.

MRS. TRAILL: The first three weeks is the time for this sort of work, I assure you, Frances. I know what I am doing.

MRS. MOODIE: I have some little reputation as a physician, and I assure you, Catherine, that you don't. Give me that child.

MRS. TRAILL: No, give it to me.

MRS. MOODIE: Catherine, I must insist—

MRS. TRAILL: Susanna, pray do not interfere—

During the last few minutes PHELIM *Brady has come on the scene from the woods, and he has been peering through the window. He is an elderly, but not decrepit, Irishman in breeches, stockings, and lace-up boots, a tightly buttoned coat, and a lamentable night-cap over which he wears a sorry top hat. He has a shrewd and even noble face, framed in Galway whiskers, and he ranges in manner between Irish bard and lowest sort of shebeener. He taps on the window.*

PHELIM: What're yez doin' there with me infant child?

All are startled by this interruption, but MRS. MOODIE *and* MRS. TRAILL *continue to struggle in a well-bred fashion for the possession of the child.*

MRS. MOODIE: Mercy on us! Who's that?

HONOUR: Sure, it's himself!

MRS. TRAILL: Susanna, I really must protest against your assumption of authority—

PHELIM: Come along now, all of yez! What kind of a game is that you're at, with your haulin' and draggin'? Open up now, and let me in!

MRS. STEWART: It's Brady, come to fetch you, Honour.

PHELIM: Make haste now, or I'll kick in your door!

MRS. STEWART: Why is he in such a temper?

MRS. MOODIE: Drunk, I suppose!

MRS. STEWART: Oh dear, I have never learned to manage drunken men.

MRS. MOODIE: Leave him to me.

She goes to the door and calls through it.

Brady!

PHELIM: *(in imitation of her tone)* Moodie!

MRS. MOODIE: What's that you say, Brady?

PHELIM: What's that *you* say, Moodie?

MRS. MOODIE: You will gain nothing by impudence.

PHELIM: Neither will you.

MRS. MOODIE: What do you want?

PHELIM: I want to see me new-born infant, to kiss it on the brow and acknowledge me paternity in the sight o' God and in the face of all this world! Now what do *you* want?

MRS. MOODIE: I want an undertaking from you that if I let you in, you will behave in an orderly and respectful manner.

PHELIM: You'll get no such promise from me, ye old petticoated grenadier, ye!

MRS. TRAILL: *(placidly massaging the child's head)* I think he resents your peremptory manner, Susanna.

MRS. MOODIE: Catherine, this is not the time to pursue a family dispute.

MRS. STEWART: Permit me to try what I can do.

She goes to the door.

Brady!

PHELIM removes his hat and bows toward her voice.

PHELIM: God bless and protect you, Mrs. Stewart, ma'am. Is that yourself?

MRS. STEWART: It is, Phelim. Will you behave yourself if I bring the child out to you?

PHELIM: And how could I help meself from behavin', before a lady such as yourself, ma'am? Wouldn't your very presence put behaviour on a skunk?

MRS. STEWART: You know, Phelim, that Mr. Stewart is from home and that we are all unprotected women here, so I must have your word that you will not make any trouble.

PHELIM: Sure, don't I know how unprotected you are, ma'am, and that heathen savage of a Sally this minute leapin' out the back door to hit me a clout with the skillet? She'd put the fear o' God into the divil, that one!

MRS. STEWART: I'll not let Sally harm you if you are peaceable. Give me the child, Catherine.

She takes it, opens the door and goes out to PHELIM. *He has refreshed himself from a snuff box, and sneezes violently on the child.*

PHELIM: Bless you, ma'am, you know the feelings of a father. Is it a boy or a child?

MRS. STEWART: A girl, Phelim, a seven-pound girl. I weighed her on the fish scales. She is rather sleepy now.

PHELIM: Drunk, eh? Well, she'll wake and start her screechin' soon enough. Where's the mother?

MRS. STEWART: You should really be ashamed of yourself, Brady. I shall ask Mr. Stewart to speak to you when he returns. You have behaved disgracefully toward that poor girl. She trusted you as a father.

PHELIM: And hadn't she a right? Amn't I a father to her and to her child as well? Can good nature go further?

MRS. STEWART: Oh Brady, you are incorrigible!

PHELIM: *(with a wink)* I am that. It's eatin' potatoes and goat's milk that does it.

MRS. STEWART: Honour, you had better come out.

PHELIM: Come out, me darlin'. I've somethin' for ye.

HONOUR *comes slowly from the house.*

HONOUR: What have ye for me, Phelim?

The ladies call him "Feelim," but HONOUR *calls him "Failim."*

PHELIM *rushes at her and kicks her spitefully several times in the rear.*

PHELIM: I've that for ye, ye great ugly baboon, ye idlin' away nine months to bring forth a scalded monkey of a girl! Oh, wait till I get ye home, me fine madam! I'll beat the divil out of yer lazy hide! I'll learn ye to breed girls! Sure, wouldn't herself that's dead and on the roof rip the soul-case out of ye if she could reach ye! A disgraceful daughter and the divil's own wife y've been to me!

MRS. STEWART: Sally!! Sally!

SALLY *rushes from behind the house, and fells* PHELIM *with a well-placed blow from her skillet.*

Oh, thank you, Sally. What a dreadful scene! I do hope you haven't killed the poor man.

MRS. MOODIE: Poor man, indeed! A shocking old villain!

MRS. STEWART: He couldn't be dead, could he?

HONOUR: It's little ye know o' the old divil to ask that. Sure, he'd live to spite the world.

SALLY: Water make him talk. I get water.

PHELIM groans.

HONOUR: The mention o' water's roused him. He can't bear to be wetted.

She kneels and shouts in his face.

Wake up, ye old conundrum! Aren't you a fright and a disgrace to the whole world!

PHELIM: Honour! Honour, me girl!

HONOUR: Well now, are ye proud of yourself?

PHELIM: What happened to me?

HONOUR: *(with gusto)* Yez were rootin' me in the rump and I got mad and levelled ye with me fist, that's what happened to ye. And I'll do it again if ye don't mind yer eye.

MRS. STEWART: Oh, Honour, what a dreadful story!

PHELIM: Ye lie! Ye never had power in yer fist to smite me the way I been smote. I been struck by lightning.

HONOUR: Ye been struck by me right hand!

PHELIM: By lightning, I tell ye! I can feel it still roarin' around in the heels of me boots. Oh, Mrs. Stewart ma'am, will ye give me a little sup o' something to put life back in me!

MRS. STEWART: No, Phelim, I will not. Honour, go into the house at once and take the child with you. You must get up, Phelim, and you must go at once.

HONOUR does as she is told.

PHELIM: And where am I to go, a poor lonely old man without a wife or a child to care for him at all?

MRS. MOODIE: You've changed your tune, Brady. You were bold as brass a few minutes ago.

PHELIM: It wasn't meself that spoke, but the drink within me. Everyone knows I'm a humble poor man, and with good reason, too.

MRS. STEWART: And whose fault is it if you are humble and poor, Phelim, when the other Irish settlers hereabout are thriving and doing well for themselves?

PHELIM: Sure, it's because they're thriving that I'm wretched.

MRS. TRAILL: That doesn't make sense.

PHELIM: Yes it does, ma'am, if I may say so, aud I can tell ye why.

MRS. STEWART: Poor fellow, you look wretchedly. Would you like a cup of tea?

PHELIM: I would that, ma'am, thank ye.

MRS. STEWART: Sally, get him some tea.

SALLY: Bad old man. You twist my skillet.

She shows him the skillet with its neck badly bent. Then she goes.

PHELIM: So that was the thunderbolt? Ah, this is a terrible, terrible country, where the savages fight with the likes o' them things.

He moves himself painfully to a stump, and sits down to rub his head.

MRS. STEWART: Now, Phelim, I'm not going to let Honour go home with you until you can tell me that your first wife is buried, and that you will marry her, and that you will promise to treat her well. You must give up drink and go to work.

PHELIM: Them's terrible hard conditions. How can I go to work when nobody around here will let me work?

MRS. MOODIE: What nonsense! As if everybody in the place were not crying out for labourers!

PHELIM: I'll have ye know that I'm no labourer.

MRS. MOODIE: And what are you then?

PHELIM: It's yerself has a right to pity me and understand me, Mrs. Moodie, for I'm one of your own kind. I'm a story-teller.

SALLY puts a cup of tea into his hand.

MRS. MOODIE: What do you mean, one of my own kind?

PHELIM: Oh, you think yerself far above me, because you can read and write. But haven't I the art of a real Irish story-teller? Amn't I the latter-day heir o' the great bards and story-tellers of the old land? I know more than five-score stories and poems in English and in the old tongue too, and I can tell ye a story will pass away a whole night from dusk till dawn. And can't I make up a new song for a wake or a wedding as quick as the fiddler can play?

MRS. MOODIE: I do not see what that has to do with me.

PHELIM: Ye can't see because you're too proud and ignorant to see. You and me is two branches o' the same old tree. Ah, sure, don't I know that you write for them maggyzines in Montreal and in England itself, and wouldn't I do the same if I could? But did ye ever have a hundred people hangin' on your lips and laughin' and cryin' as ye told them a great story? I have!

MRS. MOODIE: I am not a vain author, but I think that there is a difference between the productions of an educated and disciplined taste and a rigmarole of memorized fairy tales!

PHELIM: How wise ye are! There's a big difference, and it's this: my poems and tales are rooted deep in a mighty past, and yours are the thin and bitter squeezings from the weary fancy of a heartsore woman.

During the latter part of PHELIM's speech, Mr. Edmund CANTWELL has entered at the back of the stage and has been listening. He is a handsome man, in the Byronic-Satanic fashion of the period, and his manner is that of a gentleman of fashion. He is about thirty-five, that is to say, he is of the generation of the three women whom he now greets. He is dressed in a mixture of backwoods garb and London fashion; his fine shirt is loosely bound at the collar with a silk cravat, but he may wear a skin cap, and a buckskin wamus, and his appearance is more decorative than that of a working settler.

CANTWELL: Who speaks of a heartsore woman?

MRS. STEWART: Oh, good morning. I don't think that we have met, have we?

CANTWELL: You know that we have not met, madam, but I think you know who I am, just as I know who you are. But let us preserve the decencies, by all means: I am Edmund Cantwell, madam, at your service.

He bows. MRS. STEWART curtsies in return.

MRS. STEWART: Of course, Mr. Cantwell. It is so difficult to know how one should meet these situations in this new land, isn't it? I am Mrs. Thomas Stewart, as you surely know. Mrs. Traill, you do not know Mr. Cantwell, I believe? Mrs. Moodie, I am sure that you have heard of Mr. Cantwell.

MRS. MOODIE: I am sure that everybody has heard of Mr. Cantwell.

CANTWELL: That is an ominous remark, madam. Are you the heartsore woman to whom this ancient Hibernian made reference?

PHELIM: What's that you're after callin' me?

CANTWELL: Nothing to your discredit, my good fellow. I am an Irishman myself. You spoke of a heartsore woman; to which of these ladies did you refer?

MRS. MOODIE: Mr. Cantwell, I do not propose to be the subject of a conversation between you and this wretched creature.

CANTWELL: Then it was you, Mrs. Moodie?

MRS. STEWART: Did you come here for some purpose, Mr. Cantwell? I should not like to detain you if you have a great deal to do.

CANTWELL: I am appreciative of your concern, Mrs. Stewart, but my business is with your husband. I want to hire a yoke of oxen and a man to drive them, if that is possible.

MRS. STEWART: My husband is from home, sir. He has gone to York. And I do not think that you will easily get a yoke of oxen in this neighbourhood, or a man either. All the gentlemen have gone to York because of the rebellion, and all the other men are gathered in Peterborough to defend the town if the need should be.

CANTWELL: Ah yes, the rebellion. I had forgotten it.

MRS. TRAILL: That is more than most people can do, sir.

MRS. STEWART: The Queen has asked all the gentlemen of Upper Canada to rally to the defence of the government of York; I am surprised that you did not hear the proclaniation.

CANTWELL: I heard it, madam, but upon consideration I decided to ignore it.

MRS. MOODIE: Are we to understand that you are on the side of the rebels, then?

CANTWELL: If I were on their side I should be with Mackenzie now. No; in this dispute I am on nobody's side, and as I hope to leave Upper Canada soon I am in urgent need of a man and a yoke of oxen.

MRS. STEWART: I am sorry, but there is none to be got here, Mr. Cantwell.

CANTWELL: Are you anxious for me to be gone, Mrs. Stewart?

MRS. STEWART: Why, no sir, I said nothing of the kind.

CANTWELL: No, but I sense a certain hostility in your manner. You are, of course, too much a person of breeding to make it plain; but in the station of life to which, I think I may say, we both belong, it is not necessary to labour these hints. Now as you cannot let me have a man for my work, may I enquire if you have any need of a man—a gentleman, here? In short, is Phelim Brady making a nuisance of himself?

PHELIM: I am not, sir! Do you take me for some common settler?

CANTWELL: No, the common settlers are better dressed, and better looking, and in every way superior to you.

MRS. STEWART: Brady has been assuring us that he is far above the common run.

PHELIM: And isn't a poet and a story-teller miles beyond and above them common fellows is diggin' the ground and pullin' out stumps?

CANTWELL: That is a question which has been debated for some hundreds of years, Phelim. Take what comfort you can from this: if a poet and a story-teller is both good, and dead, he may be considered the equal or even the superior of ordinary, decent, successful men; but so long as he has the bad taste to remain alive the question will always be in dispute, and the odds will always be heavily against him.

PHELIM crosses to CANTWELL.

PHELIM: Don't I know the bitter truth of that, your honour! In the old land, now, I could get a fine living; sure, the people were that wretched they'd be glad of a tale or a song to beguile them from hunger and the thoughts of death and injustice. But here the poorest ruffian of them all has his bit o' land, and his pig, maybe, and the ones with good arms and good heads on them is thrivin' so fast they never feel the need of a story at all. They're not the people I knew, God help them. They're a strange lot entirely, with the blush o' health on their cheeks and the maggot o' respectability in their brains. They're wantin' schools for their young ones, and for me it's "Get away wid ye, Phelim; don't be wastin' our time wid yer talk." Sure, as if talk wasn't the sacred breath of all the mystery and grandeur is in the world!

CANTWELL: There is a period of struggle between poverty and affluence during which men feel no need for what you have to offer them, Phelim. And there is a sort of education which forgets that the mind needs not only to be polished, but oiled. I am still curious about the heartsore woman.

He crosses to the ladies.

PHELIM: Mrs. Moodie, ma'am, I shouldn't have made bold on ye, the way I did, but ye must see, surely, that a country that has no need for my stories has no need for yours. And now, I'll take Honour and me child and get away home.

MRS. STEWART: No, Phelim, you will not. I told you that Honour shall stay with me until your home is fit to receive her.

PHELIM: Fit, is it! And what's it been since she came to it as a child, and her own father and mother dead with the cholera morbus?

MRS. STEWART: You know very well what I mean.

CANTWELL: Mrs. Stewart no doubt refers to your uncommon fashion of disposing of your dead, Phelim. It is oddities of conduct of that sort which get poets and story-tellers their bad name.

PHELIM: I want me wife and me child. How can a poet live without a woman to tend him? This is a free country; I want me rights!

MRS. TRAILL: Oh dear, when people begin to shout about their rights I always get a blinding headache.

MRS. STEWART: If you want your rights, Phelim, you had better be careful. My husband parcels out the land in this settlement and I can't recall that he ever gave you any. You are a squatter and you have no right in law to your cabin or any bit of land hereabout. But I won't ask Mr. Stewart to be hard on you if you will do what I told you. Bury your dead: marry Honour: go to work.

PHELIM: I won't do any of 'em.

MRS. STEWART: Then go away and don't come here again.

PHELIM: Be damned if I'll budge.

MRS. STEWART: Oh dear—

She begins to laugh.

MRS. MOODIE: I see nothing to laugh at, Frances.

MRS. STEWART: No, my dear, I don't suppose you do.

MRS. MOODIE: I suggest that you ask Sally to drive him away.

MRS. STEWART: No, no; that would be cruel.

MRS. TRAILL: But you cannot remain here unprotected, with this man in a threatening mood.

MRS. STEWART: I don't think he is so very dangerous.

PHELIM: Go on. Despise me, the lot of ye, if it gives ye any pleasure. But I've more courage in me pocket than the lot of ye—yes or your savage woman o' the woods—have in all yer carcasses.

He produces from an inner pocket a case-bottle.

MRS. TRAILL: Great Heaven! Strong drink.

PHELIM: The strongest. Ye could cut this seventeen ways with holy water and it'd knock ye down still. I'll be roarin'! I'll be terrible!

MRS. TRAILL: And not a man in miles!

CANTWELL: You forget, Mrs. Traill, that I am at your service.

MRS. TRAILL: No, Mr. Cantwell, I have not forgotten. But if you had the spirit of a man, you would be in York, ready to defend the government. I cannot regard your presence, sir, as a source of reassurance.

CANTWELL: Nevertheless, madam, beggars can't be choosers, if you will excuse the bluntness of the observation. Now, if I may offer a suggestion, let us go inside the house, and talk this matter over. Phelim must remain here, for the present, as he refuses to go, and I have not yet had your instructions to remove him.

MRS. STEWART: That certainly seems the best plan. Let us go in at once.

They go into the cabin; at the door CANTWELL *bows with great elegance as the ladies pass him;* MRS. STEWART *acknowledges this courtesy with a nod and a smile, but the Strickland sisters are frosty.* PHELIM *sits on his stump, and views his bottle morosely.*

What a lot of trouble this has been. Honour, if you won't lie down, put the baby in the cradle and go and help Sally, will you? You may be here for a while, and you may as well make yourself useful. And do, for goodness' sake, bind up your hair.

HONOUR: Yes, Mrs. Stewart, ma'am.

She goes to the kitchen.

MRS. STEWART: Do sit down, my dears. And you too, Mr. Cantwell.

He declines. Here SALLY *and* HONOUR *set the table for three.*

If you are to be our protector we mustn't lessen your strength by making you stand. I know I am being foolish, but I will not send that girl and a newborn child home with that dirty old man. Probably what I am doing is quite illegal, but I know it is right.

MRS. TRAILL: If it is right it cannot be illegal. One can only deal with people like that by telling them what is good for them, and seeing that they behave themselves accordingly.

CANTWELL: That is the simple principle of government, madam, which has given rise to the regrettable revolution, in suppressing which all your husbands are at present engaged.

MRS. MOODIE: And it is an extremely good principle of government, particularly in a new country, where many settlers have more liberty, and more money, than they know how to employ.

CANTWELL: May I suggest, Mrs. Moodie, that one's opinion on that matter is likely to depend upon whether one belongs among the rulers, or the ruled?

MRS. MOODIE: You may suggest what you like, sir. I was in this country before you came, and it appears that I shall be here after you have gone. I think I know what I am talking about.

CANTWELL: Everybody thinks that, including the rebel Mackenzie.

MRS. STEWART: Let us not talk of that now. What are we going to do about Honour, and Phelim, and the baby? I don't think we need detain you, Mr. Cantwell; Phelim will grow tired of waiting after a while, and he will be reasonable in the morning.

But PHELIM has been listening to the last speech or two outside the door, and now he shouts in defiance.

PHELIM: I'll not be reasonable! Ye're hard oppressors o' the poor, the lot o' ye! I'll set fire to your house, that's what I'll do!

CANTWELL: I shall go if you wish it, of course, but you may find Phelim troublesome. Wouldn't it be the best plan to give him his girl and be rid of him?

MRS. STEWART: No, I refuse to do any such thing. He will beat her and that I will not have.

CANTWELL: If I go, as you suggest, he may come in and take her by force. Could you prevent him?

MRS. STEWART: Sally could prevent him.

CANTWELL: He is a determined old man, but not a strong one. Sally is not what I should call a clean fighter. What if she kills him?

MRS. STEWART: Oh dear, I never thought of that.

MRS. TRAILL: It is a possibility.

MRS. MOODIE: If she hit him again with the skillet, it would be a certainty.

PHELIM: *(still at the door)* Don't think I don't hear you, whispering within with himself. Sure, wouldn't your husbands be ravin' if they knew it was closeted close with himself ye were, and him the wickedest fella in Douro and some says he's the Devil himself!

CANTWELL: You hear that?

PHELIM: Hasn't he a wife that's never seen by daylight?

CANTWELL: You hear these terrible accusations?

MRS. STEWART: He seems to be very wild. Perhaps you had better stay for a time, sir, if you will. What do you think, my dears?

MRS. MOODIE: I have no fear of that drunken old man, but there may be some unpleasantness, and I suppose we should avoid it if we can.

MRS. TRAILL: I must say frankly, Mr. Cantwell, that what I know of you does not recommend you as a protector, but I agree with my sister.

CANTWELL: Indeed, Mrs. Traill? And what do you know of me?

MRS. TRAILL: Only that you are a gentleman settler who has held a large piece of land for two years, and never worked any of it; that you have avoided all your neighbours; that Mrs. Cantwell appears not to wish to make the acquaintance of any of the ladies in the district, though there are many of her own station in life; that you appear to hold dangerously, radical political opinions; and that you have not answered the Queen's call to defend the government of Upper Canada.

CANTWELL: But you do not believe that I am the Devil?

MRS. MOODIE: Pray don't trouble yourself to be facetious, sir, we are not in a mood for nonsense.

PHELIM: Beware, women; beware! He'll tempt ye! He'll have the smocks off ye! Didn't Barney Flynn see a goat fly out of his chimney last Hallowe'en?

CANTWELL: Phelim is doing his best to warn you.

MRS. STEWART: Mr. Cantwell, we must not be so ungracious as to ask you for protection and then treat you rudely. If you will stay with us for a short time, we shall be most grateful, and I hope that you will join us in our midday meal?

CANTWELL: With the greatest pleasure.

MRS. STEWART: Sally!

SALLY comes in from the kitchen.

Is the dinner almost ready?

SALLY: Uh-hunh.

MRS. STEWART: Lay a plate for Mr. Cantwell, will you?

SALLY: Uh-hunh.

MRS. STEWART: And will you be as quick as you can? We have had a rather trying morning.

SALLY: *(emphatically)* Uh-hunh!

CANTWELL: If any of you have the slightest objection to eating with the Devil, I shall be happy to take my plate out on the step. I should not wish to put you needlessly in the way of temptation.

MRS. MOODIE: You may be assured, sir, that if any of us are to be tempted, it will not be by you.

CANTWELL: *(smiling)* I have received your assurance, madam, and I shall treat it with all the respect it deserves.

MRS. STEWART: Temptation is a word I have almost forgotten, except in my prayers, of course. Here in the backwoods temptation seems very far away.

MRS. TRAILL: That is one of the very few things that can be said for the backwoods. I have remarked upon it often: the backwoods offer, as positive advantages, an unlimited supply of plant and animal life for scientific study, and a complete absence of temptation.

MRS. STEWART: Oh I shouldn't say that, my dear. Look how many men succumb to the temptation of strong drink.

By a gesture she indicates PHELIM, *though of course she cannot see him.*

MRS. TRAILL: I meant temptation of the sort to which a lady of gentle breeding and good education might conceivably fall prey.

MRS. STEWART: Oh, that sort of temptation.

CANTWELL: You make yourself sufficiently clear, madam. I have been warned.

By this time SALLY *and* HONOUR *have set the table.*

MRS. STEWART: Shall we draw up our chairs to the table? Mr. Cantwell, will you sit on my right?

MRS. MOODIE *has already taken this position of honour for herself and with polite malice* CANTWELL *places another chair for her.*

CANTWELL: It is an honour, Mrs. Stewart.

MRS. STEWART: Susanna, will you say one of your beautiful graces?

All stand, but CANTWELL *does not close his eyes.*

MRS. MOODIE: Oh Lord, who hast guided our steps thus far through the day, enable us to walk without sin toward the night. Consecrate this food to our use and bless us, thy loving servants.

MRS. STEWART: Amen.

MRS. TRAILL: Amen.

MRS. STEWART takes the lid off a fine silver dish, and an appetizing steam arises. HONOUR and SALLY are in attendance.

PHELIM: *(peering through the window)* B'God, it's the Family Compact sittin' down to their food! And where's the common people? Out in the cold, every time; out in the cold! Hurrah for Mackenzie and responsible government!

As the curtain falls, he takes a hefty swig from his bottle.

Curtain.

ACT II

When the curtain rises it is plain that dinner has been over for some time, but the ladies and their guest are still seated around the table, and their high spirits are in marked contrast to what they showed at the end of Act One. PHELIM *still sits in the dooryard, gloomy and disgruntled.*

CANTWELL: I really must stop talking. I have been monopolizing the conversation abominably.

MRS. STEWART: On the contrary, sir, I hope that you will continue, for I have not been in such good spirits since my husband went to York.

MRS. TRAILL: I have often reflected that the conversation of ladies alone is like a peal of bells without the support of the great bell; it readily becomes a clangour.

CANTWELL: You are hard upon your sex, madam. You cannot conceive what pleasure it gives me, in this backwoods place, to hear my native tongue spoken with so much of that charm and delicacy which only ladies can impart to it.

MRS. MOODIE: You flatter us, Mr. Cantwell, upon a point which is very near to our hearts. We hear the Yankees, and the Irish, and many good, humble people, but it is rarely that we hear English spoken in a fashion that recalls the society to which we were accustomed in our better days.

CANTWELL: Better days, madam?

MRS. MOODIE: Earlier days, I should have said.

CANTWELL: But you think of them as better days, and you are right to do so. Your fashion of treating a guest, Mrs. Stewart, speaks eloquently of the Ireland which we both know.

MRS. STEWART: When were you last in Ireland, sir?

CANTWELL: A month less than two years ago I was the guest of Lord Rossmore.

MRS. STEWART: Rossmore? You know him well?

CANTWELL: Intimately. I think we have other friends in common. The Wailers and the Beauforts have spoken of you; Miss Edgeworth also honours me with her friendship.

MRS. MOODIE: Maria Edgeworth? How I envy you!

CANTWELL: She sends all her new books to at least one friend in Upper Canada, for she told me so herself.

MRS. MOODIE: Yes, to Frances. We all read them greedily. They are a breath of a greater world to us here. We have little enough time to read, but half an hour now and then gives the mind something to feed on during the endless hours of sewing, mending, cooking, candle-making, preserving, gardening—all the tasks that devour our time in this Ultima Thule of civilization.

CANTWELL: It is, indeed, a demanding life. So much so that I am giving it up. And if I may say so, I think that many others might be wise to give it up, as well.

MRS. STEWART: There are many others who cannot give it up, sir.

MRS. MOODIE: And many who would be too proud to do so.

CANTWELL: It is well to rid oneself of the folly of being too proud to do what is sensible.

MRS. TRAILL: You are probably aware, sir, that our husbands are retired officers, who have their way to make in the world.

CANTWELL: And who are trying to make it as farmers upon land which has not been farmed before, without previous knowledge of farming. That is very hard.

MRS. TRAILL: You may well say so.

CANTWELL: I have watched some of those officers here in Upper Canada following the plough, and whenever they rest—which it must be said to their eternal credit is rarely—they always come to a halt facing east. I think that without knowing it they are looking toward England, as they wipe the sweat from their brows.

MRS. TRAILL: I would rather not talk about it.

CANTWELL: Forgive me; I had not realized—

MRS. STEWART: *(bridging the difficult moment)* I have a guilty conscience about Phelim. He must be growing very cold. I'll take him a cup of tea.

MRS. MOODIE: But Frances, you are punishing Phelim for his wickedness and trying to bring him to a better frame of mind. How can you do that and give him cups of tea at the same time.

MRS. STEWART: Set it down to Irish irrationality, Susanna.

CANTWELL: It is the sort of irrationality which makes our system of government endurable. If we will not permit people to run their own affairs, we are obliged to be very kind to them to make up for it.

MRS. STEWART: If you will spare me any further philosophical observations and pithy generalities, I shall take Phelim his tea now.

CANTWELL: I most humbly ask your pardon, madam.

MRS. STEWART: Pray do not; I like your conversation very much. I thoroughly enjoy having a gentleman about the place to moralize and utter weighty apophthegms while I do as I please.

CANTWELL: I shall accompany you.

MRS. TRAILL: And I. I feel the want of air.

MRS. MOODIE: I shall come too. I want to see how the man who called me a petticoated grenadier is enduring the cold.

During these speeches they have gone out-of-doors.

MRS. STEWART: Phelim, I have brought you a cup of tea.

PHELIM: Is it gentry tea, or common folks' tea?

MRS. STEWART: It is the last of the pot and strong enough even for you, I think.

PHELIM: I don't know as I ought to take it.

MRS. STEWART: Do, and oblige me. It is very hot.

PHELIM: Well, if it's to oblige you, ma'am, I don't mind draining it through me, but don't think it'll soften me heart.

During this, SALLY and HONOUR, indoors, clear the table.

MRS. STEWART: I'm sure it won't but if you are determined to stay here I cannot allow you to freeze to death at my door.

PHELIM: How wise ye are! Himself would skelp ye if ye treated me bad. I'll be waitin' here till he comes.

MRS. STEWART: Compose yourself for a long wait, then, for I do not expect Mr. Stewart for many days.

PHELIM: He's away to fight the revolution, I suppose?

MRS. STEWART: Yes.

PHELIM: A big help he'll be, and him with that delay in his right leg. There'll be great times in York, I'm thinkin', and all them fine fellas there spoilin' for a fight. I wish to God I was with 'em. Sure there's no time like wartime for larkin'. Drunk every day before noon they'll be.

He pours a generous dollop from his bottle into the hot tea, and drinks it at a gulp.

CANTWELL: And which side would you favour, Phelim, if you were there?

PHELIM: The side the bards has always been on—both sides at once. Sure, I'd make songs o' victory for the conquerors, and take a sup with them, and I'd fashion laments for the vanquished, and take a sup with them. It's what ye call the impartiality o' the artist—rejoice and mourn with everybody and hit both sides a good clout if ye can.

CANTWELL: Your philosophy of art differs from Mrs. Moodie's. She has written vigorously in support of the government side.

PHELIM: The gentry ladies are all on the government side. The Queen's proclamation was hardly dry before Moodie and Traill were squeezin' themselves into their old uniforms, and scourin' up their swords with sand, and shoutin' around in hoarse voices the way ye'd think the trees was all sojers. Hasn't this revolution been a glory and a blessed gift to them! Back to sojerin', and away from this cursed spot, and away from their wives and their debts. They've a right to be yellin' for the revolution, I'm tellin' yez!

CANTWELL: You should not speak so before Mrs. Moodie and Mrs. Traill.

MRS. MOODIE: Let him say what he pleases. He is railing so bitterly because he is on the losing side in the little battle that is being fought right here.

PHELIM: Go on! Pity me if it does ye good! But I told you this morning, me fine madam, and I tell ye again that you and me is both in one losin' battle. We're the songbirds that aren't wanted in this bitter land, where the industrious robins and the political crows get fat, and they with not a tuneful chirp among the lot of 'em!

MRS. TRAILL: How odd that poets are such bad naturalists! There are songbirds all about you, you foolish old man! Come Susanna, I am going inside. It is colder than I thought, and you have no shawl, my dear.

MRS. MOODIE: Phelim, if you think to hurt me, you must use a hickory club. I am an author, and I have winced under the lash of professional criticism. Words are powerless upon me.

She and her sister go into the house.

CANTWELL: Shall we follow them?

MRS. STEWART: Just a moment, Mr. Cantwell; I want a few more moments in the sunshine. Shall we walk in this direction?

PHELIM: Ah, ye want to say somethin' them two mustn't hear.

They ignore him, and walk to the right, out of his earshot.

MRS. STEWART: It embarrasses me to find that we have friends in common, Mr. Cantwell. I feel that I have been shamefully rude and neglectful toward you and your wife. I should have called upon her many months ago.

CANTWELL: There is no cause for embarrassment, I assure you. We did not show ourselves friendly. I presume that you know why that was so?

MRS. STEWART: I know nothing about it.

CANTWELL: You heard the rumours about us, surely.

MRS. STEWART: I pay no attention to rumours.

CANTWELL: But in this case the rumour was the truth. Mrs. Cantwell was a novice in a nunnery in Cork. She was forced into that position because her parents did not want her to marry me. I rescued her, and brought her here. She was not anxious to meet many people for some months. But now we are returning to Europe.

MRS. STEWART: To Ireland?

CANTWELL: To Italy.

MRS. STEWART: If it had been to Ireland I should have asked you to take some messages to friends there.

CANTWELL: To Miss Edgeworth?

MRS. STEWART: To her, of course; and to Lord Rossmore.

CANTWELL: Rossmore travels a great deal; I may well see him on the Continent. What shall I tell him?

MRS. STEWART: *(after some hesitation)* Oh, give him my good wishes.

CANTWELL: Nothing more?

MRS. STEWART: What more should there be?

CANTWELL: I knew Rossmore intimately. Not long before I left Ireland we were together in a day's hunting. He was thrown from his mount at a rather dangerous leap, and when he did not rise at once I feared that he might have broken his neck. There were no others near, and I knelt to examine him; his pulse beat faintly, and I opened his shirt to listen to his heart. Around his neck, on a chain, was a locket, in it was a lock of hair and a miniature of a beautiful young woman.

MRS. STEWART: You opened it?

CANTWELL: I did, madam.

MRS. STEWART: Was not that a breach of confidence?

CANTWELL: No; it was a friendly precaution. If he had been dead I should have removed the locket at once. For the portrait was not that of Lady Rossmore. Men do such things for one another, you know.

Pause.

MRS. STEWART: Do you tell that story to many chance acquaintances?

CANTWELL: I have never told it to anyone but yourself, for you alone have the right to know it.

MRS. STEWART: Why have you told it to me?

CANTWELL: Because it piques my sense of the incongruous to know of this link between a world of brilliant fashion and the backwoods of Canada.

MRS. STEWART: There is no link, I assure you.

CANTWELL: With the best will in the world, madam, I do not believe you. Indeed, I have seen that picture; I cannot believe you.

MRS. STEWART: Is my assurance nothing?

CANTWELL: You gave stronger assurance of the truth of my suspicion when I mentioned Rossmore at the table. And there is more colour in your cheek now than you know. And can you deny that you asked me to remain here with you outside the house to quiz me about him? I am not a simple man, Mrs. Stewart; I can see through a brick wall with tolerable clarity.

MRS. STEWART: If once there was a strong attachment between Lord Rossmore and me, you have no right to suggest that it endures still. I was curious about a former friend, that is all.

CANTWELL: A friend who still cherishes your memory very dearly. Do not think that I imply anything discreditable to either of you, or injurious to Lady

Rossmore, who is my friend, too. But when I see her once again in the midst of that brilliant and fashionable society, with the light of a hundred candles falling upon her jewels, shall I be able to repress a thought of you, sitting on a rush chair by the light of a backwoods fire?

Far away the note of a horn is heard, clear and mysterious in the still December air.

MRS. STEWART: I do not know Lady Rossmore, nor do I envy her her jewels or her friends.

CANTWELL: I am sure that you do not. And yet how well you would become such a life!

MRS. STEWART: I? You are absurd.

CANTWELL: No. You are beautiful, highly born, witty, and possessed of that wonderful generosity of spirit that quality of giving—which raises beauty and charm to the level of great and holy virtues. What need has the backwoods of these things? You should not be here. You chose wrongly.

MRS. STEWART: I cannot permit you to say more. Do not follow me.

Agitated, she goes out left, passing PHELIM, who raises his head slightly. CANTWELL watches her reflectively, and then goes into the house. His step is jaunty and he hums an Irish air under his breath. MRS. MOODIE and MRS. TRAILL have been unobtrusively busy during the previous scene; MRS. TRAILL has been by the fire, peacefully knitting, and her sister has sat at the table, with her back to the audience, writing busily.

MRS. TRAILL: You look glowingly, Mr. Cantwell; the air has done you good. Where is Frances?

CANTWELL: Mrs. Stewart has gone for a walk, madam, and she did not care for my company.

MRS. TRAILL: A walk? That is strange, at this time of day.

CANTWELL: I understand that she shares your enthusiasm for the study of nature, Mrs. Traill. Perhaps she has gone in search of specimens.

MRS. TRAILL: *(laughing)* Mr. Cantwell, what a droll notion! What specimens, as you call them, would she find in December?

CANTWELL: I cannot say. I am utterly ignorant of such things.

MRS. TRAILL: So it appears, sir.

CANTWELL: But not so ignorant that I have not heard of your fame as a naturalist, madam.

MRS. TRAILL: My fame is little enough. If my fame were equal to my enthusiasm, I might have cause to boast.

CANTWELL: No, fame is what I said, and fame is what I meant. When I first arrived in this country I met a Mr. Sheppard in Quebec who, when he found that I was coming to this part of the backwoods, urged me particularly to seek your acquaintance.

MRS. TRAILL: I know Mr. Sheppard only through correspondence.

CANTWELL: So he told me. But he said that your letters revealed a quite extraordinary scientific capacity.

MRS. TRAILL: That is flattering, and I wish that it were true. Mr. Sheppard is preparing a book on Canadian flora, and I was able to give him some trivial assistance in describing the great wealth of plants and flowers which we find hereabout.

CANTWELL: He told me that he had asked you to be one of three or four expert collaborators in the preparation of that work.

MRS. TRAILL: Yes, he paid me that great compliment, but I did not think that I was worthy of it, although I did what I could.

CANTWELL: You had other work, of course, which made such a collaboration out of the question.

MRS. TRAILL: That is true. The wife of a settler has no trifling day's work, as I am sure you know.

CANTWELL: Was that not a pity, madam?

MRS. TRAILL: I do not understand you, sir. I see nothing pitiful about my life. Quite the contrary; it is filled with interest. My excursions into natural science, when I have time for them, give me the greatest joy, I assure you.

CANTWELL: I did not mean to suggest that there is anything pitiful about you as a person. But is it not a pity that so much of your time is absorbed in work which is not your proper concern?

MRS. TRAILL: Really, Mr. Cantwell, you are still a stranger in Canada. No one is ashamed to do useful work here.

CANTWELL: You wilfuly misunderstand me. You are able to do work which no one else can do. Why should you waste your time in tasks of which any woman is capable?

MRS. TRAILL: I do not consider this a profitable discussion.

CANTWELL: I am being intolerably intrusive, I know. But I cannot bear to see genius wasted.

MRS. TRAILL speaks quietly, but the arrow has found its mark.

MRS. TRAILL: You abuse the word genius.

CANTWELL: It is not my word, but Mr. Sheppard's. Do you know what he said to me, madam? "If Mrs. Traill could give all her time to her studies of natural life she could do for her part of Upper Canada what Gilbert White did for Selborne."

For the second time the horn is heard, nearer but still distant. There is a pause while MRS. TRAILL considers what he has said.

MRS. TRAILL: That was generous praise.

CANTWELL: Tell me honestly; do you think it was too generous?

MRS. TRAILL: Yes; it was quite ridiculous.

CANTWELL: I asked you for an honest answer.

MRS. TRAILL: What right have you to pry in this fashion?

CANTWELL: If you have it in you to do notable scientific work is it not my concern, as a man of some education myself, to ask why you make it a bad second to the drudgery of a settler's wife?

MRS. TRAILL: You do not understand what you are talking about. A new country brings new hope, and it also demands sacrifice. Have you ever walked in our graveyard? Many stones there mark the graves of children. One of those children was—is mine. A fair hope vanished, Mr. Cantwell. And other hopes must be buried which may even be harder to give up. New countries mean not only hopes fulfilled but hopes relinquished. I must ask you not to try to estimate the claims of my duty to my husband and my children.

CANTWELL: Are you sure that you know what your duty is? Mr. Traill is an estimable gentleman, but it is no secret that he is one of the least capable settlers hereabout. He was not framed for such work, and neither are you. As for your children, it might lie in your power to pass on to them a great name.

MRS. TRAILL: Are you suggesting that my husband's concerns should play second fiddle to my work?

CANTWELL: Aha, you have said it. Your *work*. Yes, madam, I am suggesting that for your sake, and your children's sake, and for the sake of the advancement of knowledge your husband should play second fiddle to you.

MRS. TRAILL: Do you see nothing immoral—nothing contrary to the law of nature, in such a proposal?

CANTWELL: No, madam, and neither do you, in your heart of hearts. We are not animals, and the female does not live at the sufferance of the male.

MRS. TRAILL: It is not my province, sir, to ask you to leave this house, and therefore I have no choice but to leave it myself. I shall go in search of Mrs. Stewart, and I hope that when I return you will no longer be here.

CANTWELL: As you please, Mrs. Traill.

She puts on her shawl, which she has kept close at hand since her first entrance, and goes out; she asks PHELIM which way MRS. STEWART has gone, and he points out the direction; she goes the same way. CANTWELL, meanwhile, turns his attention upon MRS. MOODIE, who has been listening to the past conversation, although she has kept up a pretence of her writing; she does not raise her eyes until he speaks. His approach to her is that of the intellectual bully, in contrast to his air of calm reason when talking to MRS. TRAILL, and the romantic air which he gave to his scene with MRS. STEWART.

I fear that I have discomposed your sister. But she is a remarkable woman pretending to be an unremarkable one, and that cannot be tolerated. Now you, Mrs. Moodie, are another remarkable woman, and you know it.

MRS. MOODIE: I have no wish for a private conversation with you, Mr. Cantwell. I shall call Sally.

CANTWELL: Call her by all means, but do not forbid me to talk, for I shall certainly disobey you.

MRS. MOODIE: It is not in my power to gag you.

CANTWELL: Nor would you, if you had the power. After hearing what I said to your sister you will not be content until you have heard my opinion of you. Who ever heard a sister praised without wishing to try her own luck?

MRS. MOODIE: You are impertinent, sir.

CANTWELL: I have been told that I have the cheek of the Devil.

MRS. MOODIE goes to the kitchen door, and calls.

MRS. MOODIE: Sally, Honour, what are you doing?

HONOUR: We're braiding rags, ma'am.

MRS. MOODIE: Bring your work in here, will you? I want company.

SALLY comes in, ill-pleased, and HONOUR follows with a basket of clean rags, some braided into long strips.

SALLY: Not braid rags in best room. That kitchen work.

HONOUR: Ah, sit down and stop your talkin'. Don't ye see she has to have us here?

SALLY: No.

HONOUR: Gentry ladies can't trust themselves alone with a man. They're that frisky they'd be at him at once. It's all the rich food they eat.

MRS. MOODIE: Honour, hold your tongue.

HONOUR and SALLY sit on the floor and work during the scene which follows.

CANTWELL: Did you disagree with Mr. Sheppard's estimate of your sister's abilities, Mrs. Moodie?

MRS. MOODIE: It is not a matter in which I am qualified to judge.

CANTWELL: But Sheppard is, don't you agree?

MRS. MOODIE: Mr. Sheppard's opinion must be allowed a great deal of weight.

CANTWELL: You felt, perhaps, that I pushed the matter too far?

MRS. MOODIE: I really have no views on the subject.

CANTWELL: Perhaps I was wrong. After all, a woman's first duty is to her husband.

MRS. MOODIE: That is the accepted belief.

CANTWELL: Even when it means the subordination of her own dearest wishes—perhaps of a very great talent.

MRS. MOODIE: Most people hold that opinion.

CANTWELL: Your sister might achieve fame as a naturalist, perhaps, but it is unquestionably more important that Mr. Traill should make a farm in the wilderness.

MRS. MOODIE: *(giving a ladylike snort) Hummph!*

CANTWELL: I scarcely know how to interpret that sound, madam. Was it intended as assent?

MRS. MOODIE: I think you know how much hope there is that any of us will make a fortune at farming.

CANTWELL: Mr. Stewart seems very comfortably off.

MRS. MOODIE: Mr. Stewart brought money with him, and money begets money. To begin life here, as my sister and I have done, with all to seek, is to begin with the certainty of failure.

CANTWELL: And yet many of the humbler settlers seem to be thriving.

MRS. MOODIE: They know how to work in a sense that my husband and Mr. Traill do not; my husband can plan and contrive better than they, but he has not the strength for twelve hours of back-breaking labour, every day of the week, month in and month out. What is more, many of these humbler settlers, as you call them, sponge on us shamelessly when they need help, and why? Because we are gentry, and so are obliged to give to the needy when we have not enough for ourselves. Gentle breeding brings obligations; when it does not also bring money the obligations may grow burdensome, but they cannot be thrown off. Because we are gentry we cannot live without a few of the comforts of life which the humbler settlers have not known and do not therefore miss. Those comforts make the difference between an endurable life and what we should consider degradation; they also make the difference between a very little profit on a year's work, and debt, debt, debt! Among the gentlefolk who have come to settle in this country, Mr. Cantwell, there are few wastrels, but there are scores who have learned the bitter lesson that superior abilities may suffer the most complete frustration for the want of a few hundred pounds of capital! Good birth and gentle breeding carry with them tastes and obligations which are costly to maintain.

CANTWELL: Was there no alternative?

MRS. MOODIE: There was life as a half-pay officer in England. You know what that is.

CANTWELL: Poor Mrs. Traill!

MRS. MOODIE: Mrs. Traill?

CANTWELL: Yes, were we not talking of Mrs. Traill? Sheppard says she is a genius buried in the forest. You apparently agree with her that she must remain buried. A great pity and the world's loss.

MRS. MOODIE: A woman's first duty is to her husband.

CANTWELL: And the husband's first duty is to—

MRS. MOODIE: To his career, or to his destiny I suppose.

CANTWELL: And might not the woman's career, or destiny, sometimes be of greater importance? I have told your sister what one able scientist thinks of her.

Come, Mrs. Moodie; you and I understand and appreciate these things better, perhaps, than most people. Because a husband's hope is blighted, must his wife's even greater hope be blighted too? Merely to spare his masculine vanity?

MRS. MOODIE: It is very, very hard.

CANTWELL: Then I was right to press the matter to a conclusion with your sister?

MRS. MOODIE: It was unpardonably rude and intrusive, but I cannot say that it was wrong.

CANTWELL: I felt that you would agree with me. After all we have somewhat the same cast of intellect.

MRS. MOODIE: You and I, sir?

CANTWELL: Oh, do not imagine that I put myself on your level. You are a creator; I a critic. I once thought that I had some small talent as a writer, but it was too small for the company I kept. I was a friend of Byron, you know.

MRS. MOODIE: You knew Byron?

CANTWELL: Yes, and most of his circle. I am glad to think that he sometimes asked my opinion of his verse. You did not suppose, did you, that Maria Edgeworth was the only literary person among my acquaintance?

MRS. MOODIE: I have long admired Miss Edgeworth. Of course, to someone who has known Byron—

CANTWELL: Precisely. But I am sure that Miss Edgeworth should be proud of your good opinion.

MRS. MOODIE: Should be?

CANTWELL: You are surely aware that your abilities are in no way inferior to hers.

MRS. MOODIE: I am not aware of anything of the kind, nor do I believe it. And what do you know of my abilities?

CANTWELL: I have read many of your stories and verses in Montreal and New York journals. I think very well of them.

MRS. MOODIE: I am obliged to you. But you will hardly expect me to accept that as the approbation of Byron.

CANTWELL: No, but there was a time when, young as I was, Byron did not despise my approbation.

MRS. MOODIE: I ask your pardon; I was rude. It is only that—you see, my situation is such that—

CANTWELL: That you are unaccustomed to praise from your intellectual equals?

MRS. MOODIE: That I am unaccustomed to praise at all. I write, it is true, and I am paid for what I write, but I rarely hear any comment upon it. It is all hasty work, done when I am tired, and when I can snatch an hour from other, pressing tasks. I do it, I tell you frankly, because the money is sorely needed. That it should have any merit is more than I have dared to hope.

CANTWELL: Madam, I would scorn to flatter you. Indeed, with a lady of your intellectual stature flattery would be useless. I do not say that you always write well. I say, rather, that your writing is that of one who might, under favourable circumstances, write very well indeed. How well I cannot say, of course, but I beg that you will cease to gaze upward toward Miss Edgeworth when it is fitting that you should look her in the eye.

MRS. MOODIE: I, the peer of Maria Edgeworth!

The horn is heard for a third time, nearer but not too near.

CANTWELL: Yes, why not?

MRS. MOODIE: But I have never attempted a work of any length; I have had no opportunity to do so.

CANTWELL: Ah yes; you are in your sister's position. You must play second fiddle to the incompetence of Lieutenant Moodie.

MRS. MOODIE: How dare you speak so!

CANTWELL: How dare you, madam, pretend to me that wifely loyalty is more important than your very considerable talents as a writer!

MRS. MOODIE: You are impertinent.

CANTWELL: Of course I am impertinent. People who care greatly for anything must be so. And I care greatly for your talent, which I know, and I have no concern whatever with the ambitions of your husband, whom I do not know.

MRS. MOODIE: You should not press this discussion; it is unmanly to take such advantage of me.

CANTWELL: Humbug! You talk like a foolish girl being kissed in a corner. We are not man and woman, Mrs. Moodie, but artist and connoisseur—a vastly more delicate relationship—and I tell you that you may strangle all your children in their beds, murder Moodie with the cleaver, trample the British flag under your feet and Almighty God will find some mercy for you; but if you refuse, for an idiotic scruple, to write your best, He will put you into hellfire and I, as a critic, will applaud His judgment. Do you understand me?

MRS. MOODIE: You make my scribbling seem very important.

CANTWELL: Do you suppose that the importance of literature is diminished because nobody hereabout understands it? Would music cease to exist because your neighbours were deaf? I have said that Mrs. Traill's work is important. But that is science—a chilly business at best. Your work is art, and art is what gives form and meaning to life. Dare you neglect the sacred obligation which has been laid upon you?

MRS. STEWART and MRS. TRAILL have returned, and as they pass PHELIM he accosts them.

PHELIM: Mrs. Stewart ma'am, will ye have a little charity? I want my girl and my child, and if ye give me them two I'll go and not trouble yez any more.

MRS. STEWART: Wait a moment, Phelim. I shall attend to you very soon. Are you cold?

PHELIM: I'm perished, ma'am, and me rump's dyin' under me with the weight of the sittin' I've done.

MRS. STEWART: Be patient for a few minutes longer.

They go into the house, and she addresses CANTWELL from the door.

Mr. Cantwell, I do not think that we need detain you any longer. Phelim is quite reasonable now. You have been most kind to help us during this rather troublesome time, and I am sure that you have much to attend to.

CANTWELL: You are very kind, ma'am, but I cannot think of leaving until I have apologized to Mrs. Traill. I spoke unguardedly, and I am very sorry.

MRS. TRAILL: It is of no consequence, I assure you.

CANTWELL: I am glad that you see it in that way, ma'am. Now about Phelim—you know, of course, that once he has Honour out of this house he will beat her. Won't you, Phelim?

PHELIM has been standing outside the door and he falls into the trap at once.

PHELIM: Indeed and I will, sir! I'll scoop the heart out o' her with me naked nails! Isn't she the bold, undutiful strumpet to be troublin' her betters and defyin' me that's been more than a father to her!

HONOUR: Are yez lookin' for another clout to match the one I gave ye this mornin'?

PHELIM: Ye never hit me no clout, ye puny, sneakin' trollop! Don't I know 'twas the big savage struck me. Awww, won't I let the fresh air into yer hide!

SALLY, with an ancestral war-whoop, dashes through the door brandishing a hatchet which she has fetched from the kitchen, and puts PHELIM to flight; but with sudden courage he turns upon her, his bottle held aloft.

If ye strike me, watch out for me bottle. I didn't leave me native land to be domineered over by the likes of yourself.

MRS. STEWART: Sally! Come into the house at once! How dare you!

SALLY: I no kill, only scare. Wicked old man.

She trots obediently indoors and to the kitchen, giggling. CANTWELL closes the door at once, and PHELIM is left the master of the dooryard.

PHELIM: Go on, me lady! Keep me from what's me own, if ye dare! When himself returns I'll have me say!

He advances upon MRS. STEWART with drunken menace; when she rushes to safety in the house he sits defiantly again upon his stump, and refreshes himself from his bottle.

CANTWELL: As I was saying, once Phelim has Honour out of your sight, he will beat her. However I dare say she's used to it. Aren't you, Honour?

HONOUR: Ye never get used to beatin'. That's something only them thinks that's never been bet.

CANTWELL: And there is, of course, the delicate situation involving the corpse of the late Mrs. Brady.

MRS. STEWART: Oh, what a vexing position to be in!

CANTWELL: I sympathize with you. But I do not think that we can discuss it thoroughly in front of Honour.

MRS. STEWART: Go into the kitchen, Honour, and see to your child. How is she?

HONOUR: Och, fine—fine. I don't suppose anybody'd see it but me, but d'ye know she's a kind of an honest-lookin' little crature.

She goes.

MRS. STEWART: Honour will be a good mother. But what will the honest-looking little creature do when she comes to know her father?

CANTWELL: Mrs. Stewart, and ladies, I know that my presence here is an embarrassment to you.

MRS. STEWART: That is very frankly stated, Mr. Cantwell.

CANTWELL: I assure you that I have no wish to prolong that embarrassment for one moment longer than is needful. But if I leave you here alone, what will you do if Phelim becomes troublesome?

MRS. MOODIE: Sally has twice shown herself more than a match for Phelim.

CANTWELL: Do you intend to keep the girl here indefinitely?

MRS. STEWART: Until my husband returns. He will know what to do.

CANTWELL: When do you expect him?

MRS. STEWART: I do not know. But we shall be perfectly safe.

PHELIM: *(brooding upon his wrongs)* Ye're a pack o' female blackguards! It'd serve ye right if I set fire to your roof!

CANTWELL: You hear that?

MRS. STEWART: It's nothing but wild talk.

CANTWELL: It is a kind of wild talk which has grown into wild action in more than one backwoods settlement since the revolution began in York. I must remind you that to Phelim and people like him you settlers of the privileged class have begun to appear as oppressors. What if he collects a gang of ruffians and gives you real trouble?

MRS. TRAILL: Oh, please don't suggest such a thing. He may be listening at the door.

MRS. STEWART: We know the risks as well as you, Mr. Cantwell. But I ask you to go.

CANTWELL: Better danger than my society: is that it?

MRS. STEWART: I entreat you, if you have any gentlemanly feeling, to go at once!

CANTWELL: Very well, I shall go. But before I go I beg you to permit me to say how very sorry I am that I have disturbed you all so profoundly.

MRS. MOODIE: You have disturbed my sister, sir. You have not touched me.

MRS. TRAILL: Oh, no, Susanna; it is Frances who as been disturbed.

MRS. STEWART: What you have said to me, sir, is of no consequence. But you have taken intolerable liberties with Mrs. Traill.

CANTWELL: I assure you, madam, that was not my intention. But it is clear that I have given offence by suggesting to you all three that you are wasted in the backwoods. It was an unpardonable liberty, and I beg your forgiveness.

MRS. STEWART: Let us say no more about it.

CANTWELL: Certainly not. No such hint shall ever pass my lips again.

MRS. STEWART: I am sure that you spoke hastily.

CANTWELL: I spoke from the best feeling that was in me. Listen to me, I entreat you, and then judge me how you will. Here in the forest I meet a lady whom a poet might adore for her charm, her beauty, and her loveliness of spirit! I meet another gifted with power to see into the very heart of Nature herself and to reveal the mysteries of Nature to mankind: and as though this were not adventure enough for a single day, I meet still a third whom I know to be capable of enriching the world through acts of creation no less miraculous than the miracle of life itself. I find these three Graces hidden in the wilderness. Should I remain silent? Would you ask me to close my lips if I saw Pegasus toiling at the plough? No! I spoke. I said what lay in my heart. But it was not in that alone that I offended. My transgression was that I said what lay in *your* hearts, and you cannot forgive me.

MRS. MOODIE: You have little regard for duty, sir.

CANTWELL: I have told you, madam, where your real duty lies.

MRS. STEWART: I refuse to hear you.

CANTWELL: But you will always hear what your heart tells you. I have spoken your unacknowledged feelings; they will never be without a voice again.

MRS. STEWART: Please, please, please do not torture me!

MRS. TRAILL: Frances, what do you mean?

MRS. STEWART: Forgive me; but I think his words have deeper meaning for me than for you.

MRS. TRAILL: Can you imagine that I hear him without some pain?

CANTWELL: I do not seek to cause you pain. I beg you only to come back to the world which is rightfully yours, and which has a place for you.

MRS. MOODIE: You have caused us all pain.

CANTWELL: I have done nothing but give words to the pain which you have long felt. And is it so shameful? Is it a thing to keep hidden? Do not many settlers feel a kindred pang? Only a few weeks ago my eye was caught by some verses which an unhappy settler had sent to the Cobourg paper. Rough and simple as they were they captured a feeling common enough here. I recall a few lines:

He recites with deep pathos, and the last defences of the ladies are broken.

I canna ca' this forest home,
 It is nae home to me;
Ilk tree is suthern to my heart
 And unco' to my e'e.
I canna ca' this forest home.
 And in it live and dee;
Nor feel regret at my heart's core,
 My native land for thee.

MRS. STEWART: It is utterly impossible that any one of us should admit the truth of what you have said.

CANTWELL: I wish for your sakes that that were so, but you have admitted it already—at your heart's core.

There is a lively fanfare on a bugle offstage, and the Hon. Thomas STEWART *enters; he is a man of kindly, merry appearance, dressed like a gentleman, but with heavy boots and strains for travel. He is lame in his right leg, and limps, using a heavy stick whenever he moves. From this instant the scene changes character sharply, and moves rapidly to its climax.*

STEWART: Phelim, you rascal, what are you doing here? I've some news for you! Hello, there! Anybody at home? Nobody here to greet the survivor of the rebellion? Frances! Frances!

MRS. STEWART and the ladies have risen in haste, and with obvious relief they unbar the door and rush into the dooryard to greet them.

MRS. STEWART: Thomas! Dearest! Oh, I am so happy to have you back!

She embraces him, weeping.

STEWART: What's this? Tears? What's amiss, my pet? Eh?

MRS. TRAILL: Mr. Stewart! What joy to see you! Have you news for us?

MRS. MOODIE: I am rejoiced to see you, sir. The rebels, I presume, have been dispersed?

STEWART: Weren't you expecting me? I left Joseph and the wagon in Peterborough, and I've been sounding my bugle ever since, in the hope that someone might come to meet me.

MRS. STEWART: Oh, Thomas! I heard nothing.

STEWART: I declare. Frances, that's the first time you've ever failed to hear my bugle. Is anything wrong?

MRS. STEWART: No, nothing; nothing at all. It's just that I am so happy to have you back.

STEWART: Oh, come; you haven't been fretting have you? I was never in the least danger. But you all three look devilish queer. What's been amiss here?

PHELIM: Aha, wouldn't ye like to know, your honour. As if the three noble dames hadn't been closeted with a strange man since before noon.

STEWART: What? What's this, Frances? Who's been here?

MRS. STEWART: It is nothing of any consequence, Thomas, believe me.

MRS. MOODIE: Pay no attention to that man. He's drunk.

PHELIM hops up on his stump.

PHELIM: Not so drunk that I couldn't see what palaverin' and whisperin' and runnin' out o' the house cryin' there's been this day. Did ye think I hadn't got me eye peeled, me fine ladies? Didn't I tell ye I'd have somethin' to say to himself when he came home?

STEWART: Phelim, be silent! If there is anything that I should know, my dear, let us go inside and I shall hear it.

CANTWELL comes to the door of the house; his manner is sharply changed to an air of arrogant contempt and amusement.

CANTWELL: There is no need for a long explanation, Mr. Stewart; I can tell you all there is to know in a few words. A few hours ago these three ladies boasted to me that there was no temptation in the forest. Since that time I have tempted them, all three, and with complete success!

Curtain.

ACT III

When the curtain rises, the day has grown perceptibly darker, but inside the house the fire keeps that part of the stage bright, PHELIM *is still outside, obviously miserable with the cold, but inside* STEWART *sits at his table with the authority of the master of the house, finishing what has plainly been a fully satisfactory repast. He alone of the company is happy and at ease; he sits in an armchair which has been unused during the first two acts.* CANTWELL *sits by the door, and* SALLY *stands over him with her hatchet in her hand. On the further side of the room* MRS. MOODIE *watches him grimly, a large pistol pointed across her forearm in his general direction.* MRS. STEWART *waits upon her husband, her face marked by anxiety, in this act, for the first time, she wears her cap,* MRS. TRAILL *sits bolt upright in a chair, glaring at* CANTWELL *and knitting in an ominous manner.*

STEWART: This is delicious! The food in York was really abominable. I know of nowhere that I can eat so well as in my own home. Another slice of meat, I think, my dear. And will you be so good as to refill this tankard? Beer is a great comfort—a very great comfort. All I could get in York was rebellion whisky. Made last week I believe it was, too. Imagine, if you can, a very inferior quality of gin, hideously sophisticated with molasses and with a strong hint of untanned hides about it, and you have the flavour of rebellion whisky.

MRS. STEWART *replenishes his tankard in silence.*

I had some hope that the Archdeacon might have asked me to take a bottle of claret with him, but he had locked his wine-cellar and buried the key until the trouble was over. A Low Church action if ever I heard of one. The Governor of course, had fled to Niagara in order, I suppose, to get a clearer perspective of the fighting in York. The justices and all the more reputable lawyers were drilling with borrowed weapons on the lawn at Osgoode, and were so delighted to be soldiers, and so eager to plague poor Fitzgibbon with their notions of strategy that there was no diverting them. So you see there wasn't a house where I could get a Christian bit: or a cup of drinkable drink. Even the York ladies have forsworn tea, although their houses are full of it. Why do people become so damnably self-denying in wartime? They have decent victual; what's to be gained by not eating properly? It was the same with the rebels. "We've no time to eat," they'd cry; "we must snatch a crust on the run!" And the result was that they ate enormously, at all the wrong times, to keep their strength up.

MRS. STEWART: Thomas! You didn't mingle with the rebels?

STEWART: Let us say that the rebels mingled with me. Quite a number of them took me for one of themselves because I had no uniform and no gun.

MRS. STEWART: No gun!

STEWART: Oh, I had my pistols, but I left them at the inn.

MRS. TRAILL: It appears to me that this rebellion is being conducted in an uncommonly slipshod fashion.

STEWART: You are quite right, ma'am. I had never realized before what necessities uniforms are in a battle. Without them, how can a man decide whom he should kill? The loyalists looked such ruffians, and the rebels looked so mild that you couldn't tell which from t'other. I should think that perhaps a third of the men in York were fighting on the wrong side and didn't know it.

MRS. MOODIE: You make light of a grave matter, sir.

STEWART: I am aware of it. But pray remember that I have seen this rebellion and you have not.

MRS. TRAILL: Was there no bloodshed?

STEWART: There was a battle one evening. The loyalists marched north, and the rebels marched south, and when they met there was a battle of a kind. I'd describe it as a skirmish if it were not the only battle I've ever seen, but I don't pretend to be a judge. A handful of poor fellows were killed, and a few more were wounded, and then the rebels broke and ran. Mackenzie got away, and I suppose he will make for the States. A good many prisoners were taken and there will be some hangings; the school-children are being given a holiday to see them. It's a form of practical education which I can't say I like, but the professional educators must be allowed to know best, I suppose. You may take it from me, the back of the rebellion is broken.

MRS. MOODIE: You mean that it is all over?

STEWART: By no means. The bitterest part has just begun. But there will be no more fighting. What now remains is to hound down and punish anyone who can be associated with the insurrection. That will provide some of our people with agreeable work for a year or more.

MRS. MOODIE: Mr. Stewart, you speak very strangely. It might almost be supposed that you sympathize with the rebels.

STEWART: I bear a humble part in the government of this colony, ma'am. I do not sympathize with any armed outbreak against law and order. But a grave suspicion assails me that what we have at York is order without law. And that is tyranny, Mrs. Moodie.

MRS. MOODIE: A new country needs strong government.

STEWART: The fashion of government is changing everywhere in the world, and has been doing so since the revolution in France. This little upheaval at York is a part of that change.

MRS. MOODIE: It is Methodism which is at the root of it. Religious disunity is the trouble.

STEWART: One can pay too dear for unity of any kind. I don't really think that rebellion is such a very bad thing.

MRS. STEWART: Thomas!

MRS. MOODIE: Have you no desire for order, sir? For peace?

STEWART: There was once a rebellion in Heaven, you know—the one which sent the Devil to exercise his talents upon Earth. I have often wondered if that was the last of Heaven's troubles.

MRS. MOODIE: You are in a strange mood, sir.

STEWART: I have been compelled to question a system of which I form a part. Luckily most of my colleagues have avoided this discomfort.

MRS. TRAILL: May we expect our husbands home soon do you know?

STEWART: Set your mind at rest; the military will be needed for many months, and perhaps for a year or more. I do not know whether this is good or ill news, but Lieutenant Moodie and Lieutenant Traill are shortly to go to Niagara, to command troops there, and to remain in the service as long as they are wanted. They will be on full pay, of course.

CANTWELL: That will be good news, indeed.

SALLY: Hush, bad man!

CANTWELL: Mrs. Moodie, would you be good enough to direct that pistol at the ceiling. In the stress of your emotion you might discharge it.

MRS. MOODIE: Be silent, sir, until the Honourable Mr. Stewart is ready to address you. As for this pistol, let me inform you that I can shoot a squirrel from a branch at fifty yards.

She twirls the pistol adroitly upon her finger.

MRS. STEWART: The news from York, then, is very good.

STEWART: Yes, when we think what it might have been. Not all good though. Grimaldi is dead.

He has spoken seriously for the first time. Pause.

I see that none of you thinks very much of that. But I do. Poor old Joey! Here in the backwoods we yearn for many of the things of home, and will you believe that I have yearned for a sight of Joe Grimaldi as often as anything?

MRS. TRAILL: A clown, Mr. Stewart?

STEWART: Yes, a clown. A prince of clowns. There was a great spirit in Joey. Many a time I have laughed at him until I hurt all over. He died last May, and I heard nothing about it until I went to York to do my duty in the rebellion of Upper Canada. Did you ever see him?

MRS. MOODIE: Never.

MRS. TRAILL: Papa did not consider the theatre to be wholly serious.

STEWART: And you never saw him, I think, my dear?

MRS. STEWART: No.

STEWART: He had such a very droll way of saying the simplest things. But I mustn't run on about him. You never saw him, and you don't know what the world has lost.

CANTWELL: I saw him many times, Mr. Stewart.

STEWART: You did?

CANTWELL: And I grieve with you at his loss.

STEWART: Yes, it really is a loss isn't it? So much more than if it had been some dull, worthy fellow that one knew quite well.

MRS. MOODIE: Mr. Stewart, I warn you that you will be made a fool of! It is this man's habit to find everybody's weak spot and work upon it. Don't let him abuse your interest in this wretched clown!

STEWART: Your pardon, ma'am, but he wasn't a wretched clown.

Thumping the table.

He was the greatest clown of our day, or of any day, if you ask me. You've heard Joey sing "Hot Codlings," of course?

CANTWELL: A score of times.

STEWART: When I was at Trinity I used to do an imitation—not very good of course—

He borrows his wife's cap, puts it on, and makes a Grimaldi grin—eyes flashing, and tongue lolling out like a dog's. As he sings the song he drums with knife and fork upon his plate, tankard, and the table itself. MRS. STEWART *smiles as though accustomed to such behaviour but the Strickland sisters do not know what to make of it.*

A little old woman her living she got
By selling hot codlings, hot, hot, hot;
And this little old woman, who codlings sold,
Tho' her codlings were hot she felt herself cold.
So to keep herself warm, she thought it no sin
To fetch for herself a quartern of—

CANTWELL: *(shouts, very loudly)* "GIN!"

STEWART: Oh, for shame!

BOTH: Ri tol iddy iddy, ri tol lay.

PHELIM *hears the singing in the house and creeps to the door during the second verse. This time* STEWART *uses a plate as a tambourine, beating it on his elbows, head, knees, and, at the culminating line, on his fundament.*

STEWART: This little old woman, while muzzy she got,
Some boys stole her codlings, hot, hot, hot;
Powder under her pan put and in it round stones
Says the little old woman, "These apples have bones!"
The powder the pan in her face did send
Which sent the old woman on her latter—

CANTWELL AND PHELIM: "END!"

STEWART: Oh, you naughty man!

ALL THREE: Ri tol iddy iddy, ri tol lay.

During this verse CANTWELL *has accompanied* STEWART *by whistling and clapping his hands. At the chorus* PHELIM, *still outside, dances a lively jig and twirls his stick.*

CANTWELL: You are an excellent mimic, sir. You bring Joey to life as well as anyone I have ever seen.

STEWART: Thank you; you flatter me.

MRS. MOODIE: He does, and he'll disarm you with flattery.

STEWART: I think not. But did I not hear another voice in the chorus. Was that you, Phelim?

PHELIM: *(without)* It was, your honour, and it's a fine, strong, manly voice ye have, and you sittin' snug and easy by your fireside.

STEWART: You see, Phelim wants to disarm me by flattery, too. But I have been a magistrate too long not to be able to swallow flattery in gobs without allowing it to affect my decision in the least. As I shall demonstrate now. My dear, will you remove my plate? It detracts from the perfect dignity of the law.

Smiling, she removes her cap from his head, as well.

Thank you. Mr. Cantwell, I am now ready to question you.

CANTWELL: Before you do so, sir, may I ask what right you have to question me, and by what right you hold me here at—if I judge Sally's intentions correctly—the peril of my life?

STEWART: I shall give you an honest answer. I hold you here because I've got you here and you can't get away. It is a rather novel form of *habeas corpus*. Possession is nine points of the law, and I've got you.

CANTWELL: You are very frank. But I take it that you don't mean to kill me.

STEWART: I am only a magistrate. If I kill you it must be inadvertently.

CANTWELL: When I get away, then, what will you do if I complain to the proper authority that I have been held against my will?

STEWART: As I am the proper authority to whom such a complaint should be addressed I shall tell you to go to the Devil.

CANTWELL: There are higher authorities elsewhere.

STEWART: And I shall tell them that I held you for questioning because I suspected you of sympathy with the rebels.

CANTWELL: I shall make a counter-accusation that you yourself sympathize with the rebels.

STEWART: Nobody will believe you. Justice is not a perfect instrument, Mr. Cantwell, and you had better recognize that in this affair I am on the right side and you are on the wrong side. I have you, sir, over a barrel.

He beckons, and CANTWELL *moves to a chair across the table from him.*

CANTWELL: Very well, sir. What is the charge against me?

STEWART: I have not the slightest idea. But your accusers are at hand. Ladies, do you wish to make a joint accusation against this person, or shall I consider your grievances individually?

PHELIM, *who has been harkening at the door, bursts excitedly into the room.*

PHELIM: Lemme speak, your honour! Sure, and can't I tell the tale agin' the whole lot of 'em! Wasn't they sneakin' and whisperin' with himself when you were from home defendin' us all agin' the bloody rebels?

STEWART: Phelim, get out!

PHELIM: Yez have got to hear me evidence! I'm the main witness to the whole disgraceful affair.

STEWART: Be off! I'll deal with you presently.

PHELIM: Ain't I a sufferer from him? Didn't he stay here the whole day to keep me from me lawful child and me nearly lawful wife?

STEWART: If there is one thing I cannot abide in a court it is lack of discipline! Sally, give me the poker. Now do you see this, Phelim? This is the mace of this court. I lay it here on the table before me. So long as the mace is in its position the court must be obeyed without question. If you raise your voice again I'll remove the mace from its place of honour and give you a good skelping with it. Now—sergeant-at-arms! Sally, I mean you! Remove the man Phelim Brady; he has no place here; he has merely come inside to get warm! Phelim, wait in the witness room until I call you.

PHELIM: Sure and where's the witness room, your honour?

STEWART: It is all of Upper Canada except this chamber, Phelim. Out you go!

SALLY *hastens* PHELIM *out into the cold; as soon as the door is closed he creeps back to listen.*

Phelim has hinted at misconduct of a particular kind in which you ladies and Mr. Cantwell were involved. I may say at once that I regard any such accusation as too ridiculous to be entertained.

CANTWELL: Of course such a notion is ludicrous!

STEWART: Mr. Cantwell, one of these ladies is my wife, and so far as I am concerned, above suspicion. On behalf of Mrs. Moodie and Mrs. Traill, I repeat that such a notion is ridiculous, but you show very little feeling for words when you suggest that it is ludicrous.

CANTWELL: Your gallantry, sir, is obviously greater than my own.

STEWART: Very likely.

MRS. TRAILL: I resent this masculine exchange, which I feel to be derogatory to myself and my sister. It is not by our beauty or our attractiveness to your sex that we seek to justify our existence.

MRS. MOODIE: And it was not through these agencies that Mr. Cantwell sought to offend us.

STEWART: Then pray how did he offend you?

MRS. TRAILL: Do you suppose, sir, that a woman has no feelings save those of female vanity?

STEWART: No, madam, I do not suppose anything so stupid, and I must ask you not to fly at me when I am trying to help you.

MRS. TRAILL: I have not flown at you, as you put it.

STEWART: Come now, Catherine, don't be vexed. What has he done?

MRS. TRAILL: It is by no means easy to say precisely what he has done.

STEWART: Was he rude toyou?

MRS. TRAILL: No, nothing so trivial.

MRS. MOODIE: We are not children, Mr. Stewart, to take offence at trifles.

STEWART: Did he employ any violence—any physical force?

CANTWELL: Do I look like a brigand, sir?

STEWART: If I ask if it is a case of offensive language I am rebuked by the plaintiffs. If I suggest that it was physical assault I am sneered at by the defendant. The position of a judge under such circumstances is an impossible one. Frances, will you be good enough to tell me what is the matter? Why did you all insist when I came home that I do something desperate to Mr. Cantwell at once?

MRS. STEWART: I suppose that we were overwrought, Thomas.

STEWART: Well? What put you in such a state?

MRS. STEWART: It was his horrible words about what had gone on this afternoon.

STEWART: He said that he had tempted you all. Was that it?

MRS. STEWART: Yes.

STEWART: That remark, and the violent exception which you ladies took to it, persuaded me to put Mr. Cantwell under this rather crude form of arrest. Why can you not tell me what he has done?

MRS. STEWART: Thomas, dear, you have created an atmosphere in which that is very difficult.

STEWART: I am sorry for that, Frances, but it is the only atmosphere I knew for an enquiry.

MRS. STEWART: But you treat the whole thing as an elaborate joke.

STEWART: Well—consider, my dear. This fellow says that he has tempted you, and Mrs. Moodie and Mrs. Traill—all in an afternoon. I know you all three far too well to attach the obvious meaning to his words. And if he didn't mean the obvious thing, what serious meaning can they have? Shall I ask Cantwell himself to explain what he has done?

MRS. STEWART: No, Thomas, pray don't do anything of the kind.

MRS. TRAILL: No, that would certainly be most undesirable.

MRS. MOODIE: He would merely make worse a situation which is already bad enough.

STEWART: But why is it bad? Will no one tell me?

MRS. MOODIE: Yes, Mr. Stewart. I shall tell you. He has made fools of us. That may not sound impressive. I assure you that it feels very painful.

STEWART: Made fools of you? How?

MRS. MOODIE: Perhaps I should speak only for myself. Mr. Cantwell, by playing upon a foolish side of my nature, led me to feel emotions, and to admit ambitions, to which I had no right.

STEWART: And am I to know more? I mean, were these emotions and ambitions of a very private nature?

MRS. MOODIE: Yes.

MRS. TRAILL: You understand, Mr. Stewart, that in every heart there are desires which can never be fulfilled, and which are cherished all the more closely for that reason. Many worldly people think that only carnal desires are nourished and grieved over in that way. But some of us know that intellectual passion can hurt as terribly as any flame of love. People laugh at intellectual women, as cruel people laugh at ugly women, and mock their yearnings and disappointments. But a devoted and loving wife may know an agony of frustration which has nothing at all to do with her marriage; it is the frustration of the mind.

STEWART: I begin to see what has been happening here. It is something far beyond the jurisdiction of this enquiry or of any court I have ever heard of. What a scoundrel you are, Cantwell!

CANTWELL: Am I? You are delivering an emotional judgment upon a supposed emotional injury which these ladies think that I have done them. How do you know that, if you were not in such high spirits about the failure of the rebellion in York, you might not dismiss the whole thing as a foolish female vapour?

STEWART: I have no wish to split hairs. I don't intend to pry into things which are unanswerable.

CANTWELL: But I delight in splitting hairs, and unanswerable problems are the only ones which can hold my attention for two minutes. You have called me a scoundrel without hearing my side of the case. What sort of a judge do you call yourself?

STEWART: I am not upon trial, sir.

CANTWELL: These ladies will tell you that I have not laid a hand upon them, nor have I said a word to them, which they bade me unsay. Mr. Magistrate, you find yourself presiding over a court which is faced by a moral issue, and I suggest that you drop your jocular manner and sharpen your wits.

STEWART: How dare you speak to me like that?

CANTWELL: The ladies will tell you that I dare to say what other men fear to say.

PHELIM: *(outside)* Watch him now, your honour! Mind, or he'll have you destroyed!

SALLY opens the door and speaks directly into PHELIM's face:

SALLY: Quiet!

MRS. MOODIE: I think that Mr. Cantwell has shown the matter in its true light. His offence was a moral one, and not capable of judgment here or perhaps anywhere. Let us drop the matter.

STEWART: Good God, madam, are you his accuser or his lawyer?

MRS. MOODIE: Any offence which Mr. Cantwell gave me was made possible by my own foolishness and vanity. I am as much to blame as he.

MRS. TRAILL: I think that I may say the same. Perhaps we should go home now.

STEWART: Frances, will you tell me what has been going on? I am utterly flabbergasted by the whole business.

MRS. STEWART: I think that Catherine and Susanna are too noble, too self-accusing. I have no wish to pursue any enmity against Mr. Cantwell myself. I think, however, that they should at least have an apology.

STEWART: I am not an inquisitive man. I hear enough of other people's troubles without inviting confession. But I return to my home. A man greets me with the news that he has successfully tempted my wife and her two closest friends. I cannot get one crumb of undisputed, factual information as to what he has done. Everybody accuses everybody else—including me—and now two of the complainants have decided to accuse themselves. This business has driven me to a pitch of curiosity which I cannot sustain much longer without internal combustion.

CANTWELL: The ladies feel that you lack the subtlety of intellect to understand their difficulty.

STEWART: I resent that suggestion; I am as subtle as is good for anybody to be.

CANTWELL: You will not be contented with an apology, then?

STEWART: No. There is nothing I despise so much as an apology.

CANTWELL: *(rising)* That's as well, for I have no intention of apologizing. I have done nothing which appears to me to call for retraction on my part. I tempted these ladies; I did so intentionally; I succeeded and I am satisfied. How long have I been your neighbour, Mr. Stewart?

STEWART: I don't know.

CANTWELL: You are the great man in these parts. Wasn't it your business to know?

STEWART: Your settlement papers were in order. That was all that concerned me.

CANTWELL: Was it nothing that I was a man of your own class, a countryman of yours? Are Irish gentlemen so common here that you feel no curiosity about them?

STEWART: If you are complaining that I did not make a social call upon you I assure you that I am too busy for such formalities.

CANTWELL: And Mrs. Stewart was too busy to call upon Mrs. Cantwell?

STEWART: My wife uses her own discretion in such matters.

CANTWELL: And it would have been indiscreet to call upon Mrs. Cantwell because rumours about her had reached you from Ireland?

MRS. STEWART: That is unjust, sir.

CANTWELL: No, not unjust; merely a statement of disagreeable fact. You put a slight upon me and my wife.

STEWART: *(uncomfortably)* In time we would have made your acquaintance. Don't exaggerate, man.

CANTWELL: Perhaps you do not realize what a tight, snug, unapproachable little society you have here in Upper Canada. I am not surprised that you have brought a rebellion upon yourselves.

MRS. MOODIE: Do you mean that you did what you did in revenge upon us?

CANTWELL: Do you recall your boast to me, this morning, that there was no temptation in the forest? It was you, Mrs. Traill, who said that there was nothing here which might lead ladies of gentle birth and good education astray. You were mistaken.

STEWART rises and takes the poker back to the fire.

STEWART: How were you led astray? You can't have let this man pop some wicked idea into your heads.

MRS. MOODIE: Yes. That is exactly what we did do.

STEWART: Well, God bless my soul! But surely that's simple enough. Pop the idea out again.

CANTWELL: Let them do so if they can.

STEWART: You have a great opinion of yourself as a tempter haven't you?

CANTWELL: Yes.

PHELIM: *(outside)* He's the Devil, I'm tellin' yez. Why haven't yez got the sense to hear what I'm saying?

STEWART: I wish Phelim would stop shouting that you are the Devil. We don't have the Devil in the nineteenth century, and we certainly don't have him in this country.

CANTWELL: These ladies have nothing to worry about then. Now may I go?

STEWART: I can see no reason for detaining you, though I do wish that somebody would tell me what the idea was that caused so much commotion.

CANTWELL: Now that you have virtually acquitted me of injuring these ladies, I shall be happy to tell you myself. I have observed that there is one temptation which only the strongest spirits can resist. It is the temptation of discontent.

STEWART: Discontent?

CANTWELL: Yes. It is only the crude seducer who takes a woman's honour, and in order to do that he must have some liking for her. It is a more lasting and serious injury to rob her of her peace of mind. These ladies will never, I think, know perfect content again. They will say to themselves that my temptation was beneath contempt, but they will never be free from it. It will always linger at the heart's core. And yet a little humility this morning, and a little charity toward Mrs. Cantwell a few months ago, might have spared them this distress.

MRS. MOODIE: Who are you, to cast our sins of omission in our teeth, and to stand in judgment upon us?

CANTWELL: That, Mrs. Moodie, is a matter which I prefer to leave in doubt.

MRS. MOODIE: And all that you said—you whose opinion Byron valued—was flattery? No grain of truth in it?

CANTWELL: That also I prefer to leave in doubt.

MRS. MOODIE: If it gives you satisfaction, sir, that doubt will gnaw at me all my life.

CANTWELL: That is as I intend it, madam. You have no further need of me, I believe? Then permit me to make my adieux.

He bows to MRS. MOODIE and MRS. TRAILL in turn, and good breeding demands that they curtsy; he crosses to MRS. STEWART who stands by the door, ready to hand him his cap.

Mrs. Stewart, I shall not forget your message.

He says this just loud enough for STEWART to hear, and as she curtsies he gives STEWART a look of triumph. He goes into the yard, and there eyes PHELIM, who backs away from him in fear.

Phelim, you are ninety different kinds of a scoundrel, but I think you have the best pair of eyes in these parts. Drink my health at your wedding.

He throws him a coin, and goes, humming his Irish jig. PHELIM *rushes into the house.*

PHELIM: He's gone! Are yez all unharmed?

STEWART: Perfectly unharmed, Brady—I think.

PHELIM: Then please, your honour, can I have me justice now? It's bitter cold outside.

STEWART: Very well. Justice hot and strong for you, Phelim. Sally, tell the girl to come in.

SALLY *admits* HONOUR *from the kitchen; she has the child in her arms.*

STEWART: Now, Honour, do you want to marry this old rascal?

HONOUR: I promised his late wife I'd do so, and I'm a woman of me word.

MRS. STEWART: But Thomas, the girl cannot go to Phelim's cabin so long as you-know-what is on the roof.

STEWART: I quite agree, my dear. But you-know-what is no longer there. I passed your cabin on my way home, Phelim, and I ordered Barney Flynn to bury your late wife at once. Now you get away before nightfall to Father Clary and make your peace with him as best you may, for I will not have any more of your unchristian antics in the range of my jurisdiction. And if Father Clary permits—and I have my reasons for thinking he will—you and Honour can be married in three days. Meanwhile she is to remain here. Now, Honour, I want you to keep this man in order, and if he lets a rebellious thought out of him, you are to tell me at once.

PHELIM: Yez'll permit me just one harmless kiss, your honour, from the girl that's to be me bride?

HONOUR: Yez have had all the kisses ye'll get from me, Phelim, for a good year and maybe more. Get away to Father Clary at once, as his honour says.

PHELIM: Look at her, would yez—as conceited as if she'd cut a dead dog in two with a dull knife! Ah, wasn't I the big fool to take his coin! And sure I'll be in the Devil's own hand from this day!

He goes, and is seen to wander disconsolately off into the forest. HONOUR *goes to the kitchen with her child.*

STEWART: Well, does that tie up everything with a bit of blue tape?

MRS. STEWART: You have done very well, my dear.

SALLY *puts two lighted candles upon the table, for it is now winter dusk outside.*

MRS. TRAILL: We too should go if we are not to be very late in getting home.

STEWART: Quite out of the question. Anyhow, you haven't heard half my news. Susanna, I hear that Moodie is to have a government post.

MRS. MOODIE: You couldn't possibly be mistaken?

STEWART: No. It's quite certain. It will mean giving up his farm.

MRS. MOODIE: Giving up his farm? Giving up this backwoods life? Giving up uncertainty, and poverty and debt? Oh, God!

She bursts into tears.

MRS. STEWART: Catherine, will you take her into the back bedroom. It shall be yours tonight. You need rest, my dear. Later we shall have supper.

She gives MRS. TRAILL one of the candles.

MRS. TRAILL: Come along, my dear. You must try to compose yourself. We mustn't give way before the servants.

They go through the door to the kitchen quarters.

STEWART: If I had known that she would take it so hardly I should have told her later, when fresh tea was made.

MRS. STEWART: I am sure that there is no harm done. It has come as a great relief.

STEWART: They'll be set up for life, now. I suppose the thought of getting away from that wretched farm, combined with today's trouble, and the thought of the rebellion and all, has discomposed her.

MRS. STEWART fetches a chair to the fire for him, and places a footstool for his lame foot.

MRS. STEWART: Catherine and Susanna were not too much concerned about the rebellion. Not about their husbands, I mean. They know what soldiering is. I don't. I am so happy to see you safely back, Thomas.

STEWART goes to her, and sits in the chair.

STEWART: Thank you, my dear.

MRS. STEWART: Would you like to have your slippers?

STEWART: You don't think that Susanna and Catherine would consider it a trifle offhand if I wore them?

MRS. STEWART: Oh I'm sure they wouldn't.

STEWART: Then I should like them more than anything.

MRS. STEWART brings them from under the bunk, right. She kneels at his feet and draws off his boots. He winces as she draws off the boot from the lame leg.

MRS. STEWART: Would you like me to rub your leg, Thomas?

STEWART: Thank you.

She does so.

That helps. It is very kind of you to do this.

MRS. STEWART: Is it particularly kind today? I have done it often.

STEWART: Yes; particularly kind today. I am never unconscious, my dear, that as a husband I lack something in beauty, and agility.

MRS. STEWART: Oh, Thomas, what nonsense!

STEWART: You could have done better. Don't think I don't know it.

MRS. STEWART: When you fish for compliments, Thomas, you should take more care to hide your hook.

STEWART: Ah, I see that you have been spoiled for my conversation by the polished style of Mr. Cantwell.

MRS. STEWART: That detestable man!

STEWART: An insinuating fellow, all the same. Anyone who could find a chink in the armour of Susanna and Catherine is no fool.

MRS. STEWART: Do you mean that a fool could find the chink in mine, Thomas?

STEWART: No, my dear, I do not mean that. Was it very painful?

MRS. STEWART: It was—unexpected.

STEWART: I had always expected that some day someone would appear who would talk to you about Rossmore.

MRS. STEWART: Then you guessed what my temptation was?

STEWART: I believe that many husbands think from time to time of the men their wives might have married.

Pause.

The message of which Cantwell spoke was for Rossmore, I suppose?

MRS. STEWART: Oh Thomas, after so many years, are you jealous?

STEWART: No, but I am not complacent, either. I have never taken you for granted, Frances. I do not suppose that a day passes that I do not thank God for the blessing of our life together.

MRS. STEWART: You make me feel very humble, Thomas.

STEWART: I did not intend to do so; I thought that I was the one who should be humble.

MRS. STEWART: But today—when that man put discontent into my heart—I should have thought of you.

STEWART: Is there a man anywhere who is capable of filling the whole of a woman's heart forever? I know that such fellows exist in romances, but I doubt their reality.

Pause.

If I may ask—you needn't answer—is Rossmore that sort of man?

MRS. STEWART: How can I possibly know? It is many years since last I saw him, and when I think of him now, which is rarely, I think of him as he was then, and I see him, sometimes, with the eyes of a girl. But if we were to meet again I am sure that the whole thing would dissolve. That was where Cantwell was so clever, and so cruel; from something which was past he created, only for a few moments, something which had never been. What he roused in me was not regret, but discontentment, disguised as regret.

STEWART: Hoping, I suppose, that it would work like slow poison.

MRS. STEWART: But he had reckoned without you.

STEWART: He had reckoned without us.

She is now sitting on the floor beside his chair and they are both looking into the fire. A happy pause.

MRS. STEWART: I should be getting tea, and calling Susanna and Catherine.

STEWART: Do not be hasty, my dear. Let us enjoy our victory a little longer.

During the last scene it has become much darker outside and the first flakes of snow have begun to fall.

Curtain.

THE KOMAGATA MARU INCIDENT

SHARON POLLOCK

HISTORIOGRAPHY AND *THE KOMAGATA MARU INCIDENT*

GEORGE BELLIVEAU

In May 2014, to commemorate the centenary of the *Komagata Maru* incident, a series of important events took place in British Columbia. Of note were theatrical representations of the 1914 incident, with selections from three plays: Sharon Pollock's *The Komagata Maru Incident* (first performed in 1976; in English),[1] Ajmer Rode's *Kāmāgātā Mārū* (first performed in 1979; in Punjabi),[2] and Sadhu Binning and Sukhwant Hundal's *Samundari Sher Nal Takkar* or "*The Conflict with the Sea Lion*" (published in 1989 in *Piket Lain*; in Punjabi).[3] Staging excerpts of these three plays in English and Punjabi in Vancouver and Surrey provided a forum for "a broader conversation about the significance of the *Komagata Maru* incident and what it represents in the history of Canada, [turning] the lens back on white society to complicate and highlight contradiction and dissent within it."[4] The theatrical presentations were sponsored and hosted by the University of British Columbia and the Surrey Arts Centre.

Herbert Lindenberger suggests "that by a strict definition one cannot categorize historical dramas as a genre at all, though one can speak of specific forms of historical plays which prevailed at certain moments in history."[5] For

1 Sharon Pollock, *The Komagata Maru Incident* (Toronto: Playwrights Co-op, 1978).

2 Ajmer Rode, *Kāmāgātā Mārū* (Amritsar: Nanak Singh Pustakalaya, 1984).

3 Sadhu Binning and Sukhwant Hundal, *Pikat Lain: Nātak Sangraih*. (Chandigarh: Balraj Sahni Yadgar Prakashan, 1989).

4 Anne Murphy, "Performing the Komagata Maru: Theatre and the Work of Memory," *Studies in Canadian Literature* 40.1 (2015): 45–73.

5 Herbert Lindenberger, *Historical Drama: The Relation of Literature and Reality* (Chicago: U of Chicago P, 1975), ix.

his part, Ric Knowles notes that since the early 1970s, Canadian playwrights have been making use of a specific form of historical play—historiographic metadrama. He suggests that this genre of drama incorporates "self-reflexive, metadramatic forms to highlight the instability both of history and dramatic texts."[6] In a historiographic drama, historical events are subjectively presented to suit the goals of the playwright. It is difficult to pinpoint precisely what elements a play must incorporate in order to be historiographic. However, if we define some of the differences between a historiographic drama and historical fiction, then we are better able to place Pollock's play within the first genre. On the one hand, *historical fiction* more often than not involves the imaginative creation of plausible but fictional private conversations or situations wherein the facts of the case are not known; on the other hand, *historiographic drama* generally contains self-conscious dramatic devices that make the audience aware that the play they are watching is a representation of the past. Pollock's *The Komagata Maru Incident* clearly focuses on the latter, as she consciously makes the audience aware that what they are watching is a representation of the past, a possible version of what happened. Most historical dramas raise questions about how the past is reconstructed; however, what makes a historiographic drama distinct is that it also raises awareness about the assumptions and conventions according to which we reconstruct that past.

Sharon Pollock's *The Komagata Maru Incident* premiered in 1976 at the Vancouver Playhouse. It is the story of the 376 would-be immigrants of Punjabi origin aboard the steamer *Komagata Maru* who were denied entry into Canada. Set in 1914 Vancouver, the play makes use of a carnival-like circus atmosphere. Pollock's T.S.,[7] the master of ceremonies, reconstructs history by theatrically presenting the Canadian government's success in denying the ship's mostly Sikh passengers rightful entry into the country. T.S. opens the play by directly addressing the audience from the outer ring, or runway arc, of the playing space: "This is Vancouver, ladies and gentlemen, the 21st day of May, nineteen hundred and fourteen." He gradually directs the audience to pay attention to the action taking place inside the circus ring, creating the sensation that spectators are viewing a circus show. From the beginning, T.S. openly demonstrates his puppeteer-like control over events and characters, making the audience aware of Pollock's deliberate presentation of history as theatrical retelling. With a snap of his fingers, T.S. makes a spotlight appear on himself, then with a bang of his

6 Richard Paul Knowles, "Replaying History: Canadian Historiographic Metadrama," *Dalhousie Review* 67 (1987): 228.

7 Pollock's T.S. is an abbreviation for The System.

cane he makes Hopkinson (an inspector in the immigration office) and Evy (a brothel proprietor) come to life. With another bang of his cane, they freeze, and the spot returns to him. T.S. performs the same magical feat with Georg (a German patron of the brothel) and Sophie (a prostitute working for Evy) in the opening scene. Finally, by pulling a cover he reveals the Sikh Woman—representative of all the Punjabis involved—on board the *Komagata Maru*.[8]

In setting up her metadramatic play-within-a-play frame, Pollock implicates the paying audience in the incident, as they become bystanders and participants in the racist sideshow. Knowles suggests that the central subject of the play "is its predominantly white audience, for whose benefit both Hopkinson and the theatre company act."[9] He later comments that "we are confronted with our ability to detach ourselves from action that 'doesn't concern us,' but for which we are necessarily passive accomplices."[10] Robert Nunn notes that "as an audience, watching *The Komagata Maru Incident* we are alienated from an automatic acceptance of the predominance of the White Race in our country: it didn't just happen; choices were made and continue to be made to maintain it. The play forces us to either criticize or justify the state of affairs: we cannot take it for granted."[11] Both critics suggest that Pollock questions and implicates her audience regarding its inaction on the subject of blatant racism.

One of Pollock's first stage directions is: "T.S. observes the audience entering [while] the other characters are frozen on stage." This reverses traditional roles as the audience becomes the focus of interest for those on stage. The actors wait for their onlookers and T.S. makes the audience aware of the play's metatheatricality with his solicitations: "Hurry! Hurry! Hurry! Right this way!" His invitation enhances the spectators' participation. Pollock's use of metatheatricality allows her to compare the play's audience and the historical "spectators" to the 1914 incident, suggesting that the play's audience inadvertently perpetuates racism by remaining indifferent to it in their daily lives in a way that parallels the casual racism prevalent in 1914 Vancouver. An example of this occurs early in the play, when Evy vividly recounts to Hopkinson a fight she saw from a tram window. She describes how a Sikh was violently beaten by (presumably white) men while waiting in an employment line: "They knocked him down,

8 Pollock's stage direction suggests that a curtain was used to mask the Sikh Woman: "*T.S. pulls cover to reveal woman who bends over child on deck. T.S. bows. Spot is out.*"

9 Knowles, 238.

10 Ibid., 239.

11 Robert C. Nunn, "Performing Fact: Canadian Documentary," *Canadian Literature* 103 (1984): 56.

the man in the turban they were kicking, and then pushing and shoving to get in a blow—and the tram pulled away . . . it was gone. As if I'd imagined it. It had never been . . . I should have done something . . . And I just sat on the goddamn tram and came home." Evy then looks "out the window" to the theatre audience and says: "There are . . . people at the end of Burrard, staring out at that ship . . . They look like the men in that line." The scene invites audience members to reflect on their own inaction with regard to instances of overt racism, and the stage direction directly implicates them in allowing such acts to continue. According to Reid Gilbert, Pollock exaggerates the violence and hatred in an effort to shock her audiences and force them to acknowledge their role in this historical (and arguably ongoing) act of racism.[12] In her Programme Note for the first production of *The Komagata Maru Incident*, Pollock supports this claim: "The attitudes expressed by the general populace of that time (1914), and paraphrased throughout the play, are still around today and, until we face this fact, we can never change it."[13] In doing so, Pollock triggers the audience's cultural memory and actively asks it to consider racism today.

By the end of the play, it becomes evident that Pollock's T.S. has manipulated and controlled every aspect of the play-within-a-play. After the government officials have forced the *Komagata Maru* out of the harbour, T.S. imaginatively leads the audience to the courtroom. During this final scene, T.S. steps into the action and plays the roles of judge, prosecuting attorney, and narrator—all positions of power. He describes how Inspector Hopkinson attempts to redeem his inner guilt but points out that it is too late: while he is approaching the courtroom, Hopkinson is gunned down by Mewa Singh, a Sikh nationalist. The audience realizes that Hopkinson has played the "middle man" in the negotiations, and that he has done what his superiors told him needed to be done. In the play-within-a-play, Hopkinson is manipulated like a puppet by the government officials (played by T.S.) and it becomes clear that T.S. is not only the master of ceremonies but also the puppet master controlling the entire play. This omniscient power has allowed T.S. to manipulate the dramatic characters and to focus the action in the direction he wishes. This is exemplified in Pollock's final stage directions: "*T.S. touches HOPKINSON with the cane. HOPKINSON's head falls forward . . . T.S. does a soft-shoe shuffle, stops, looks out, raises his arms, pauses, and makes a large but simple bow. Black.*"

12 Reid Gilbert, "Sharon Pollock," in *Profiles in Canadian Literature, Vol 6*, Jeffrey Heath, ed. (Toronto: Dundurn, 1986), 116.

13 Qtd. in Gilbert, 7–8.

The play-within-a-play in *The Komagata Maru Incident* reminds the audience how, to a certain extent, history is shaped by whoever is retelling it and that Pollock, via her dramatic characters, is interpreting the circumstances that led Hopkinson (and the Canadian government) to deny entry to the passengers on board the *Komagata Maru*. In their essay "Documenting Racism: Sharon Pollock's *The Komagata Maru Incident*," Sherrill Grace and Gabriele Helms note the difference between how the *Komagata Maru* incident is interpreted in Sarjeet Singh Jagpal's *Becoming Canadians: Pioneer Sikhs in Their Own Words* (1994) and in Robert Jarvis's *The "Komagata Maru" Incident: A Canadian Immigration Battle Revisited* (1992): "Jarvis sees William Hopkinson as 'a Canadian martyr and hero' (Jarvis 1) and Mewa Singh as 'the Sikh terrorist and murderer of William Hopkinson' (43), while for Jagpal and the Sikh community, Hopkinson is the 'corrupt immigration official' and Mewa Singh a Sikh martyr' (Jagpal 34)."[14] Jarvis and Jagpal presumably worked from the same available source material, yet their interpretations of these sources, and no doubt personal politics, steered their rewriting of history in particular directions.

Like Jarvis and Jagpal, Pollock's interpretation of historical "facts," as well as her politics, determines how she represents the events addressed in her play. By using T.S. as a master of ceremonies who presents and theatricalizes the events of 1914, the playwright provides her perspective on what transpired during the *Komagata Maru* incident. The metatheatrical atmosphere ensures that the play never presumes to replay the story as it "really" happened or to explain the reasons why this incident occurred. Pollock's Playwright's Note contains the following disclaimer, which allows her to stray from documented accounts of the incident: "*The Komagata Maru Incident* is a theatrical impression of an historical event seen through the optique of the stage and the mind of the playwright. It is not a documentary account, although much of it is documented. To encompass these facts, time and place are often compressed, and certain dramatic license is employed."[15] The word "optique" is fitting because it calls to mind the subjectivity involved when elements are viewed through a particular lens. Pollock's political intent in *The Komagata Maru Incident* is quite overt. For

14 Sherrill Grace and Gabrielle Helms, "Documenting Racism: Sharon Pollock's *The Komagata Maru Incident*," in *Painting the Maple: Essays on Race, Gender, and the Construction of Canada*, Veronica Strong-Boag, Sherrill Grace, Avigail Eisenberg, and Joan Anderson, eds. (Vancouver: UBC Press, 1998), 91. See also Sarjeet Singh Jagpal, *Becoming Canadians: Pioneer Sikhs in Their Own Words* (Vancouver: Harbour, 1994) and Robert Jarvis, *The "Komagata Maru" Incident: A Canadian Immigration Battle Revisited* (Toronto: Citizens for Foreign Aid Reform, 1992).

15 Pollock, *Komagata*, 1.

example, the audience, in listening to T.S., cannot ignore the bitter sarcasm in his voice. In one instance, the master of ceremonies describes the situation at hand this way: "A Japanese steamer chock-full of brown-skin Hindus headed for a predominantly pale Vancouver, and entry into whitish Canada. The *Komagata Maru* in blue Canadian waters!" One does not have to look very far, then, to see the perspective that steers the play.

Pollock acknowledges the impossibility of presenting an authentic truth and a definitive history. *The Komagata Maru Incident* highlights how history, in this case British Columbia's history, is recreated each time it is retold or restaged. The historiographic approach and use of metadramatic devices encourages audiences to rethink the events surrounding the *Komagata Maru* incident, seeing them as explicit acts of racism. The staging approach of setting the theatrical frame within a circus ring brings a historical past vividly into the present, provoking audience members to look at one another and consider how this 1914 "*incident*" might still resonate today.

The Komagata Maru Incident was first produced at the Vancouver Playhouse in January, 1976, with the following company:

T.S.: Allan Stratton
Hopkinson: Richard Fowler
Evy: Heather Brechin
Georg: Leroy Schulz
Sophie: Nicola Cavendish
Woman: Diana Belshaw

Directed by Larry Lillo
Designed by Jack Simon
Stage Managed by Paul Reynolds

The Komagata Maru Incident was subsequently produced by the Citadel Theatre, Edmonton, in January, 1977, with the following company:

T.S.: Ray Hunt
Hopkinson: Michael Ball
Evy: Peggy Mahon
Georg: Jean-Pierre Fournier
Sophie: Angela Gann
Woman: Patricia Lenyre

Directed by James DeFelice
Designed by David Lovett
Stage Managed by Marion Brant

CHARACTERS

T.S.: The Master of Ceremonies, who plays many roles
William Hopkinson: Department of Immigration Inspector
Evy: A prostitute involved with Hopkinson
Sophie: A prostitute involved with Georg
Georg: A German national
A Woman: A Sikh immigrant, British subject

SCENE

A brothel, Vancouver, 1914.

PRODUCTION NOTE

It is important that the scenes flow together without blackouts and without regard to time and setting. The brothel is the major playing area. Surrounding it is an arc or runway used by T.S. and Hopkinson for most of their scenes. Although T.S. cannot intrude upon the Woman's space, he is free to move anywhere else on the set to observe or speak. As the play progresses, T.S.'s scenes move from the arc into the brothel area.

The characters never leave the stage. When not involved in the action, they sit on benches placed on the extreme stage right and stage left ends of the arc. The Woman is on a level above and behind the area used by the other characters. An open, grill-like frame in front of her gives both the impression of a cage, and of the superstructure of a ship. T.S. observes the audience entering. The other characters are frozen on stage; the grill-like frame, with the Woman behind it, is concealed by a sheet. The child accompanying the Woman is not visible or present.

The houselights fade out and a faint light comes up on T.S. *who moves to a stool set in the centre of the arc. On this stool are his gloves, hat, and cane. He carefully puts on the gloves while surveying the audience.*

T.S.: Good . . . gooood.

He pauses for a moment.

Do you like the suit?

T.S. *puts on his top hat, gives it a tap with the cane, looks toward the lighting booth, and snaps his fingers. A spot comes up on him.*

Hurry! Hurry! Hurry! Right this way, ladies and gentlemen! First chance to view the *Komagata Maru*! At this very moment steaming toward picturesque Vancouver Harbour. Yes sireee! The *Komagata Maru*! A first-class—let the buyer beware—Japanese steamer, 329.2 feet in length, 2,926 gross tonnage! Captained by one Yomamoto, remember that name. And Japanese crew, carrying a cargo of coal! And 346 Sikhs, count 'em! Plus 30 East Indians, religious affiliation unknown! Add 'em all together and what do you get? That is correct, sir! Give the man a cigar! Three hundred and seventy-six is the answer! Three hundred and seventy-six Asians, to be precise, and all of them bound for Oh Canada, We stand on guard for thee!

T.S. *salutes, holds it for a moment, then lets it drop as he moves into the brothel area.*

This is Vancouver, ladies and gentlemen, the 21st day of May, nineteen hundred and fourteen . . . And may I direct your attention to my hat . . . I place the hat on the table . . . I pass my hands over the hat . . . and what do we have inside the hat?

A pair of gloves! I give you Inspector William Hopkinson, Head of Intelligence, Department of Immigration!

T.S. slaps the gloves into HOPKINSON's hand, looks at him for a second, then continues.

Ladies and gentlemen, the hand is truly faster than the eye . . . you see this box . . . and now you don't . . . and here it is again.

He passes it behind his back.

I open it, it's empty, I close the box.

He looks at EVY, then places it in her hands.

May I present *(stepping back)* Miss Evy: Entrepreneur!

T.S. bangs his cane, spot out. EVY and HOPKINSON are lit and animated.

EVY: What is it?

HOPKINSON: It's a present.

EVY: Don't tell me, silly.

HOPKINSON: You asked.

EVY: But I don't want you to tell me.

HOPKINSON removes his hand from her eyes.

Oh, Bill.

She opens the box which contains a brooch.

It's beautiful. Here, pin it on me.

HOPKINSON bends over her to do so. T.S. bangs his cane, they freeze, spot on T.S.

T.S.: Ladies and gentlemen! Your attention, please! Now the pocket's empty. Not so now.

He takes out a billfold and visa.

I have here one billfold and one German visa for one Georg Braun!

He throws it on the floor near GEORG.

And here! Behind an ear, a chocolate!

He places it in SOPHIE's hand.

Allow me to introduce, one Georg Braun and Sophie!

T.S. bangs his cane, spot out. SOPHIE goes to eat the chocolate, GEORG attempts to embrace her, and she pushes him off.

SOPHIE: Not so fast.

GEORG: Eh?

SOPHIE: No tickee, no washee.

GEORG: I . . . ?

SOPHIE: *(putting her hand out)* Mon-ey.

GEORG: Oh.

GEORG feels for his billfold, finding it on the floor as T.S. knocks.

SOPHIE: Somebody get the door!

Plucks the billfold from GEORG's hand.

Thank you.

GEORG amorously tries to embrace SOPHIE again as she counts the money.

T.S. knocks. SOPHIE pushes GEORG away.

Wait a minute! Are you deaf? There's someone at the door.

SOPHIE moves off stage right with the billfold. After a moment of indecision, his billfold gone, GEORG moves after her.

GEORG: Ah—Sophie?

A spot on T.S.

T.S.: *(laughing)* Ladies and gentlemen. Lest we forget. The *Komagata Maru*. A Japanese steamer chock-full of brown-skin Hindus headed for a predominantly pale Vancouver, and entry into whitish Canada. The *Komagata Maru* in blue Canadian waters!

T.S. pulls cover to reveal WOMAN who bends over child on deck. T.S. bows. Spot is out.

WOMAN: Go to sleep. Go to sleep. Shut your eyes, go to sleep.

It's very hot and WOMAN turns from the child, wipes her forehead, and looks out with a sigh, then turns back to the child.

Still not asleep?

HOPKINSON pins the brooch onto EVY's top.

HOPKINSON: There. Everything's forgotten. All right?

EVY: All right.

HOPKINSON: But you have to thank me for the brooch.

EVY: Thank you, Billy.

HOPKINSON: Don't tease. You know I don't like Billy.

EVY: Thank you, Bill.

HOPKINSON: That's better.

EVY: Now you sit down, and I'll get you a drink.

HOPKINSON checks his watch.

Oh—not the time again? You just got here.

HOPKINSON: Can't be helped. I'm sorry.

EVY: You always have to go.

HOPKINSON: Don't be mad. I won't be long, it's just an appointment.

EVY: Bill?

Still holding the billfold, SOPHIE crosses round to stage left with GEORG following.

SOPHIE: You may as well get used to it. That's what it's like around here. Half the time I'm running messages for him.

GEORG: For who?

SOPHIE: Mr. Hopkinson. Evy's friend with Immigration.

GEORG: Immigration?

SOPHIE: I'm sick of answering that damn door for him.

GEORG: Sophie, do you think—?

SOPHIE: *(at door stage left)* There's a man out back for Mr. Hopkinson!

HOPKINSON: *(from inside room)* Who is it?

SOPHIE: He says tell Mr. Hopkinson that Bella Singh is here.

EVY: Your rat again.

HOPKINSON: *(preparing to leave)* Don't call him that.

EVY: I don't like rats coming round.

HOPKINSON: Let's not start this again.

EVY: He's always coming round and when he does, off you go, poof!

HOPKINSON: It'll only take a minute.

EVY: My mother always said, don't snitch, and don't play with snitchers. Didn't your mother ever tell you that?

HOPKINSON: Evy, we've settled all this.

SOPHIE: Mr. Hopkinson! Did you hear me!

HOPKINSON: Now don't pout, you'll get wrinkles.

EVY: Oh, get out.

HOPKINSON: I'm going.

HOPKINSON goes to the door.

SOPHIE: Come on, Georg.

GEORG: Mr. Hopkinson?

HOPKINSON: Who's this, Sophie?

GEORG: Georg Braun, sir, if I could—

WOMAN: See the birds? Land must be near . . . Mountains, trees, then the island, through the pass. Your uncle will meet us . . . Look! Soon we will enter the harbour. See where your uncle lives? That is where we'll live.

GEORG: Thank you, sir.

SOPHIE: Georg!

GEORG goes to the bench. HOPKINSON turns back into the room.

HOPKINSON: Evy? That fellow with Sophie.

EVY: Georg Braun?

HOPKINSON: I've, ah, asked him in for a drink when I get back.

EVY: Oh?

HOPKINSON: I want to meet him.

EVY: You've already met him.

HOPKINSON: Talk to him, then.

EVY: I thought brown rats were your specialty.

HOPKINSON: Bella Singh's a loyal British subject.

EVY: Well, Georg Braun's no British subject! You're setting up no rats in my house!

HOPKINSON: I'll do just as I please in your house! It's me that keeps you open, and don't you forget it! A nod from me, and you'd be buried under warrants. Oh Evy, Evy, Evy . . . what's good for me is good for you, eh? . . . Eh, Evy? All I want to do is meet him, get to know him better . . .

EVY makes a murmur of protest.

I get ahead, Evy, do you know how I do that? I look ahead, I'm always thinking. Now, you read the papers, you stop and think . . . With Kaiser Wilhelm and all, something in here tells me a German can do me some good. Eh? Perhaps not today or tomorrow, maybe next year, who knows. Now you can understand that, can't you?

EVY: I just don't like—

SOPHIE: Bella Singh's at the end of the yard! He wants to see you!

HOPKINSON: The German's coming in for a drink, Evy.

HOPKINSON exits.

EVY: If—if you say so.

T.S.: Hopkinson!

HOPKINSON joins T.S. downstage right arc.

HOPKINSON: Yes, sir.

T.S.: The *Komagata Maru*'s in port with three hundred and seventy-six potential immigrants.

HOPKINSON: Yes, sir.

T.S.: So? What do you know about them?

HOPKINSON: I've spoken to my man, Bella Singh, sir. He tells me they're Sikhs from India, British subjects, and as such they do have right of entry to Canada, sir.

T.S.: The word is no entry.

HOPKINSON: I realize that, but we may have a problem.

T.S.: A what?

HOPKINSON: Many are veterans of the British Army, sir; they're sure to plead consideration for military service.

T.S.: You can put it this way—we don't mind them dying for us, we just don't want them living with us. *(laughing)* Get the point?

HOPKINSON: *(laughing)* Yes, sir . . . but if they should go to the courts—

T.S.: They won't go to the courts. He hasn't done his homework. Have you forgotten our two orders-in-council? If an immigrant wishes to enter the country through a western port, he must make a continuous voyage from his own country to here. Have they done so?

HOPKINSON: No, sir, they haven't.

T.S.: And that's no surprise. There's not a steamship line in existence with a direct India-to-China route and for our second ace-in-the-hole—a tax, two hundred dollars per head, to be paid before entry. Do they have it?

HOPKINSON: Bella Singh says they do not, however—

T.S.: Again, not surprising. In the land of his birth, the average Indian's wage is nine dollars per year. There—you see how we operate, Hopkinson? Never a mention of race, colour, or creed—and yet, we allow British subjects; we don't allow them to enter.

HOPKINSON: Thank you, sir. However, I must inform you that Hermann Singh says—

T.S.: Sh, sh.

HOPKINSON: *(lowering his voice)* Hermann Singh says that the local Sikhs have raised the money for the head tax.

T.S.: That's not so good.

HOPKINSON: It's possible that a launch—

T.S.: It is possible? Do you pay for information like that?

HOPKINSON: Bella Singh says a launch will deliver the head tax to those on the ship late tonight.

T.S.: The word is no entry, Hopkinson.

HOPKINSON: Yes, sir.

SOPHIE rushes into the room followed by GEORG.

SOPHIE: Listen everybody! Here it is! *(reading from paper)* "Immigration Officials Intercept Head Tax in Vancouver Harbour."

EVY enters stage right. WOMAN enters from arc.

WOMAN: Look! A launch is coming! Maybe it's your uncle.

SOPHIE: There's your name right there! Inspector William Hopkinson.

WOMAN: Be careful! You'll fall!

SOPHIE: Look, Georg! Look, Evy!

WOMAN: The Immigration boat is stopping the launch.

SOPHIE: There it is again, "Hopkinson declares—"

WOMAN: Shhhhhh. Don't be afraid.

SOPHIE: You read it, Evy, what's it say?

HOPKINSON: I can tell you what it means. British Columbia wants no Calcutta coolies. We've Chinamen and Japs running our shops, Greeks running our hotels, Jews running our second-hand stores, and we don't want Hindus running our mills.

EVY: For God's sake, Bill, have a drink.

T.S.: Have a drink.

HOPKINSON: *(offering bottle)* Georg?

GEORG: Please. The Sikhs on the ship would pay the head tax with the money from the launch, eh? And what is legal? Can you intercept it like that?

HOPKINSON: Well, we did. Another bottle, Evy. The Calcutta coolie, Georg, belongs in India.

GEORG: Do you know India, sir?

HOPKINSON: Do I know India? He wants to know if I know India, Evy.

EVY: Does he know India!

EVY gives him a bottle, sits at the table, and begins to play cards.

HOPKINSON: I know India, and I know its people. When I was a child, my father was stationed in the Punjab— He had only to shout "*Quai Hai*" to summon a slave—a servant—no, goddamn it, a slave, to summon a slave, to scrawl his initials on a chit, and there was a felt carpet from Kashmir, brass ornaments from Moradabad, silver for pocket money, cigars, a horse, a dog, anything he wanted. Show him your brooch, Evy. It belonged to my father. Wonderful craftsmen, the natives.

GEORG: It's lovely.

HOPKINSON: Did you know "loot" was an Indian word?

GEORG: Is it?

SOPHIE: *(examining brooch)* Really beautiful.

HOPKINSON: My father was a big man, blond curly hair, wonderful moustache he had, looked like a prince in his uniform. A prince—surrounded by little beige people. *(laughing)*

SOPHIE: What about your mother?

HOPKINSON: "*Quai Hai!*" That's all, and they'd scuttle like bugs.

SOPHIE: Did your mother like it there?

HOPKINSON: She never said. You've no idea, Georg, of the size, the immensity, and the millions. *(smiling)* When I was a boy I used to like to read at night, alone, in a room that had dimensions.

GEORG: Sophie tells me you yourself served in the Punjab.

HOPKINSON: Oh, yes. Lahore Police Force. Six years service.

GEORG: And how do you end up in Canada, sir?

HOPKINSON: Promotion was blocked in Lahore.

GEORG: That's hard to believe for a man like . . . yourself.

HOPKINSON: Quite simple, Georg. Cliques. And I learnt something from that. So. I answered an ad and here I am.

GEORG: Your life has been very exciting—

SOPHIE: Sophie can make your life exciting too, yes, she can. Let Sophie sit on Georg!

SOPHIE lifts her skirts and plunks herself on him. They both fall over on the floor as T.S. bangs his cane. They freeze.

T.S.: Ladies and gentlemen! The turbanned tide is flowing! May 23rd, 1914. The first wave of an Asian Invasion sits at anchor in Vancouver Harbour!

WOMAN: They won't let us land! I've told you. We've asked a judge to rule on the orders-in-council. Now go! . . . Our food and our water are rationed. How long must we wait?

T.S.: Today's lesson is taken from the Department of Immigration's handbook, Regulation 23, Paragraph 4. I am talking about Checks and Balances of Power. Now, I am the Department of Immigration, I have the power to hold proceedings, make decisions, give orders. I can detain and deport any person or potential immigrant on any grounds whatsoever, unless that person is a Canadian citizen. You are the courts. You have the power to review, reverse, and restrain, quash, and otherwise interfere with my power to hold, to make, and to give, to detain and deport. And you do. Fairly often. It's annoying. So what do I do? Quite simple. I pass Catch 22, Regulation 23, Paragraph 4, which states: "No judge and no court and no officer thereof shall have any jurisdiction to review, reverse, and restrain, quash or otherwise interfere with my holding and making and giving, detaining, deporting."

We are gathered here in the sight of God, and in the spirit of the British Empire to rule on the *Komagata Maru*'s contention that Catch 22, Regulation 23, Paragraph 4 is invalid. They maintain that the Department of Immigration has not the authority to deny immigrants access to the courts. If we give them access, then a judge or a court or an officer thereof could overthrow our orders-in-council of which we have two denying them entry—And that, my good friends, would open the floodgates!

T.S. bangs his cane. GEORG picks himself up in embarrassment, pushing SOPHIE aside.

GEORG: My . . . my feelings are this, sir. If you examine the world and its history, you will see that the laws of evolution that have shaped the energy, enterprise, and efficiency of the race northwards have left less richly endowed the peoples inhabiting the southern regions.

HOPKINSON: Go on.

GEORG: Yes. This . . . this process is no passing accident, but part of the cosmic order of things which we have no power to alter. The European races must administrate; all that's needed to assure their success is a clearly defined conception of moral necessity. Do you agree, sir?

HOPKINSON: Agreed. It's a pleasure to talk to you, Georg. I feel as if you're a friend, a good friend.

GEORG: I'm honoured.

HOPKINSON: I have very few friends. A man in my position, Head of Intelligence, has very few friends.

GEORG: Please consider me one of them.

HOPKINSON: I'm thought of most often as a dose of salts; not palatable, but essential for the health of the body. I accept this.

GEORG: You are—

HOPKINSON: But! If I may make a small observation? It's truly amazing the number of people who use laxatives regularly, and lie about it. Eh? *(laughing)* You follow me, eh?

HOPKINSON laughs and GEORG joins in.

Yes, I have my job, and I do it. And damn well, if I say so myself.

GEORG: You've a good network of men.

HOPKINSON: Uh uh, more than that. It's a sense of responsibility, that's what it is. I take the risks, and I find my reward in the fulfillment of my task. Now there's your difference between white and coloured—the Gift of Responsibility.

EVY looks up from her cards.

EVY: What's the difference?

HOPKINSON: You see that's why we're sitting in here, and the *Komagata Maru*'s out there scratching at the door.

EVY: Why?

HOPKINSON: For Christ's sake, Evy, if it weren't for the British, they couldn't construct a canoe, much less charter a steamer.

EVY: *(back to her cards)* You should know, I suppose. You lived with them.

HOPKINSON: I did not live with them!

EVY: Well, you were there, God knows I've heard it often enough. It's hard to keep straight where you were when, and with who.

HOPKINSON: I was brought up in India! I know them, if that's what you mean. Keep your mouth shut when we're talking!

He picks up the bottle and starts off.

Come on, Georg, I've a chess set, hand-carved from ivory.

He moves off, with GEORG *following.*

Marvellous chess player, my father.

WOMAN: I saw what you did! Do you think because I have no man you can steal food from my child? If you steal again, I will come when you sleep and I'll kill you!

T.S. is downstage right, in arc.

T.S.: Ah, Hopkinson.

HOPKINSON: I have observed suffering and deprivation on the *Komagata Maru.*

WOMAN: The child cries! He is thirsty!

T.S.: What else?

HOPKINSON: Our policy of disallowing the supplying of the ship is sound. It weakens their morale. It's only a matter of time till they question their leadership . . .

T.S.: Continue.

HOPKINSON: As . . . conditions deteriorate, we could, at some future date, offer supplies as an incentive to leave.

T.S.: Very good. Very good.

HOPKINSON: There is . . . a woman and child on the ship.

T.S.: Irrelevant.

WOMAN: It's hard to explain to a child . . . Your father was a soldier, he died fighting for the king, so we come to live with your uncle. But first—we must wait . . .

SOPHIE: My feet hurt.

EVY: Mmn?

SOPHIE: I don't know why. I'd have thought it'd be my back.

EVY looks at SOPHIE and laughs.

What? *(laughing)* Noo. Back trouble runs in the family.

EVY: Oh.

SOPHIE: In the women, that is. With the men it's always having to, you know, piss when they're older.

EVY laughs.

Yeah, I guess if I had my druthers, I'd rather have a bad back . . . In the night when the pot was full, Grampa would piss out the window . . . Unless the wind blew from the east. Then he pissed out the door.

EVY: Why?

SOPHIE: It blew back at the window. The window faced east.

EVY: Oh, Sophie.

They both laugh.

SOPHIE: It's true . . . I used to lie on my back in the field and Mama would scream "Sophie, Sophie!" and I'd lie there and think, "Sophie, get out of here, better yourself!" . . . And Mama would scream "Sophie! I know you're hidin'." . . . and I'd just lie there . . . Mama always said I was lazy. Maybe I am, but you don't see me emptying piss pots. I got out of there.

EVY: Don't stop here, Sophie.

SOPHIE: My back's not breaking from too many kids and carrying milk cans.

SOPHIE looks at her foot.

EVY: *(as she exits)* Find a nice man, and move on.

SOPHIE: Maybe I sprained it.

WOMAN bends over, retching, dry spasms. When she's finished she draws in several deep breaths. She attempts a smile for the child.

WOMAN: Don't worry . . . smile, it's only the water. Don't worry. You are a very brave boy. Your uncle will like you. Come, we'll sit on the side where there's shade.

T.S.: I don't understand.

HOPKINSON: I've promised them food and water.

T.S.: Really?

HOPKINSON: I've given my word.

T.S.: And what did you hope to gain from that?

HOPKINSON: Sir—

T.S.: Surely not plaudits from me.

HOPKINSON: Sir, when I boarded the ship for inspection, they seized me and were ready to take off in our launch and head for shore, patrol boats or not. They were desperate. They say they'd rather be shot than die of hunger and thirst. I felt it only—humanitarian to grant one week's provision.

T.S.: You've enabled them to hang on. That's what you've done!

HOPKINSON: I saw the mother and child—

T.S.: Now where's that incentive to leave?

HOPKINSON: Their case is still pending.

T.S.: Never initiate action when you haven't the guts to carry it through. It's a sign of weakness, Hopkinson.

HOPKINSON: Yes, sir.

T.S.: You disappoint us.

HOPKINSON: Yes, sir.

T.S.: We brought you up. We can put you down.

HOPKINSON: Yes, sir.

T.S.: We trust that our meaning's sufficiently clear?

HOPKINSON: Yes, sir.

EVY enters the room stage left.

EVY: Bill!

SOPHIE: Evy!

EVY: Bill!

SOPHIE: Mr. Hopkinson!

HOPKINSON enters stage right.

HOPKINSON: What's the matter?

EVY: Oh, Bill.

SOPHIE: I thought you went shopping.

EVY: I just—sat on the tram. A round trip. I never got off it.

HOPKINSON: Come on, Evy.

SOPHIE: Are you sick?

EVY: I . . . was on the tram. I had a seat by the window. When we . . .

HOPKINSON: Come on now.

EVY: When we came round by the creek there was a queue for employment, a long line of men looking for work. They were standing in line, we'd stopped for a fare, and then . . . the line . . . all of a sudden it . . . there was a man in a turban at the end of the line, his eye had caught my eye as I looked out the window—he looked so—solid—and I smiled . . . and he smiled . . . and as he smiled a man stepped in front of him, and he was back at the end . . . Then, I don't know, it happened so quickly, he touched the man on the shoulder, the man turned . . . and the long line of men, it seemed to turn. The man in the turban started to speak, he got out a few words, I didn't sense anger—and then it exploded. They knocked him down, the man in the turban they were kicking, and then pushing and shoving to get in a blow—and the tram pulled away . . . it was gone. As if I'd imagined it. It had never been.

HOPKINSON: You were frightened, that's all.

EVY: I should have done something.

HOPKINSON: You should have come home and you did. Come on now, you saw a fight. You've seen fights before.

EVY: No, it wasn't a fight! And I just sat on the goddamn tram and came home.

HOPKINSON: *(to SOPHIE)* Get her a drink.

EVY goes to look out the window, at the audience, where the Komagata Maru *sits.*

EVY: There are . . . people at the end of Burrard, staring out at that ship . . . They look like the men in that line.

HOPKINSON: That's why we're sending the *Komagata Maru* back, so things like your fight won't happen. We don't want them here.

SOPHIE exits after giving him the drink.

EVY: But why does it happen?

HOPKINSON: All I know, Evy, is my father didn't die in the service for the world to be overrun by a second-rate people.

EVY: You don't make sense. Who's second-rate when you run out of brown people?

HOPKINSON: Drink your drink.

EVY: I don't want a drink! *(exiting stage right)* You belong on Burrard.

HOPKINSON follows her.

HOPKINSON: Evy!

T.S.: Mr. Speaker; Prime Minister; Honourable Members. Today I am opening my heart to you. I am telling you my fears—fears that affect each and every Canadian today . . . I fear for my country, and I fear for my people . . . I am not ashamed, nor should you be, to state that this is white man's country! And I can tell you that our British legacy, our traditions, those things that we hold dear, that we have fought and died for, is placed in jeopardy today by a massive influx of coloured foreigners! The class of East Indian that has invaded British Columbia is commonly known as Sikh—having been accustomed to the conditions of a tropical clime, he is totally unsuited to this country. He is criminally inclined, unsanitary by habit, and roguish by instinct. The less we speak of his religion, the better. Suffice it to say that unless his ridiculous forms of worship are relinquished, he is an affront to a Christian community. His intelligence is roughly that of our Aborigines. He indeed belongs to a heathen and debased class. Honourable Members, stand up and be counted! Admit the honest fears of your constituents! Will the Sikh work for cheaper wages, and thus take away their jobs? Will he bring out his women, children, relatives, and friends. Will Canadians step on a tram next week to ride from home to work and never hear a word of English spoken? And once at work, if they still have a job, who will they eat their lunch with? Men, honest and true like ourselves, whose fathers made this country what it is today—or will they be surrounded by coloured men with foreign food? Canadians have rights! Our fathers died for them! Let any man who is not willing to do the same step down! I've told you here today what's in my heart. For God's sake, show me what's in yours!

HOPKINSON enters stage left.

HOPKINSON: Evy!

EVY enters stage right.

EVY: I'm here.

HOPKINSON: Was Bella Singh around?

EVY: Don't ask me.

HOPKINSON: Where's Sophie? Sophie!

SOPHIE enters stage right.

SOPHIE: What?

HOPKINSON: Was Bella Singh around?

SOPHIE: When?

HOPKINSON: Day before yesterday, goddamn it, was he here?

SOPHIE: Maybe. I don't remember.

HOPKINSON: What the hell do you mean, you don't remember?

EVY: Look, Bill, my girls don't keep track of your rats.

HOPKINSON: If they don't, they better start. Customs picked up three men at the border today. Sikhs smuggling guns for the *Komagata Maru*. And my head's on the block! That's the kind of information I'm paid to deliver! And I knew nothing. Do you hear that? Sweet bugger all! Was Bella Singh around or not?

EVY: You can leave now, Sophie.

HOPKINSON: She'll leave when I tell her. Did you forget a message, Sophie?

EVY: You run your business, I'll run mine; Sophie, get out!

HOPKINSON: *(grabbing SOPHIE)* By Jesus, I want an answer!

EVY: Me! It was me! Bella Singh came round, he left a note, I threw it out!

HOPKINSON releases SOPHIE. She leaves.

HOPKINSON: Why did you do that?

EVY: I don't pass notes.

HOPKINSON: It's me they come down on. Don't you realize that? If I don't deliver, I'm the one that pays—not Bella Singh. Why did you do it?

EVY: I'm sorry.

HOPKINSON: No you're not.

EVY: No, I'm not.

HOPKINSON: You wanted to make me look bad, is that it?

EVY: No.

HOPKINSON: I look bad enough then they'll dump me. Is that what you want?

EVY: No.

HOPKINSON: And off we go! Something else, somewhere else, eh?

EVY: What's wrong with that? People do it!

HOPKINSON: Not me.

EVY: Don't you like honest work?

HOPKINSON: That's a funny remark from a whore!

EVY: You want to know why I threw out your note? I'll tell you why! I'm a whore and what you do is offensive to me! What you do would gag me! I'm a whore and when I look at your job, I could vomit!

HOPKINSON slaps her.

WOMAN: Don't look at the crowd on the shore! . . . don't listen, pretend they aren't there . . . the sky is a blue, a beautiful blue . . . look at it! Don't look at them on the shore, they are ugly!

WOMAN turns her back and begins to sing to the child.

HOPKINSON: I never think of the woman and child they never enter my mind . . . Mewa Singh is a mill worker and priest caught crossing the border with guns. Mewa Singh is a trusted man in the Sikh community. Mewa Singh is a man I could use . . . I speak to him in his jail cell. I begin with loyalty, move on to money, end up with threats. Mewa Singh says nothing. He looks me straight in the eye. I don't always like that, with some it's an act of defiance . . . In Mewa Singh's eyes there is an infinite sadness, and surrounding him is a pool of silence, and as I speak and the words fall on my ears as if from a distance . . . I think of an incident when I was a child . . . there was trouble at the bazaar . . . the soldiers had to come in on their horses . . . and the next day I walked through . . . I saw blood, like clots of dark jelly still on the streets . . . but no people . . . an empty bazaar. Do you have any conception of how strange that is? I remember standing very still, scrawny and pasty, very still, afraid to move . . . in the middle of silence, listening, like a mouse on a pan, listening, for the beat of the wings of the owl . . . very still . . . And then as I stood there, I saw a figure approaching from one of the streets. Some native person. He stopped in the shadow of the huts . . . he extended his arms toward me . . . and I . . . turned around . . . and ran home. I was frightened . . . Mewa Singh . . . when I finish my mixed bag of offers Mewa Singh turns his head toward the window. It's narrow and barred. He has dismissed me. His answer is no. Goddamn it! I need a man who they trust! I'm the one who has something to lose!

T.S.: Relax! Don't worry! Congratulations are in order . . . The courts have come through! Catch 22, Regulation 23, Paragraph 4 still stands!

Carnival music, the air of a party. SOPHIE, GEORG, *and* EVY *join* HOPKINSON *on stage.*

Hurry! Hurry! Hurry! Final Immigration ruling on the *Komagata Maru*! Right this way, folks! Right this way! July 16th, 1914! Last and final chance to view the *Komagata Maru*! Anchored in picturesque Vancouver Harbour these last six weeks and two days! Yes sireeee! A decision is made! Of three hundred and seventy-six Asians, twenty individuals have proven to Immigration Officials the legality of their Canadian domicile; ninety suffering from disease are ordered deported and the rest can just shove off! The Immigration Department reigns supreme! To hell with the judges, the courts, and the officers thereof! Last chance to view! The *Komagata Maru*! Take it away, Bill!

Everyone's been drinking and it shows.

HOPKINSON: Fare thee well, *Komagata Maru*! Have a pleasant journey!

GEORG: Fare thee well!

HOPKINSON: Bon voyage! You had your day in court—

SOPHIE: Goodbye you Hindus!

HOPKINSON: Now you and yours can eat crow from here to Calcutta! Crow with seagull, crow with seaweed, or crow with seawater!

SOPHIE: *(laughing)* Crow!

HOPKINSON: Fare thee well! Fare thee well!

They're all roaring with laughter, except EVY.

Fare thee well *Komagata Maru*!

EVY: Is it moving yet?

HOPKINSON: Not yet, but any minute.

SOPHIE: That's funny.

HOPKINSON: Have a drink, Evy.

SOPHIE: That's very funny. Why would they want to eat crow with seawater?

GEORG: Who knows what Hindus eat?

GEORG and SOPHIE are laughing still.

SOPHIE: Still, crow and seawater? It would make you sick. It would make me sick.

GEORG: You aren't a Hindu.

SOPHIE: It'd make anybody sick!

GEORG: Silly, silly, Sophie.

HOPKINSON: See, Evy? It's all over.

SOPHIE: You wouldn't eat that unless you had nothing else to eat, that's for sure.

GEORG: Silly, silly.

SOPHIE: Hey, crow and seawater sounds awful too.

HOPKINSON: Forget it, Sophie.

SOPHIE: Eh?

HOPKINSON: It's just an expression.

SOPHIE: So what's it mean?

HOPKINSON: Come on, Evy.

SOPHIE: *(louder)* Eh?

HOPKINSON: To submit humbly!

EVY: Surely that rings a bell, I mean, it does for me.

SOPHIE: What?

HOPKINSON: Don't be like that. Say you're sorry. I'm sorry.

SOPHIE: Come on, Georg.

GEORG embraces SOPHIE.

Where's the music—you gotta have music for a party!

HOPKINSON: Sophie's right.

GEORG: What we'll have is a polka!

GEORG and SOPHIE wind up the gramophone.

HOPKINSON: It's a party! Come on, Evy, let's dance.

SOPHIE: I love to polka! It's hard on the feet, but I love it!

They dance to the music.

T.S.: Hopkinson!

HOPKINSON stops dancing.

There's someone at the end of the yard. Bella Singh's at the end of the yard!

HOPKINSON exits. EVY follows him for a step or two, then stops. SOPHIE and GEORG dance, carry the bottle, and laugh.

WOMAN: We hear them rejoice on the shore . . . They say we are beasts; physical death is no evil for us, it may be a blessing, else why pestilence and famine? They say we are the enemies of Christ, the Prince of Peace; they will hate us with a perfect hatred; they will blast us with grape shot and rockets; they will beat us as small as dust before the wind!

The music stops. SOPHIE and GEORG collapse.

They say our appeal to the courts is dismissed. They say tonight the *Komagata Maru* will sail for India.

T.S.: *(winking)* Guess again!

HOPKINSON: The bastards!

WOMAN: On the ship a meeting is held. I vote in the place of my son who is five. It is right that we're here!

HOPKINSON: *(gazing out at the ship)* Sit tight in the harbour, will they?

EVY: Drink up, everyone.

HOPKINSON: The foolish bastards. They must think it's a cricket game with the officers. Fair play. Your wicket. Pass the crumpets.

GEORG: So what can they do?

HOPKINSON: Bugger all. A move can't be made nor a word whispered, on the street, in the temple, on the waterfront, without my knowing it.

EVY: He has his men! His men produce! Eh, Bill?

HOPKINSON: If they don't, they'll find themselves in steerage on the next ship out!

EVY: *(drunkenly)* You know something?

HOPKINSON: I'll seal the *Komagata Maru* off tighter than paint on a wall.

EVY: You sound worried.

HOPKINSON: I'll see it wrapped round with rot and rust and manned by skeletons before one bastard disembarks!

EVY: Come on, everyone! It's a party!

HOPKINSON: That's right! Glasses up, glasses up! Here's to the *Komagata Maru*—stuck in picturesque Vancouver Harbour! It gives me great pleasure to extend to you the hospitality of the Canadian people! Enjoy your anchorage! Sip our rain and eat our air! And when you've had your fill—India lies westward!

T.S.: Ladies and gentlemen! It walks! It talks! It reproduces! It provides cheap labour for your factories, and a market for your goods! All this, plus a handy scapegoat! Who's responsible for unemployment? The coloured immigrant! Who brings about a drop in take-home pay? The coloured immigrant! Who is it creates slum housing, racial tension, high interest rates, and violence in our streets? The coloured immigrant! Can we afford to be without it? I say "No!" It makes good sense to keep a few around—when the dogs begin to bay, throw them a coloured immigrant! It may sound simple, but it works. Remember though—the operative word's "a few"— For reference, see the Red, the White, the Blue, and the Green Paper on Immigration, whatever year you fancy!

EVY: *(still drinking)* This place is a pigsty.

SOPHIE: That's old news, Evy.

EVY: This place is a pigsty.

SOPHIE: At least it's a profitable pigsty—isn't it?

EVY: Money isn't everything.

EVY laughs as no one else reacts.

. . . eh?

SOPHIE: Don't be silly.

EVY: Did you know that if a pig falls in a trough, the other pigs would eat him. *(playing cards)* Gobble, gobble, gobble . . . I think pigs are all right . . . I've known some not bad pigs . . . it's the goddamn pigsties that turn them nasty . . .

GEORG sits reading a German paper.

GEORG: I would not want to be Kaiser Wilhelm today . . .

EVY: Why? Isn't he feeling well.

EVY laughs as no one else reacts.

Oh, well . . . that's too bad . . . maybe tomorrow? . . .

SOPHIE: It's so hot. At home you always get a breeze off the water.

EVY: In Manitoba you don't.

GEORG: *(turning page)* If war should break out . . . well . . .

EVY: *(brightly)* People will die, eh?

EVY looks at HOPKINSON who stands staring out at the ship.

Bill? . . . Bill, a watched pot never boils.

T.S.: *(speaking very quietly, his stance mirroring HOPKINSON's)* What we need is a reason to board her. To mount a police action, preliminary, whatever. To arrest those aboard.

EVY: Leave the window alone, Bill.

T.S.: We could board them, arrest them, escort them to the open sea, and once there, release them, pointed toward India.

EVY: Come talk to me.

T.S.: Now if the captain and crew charged the Sikhs with mutiny, we'd be away, eh?

EVY: Bill?

T.S.: The captain refuses to press charges? Really? You know, I can't help but feel you don't give full vent to your powers of persuasion. One begins to wonder whose side you're on, someone should check out your file. A good man would find a reason to board her.

HOPKINSON: Yes.

SOPHIE: It's the heat. It's so hot.

SOPHIE gets up and exits.

HOPKINSON: It's July . . . It's supposed to be hot . . .

T.S. howls in a boy scout position, on his haunches, two fingers of each hand at his temples.

T.S.: Akela says "Be Prepared." *(howling)* Akela says "Do your Duty for God and the King, and Obey the Law of the Pack."

T.S. continues howling, then stops abruptly and rises.

Akela says I have three merit badges for the boy who comes up with a first-rate reason to board the *Komagata Maru*!

EVY: What're you writing?

HOPKINSON: Nothing.

EVY: Are you writing in German, what is it?

HOPKINSON: It's nothing . . . now . . . clear off, I'm busy.

EVY wanders off stage left.

WOMAN: This is not where we live . . . we shall not see your uncle . . . but we can't cross an ocean without water or food . . . You must not be afraid, for hundreds of years the Khyber Pass has run with our blood, we're not afraid to spill more of it here! Do you hear me ashore! We have suffered, but we have endured! We are tempered like steel! We are ready!

HOPKINSON: Georg?

GEORG: *(from behind paper)* Mnn?

HOPKINSON: I was wondering.

GEORG: Yes?

HOPKINSON: I have a small problem . . . perhaps you could advise me . . .

GEORG: Certainly. What is your problem?

HOPKINSON: It's the *Komagata Maru.*

GEORG: *(laughing)* You call this a small problem?

HOPKINSON: *(doesn't like the laugh)* Compared to, say, Kaiser Wilhelm, of course. Compared to that of an enemy alien in this country if war should break out, yes, I think a small problem, don't you?

GEORG gets the point.

T.S.: It's not what you call subtle, but it works.

HOPKINSON: I wish to make the *Komagata Maru* an offer—to give them supplies, to make some vague promise of promises, to recompense them for their cargo of coal, to entice them to sail. I wish the whole transaction kept quiet.

GEORG: And what is your problem?

HOPKINSON: If my offer got out, it might look like some kind of acknowledgement of their rights, and in this affair, they have none.

GEORG goes to speak.

As for Bella Singh and the rest, well, to be blunt, I don't trust them—trustworthy as they are, have been in the past, will be in the future, I do not totally trust them in this endeavour. A very slight qualm of mistrust.

GEORG: I see.

HOPKINSON: What do you advise, my good friend, Georg?

EVY enters unobserved. She's come in for a bottle but stops to listen.

GEORG: You're looking for someone to carry your offer out to the ship?

HOPKINSON: That's correct.

He draws out an envelope.

This particular offer—a man I can trust—a man for whom I possibly could do a small favour sometime in the future in return for this favour . . .

GEORG: And with some small financial reward, I suppose?

HOPKINSON: Correct. I will provide a boat, and one of our patrols will study the night sky as you slip through the—oh—excuse the use of the pronoun.

GEORG: Quite all right. Quite—all right—in fact, is there any reason why I myself, Georg, cannot act on your behalf in this matter?

HOPKINSON: Ah.

GEORG: Shall we drink to it?

GEORG moves to do so.

HOPKINSON: First the details—

They catch sight of EVY.

EVY: Hello.

GEORG: Hello, Evy.

HOPKINSON lowers his voice slightly as EVY hovers in background.

HOPKINSON: First the details, then the drink— Note, the envelope is sealed, and must remain so.

As he passes the envelope to GEORG, EVY takes it.

EVY: What's this?

GEORG: *(looking to HOPKINSON)* Ah?

EVY: A letter home?

GEORG: Yes. May I have it?

EVY: A letter to Germany—but it has no address.

HOPKINSON: Give him his letter.

EVY: A letter to Germany—what if—someone should open it. What's in it?

HOPKINSON: Evy—

EVY: Georg, where's your head? We're practically at war. The only thing worse than a letter to Germany is a letter from Germany. Governments are paranoid. Ask Bill.

GEORG: Eh?

HOPKINSON: She drinks too much.

EVY: I just had an idea! What if—

HOPKINSON makes a grab for her arm and misses.

HOPKINSON: Give it to me!

EVY: I'm not finished! What if a letter containing—who knows what—was carried by a German national out to the *Komagata Maru*—

HOPKINSON: Shut your mouth.

EVY: —and intercepted by the Department of Immigration—what if, eh?

GEORG: *(shrugging)* What if?

EVY: A plot between the Germans and the Sikhs!

GEORG: A plot between . . . ?

GEORG laughs with a tinge of nervousness and a look to HOPKINSON.

Give me the letter.

EVY: He wants a good solid reason to board the *Komagata Maru* and by Jesus I'm looking at it!

HOPKINSON: You're going to end up in a sailor's bar, Evy.

EVY: I won't let you do this!

HOPKINSON: Two-bits-a-crack in a dark alley.

EVY: Georg—

EVY gives him the envelope.

Open it.

GEORG: This is an offer to—

HOPKINSON: That's enough.

EVY: It's a trick. Open it!

HOPKINSON: Return it, or deliver it sealed.

GEORG: You don't understand—

HOPKINSON: No trust, no deal.

EVY: Don't you know who he works for?

GEORG: Evy, he works for the government.

EVY: Oh, yes! . . . Oh, yes . . . and I can tell you a story about governments . . . a bedtime story—

T.S. & EVY: Once upon a time—

The characters freeze as T.S. moves among them. T.S. continues the story.

T.S.: There was a little boy who came to Manitoba with his mummy and daddy and sisters and brothers and many others very much like him. Their skin was a pale ivory, their eyes a light blue, and their hair dark—without being too dark—and curly—but not too curly! They were running from persecution and injustice . . . and Canada said: "You wish to own farmland communally? No bother at all! You will not swear allegiance to the Crown and the flag? Weeeelllll, what is it, after all, but headgear and a piece of cloth? You do not wish to fight wars? That too can be arranged; exceptions can be made." The daddies worked to earn money for seed and supplies, and the mommies harnessed themselves to the plough and pulled it, breaking the hard brown earth of Manitoba and the soft white flesh of their backs till the red blood ran down, and the little boy walked beside the plough picking bouquets of tiny blue flowers. By and by, the mommies and daddies had homes and barns and food for the winter and seed for the spring and horses for the plough. Then others came and saw what they had. And Canada said—"Now about this allegiance! And which of you owns this particular piece of land? Be precise and sign here! And my goodness, friends, isn't all this worth killing and maiming for? What kind of people are you?" The mommies and daddies and sisters and brothers set out on a pilgrimage. They walked to Yorktown and along the tracks toward Winnipeg.

T.S. bangs his cane. The others unfreeze, and GEORG turns to HOPKINSON.

GEORG: About this letter!

GEORG extends the letter.

EVY: Listen to me! I watched them walk past—

T.S. bangs his cane. They freeze.

T.S.: It was snowing. They had little to eat, and then nothing to eat, for the Mounties cut off their supplies—and it snowed. People dropped by the tracks and a special train came along and returned everyone to Northern Manitoba.

And those who would not sign and swear allegiance were driven from their land with only what they could carry!

T.S. bangs his cane.

HOPKINSON: *(snatching letter)* I'll make other arrangements!

T.S. bangs the cane. They freeze.

T.S.: Then people whose skins were so fair as to be opalescent, whose eyes were so light they shone in the dark, whose hair sparkled like dust motes in the sun, with each strand hanging in a manner that can only be described as poker straight—these people stormed the land office for homesteads and barns and harvests still in the fields.

EVY: My brother stood in line for three days, he got a section—next to my father's.

T.S.: And they all lived happily ever after! . . . There now. Goodnight, sleep tight, don't let the bedbugs bite . . . Shhhhhhhhhh!

T.S. tiptoes away.

EVY: It can happen to any of us.

HOPKINSON: Go to bed.

EVY: Look at him. He'd cut off his hand before he'd make the *Komagata Maru* an offer. *(laughing)* He's got a thing about race, about colour, haven't you noticed?

HOPKINSON: You're boring and stupid, Evy.

EVY: Why do you suppose that is?

GEORG: I—

EVY: He goes to the temple.

GEORG: Eh?

EVY: Gets himself all dolled up, goes to the temple in disguise—he thinks he looks like a Sikh. I bet the Sikhs think he looks like an ass.

HOPKINSON: Goodnight, Georg.

GEORG: About—

HOPKINSON: Goodnight.

GEORG gives a little bow and leaves.

EVY: I've been thinking. Funny thing, your background—

HOPKINSON: That's enough.

EVY: Birthplace, things like that, where were you born, Bill?

HOPKINSON: Get the hell upstairs.

EVY: Where?

HOPKINSON: England.

EVY: Where in England, be specific.

HOPKINSON: Yorkshire!

EVY: Yorkshire? Yorkshire! Now that's a new one, Yorkshire, eh? . . . That's not what I think.

HOPKINSON: Evy!

EVY: Quick, Georg *(pretending GEORG is still there)* without looking, what colour's his eyes, wanna bet? I'd say brown.

Sometime during this scene, HOPKINSON begins to subtly stalk her. She, as subtly, avoids him.

HOPKINSON: You filthy bitch!

EVY: Blue, did you say? Well then I bet his mother's eyes were brown.

HOPKINSON: My mother's dead.

EVY: Born in Punjab, served by Yorkshire.

HOPKINSON: Born in Yorkshire!

EVY: So are they blue or brown?

HOPKINSON: Blue!

EVY: Your mother's eyes, now what were they?

HOPKINSON: My mother's eyes were blue, you bitch! I'll kill you.

EVY: First you'll have to catch me.

HOPKINSON chases her; she avoids him.

You're stupid, Bill, you're stupid . . . it's not me that's stupid, it's you. Stupid, stupid, Bill! They all use you, Bill, yes, they do . . . You think that you use Georg, you think that you use Bella Singh, you think that you use me, but you're the one that's being used . . . they're using you and Billy Boy's too dumb to know and stupid dumbo Billy will keep on being used cause Billy Dumbo's stupid! Stupid dumbo Billy's stupid dumbo Billy.

HOPKINSON catches EVY; she speaks softly.

And Billy's mother's brown.

HOPKINSON slaps EVY; she speaks louder.

And Billy's mother's brown!

HOPKINSON slaps EVY; she speaks louder.

And Billy's mother's brown.

HOPKINSON throws EVY down, kneels, and shakes her.

HOPKINSON: Don't say that. Don't say that! I'll kill you if you say that to me!

He's slowing down his attack on her.

Evy, don't say that. Please don't say that . . .

He stops.

I . . . I love you, Evy, don't say that to me . . .

EVY reaches out and draws his head to her.

EVY: Oh . . . oh . . . poor, poor, Billy.

T.S.: Hopkinson!

HOPKINSON moves very slowly and speaks without expression. It's an effort for him to get up.

What're you waiting for . . . Where's your report?

HOPKINSON: Sir.

T.S.: You've come up with what?

HOPKINSON: Sir.

T.S.: A reason to board her, remember?

HOPKINSON: Sir.

T.S.: Kindly observe. *(clearing his throat)* Captain Yomamoto! Captain Yomamoto! Is there a Captain Yomamoto in the house? Ah, my dear Captain, there you are. If you wouldn't mind taking a seat.

T.S. indicates a chair for the captain, who is exceedingly short.

How many times have we had this conversation? How many times must we have this conversation? Yes, yes, I know what you said before: "strictly speaking" your passengers have not mutinied, hence you are reluctant to lay a charge . . . Truly a commendable stance—however. Let us forget "strictly speaking" for a moment. How about trying "laxly speaking," "loosely speaking," "informally speaking"—could you find it in your heart to lay a charge "loosely speaking" against the passengers of the *Komagata Maru*? . . . Nothing has changed, huh? . . . Not so quick, Captain, one more minute please . . . While casually flipping through my classified copy of condensed Canadian law "What to Do in a Pinch" I found the most interesting—oh, I'm sure you'd be interested—you see it says right here, as I interpret this small item here . . . Yes, right here in very small print— You can't see it? But my dear Captain, I assure you I can. It states: If given formal notice to sail, then sail you must, *tout de suite*—it's a bilingual law—or be subject to a fine of $500.00. That's per person aboard. "With-the-Power-Vested-in-Me-by-His-Majesty's-Government-I-Hereby-Give-You-Formal-Notice-to-Sail!" Now, let me see, 500 times 356, that's put down the zero, carry the three—what was that you just said? You wish to press charges? Mutiny, sedition, treason, and—blackmail? Be serious, my dear fellow, the first is sufficient . . .

Mutiny!
M–that's militia for instilling fear,
U–Union Jack which God knows we hold dear,
T–for a tugboat, one you can't sink,
I–for informant, a nice word for fink,
N–for our navy of fine volunteers,
Y–for Yomamoto, who finally signed

Here!
Hopkinson! Here are your papers.
Now, my good man, do your duty.

GEORG helps HOPKINSON on with his jacket.

GEORG: I'm sorry about the letter. I pay no attention to her. She's a stupid woman.

HOPKINSON: Yomamoto has signed, pressed charges of mutiny. The militia is lining the dock, they are armed, they wait in reserve . . . We will engage the *Komagata Maru* at sea!

GEORG: In the harbour, you mean.

HOPKINSON: In the harbour. *(addressing a crowd)* We will mount an attack from the *Sea Lion*, the largest ocean-going tug in the port! Police Chief MacLennan shall lead 120 policemen and 40 special Immigration Officers—

GEORG: May I volunteer my services, sir?

HOPKINSON: In a paramilitary attack on the ship.

GEORG: Will I come under fire, sir?

HOPKINSON: On board the *Komagata Maru* are veteran soldiers.

GEORG: Are they armed?

HOPKINSON: Reliable sources inform me that weapons abound on the ship. They have made clubs from floating driftwood, possibly spears from bamboo poles.

T.S.: He's forgotten the cargo of coal.

HOPKINSON: Force will be met with force. Rifles will be issued before we embark . . .

T.S.: *(prompting)* I expect every . . .

HOPKINSON: I expect every man to do his duty. No doubt we will meet with stubborn opposition, but remember, we are a formidable force!

T.S.: In an orderly manner.

WOMAN: They are coming.

T.S.: Board the *Sea Lion.*

WOMAN: *(softly) Jai Khalsa . . .*

GEORG: It was fair-sized for a tug, but not large enough for a company of men such as we were.

WOMAN: Stand back from the rail.

GEORG: Four reporters came along for the ride. "Hoppy," they cried, "How about a smile for the press!" Mr. Hopkinson smiled.

WOMAN: Get below.

GEORG: It looked like a very big ship and the closer we got—

WOMAN: They have guns.

GEORG: The more quiet we were . . . silence . . . The *Sea Lion* rode low in the water . . . as we looked up we saw them . . . lining the rails were great turbanned figures . . . We stared up at them . . . they stared down at us . . . then . . .

T.S.: *(low)* Throw out the grappling hooks.

WOMAN: *(screaming) Jai Khalsa*!!

GEORG: All hell broke loose!

WOMAN: *Jai Khalsa*!

GEORG: From three hundred odd throats came a yell!

WOMAN: *Jai Khalsa*!

GEORG: Followed by bricks from the boiler settings, scrap iron, and coal!

WOMAN: Hide!

GEORG: Mostly coal!

WOMAN: Hide below!

GEORG: Coal rains around us!

WOMAN: *Jai Khalsa*!

GEORG: Hopkinson's hit again and again!

WOMAN: *Jai Khalsa*!

GEORG: They can see the gold braid on his hat!

HOPKINSON: I look for the woman and child.

GEORG: Get down! For God's sake get down!

WOMAN: *Jai Khalsa*!

HOPKINSON: I stand as straight as I can.

GEORG: Take off your hat and get down!

GEORG raises his gun to fire.

HOPKINSON: There's no order to fire! Don't fire!

WOMAN throws the missile of coal which knocks HOPKINSON down.

WOMAN: *Jai Khalsa*!

A pause with HOPKINSON lying on the floor. EVY enters slowly with SOPHIE. They help HOPKINSON to the sofa and press a cloth to his head.

GEORG: It was a total and humiliating defeat. What else can you expect? It was ridiculous. We go out with rifles and then never use them. The whole thing was poorly conceived. However, compared to the execution of the scheme, the conception was an act of genius!

SOPHIE: What do you mean?

GEORG: It was a stupid thing to do.

EVY: Hold the cloth to your head, Bill. It's cold. It'll help.

HOPKINSON: I'm all right. I just want something to wash with.

SOPHIE: *(laughing)* I don't wonder. He looks like a chimney sweep, doesn't he, Georg?

GEORG: There you sit, a servant in His Majesty's government, battered and bruised by a bunch of Hindus.

HOPKINSON: Get me some water!

SOPHIE: If you yell you can get it yourself.

GEORG: Tell me the point of carrying rifles if nobody uses them? . . . And there he stood with his hat. The smart thing to do was remove it. No, there he stood. Every time he was hit, they all cheered. The air rang with cheers!

SOPHIE: I just thought of something . . . *(laughing)* Mr. Hopkinson, I guess it was you that ate crow, eh?

SOPHIE nudges GEORG, who chuckles after a slight effort to restrain himself.

It was him that ate crow!

HOPKINSON: Get out! Get out and leave me alone!

SOPHIE and GEORG move to exit stage left.

SOPHIE: It was him that ate crow.

They're still chuckling.

GEORG: Sophie.

They exit. WOMAN is at a meeting on the ship.

WOMAN: We have gained nothing but time! We've driven them off for only a while, what now we must press for is food! I say it is better we starve on their doorstep than out on the sea!

HOPKINSON: Do you remember when I gave you your brooch?

EVY: Yes.

HOPKINSON: Do you like it?

EVY: Yes, I do.

T.S.: Order! Order!

HOPKINSON begins to adjust his clothing.

EVY: Bill—this time don't go.

T.S.: Order!

EVY: Say to hell with it.

T.S.: Are you assembled?

EVY speaks as HOPKINSON joins T.S.

EVY: Don't go, Bill.

T.S.: The meeting will come to order . . . Well now, that was a bit of a balls-up yesterday, wasn't it? . . .

HOPKINSON goes to speak.

However, we aren't here to assign guilt, we can do that later. What's the next step, that's the question. Any suggestions, Hopkinson?

HOPKINSON shakes his head slowly.

I thought not. Well, luckily we have in our midst a man with courage and foresight. He has had refurbished, refitted, and manned a second-class cruiser at Esquimalt, the *Rainbow*, length 300 feet, 3,600 gross tonnage with two six-inch guns and six four-inch guns. A small hand, please, for Harry Stevens, our federal M.P. . . . I think we can do better than that.

HOPKINSON claps.

Ah, yes . . . Mr. Stevens has worked diligently since the arrival of the *Komagata Maru* in our waters. Diligence, perseverance, and patriotism always pay off. Let the *Rainbow* push through the Narrows; let her anchor near enough to the *Komagata Maru* for the sun to glint on her guns. Let our next message be—we won't necessarily fire on you—but we will fire on you if necessary!

T.S turns to leave.

HOPKINSON: Sir! . . . My informants in the Sikh community inform me—

T.S.: Informants inform you? *(laughing)* You're being redundant, my boy.

HOPKINSON: My people in the Sikh community tell me that threats have been made. Death threats.

T.S.: You've stirred up a hornet's nest, haven't you? You've opened up Pandora's box. You've created a maelstrom.

HOPKINSON: I was following orders.

T.S.: Let me tell you something—there's someone at the end of the yard . . .

HOPKINSON: Bella Singh?

T.S.: Not Bella Singh . . . Someone who's not Bella Singh waits at the end of the yard . . .

EVY: Who is it out there?

HOPKINSON: One of my men, I imagine.

EVY: Why don't you go out?

HOPKINSON: Later, perhaps . . . Let him wait.

WOMAN: *(laughing)* Do you know something? My son's lips have swollen and burst from the thirst—they are covered with grease from the engines. My legs are like sticks—if I smelled a real meal I would vomit—and you think a few guns will make our knees knock? *(stops laughing) Sale Haramazaade*! Give us supplies and we'll leave!

HOPKINSON: See the cruiser . . . it has guns trained on the *Komagata Maru*.

EVY: Will they fire on it?

HOPKINSON: That—is not my concern.

EVY: Don't you feel anything for them?

HOPKINSON: You wouldn't understand.

EVY: Yes I would. I would try.

HOPKINSON: One has to make decisions. Commitments. To one side or another.

EVY: What side are you on?

HOPKINSON: The winning side.

EVY: Are you winning?

HOPKINSON: This time the *Komagata Maru* will sail.

EVY: Do you think then you'll have won?

HOPKINSON: I'm . . . tired. Let's go to bed.

HOPKINSON starts off.

EVY: Not right now.

HOPKINSON stops, turns to look at EVY.

HOPKINSON: Lie beside me. That's all.

EVY: I don't want to.

HOPKINSON: I don't have to ask! I can order!

EVY looks at him, then picks up her cards, begins to lay them out. After a moment, HOPKINSON leaves. Carnival music plays.

T.S.: Hurry! Hurry! Hurry! Absolutely the last and final chance to view the *Komagata Maru*! Anchored in picturesque Vancouver Harbour for two, count 'em, two glorious months! Note the cruiser standing by to the right, see the sun on its guns, what a fantastic sight! Ladies and gentlemen, can you truly afford to bypass this splendid spectacle? Run, my good friends, you mustn't walk, you must run! Cotton candy, taffy apples, popcorn, and balloons! All this and a possible plus, the opportunity to view your very own navy in action with no threat to you!

Music stops.

SOPHIE: It's all so exciting . . . now tell me what are all the little boats doing?

GEORG: Some of them are harassing the Sikhs, some of them are supplying the ship—the government is giving them provisions.

SOPHIE: And what about the cargo of coal—if there's any left.

GEORG: I hear the government may recompense them. My friends tell me they have promised them everything and will give them nothing. That's called diplomacy, eh, Bill?

SOPHIE: Oh look, everybody! Look! There's black smoke coming out of the smokestack . . . look the *Rainbow*'s moving . . . it's moving in . . . what's it going to do . . . I bet it's going to shoot, I hope it's going to shoot, it's . . . Look, Evy! Come look! It's . . . It's . . . it's moving—The *Komagata Maru*'s moving—and the *Rainbow*'s going right alongside . . . We won! We won! Didn't we, Georg? Didn't we, Mr. Hopkinson? Aren't you even going to look? It's over and we won!

A bang of the cane and they freeze.

T.S.: Over? . . . A note, Mr. Hopkinson, from the man at the end of the yard . . . "When the affairs were past any other remedy, I thought it righteous to draw my sword."

HOPKINSON looks at the note.

WOMAN: *(hard, not sentimental)* We go back. My husband is dead. He died in their war. His father is dead. He died when they cut back the famine relief. I am a British subject, and my people's taxes have gone to their king. I am not a possession, a thing. I am myself and I will fight for myself and my son and my people. I am strong.

GEORG: The whole thing has been most educational. I should thank you. I have made many valuable friends and good contacts. I owe it to you, Bill . . . Can I get you a drink, Sophie, get him a drink.

HOPKINSON steps out to T.S.

HOPKINSON: I have good men in the Indian community . . . good men . . . they produce . . . Bella Singh, Baboo Singh, Hermann Singh, Gunga Ram—

T.S.: Mewa Singh?

HOPKINSON: Not—Mewa Singh.

T.S.: For God's sake, get on.

HOPKINSON: Their lives are in danger . . . the community feels that they're traitors, surely they're loyal British subjects, like myself.

T.S.: Hurry up.

HOPKINSON: My own life has been threatened . . . I ask for—

T.S.: Extra! Extra! Read all about it! War Declared! Recession Recedes! Factories Hum the National Anthem! Send your sons overseas! See all of Europe at federal expense! Check your programme for casting—the enemy's the Kraut! The Sikh's on our side! Extra! Extra! Read all about it!

GEORG: *(picking up paper)* This can't help but work nicely for me.

HOPKINSON: What?

GEORG: I say the war shall increase my use to your department.

SOPHIE: Isn't he smart, Evy? Georg is going places—and so is Sophie.

EVY looks up from her cards.

EVY: Christ, Sophie, it's a war.

GEORG: It's also a good business deal.

EVY spits on the floor.

You should teach her some manners.

SOPHIE: You're jealous.

EVY: Oh, Sophie.

SOPHIE: It's true—you're jealous of me—Georg's up and doing—he gets around—we have a good time. Look at him—he doesn't do anything since the *Komagata Maru*. And you're just as bad. This place is just like a morgue. Who wants to live in a morgue? I'll leave if I want to—I can, you know—I'll leave anytime I want.

HOPKINSON: No you won't.

SOPHIE: Yes I will. Won't I, Georg? Whenever Georg wants.

HOPKINSON: Georg wants what I give him! When I say move, you bloody well move, when I say jump, you say how high. In this stinking world there's two kinds, there's the ruler and the ruled—and when I see the likes of you, I know where I stand! *(beginning to weaken)* Some people talk, and some people listen, but by God, I act, and if . . . it weren't for people like me . . . people like you . . . would still be down in the slime . . . I have my . . . I have my . . .

T.S.: Bill?

HOPKINSON: I have . . .

T.S.: Mewa Singh waits at the end of the yard.

HOPKINSON: Yes.

EVY moves to him.

WOMAN: We dock at Budge Budge fourteen miles from Calcutta. We are to be herded aboard trains and returned to the Punjab although many of us have not been there for years. We resist. Police, reinforced by soldiers, open fire. Men who shared their rancid flour with my son are dead. *(threatening)* We will remember them.

T.S.: Order! Order! The court will come to order! Will the Inspector take the stand! Do you swear to tell the truth, the whole truth, and nothing but the truth, as it befits this case, so help you God?

HOPKINSON: I do.

T.S.: Might I ask if you were acquainted with one Hermann Singh?

HOPKINSON: I was.

T.S.: What was his character?

HOPKINSON: He was a quiet, unassuming man, intensely loyal to his king.

T.S.: What was the nature of your relationship?

HOPKINSON: He rendered assistance to the government in the *Komagata Maru* Incident.

T.S.: Five and one-half weeks after the departure of the *Komagata Maru*, one Pirt Warnes was walking along a little used trail on the Kitsilano Indian Reserve. It was quite a pleasant trail . . . he noticed what at first glance appeared to be a bundle of rags behind a log close to the path. He examined it. It was the badly decomposed body of an East Indian. The turban was wrapped round the ankles. Beside the body lay a leather satchel, an empty brandy flask, and an open straight razor. When he touched the head it came off in his hand. It was Hermann Singh. Let me ask you, Inspector, from your intimate knowledge of the Asian mind, would you say the facts as related are consistent with . . . suicide?

HOPKINSON: No, I would not.

T.S.: Ah . . . and if indeed it were murder, can you suggest a possible motive?

HOPKINSON: By informing, Hermann Singh had incurred the hatred of his people.

T.S.: You may step down.

EVY: Why don't we go away? . . . Why can't we? . . . Bill? . . . Bill, talk to me! . . . I can leave. I can leave. And I will.

EVY exits off stage.

T.S.: Six weeks after the departure of the *Komagata Maru*, Arjun Singh shot through the back of the head from behind!

HOPKINSON: Arjun Singh is dead.

GEORG is on the sofa, feet up, reading the paper.

GEORG: He'll have to get a new stable of fellows, eh?

SOPHIE is playing cards.

SOPHIE: Where would he find them, eh?

GEORG: *(laughing)* Good point . . . where is he going to find them?

T.S.: September 5th, 1914 . . . early evening . . . Bella Singh goes to the temple. Inside the temple, people are singing. They're singing hymns for Arjun Singh, Hermann Singh . . . Bella Singh takes off his shoes . . . Bella Singh enters the temple . . . Bella Singh moves to the back . . . Bella Singh sits in a corner . . . Bella Singh takes out a gun . . . he fires ten shots, scores nine out of ten, seven wounded, two dead. He never speaks till arrested.

GEORG: Do you know what he says, Sophie? He says that he acted in self-defence, he says Bill will verify that . . . will you testify, Bill?

HOPKINSON: Yes.

T.S.: October 21st, 1914 . . . My God, what a day! Look at that sky . . . and the leaves all russet and gold . . . the mountains like sentinels, just a light breeze, the city set like a precious gem on the Pacific . . . breathe in . . . breathe out . . . breathe in . . . breathe out . . .

HOPKINSON: I leave the house early. I walk to the court house . . . It's fall . . . I feel like a toy man walking through a toy town. Everything's working. My arms and my legs move so well together, there is . . . a mechanical precision to everything . . . I notice the houses seem neater than usual, a certain precision . . . at the same time, it's slower, things are slower, but very precise . . . there are no clouds in the sky, and it's blue, a deep blue . . . there's a slight breeze . . . the veins in the leaves protrude as if swollen . . . toy mountains frame my toy town . . . I'm just a bit late because of the walk. I enter the courthouse from Howe Street. As I wait for the lift to take me up to the court, I place very carefully one hand on the wall, feeling the wall, and feeling my hand on the wall, in this tiny toy court . . . I open the door of the lift, I step inside, then I close it. I think of the peace of the coffin. I think of the safety of the cage. I open the door. I step out. I walk down the corridor. I see no one I know . . .

T.S.: Mewa Singh waits in the witness room.

HOPKINSON: I stop at the witness room.

T.S.: Mewa Singh steps out of the witness room. In each hand he carries a gun.

HOPKINSON: When I see him, I feel myself bursting. My toy town is destroyed in an instant. He is large, he encompasses my world, I feel myself racing toward eternity . . . They say I grapple with him. I do not. I open my arms, I say: Now!

Dazzles the sparkle of his sword
Who is utterly dreadful and is contained not
By the elements. And when he performeth
His death-dance, how dolefully his bells
toll and knell.
He, the four-armed one, of a lustrous hair bun,
He wieldeth the mace and the club,
And crushes the swollen head, even of death.
His auspicious tongue of blazing fire
Licketh all that is unholy.
When shrieks his horrid conch
The whole universe reverberates with its
raucous notes
How tintinnabulating are thy ankle bells,
And when thou movest, thou stampest the earth like a quake,
And thy immense gongs strike deep resonant notes.

T.S.: Mewa Singh fires three times. A bullet pierces Hopkinson's heart.

T.S. touches HOPKINSON with the cane. HOPKINSON's head falls forward.

WOMAN: Mewa Singh will be hanged by the neck till he's dead. Mewa Singh says on the gallows: "I am a gentle person, but gentle people must act when injustice engulfs them. Let God judge my actions for he sees the right and the wrong. I offer my neck to the rope as a child opens his arms to his mother."

T.S. does a soft-shoe shuffle, stops, looks out, raises his arms, pauses, and makes a large but simple bow. Black.

The end.

ANGÉLIQUE

LORENA GALE

DEDICATION

I dedicate this book to my mom, the late Lillian Madden, who slaved all her life for minimum wage and still managed to house, feed, clothe, and educate five children. And to my son Clayton Cooper. May he never know the hardships previous generations have endured.

ACKNOWLEDGEMENTS

The playwright acknowledges the assistance of the 1997 Banff Playwrights Colony—a partnership between the Banff Centre, the Canada Council for the Arts, and Alberta Theatre Projects; the Canada Council for the Arts (Theatre Section); Canadian Heritage (Writing and Publishing); the Province of British Columbia (Recommender Program); as well as the Canadian Centre For Architecture, Women in View, the National Arts Centre, the Canadian Stage Company, Playwrights' Theatre Centre, Nightwood Theatre Company, Western Canada Theatre Company, Headlines Theatre Company, Brenda Leadlay, Jackie Maxwell, Diane Roberts, Bob White, ahdri zhina mandiela, Alison Sealy-Smith, John Cooper, and Denyse Beaugrand-Champagne.

STAGING CONTESTATIONS: LORENA GALE'S *ANGÉLIQUE*[1]

NAILA KELETA-MAE

Theatre has an uncanny ability to examine perceptions of what was then and what is now, to face the past as the present and the present as the past. It is through the sustained engagement with then and now that theatre reveals, especially in Canada, its remarkable capacity to expose historic omissions in dominant epistemes and stage productive contestations against established narratives.

Angélique is based on the historical account of Marie-Joseph Angélique, born into slavery in Madeira, Portugal, circa 1710; sold into slavery in New France in 1725; and accused of burning down the city of Old Montreal in 1734. Once convicted, Angélique was tortured, hanged, and burned.[2] Lorena Gale's play is a mix of fact and fiction that centres primarily on Angélique's life in the 1730s as an enslaved person in Old Montreal, where slave ownership was a symbol of wealth and social standing. As much as *Angélique* is a historical representation, it is also deeply invested in producing the present; this is made explicit in Gale's description of the play's time period as "The present and 1730s. Then is now. Now is then." Gale's constant blurring of the lines between past and present (through costumes, music, and references to current affairs) transforms the play

1 This introduction is a revised version of "Performance as Reappearance: Female Blackness in History and Theatre," a chapter that first appeared in *In Defence of Theatre: Aesthetic Practices and Social Interventions*, Kathleen Gallager and Barry Freeman, eds. (Toronto: U of Toronto P, 2016), 129–42.

2 See Lorena Gale, *Angélique* (Toronto: Playwrights Canada, 2000); Afua Cooper, *The Hanging of Angélique: The Untold Story of Canadian Slavery and the Burning of Old Montreal* (Toronto: HarperCollins, 2006); Katherine McKittrick, *Demonic Grounds: Black Women and the Cartographies of Struggle* (Minneapolis: U of Minnesota P, 2006).

from a dramatization of Angélique's life in New France in the early eighteenth century to an exploration of the lives of people in bodies read as female and Black in Canada today.[3]

Attempts to control female Blackness have occurred in the Americas since, at least, the advent of the transatlantic slave trade in the sixteenth century. Identifying the contemporary impact of the transatlantic slave trade is particularly difficult in Canada, where the dominant narrative of the nation's implication in this historical episode is that of Canada as the place to which runaway slaves from the United States of America escaped to be free. This narrative holds within it telling omissions. As Katherine McKittrick asserts, *Angélique* challenges Canadian historiography by calling "into question the workings of the Canadian nation by shattering the safe-haven myth—one of the key ways in which the nation secures both its disconnection from Blackness and its seeming exoneration from difficult histories." Furthermore, the play exposes Canada "as both materially complicit to, and discursively innocent of, racial domination."[4] One of the prevalent stories of female Blackness is that of Harriet Tubman, famed for her leadership of a secret network called the Underground Railroad. Although slavery was abolished in Canada in 1834, Canada only became a destination on the Underground Railroad more than sixteen years later, when the Fugitive Slave Act was passed in the United States requiring that enslaved people who ran away be returned to their owners. Even though Angélique was bought, further exploited, and hanged in Old Montreal 125 years *before* Tubman crossed Canadian borders to lead enslaved people to freedom, it is Tubman that is given centre stage in established recitations of Canadian history—it is Tubman who emerges as the protagonist in the "safe-haven myth." The historiographical emphasis on Tubman as protagonist in the "safe-haven myth," and as representative of histories of female Blackness in Canada, is specious in at least two ways: it erases the presence of enslaved Black people and Black labourers who were in Canada long before the advent of the Underground Railroad; and it incorrectly locates the origins of female Blackness in Canada in the United States.

By placing Angélique at centre stage, Gale "uses the moment of performance to destabilize the narratives that have historically secured Canadian

3 I use the term "people in bodies read as female and Black in Canada" in an effort to make visible the roles of spectator and geographic location in the performance of female Blackness. I also place the word "female" before the word "Black" in order to foreground sex as a primary site of inquiry.

4 McKittrick, 119.

nationhood,"[5] challenging not only the historiographical omission of slavery's role in Canada's past, but also the erasure of female Blackness from the national imaginary and linking these two occlusions through the life of Angélique. The play's ability to directly address modes of exclusion has been no more evident to me than when I have brought *Angélique* into the undergraduate classroom. I have yet to teach a student, educated in Canada, who has not heard of either the Underground Railroad or Harriet Tubman, but in almost every instance when I teach the historiography of Angélique, students are surprised about her existence and shocked that the transatlantic slave trade took place in Canada. Inevitably, the students' surprise leads them to pose some iteration of the question "Why wasn't I taught this in school?" Like many of my students, I attended public elementary, middle, and high schools in Canada, and these aspects of Canadian history were also absent from the curricula that I was taught. Like many of my students, I too was surprised when I first heard the story of Angélique; though I had already learned, outside of the classroom, that the transatlantic slave trade had operated in Canada, reading *Angélique* concretized this knowing in visceral ways. According to McKittrick, this experience of surprise is particularly telling of how Blackness is often constructed within narratives about Canada:

> Blackness is surprising because it should not be here, was not here before, was always here, is only momentarily here, was always over there (beyond Canada, for example). This means, then, that black people in Canada are also presumed surprises because they are "not here" and "here" simultaneously: they are, like blackness, unexpected, shocking, concealed in a landscape of systemic blacklessness . . . In Canada, blackness and black people are altogether deniable *and* evidence of prior codes of representation that have identified blackness / difference as irrelevant. But black existence is an actuality, which takes on several different forms that do not (much to the surprise of some) always conform to the idea of Canada.[6]

Angélique dramatizes Canada in ways that challenge students to productively contemplate relationships between history, gender, race, and nation, and to reflect critically on how their understandings of themselves and the nation are affected by what is and is not included in dominant discursive formations.

5 Alan Filewod, "'From twisted history': Reading *Angélique*," in *African-Canadian Theatre*, ed. Maureen Moynagh (Toronto: Playwrights Canada, 2005), 31.

6 McKittrick, 93.

Angélique demonstrates that theatre can also be a productive site of contestation that shifts the emphasis of official narratives, imagines personal agency, and explores the conditions that make hope possible. In the play's opening scene, Gale uses a nuanced combination of imagery and language to contest an authoritative account and shift its emphasis. The initial stage directions call for "[t]he featureless silhouette of a woman dancing with a book against a backdrop of red, oranges, and yellow, suggestive of flames." Gale makes the woman on stage, presumably Angélique, indistinguishable apart from her sex, and instead emphasizes the presence of an authoritative document—a book. The play's opening words further usurp the woman's presence, with a voiceover that states, presumably reading from the book, "And in seventeen thirty-four a Negro slave set fire to the City of Montreal and was hanged." With this utterance, Gale reproduces what was, at the time of the play's writing,[7] the official interpretation of the events that led to Angélique's conviction and sentence. However, Gale's reproduction contains a subtle disruption that calls the sequence of events into question. Gale begins with a conjunction ("and") but does not include the requisite preceding clause with which the conjunction would connect—signalling that information is missing, suggesting the larger idea of the event is incomplete. Gale further contests the authoritative account with a painstaking and methodical exercise in revision and repetition, removing the first word or two of the opening sentence and restating the remainder, concluding with the single word "hanged." This draws attention away from the historical era, the slavery, the location, and the fire, and places it firmly on the state-sanctioned killing of Angélique. Because the play establishes the interchangeability of then and now, this seemingly simple shift in focus catapults the play from a representation of a specific historic moment into a provocative conversation about the activities of the state in contemporary times. The scene ends with a stage direction, "The crackling sound of fire." And while this certainly alludes to the burning of Old Montreal, it can also be read to suggest, through images and performance, a burning away of an authoritative account, a razing over of an official historical narrative in order to focus on an under-examined perspective on the story.

Angélique also acts as a productive site of contestation in the moments when Angélique imagines the scope of her own agency. Gale does not stage these moments as forceful declarations; instead, Angélique's imaginings occur in tentative, hushed tones. In a conversation with César, Angélique remembers her life before coming to New France. Comparing her experience of the slave trade in

7 In the years following the initial stage productions and publication of *Angélique*, historians' analyses of relevant historical documents brought into question whether or not Angélique set the fire and whether or not the fire was an act of arson.

Portugal with the one in New France and concluding with an indictment of the brutality of her treatment in the latter, Angélique does not propose that she and César match the violence of their owners with their own—instead, she imagines the possibility of freedom. "We could run," Angélique cautiously suggests—a clear disruption of the narrative that Canada was a place that slaves ran to. "We could run," Angélique says, cognizant of the vicious physical punishments they would suffer if captured. "We could run," Angélique says anyway—a lucid example of the glimpses of agency that can exist even within a context as violent as slavery, where the litmus test for whether or not one is treated as a human being consists of the visibility of the melanin in one's skin. "We could run" is a poignant reminder to readers and spectators, especially those in bodies read as female and Black, that alternate realities can be imagined even in circumstances laden with gendered and racial oppression.

Finally, Gale unflinchingly stages the conditions within which hope can arise. The reward, and relief, that a moment of hope can offer does not come easily. *Angélique* requires audiences and readers to witness a wide range of violence—from the sale of a human being, to rape, to infanticide, to torture, to hanging. What I find most unsettling, however, is Gale's insistence that readers and spectators witness Angélique's articulation of her hopes for a life in slavery that includes some modicum of human dignity. By the time Angélique delivers her first monologue, soon after she is purchased by de Francheville, Gale has already foreshadowed that Angélique will remain enslaved, she will be raped, and she will be killed. The monologue opens and closes with the same lines—"This time will be different"—clearly indicating that Angélique is not interested in reliving the past. She survived those experiences, but now she aspires to something different—a life that is "good." Hers is a reasonable hope that readers and spectators know will be almost impossible to obtain. With this knowledge, readers and spectators are forced to witness Angélique express her hopes that "This time everything will work out for me," that "This time, / I will be treated with loving kindness and understanding," and that "It will be good this time."Angélique demonstrates a measured and strategic hopefulness—one shaped by her astute assessment of the possibilities afforded to her given her sex, skin colour, and the geographic and historical contexts that inform perceptions of her corporeality. Angélique's hopefulness is pragmatic, and in order to actualize it she commits to being obedient, following her master's and mistress's orders, and knowing her place. And despite having been born into slavery in Portugal, Angélique is hopeful that a different kind of slavery might be possible in New France. Angélique's hopefulness is specific; she describes the mundane, everyday activities that in her purview would make her life "good"—holidays, laughter, and private moments. And when she attempts to articulate the kinds of experiences that would constitute a good life beyond the possibilities that life in her body has thus far permitted, she runs out of concrete examples and says instead, "and . . . / and . . . " Gale insists on hopefulness in these moments too, using ellipses and full returns as placeholders for the possibilities Angélique's future might hold.

In a play in which "Then is now. Now is then," these ellipses and full returns can also resonate profoundly in the contemporary lives of readers and spectators. Gale's placeholders act as reminders of a shared present and future that have yet to be realized, but for which there is ample room to be hopeful in measured and strategic ways. When there is no clear delineation between then and now, theatre has the potential to intervene in the lives of its spectators, readers, and practitioners, and unmoor them from the constraints of the past. It is precisely in these moments that theatre can inspire us to work and hope, in measured and pragmatic ways, for a more just future.

Angélique was first produced by Alberta Theatre Projects, D. Michael Dobbin, Producing Director, as part of the PanCanadian playRites '98 Festival, January 1998, with the following company:

Thérèse: Tracey Ferencz
Claude: Dennis Fitzgerald
François: Andrew Gillies
Ignace: Grant Linneberg
Angélique: Karen Robinson
Manon: Alexandra Thomson
César: Nigel Shawn Williams

Directed by Sandhano Schultze
Set Design by Scott Reid
Costume Design by Judith Bowden
Lighting Design by Brian Pincourt
Stage Managed by Colin McCracken
Dramaturgy by Rob Moffatt

CHARACTERS

Marie-Joseph Angélique: A slave, in a Canadian history book, twenty-nine

François Poulin de Francheville: Montreal merchant, owner of the St. Maurice Ironworks and the slave Angélique, forty

Thérèse de Couagne: Wife of François. A few years older than Angélique, thity-five

Claude Thibault: The Franchevilles's indentured servant. Angélique's lover, thirties

Ignace Gamelin: Entrepreneur/Montreal merchant. François's business partner, around forty

César: Slave owned by Ignace Gamelin. Lover to Angélique, thirties

Manon: Indian slave owned by the de Berays, next door neighbours of the de Franchevilles's, early twenties

Reporter, Margeurite, Hypolite, Marie Louise, Marie Josephe, Jean Josephe, and François de Beray: These characters are to be played by the members of the main cast.

TIME

The present and 1730s. Then is now. Now is then.

PLACE

Montreal, 1700s.

NOTE

Unless otherwise stated, the slaves are working in every scene in which they appear, either in a modern or historical context. Although the specifics are not written into the text, what can be explored is the concept of witnessing. As servants and slaves are essentially invisible, experiment with who sees what, who knows what.

ACT I

SCENE I

The sound of African drumming. The featureless silhouette of a woman dancing with a book against a backdrop of red, oranges, and yellow, suggestive of flames. VOICEOVER*—building in a rapid repetitive delivery.*

VOICEOVER: And in seventeen thirty-four a Negro slave set fire to the City of Montreal and was hanged.
in seventeen thirty-four a Negro slave set fire to the City of Montreal and was hanged.
seventeen thirty-four a Negro slave set fire to the City of Montreal and was hanged.
a Negro slave set fire to the City of Montreal and was hanged
slave set fire to the City of Montreal and was hanged
set fire to the City of Montreal and was hanged
fire to the City of Montreal and was hanged
to the City of Montreal and was hanged
City of Montreal and was hanged
Montreal and was hanged
and was hanged
was hanged
hanged.

The crackling sound of fire.

SCENE II

FRANÇOIS Poulin de Francheville in a pool of light. He is dressed in full 18th century garb. He talks directly to the audience, with the cocky confidence of a Donald Trump on a roll.

FRANÇOIS: I was hot. I tell you, everything I touched would turn to gold. Or should I say iron. The interest on the loans I paid out was rolling in. And well . . . there seemed to be no end to the number of furs that could be traded. Something went bing! in my mind. Iron . . . iron is the wave of the future. So Ignace Gamelin and I laid down the foundations for the Ironworks. Wrote to the Minister of Marine requesting a twenty-year monopoly on the deposits in St. Maurice. And ba-da-bing ba-da-bang! Request granted from the first day of smelting! Not only that, but the right to exploit cultivated and uncultivated lands next to my own. I felt like a king! Better than Louis! I felt like Midas! With an iron touch. Which is better because iron is stronger and sometimes more valuable than gold.

But do you think I can put a smile on my wife's face?

Our daughter, Marie Angélique, had been dead for two years. Still, Thérèse cried all the time . . . Don't get me wrong. I think of Marie and I feel sad. Yes! But hey . . . life goes on. And we could always have another child.

Beat.

Do you know how hard it is to get close to someone who breaks into tears every time you touch her?

One day I met this really annoying little guy named Bleck. Nicholas Bleck. A Flem. You know what they're like. Just arrived in New France. "With a very rare and special cargo," he says. "Slaves. African slaves. Not those wild things fresh from the jungle. But directly from Portugal. Handsome servants experienced in the ways of Europeans and trained to cater to our every pleasure." A luxury only a fine gentleman like myself could appreciate. And a steal at any price. I wasn't really interested. But the guy was so determined to make a sale, I knew he wouldn't let me go before he displayed his merchandise. So I said I'd take a look. What does it cost to look?

ANGÉLIQUE in shadows.

The figure of this fine creature could not but attract my particular notice. She was standing off to the side with some others. Perfectly straight . . . with the most elegant shapes that can be viewed in nature. Her chestnut skin shone with double lustre. Her large ebony eyes with their inward gaze. Her proud face . . . immobile . . . I don't know . . .

Do you know what it's like to be flush? To say, "I want that!" And without giving it any more thought, to just reach out and take it. To be able to buy anything or anyone . . . there is no more powerful feeling in the world! Eight hundred pounds later . . .

I thought maybe I could give this creature to Thérèse as a special surprise. Make her the envy of female society. Maybe she would be happy . . . Want to be close . . .

What would you pay for your wife's happiness? What would you pay for your own?

SCENE III

Lighting change. ANGÉLIQUE, *dressed in a white domestics uniform, in a spot.* THÉRÈSE *de Couagne dressed in early 18th century in another spot.* ANGÉLIQUE *directly addresses the audience as documentary,* THÉRÈSE *as commentary.*

ANGÉLIQUE: Angélique . . . Marie-Joseph . . .

THÉRÈSE: After my sister, Marie-Joseph de Couagne.

ANGÉLIQUE: Angélique . . .

THÉRÈSE: After . . .

Unable to speak the name of her dead daughter, she turns away.

ANGÉLIQUE: Negro slave born around 1710. Baptized in Montreal June 28, 1730. Hung in Montreal June 21, 1734.

THÉRÈSE: Property of François Poulin de Francheville. 427 rue St. Paul.

The lights come up. THÉRÈSE *has been informing* ANGÉLIQUE *of her duties. She does so lightly and politely, but with the easy authority of one who is in command of her household.* FRANÇOIS *stands by her.*

Beds each morning, change the linen every other day or so. Bathrooms every other morning. Vacuum the main living spaces—bedroom, living room, stairs—daily . . . Don't worry. We have a deluxe machine. I hear it makes vacuuming a breeze . . . Floors swept and washed every day. Waxing every third week. Are you getting all this?

ANGÉLIQUE: *(eager to please) Oui*, Madame.

THÉRÈSE: I am very sensitive to dust. You'll have to dust each day. Metal and wood surfaces polished. Mirrors and windows clear. Without streaks . . .

ANGÉLIQUE: *Oui*, Madame.

THÉRÈSE: Let's see. What else is there? Laundry, including dry cleaning, is Tuesday and Friday. Handwashing daily. Mending as necessary. Marketing is Saturday.

ANGÉLIQUE: *Oui*, Madame.

THÉRÈSE: We breakfast at eight, take luncheon at one, and dine between six and six-thirty.

CLAUDE, the de Franchevilles's indentured servant, walks across the stage carrying a ladder. He wears modern clothing. THÉRÈSE notices him.

ANGÉLIQUE: *Oui*, Madame.

THÉRÈSE: Yours is the little room off the kitchen. Claude will show you where it is. Claude . . . This is . . .

ANGÉLIQUE: Angélique . . .

THÉRÈSE: Yes . . . See that she gets settled down to work.

CLAUDE: *Oui*, Madame.

THÉRÈSE: There is a place for everything in this house and everything has its place, do you understand?

ANGÉLIQUE: Oh *oui*, Madame. I keep a very clean house. You will not be disappointed.

THÉRÈSE: Good.

CLAUDE and ANGÉLIQUE exit.

FRANÇOIS: So . . . ? What do you think?

THÉRÈSE: Does it matter what I think?

FRANÇOIS: Of course, Thérèse. Your opinions are important to me.

THÉRÈSE: Then I think that we don't need a slave.

FRANÇOIS: I didn't buy her because we needed her.

THÉRÈSE: Why did you buy her?

FRANÇOIS: Because . . . Because I thought you would want one.

THÉRÈSE: For me.

Beat.

Thank you. But next time, instead of asking what I think, try asking what I want.

She exits.

FRANÇOIS: *(to himself)* What do you want, Thérèse? What do you want?

SCENE IV

Jungle music on a boom box. "Agony" by Angie Angel. The repetitive, upbeat tempo like the accelerated drumming of a slave driver. ANGÉLIQUE *with a mop, moving though space in an abstracted dervish of cleaning.* CLAUDE *and* FRANÇOIS *witness.*

ANGÉLIQUE: This time will be different.

This time everything will work out for me.
This time, I will not just
"live in."
This time, I will
"live with."
I'll make this strange new land—my land!
This house—my home!
These new people,
my people!
This time I will live in reasonable peace.

These people will be different.
These folk will be decent and good.
This mistress will be firm but gentle.
This master will be honest and fair.
There will be no
harsh looks or cruel words,
this time.
This time,
I will be treated with loving kindness and understanding.

I will work hard.
From sun to sun.
Do exactly as I'm told.
I will perform each duty with pride and obedience.
I will maintain their order.
Everything will go smoothly.
I'll know my place.

I will give freely of myself.
Repaying their humanity with loyalty.
Earning their protection and their care.
They'll wonder how they ever lived without me!

Life will be different this time.

There will be holidays . . .
and happy days . . .
and good times . . .
occasional laughter . . .
and private moments . . .
and . . .
and . . .

It will be good this time.

This time will be different.
This time will be different.
This time will be different.

SCENE V

Light change. Night. FRANÇOIS *sits at a small table with a candle and a pitcher of water.* CLAUDE *and* THÉRÈSE *witness.*

FRANÇOIS: *(whispered)* Angélique . . . Angélique?

ANGÉLIQUE: *Oui*, Monsieur?

FRANÇOIS: *Viens.* Come.

ANGÉLIQUE: Is there something wrong, Monsieur?

He tries to put her at ease.

FRANÇOIS: No, no. I just wanted . . . uh . . . pour me a glass of water. Please.

ANGÉLIQUE: *Oui*, Monsieur.

He watches intently as she goes to the table, pours him a glass, which she sets beside him. He smiles at her and drinks. There is a moment of awkward silence.

Will that be all, Monsieur?

FRANÇOIS: Yes . . . uh . . . no. *(wanting her to like him)* I have something for you. A present. You like? *Castor.* Beaver. Its worth improves with wear. *Castor gras* . . . even more valuable. Not to mention warm. It's yours.

ANGÉLIQUE: *(perplexed)* Thank you, Monsieur.

FRANÇOIS: Don't mention it.

He puts the fur around her shoulders and considers her carefully a moment.

Now come . . . Stand over here. I want to take a good look at you.

There is yearning in his observation.

Turn around. Slowly. That's it. Nice. Very nice. Yes . . . You are a beauty . . . I wonder . . . *(with earnest curiosity)* Is it true what they say about African women?

ANGÉLIQUE: *(stiffly)* I'm sorry, Monsieur. I don't know what they say.

FRANÇOIS: That you're wilder? Freer? Hot like the sun that scorched you?

She does not reply.

I would like to know for myself . . .

ANGÉLIQUE: Please, Monsieur . . .

FRANÇOIS: No . . . Don't fight it. You'll disturb Thérèse.

She stops resisting.

See? I'm not so bad. I'm better than sleeping in the snow. If you get my drift.

Beat.

Come on . . . smile. I will not hurt you. If you obey. I won't hurt you.

SCENE VI

CLAUDE in a spot.

CLAUDE: This indenture made the 17th of August, 1729, between me, Claude Thibault, also known as Claude de la Butanne, aged twenty-nine, and François Poulin de Francheville witnesseth that I do covenant, promise, and grant to François Poulin, from my first arrival at Montreal and after, for the term of three years, to serve in such service as he François Poulin shall there employ him.

ANGÉLIQUE enters and begins her cleaning dervish in silence. CLAUDE continues to speak as if he has been doing so for a while.

Yep. This little piece of pounded wood is all that ties me here. One day I'm going to wipe my ass with this and stick it to Francheville's forehead. Take off across the river and not look back till the earth turns to sand beneath my feet and the sea stretches out unbroken before me!

ANGÉLIQUE: But why, Monsieur? What has Monsieur done to you?

CLAUDE: Nothing, I guess. I just don't plan on shovelling his horseshit for the rest of my life, that's all. Until then . . . I guess I'll just have another drink.

He takes a flask out of his shirt and drinks.

You want some? It's on the house.

ANGÉLIQUE: No thank you, Monsieur.

CLAUDE: Come on. Just take a swig. I hate to drink alone.

ANGÉLIQUE: But, Madame . . .

CLAUDE: Fuck Madame! Yeesh! That's a scary thought.

Beat.

Just take a sip. It'll do you some good.

ANGÉLIQUE: If you insist, Monsieur.

CLAUDE: And drop the "Monsieur" bullshit. I'm not one of them. Call me Claude or call me Thibault as long as you call me, okay?

ANGÉLIQUE: You could be one of them. You look like one of them.

CLAUDE: Yeah, right. I guess to you we all look alike. No, don't confuse me with the rest of my species. I'm just a peon. Like you. Something to pee on. Cheers.

He drinks and hands the flask to her. She drinks.

ANGÉLIQUE: Look . . . ! *(referring to an imaginary window)*

CLAUDE: The first snow is always the best. You see how it melts when it hits the ground. The earth isn't ready. Still too warm. It's not going to stick. Whatever falls will be gone by this afternoon. You see? It's already turning to rain. It will all get washed away. But the next time will be a blizzard and then you'll see.

ANGÉLIQUE: It's beautiful.

CLAUDE: You think so now, but after six or seven months of freezing your ass off you'll change your mind. Snow's a bitch. Let's drink to that.

ANGÉLIQUE: You drink too much.

CLAUDE: And you don't drink enough.

He drinks.

Eau de Vie! The spirit of life! Warms the soul, kills the pain! Here.

ANGÉLIQUE: I am not in pain.

CLAUDE: Keep telling yourself that and maybe one day you'll believe it. In the meantime, drink up.

She drinks, then gives him back the flask.

ANGÉLIQUE: Claude? Where will you go? When your time is up?

CLAUDE: I don't know. Back to Franche Comte, maybe. Or the Islands. No snow in the Islands. Yeah . . . The Islands . . . that's the place to be. Warm winds, blue horizons, women running around naked all the time. That's what I hear. Is it true?

ANGÉLIQUE: How should I know?

CLAUDE: Sorry. I guess that's not the kind of question to ask a lady. But you can't blame a man for asking.

Beat.

I don't know. What island are you from?

ANGÉLIQUE: Not the ones you're thinking of. Madiere . . . Across from Portugal. A jewel in the Atlantic.

CLAUDE: Sounds good to me. Maybe there. You want to come?

ANGÉLIQUE: Don't make me laugh.

CLAUDE: Why not? You're pretty when you laugh.

SCENE VII

Black. FRANÇOIS with a deer skin and a BIC lighter. He flicks. The light reveals him.

FRANÇOIS: *(whispered)* Angélique . . . Angélique?

Black. Beat. FRANÇOIS flicks again. The lights bump up. He is closer.

(whispered) Angélique . . . Angélique?

Black. FRANÇOIS with a deer skin.

(whispered) Angélique . . . Angélique?

ANGÉLIQUE in a spot.

ANGÉLIQUE: Angélique became the mistress of Jacques César, a Negro slave owned by Ignace Gamelin, with whom she had a son, Eustache, born in January 1730 and in May 1732, she gave birth to twins; Louis and Marie Françoise.

SCENE VIII

In the darkness we hear . . .

ANGÉLIQUE: *(whispered)* Brother? What are we doing here?

CÉSAR: Didn't they tell you?

ANGÉLIQUE: No.

Lights come up to reveal IGNACE *Gamelin, in full period dress on one side of a two-way mirror. He speaks in a clinical, scientific manner.*

IGNACE: It's very interesting. Notice how they just stand there. It would seem like nothing is going on between them. But look . . . his eyes . . . her mouth. Fascinating. See. He is putting some distance between them in order to get a better look.

Beat.

I am surprised he's so contained. I've owned him for years and he hasn't had a woman.

FRANÇOIS *enters the mirror.*

FRANÇOIS: That you know of . . .

IGNACE: Touchée.

THÉRÈSE *enters. The three are framed as if in portrait.*

THÉRÈSE: Why do they not speak, Ignace?

FRANÇOIS: Perhaps they are shy.

IGNACE: Perhaps they are like dogs. Two males pass on the street and they growl or bark to indicate status and territory. But a bitch in heat struts past and the first thing that happens is they sniff each other out. Circle and sniff. Most animals do that. Hey François, maybe we should make a study of this. The unusual mating practices of the African in captivity. Imagine, we could be scholars as well as merchants.

FRANÇOIS: *(guarded jealousy)* She won't go for him . . .

THÉRÈSE: Why not? I would . . .

The men turn to her.

If I were her.

IGNACE: Care to place a little wager?

IGNACE takes out his purse.

FRANÇOIS: I hate to take your money.

THÉRÈSE: Shh . . .

IGNACE: The sniffing has begun.

The lights come up on ANGÉLIQUE and CÉSAR, IGNACE's slave. They whisper.

CÉSAR: My master says that you are to be with me now.

ANGÉLIQUE: What!

THÉRÈSE: What are they saying?

IGNACE: Look.

CÉSAR: You have been chosen for me.

ANGÉLIQUE: I don't even know you . . . And we're supposed to!?

CÉSAR: I guess.

ANGÉLIQUE: What if I refuse?

CÉSAR: I don't know.

ANGÉLIQUE: And you agreed to this?

CÉSAR: It's been a long time, Sister. I don't come into contact with too many of our people. Let alone women.

Pause.

I need . . . someone.

ANGÉLIQUE: And anyone will do?

CÉSAR: Someone . . .

ANGÉLIQUE: Then you are no better than they are!

Beat.

Come on. Let's get this over with.

She lies down, opening her legs.

This is what it's all about? Well, take it. Here it is. Come on and take it. Just take it. I won't fight you. I've been chosen for you. Well, here I am. Only make it fast. I don't have all day. I have other work I have to do.

IGNACE: All right César, old boy! The sexual prowess of the African male is legendary. Let this be a lesson to you, François. Don't bet with the best 'cause the best only bet on a sure thing. Those two will turn a profit for us in no time.

FRANÇOIS reaches for his purse.

Oh . . . Put that away. We are, after all, gentlemen.

The two men exit. Lights out on THÉRÈSE who watches with fascination.

ANGÉLIQUE: Well? What are you waiting for?

CÉSAR: Get up off of that floor. You think I want it to be like this?

ANGÉLIQUE: I don't care what you think.

CÉSAR: What am I supposed to do? Just say no? All I did was ask permission to court a woman. I thought he'd just let me find one on my own. There's an Indian girl I see sometimes. I guess my master thought he was doing me a favour.

ANGÉLIQUE: Real generous of him.

CÉSAR: Real generous of your master, for he would have to give permission too. If it makes you feel any better, now that I've seen you up close I'm not much taken by you either. But we've been paired together. And there is no getting away from it.

Pause.

ANGÉLIQUE: What do we do?

CÉSAR: Make the best of it, I guess. We can start by trying to be friends. Yes? Maybe we can pretend that we are meeting again. In another time, another place. Under more pleasant circumstances. Yes? Sister?

He pretends.

Hello. Wonderful woman of the great homeland. I haven't seen you before. I am César. Jacques César.

ANGÉLIQUE: I am . . . Angélique. Marie-Joseph Angélique.

SCENE IX

The painful sounds of childbirth. IGNACE and FRANÇOIS are smoking and waiting. CLAUDE in the shadows. CÉSAR waits expectantly off in a corner. CÉSAR jumps up.

IGNACE: Relax, old man. There is nothing you can do. You will only be in the way. The women have everything under control . . .

THÉRÈSE: *(off)* It's a boy . . .!

FRANÇOIS: A boy . . .

IGNACE: It's a boy! Congratulations, César old man. Or should I say Papa.

CÉSAR: *Merci*, Monsieur. I am very proud to have a son.

IGNACE: If he is anything like you, César, he'll be a strong lad.

FRANÇOIS: And a strong man. He'll fetch a good price when the time comes.

IGNACE: You scoundrel. Don't run off with the profits. I lay claim to half.

THÉRÈSE enters with a bundle.

THÉRÈSE: It's a boy, François.

FRANÇOIS: Beautiful.

He turns away. She addresses CÉSAR.

THÉRÈSE: Would you like to hold him?

CÉSAR: Thank you, Madame.

She delicately hands the baby to CÉSAR. They admire it in silence for a moment.

IGNACE: *(looking at baby)* He's awfully fair.

They all turn to him.

Which only goes to show that everything is born pure. Perfect!

Beat.

His face all screwed up like that—you know who he reminds me of?

FRANÇOIS: *(quickly)* Who?

IGNACE: Eustache, the foreman at the Ironworks.

FRANÇOIS: Eustache?

IGNACE: All this baby is missing is his moustache.

FRANÇOIS: *(relieved)* Yes . . .

He laughs.

Yes, it does look like Eustache. All red face and hairy. Then that's what we will call it. Eustache.

IGNACE: *(to CÉSAR)* Well, we better be heading back. Plenty of time to play daddy ahead of you.

FRANÇOIS: Claude. See to Monsieur Gamelin's carriage.

CLAUDE: *Oui*, Monsieur.

CLAUDE exits.

IGNACE: By the way, how is the mother doing?

THÉRÈSE: Fine. She's just fine.

IGNACE: Now hand him back.

CÉSAR hands the baby to THÉRÈSE.

FRANÇOIS: I'll see you to the door.

They exit. THÉRÈSE is left holding the baby. She studies its face.

SCENE X

ANGÉLIQUE alone with her baby. The sound of a new heart beating. She stands, gently swaying, rocking the child in her arms.

ANGÉLIQUE: In the beginning there was Darkness.
Dense
profound
Darkness.
Like a thick black blanket
stretching
into seamless infinity.
Darkness was all and all was Darkness.
Is.
And would ever be.
And Darkness slumbered,
complete
in her ebony world.

Till one day there was a movement, a stirring, a rumbling
somewhere
deep inside.
An unacknowledged longing to be
more
than everything.
Growing like the sound of distant thunder.
Unsettling her dreams,
but not enough to wake her.

The stirring grew into a churning.
The darkness swirled and eddied.
Rising

and crashing
in
on herself.
She rocked.
She reeled.
Until she woke.
And then she knew
that she would
never
sleep again.

"Something has changed in me. I can no longer bear to be alone."

And with that thought,
Darkness heaved and pushed.
Heaved and pushed.
Forcing
desire from her depths.
Giving birth to
Light.

Light was small.
No bigger than a spark.
But in It,
Darkness could
see
the full extent of herself.

"I am so much more than what I thought I was."

And Light blinked
with the bright eyes of a newborn.
Dazzling.
Delighting Darkness.
And a great heat she had never before noticed
spread through Darkness
as she closed
protectively
around Light. Like
mother
cradling
child.

Light,
unlike Darkness,
came into being
complete
with its own self knowledge
which it fed on with a ferocious hunger,
growing fatter,
and pushing back
Darkness in defiance.

Darkness,
being everywhere, still
encompassed Light no matter how she strained
to give It room.

Light,
fuelled by it's own existence, grew
hotter
in confinement.

"I am so much more than what I am. At least as much as Darkness, which is everywhere. Why must I be contained? Without me Darkness has no Knowledge of itself. Therefore, I am everything! And Darkness is nothing!"

Light burned with greater arrogance.
Growing hotter and denser with a simmering anger,
which bubbled
and popped
beneath its surface of brilliance.
And still
Darkness
closed around it.

"I am more . . . I am more than . . . I am more than this," Light seethed.

Till it was so
full
of itself
It exploded.
Sending shards of its being
hurling through Darkness.
Lighting up
the void.

Light
was now everywhere.
Cutting through darkness with the sharpness of
an axe.
Cruelly
severing
the umbilicus between them.

Darkness
was so blinded by the light
she could no longer
see,
and so retreated
to where she could have some sense of herself.
Though Light still pierced her,
as a reminder that It
now
ruled
every
thing.

Light and Darkness.

That is how the two became separate forces.
In constant opposition.
Light in the forefront
and Darkness . . .
waiting . . .
on the edge
of everything.

But there is something else we know, my child. That in the end, Darkness reclaims everything. The stars will fall. The sun will cease to shine. Light will collapse in on itself. Till once again, it is nothing more than just a little spark. That flickers. Sputters. Pops itself out. Then Darkness will resume her peaceful reign.

That day is a long way off. I will ever see it. Neither will you, my baby . . . So light . . . So powerfully dark.

VOICEOVER: *(whispered)* Angélique . . . Angélique?

Puts her hand over the baby's face, smothering it. The heartbeat stops. Silence.

Fly home and greet the darkness. There are others waiting there. Mama loves you and will join you soon.

THÉRÈSE enters. She regards ANGÉLIQUE compassionately and speaks from her own pain.

THÉRÈSE: Children don't live too long here. Most babies born in the winter don't live to see the spring. I don't know why . . . Best it happened early on. That way you don't get too attached.

She looks at the dead baby.

I had a child once . . . A girl. Marie Angélique. Eight winters she lasted. Eight sweet years . . . And then she caught a fever she was just too young to fight . . . So you're lucky it happened sooner.

SCENE XI

FRANÇOIS looking over a file folder of documents. THÉRÈSE regards him for a tense moment, then begins tentatively.

THÉRÈSE: God forgive me, but I am glad it's dead.

No response.

At least now we don't have to bear the embarrassment of her bastard running around the streets.

He pays little attention.

I find it difficult to believe that César was the father . . . the baby was so pale.

FRANÇOIS: *(still engrossed in his work)* What does it matter? It's dead now. It's gone.

THÉRÈSE: Do you know who the father was?

FRANÇOIS: César.

THÉRÈSE: No.

FRANÇOIS: Then how should I know? It could be anyone for all we know. Claude even . . .

THÉRÈSE: Or you . . .

Pause.

FRANÇOIS laughs.

FRANÇOIS: Really, Thérèse. I have more important things to worry about.

THÉRÈSE: *(softly)* I have wrestled with that possibility since that child was born.

Beat.

I understand how tempting it could be . . . when it is so readily available. To succumb to temptation . . .

FRANÇOIS: I don't think I like what you are implying.

THÉRÈSE: *(quickly)* Did you?

FRANÇOIS: Did I what?

Pause.

THÉRÈSE: I think we should get rid of her, François.

FRANÇOIS: And what do you propose I should do with her?

THÉRÈSE: Sell her. Give her away.

FRANÇOIS: Just give her away?

THÉRÈSE: I don't know. Anything. Just get her out of here.

FRANÇOIS: Why?

THÉRÈSE: Because I'm your wife and I am asking you.

FRANÇOIS: *(irritated)* You're being ridiculous. What's gotten into you, Thérèse? First you accuse me of being an adulterer and now you want me to give up a valuable piece of property just because of some crazy idea you've got?

THÉRÈSE: Please, François.

Beat.

FRANÇOIS: *(softer)* Listen to me. You are my wife. I love you. Believe me when I tell you that you have nothing to worry about.

He kisses her forehead.

Now, all this nonsense has interrupted my work. I'm going off to collect my thoughts.

THÉRÈSE: François . . . Tell me you will consider it? Out of respect for me?

FRANÇOIS: You have nothing to worry about.

SCENE XII

The sound of one lone drum beating in a slow Native rhythm. MANON, *a* panisse, *a young Native slave/servant carries a basket of wet clothes.* ANGÉLIQUE *enters with a basket of wet clothes, notices* MANON, *and halts. She stares.* ANGÉLIQUE *returns her gaze with similar curiosity. Another drum beating to a corresponding African rhythm joins with the first. They do not clash. They complement.* MANON *puts her basket down and starts to shake and hang the clothing at the opposite end of the clothesline to* ANGÉLIQUE. *As she does so she begins to sing to herself in her Native language. It is a mournful song.* ANGÉLIQUE *starts to hang her wash and once again responds to* MANON *singing with her own song in an African language. The two songs blend in a call and response style and in rhythm to the beating of the two drums. The women work and sing. All the while getting closer and closer. Freer and freer. Becoming jubilant. They meet in the centre, neither capable of hanging more clothes. They regard each other for a moment. They smile in their song, uncomfortable but friendly. They are about to speak when* THÉRÈSE *enters.*

THÉRÈSE: Stop. Stop that noise immediately.

She tears the laundry from the line in her anger.

How many times do I have to tell you that it's strictly forbidden. I should have you both whipped. Maybe then you would understand that we are a civilized people and won't tolerate that sort of . . . savage behaviour.

(to MANON*)* Now you get out of here. And don't think I won't mention this to Madame de Beray, because I will.

SCENE XIII

ANGÉLIQUE *drags a carpet or a panel of heavy drapes or a manageable wall tapestry out and hangs it over the line.* THÉRÈSE *waits silently while* ANGÉLIQUE *toils. When* ANGÉLIQUE *is finished, she stands beside the hanging.* THÉRÈSE *then commences to beat the rug, each blow being a complete and separate beating in itself, meted out over the course of time.*

ANGÉLIQUE *responds as if she herself is being struck—first with pain, then with growing endurance and compressed rage.* FRANÇOIS *enters and watches from the side and* MANON *watches from the shadows.*

THÉRÈSE: Because you dropped the serving bowl. *(smack)*
Because you were late coming back from the market. *(smack)*

Because you forgot to put oil in the lamps. *(smack)*
Because you were whistling in the kitchen. *(smack)*

ANGÉLIQUE: Each stroke a reminder.

THÉRÈSE: Because the bread didn't rise. *(smack)*
Because he went to you again last night. *(smack)*
Because you burnt the edges of the waffles. *(smack)*
Because he is my husband and I love him. *(smack)*

ANGÉLIQUE: Each stroke a reminder.

THÉRÈSE: Because he stared at you through dinner. *(smack)*
Because I have to pretend this isn't happening. *(smack)*
Because I wish you'd disappear. *(smack)*
Because there is nothing else I can do. *(smack)*

THÉRÈSE crosses to FRANÇOIS and they exit together.

ANGÉLIQUE: Each stroke . . .

SCENE XIV

ANGÉLIQUE is drinking Eau de Vie. *CÉSAR is rubbing her back.*

CÉSAR: . . . eleven times, this slave and his Indian wife. Ten times they ran away. Ten times they were caught. First time they got caught, the master cut off one of their feet. Next time a hand. Next time an ear. Next time a nose. Next time . . . whatever. These two so cut up makes you wonder how they were still standing. But the eleventh time . . .

He finishes rubbing her down.

Hey . . . slow down.

He takes the flask from her.

There.

He pats her stomach.

This one is mine and I don't want nothing to happen to it.

ANGÉLIQUE: Well, you just march up there and tell that to Madame. Say, "Madame, I want you to give my Angélique the day off." She'll laugh in your face. These people work me harder than they work their horses. *(cautiously)* Do you remember what it was like before?

CÉSAR: Before what?

ANGÉLIQUE: Before . . .

CÉSAR: I have no before. I don't remember my mama or my papa. Probably sold or died off before I could get a good fix on 'em. I got sold to a fur trader when I was still a boy, and come up north. Been here ever since.

ANGÉLIQUE: I remember. Before this Montreal. This New France. Before this Canada. I remember Madiere. Picking coffee with my mother and my father. The coffee beans. Their tender green. Their firmness between my little fingers. We toiled for them. Yes! But it was work. Just work. Hard work is a part of life. And at least we were together.

On the days of rest and celebration we would all descend on the beach. We would build a fire in conjunction to the line of the horizon. As the sun set, the orange and red and yellow of day's transition into night would blend with the colours in the fire. Everyone would gather round. And to the beating of a drum, they would tell the stories of our ancestors. Our warriors dancing the great battles. Our hunters re-enacting their kills.

The little me would stand on the sandy shore and look out across the inky water. And imagine I could see the land of my ancestors. It was that close. It was that far away.

Pause.

I cannot understand this coldness and this cruelty. I may have always been a slave. But I did not feel like one until I came to this land . . . *(carefully)* We could run.

CÉSAR laughs.

CÉSAR: Sure. You wait here while I pack my belongings. Hey! I've got everything. Let's go!

ANGÉLIQUE: We could!

CÉSAR: Look Angélique, everywhere we go we're going to be slaves. There's nowhere to hide. And even if there was we can't hide forever. They'll find us. Snap the chains back on or worse. I don't fancy clomping around the rest of my life with one foot. Gamelin isn't too bad a master. And I have you now. And a baby coming. It may not seem like too much. But the one thing I have learned, is to take what happiness I can when I can get it. And everything I have is right here.

ANGÉLIQUE: But don't you want to be your own man? Wake up in the morning and decide what you want to do . . .

CÉSAR: I am just trying to accept what life has put before me.

ANGÉLIQUE: Accept . . .

CÉSAR: That's right. Accept. 'Cause there is nothing I can say or do that's going to change my lot in this life. If I am going to have any kind of happiness I have to come to terms with that fact. I suggest you do too. Find some way to live. Something to live for. And life will seem a little easier.

ANGÉLIQUE: But what about those eleven times? Don't they tell you something.

CÉSAR: Yeah. They made it the eleventh time. Into Heaven. They were found wrapped in each other's arms. Froze to death. In the snow.

FRANÇOIS: *(whispers, off)* Angélique? Angélique?

CÉSAR: Just take what happiness you can—when you can.

SCENE XV

Light change.

CÉSAR: Eustache. Natural son of Marie-Joseph Angélique and Jacques César. Baptised, January 11, 1731. Buried, February, 12, 1731. Age . . .

ANGÉLIQUE: One month.

CÉSAR: Louis: *fils naturel de la même negresse* and brother of the previous. Born and baptized May 26, 1732. Buried the next day. Age . . .

ANGÉLIQUE: Two days.

CÉSAR: Marie Françoise, twin sister of the preceding. Buried October 29, 1732. Age . . .

ANGÉLIQUE: Five months.

CÉSAR: Father—unknown. Though the mother declared it to be Jacques César.

CÉSAR exits.

SCENE XVI

FRANÇOIS enters and stands behind ANGÉLIQUE. CLAUDE works quietly in the background. Every once in a while he looks in the direction of ANGÉLIQUE. He is aware of what is happening with her but cannot watch openly. From behind, FRANÇOIS reaches around and removes ANGÉLIQUE's uniform, revealing period undergarments beneath her modern clothing. He then commences to dress her up again, only this time, in period clothing. ANGÉLIQUE does not resist.

ANGÉLIQUE: A dog barking . . . A baby crying . . . Footsteps . . .
The wind whistling, low and breathy . . .

THÉRÈSE enters and watches in the shadows.

The faint creek of wood giving way to weight . . .
Someone stepping stealthily on the fourth floorboard
before the doorway to my room.
There is no sneaking in this house where every sound
betrays.
A cat scowling . . .
Perhaps the dog has caught the cat.
Or maybe,
the cat has caught the dog.

FRANÇOIS places a corset on ANGÉLIQUE.

I could leave here. Right now!

She takes a step away from him. Then another and another which has the effect of tightening the corset.

I am walking toward the door . . . I am opening it . . . I am stepping outside and . . .

She falls forward. Her arms spread like a bird. She is kept aloft by the laces of the corset which FRANÇOIS holds like reins on a wild horse. But he doesn't notice anything that's happening with her. He pumps her, like he's fucking her from behind.

I'm freeeeeeee! I'm free! I'm free! I'm free! Look at meeee! I'm running through the gates of the city. I'm racing across the land. I'm floating across the big river. I am washed up on the shores of my beloved Madiere . . .

He pulls her back to him and ties the corset.

But I am not really out there . . .

She steps into the dress.

I am here.
I see.

The dog has caught the cat. The cat has a mouse in its jaws. The mouse is playing dead.

You think you own me. This body. That complies. That never fights. The heat you feel is white-hot rage scorching the inside of my mind. A blazing fury I bite back. Fire—I would spit into your face. If you would face me, you coward, you would know . . . One day . . .

SCENE XVII

CLAUDE whistles cheerfully to himself, carries two pails of water which we are to believe he has hauled from a well. He carries them to a large black kettle and pours them in. He speaks with great caution, as he works.

CLAUDE: There's a place. Not too far from here. South. Called New England. Ever heard of it?

She does not respond.

I went there once with Monsieur de Francheville. Not much different from here. Only everyone speaks English. And free Blacks too.

ANGÉLIQUE: *(cautiously)* How do you know they're free?

She takes up her old clothing and puts it in the kettle.

CLAUDE: We took the horses to the blacksmith. Right next door was a small house. In need of some repair. But it looked safe. Three little African children playing in the yard. I figured they must be his.

ANGÉLIQUE: That doesn't make them free. Makes them children.

Takes a bucket and pours it in the kettle

CLAUDE: He spoke to Monsieur de Francheville directly. Monsieur paid him directly, though he complained about the price. Every man who came into the smithy's shouted at him like he was their slave. But when they left they paid him like a free man.

ANGÉLIQUE: How do you know his master didn't hire him out? Make himself more money?

CLAUDE: I don't. But I'm willing to wager that I'm right and you're wrong.

ANGÉLIQUE: I'm not willing to bet my body parts on your view of the world.

CLAUDE: *(seriously)* I'll prove it. It's about two, maybe three weeks journey. Depending on time of year, weather. Weather's great now. Let's go. I know the way.

ANGÉLIQUE: We can't just walk out of here.

CLAUDE: It's that easy. Just put one foot in front of the other. Come on. I'll show you.

ANGÉLIQUE: Why? Why should I trust you?

He takes her hand and kisses it.

FRANÇOIS: *(off)* Angélique! Angélique . . .

CLAUDE: Anytime you want out . . . I know the way.

FRANÇOIS enters.

FRANÇOIS: Angélique . . . *(surprised)* Oh, Claude . . .

ANGÉLIQUE takes a bucket and pours it in the kettle.

CLAUDE: What can I do for you, Monsieur?

FRANÇOIS: Uh . . . The Mercedes. I think you should take it in and have it looked at.

CLAUDE: Sure thing.

He lights a fire under the kettle.

You leaving town again?

FRANÇOIS: Soon. Real soon.

He regards CLAUDE with cloaked suspicion. ANGÉLIQUE takes a bucket and pours it into the kettle.

Angélique . . . Watching you pour that water has made me real thirsty. Why don't you go and get me a cup.

ANGÉLIQUE: *Oui*, Monsieur.

She exits.

FRANÇOIS: You're a really useful guy to have around the house.

CLAUDE: That's why you pay me the big bucks.

FRANÇOIS: Yeah, well, maybe you should come out with me to the Ironworks. We could use someone like you out there.

CLAUDE: What about Madame? How will she cope?

FRANÇOIS: Is it Madame you're concerned for? Or Angélique?

ANGÉLIQUE enters. CLAUDE notices but doesn't say anything.

You've been fucking her, haven't you?

CLAUDE: No, Monsieur.

FRANÇOIS: But you want to.

She spits in the water. Stirs it with her finger.

I don't blame you. Everyone should get a taste of brown sugar.

ANGÉLIQUE: Your water, sir.

FRANÇOIS: *(with great show)* Why, thank you.

(to CLAUDE) Salute.

He drinks.

Mmmm. That was the coolest, sweetest water I ever tasted. Thanks again.

He smiles at ANGÉLIQUE and tosses CLAUDE the keys.

I want the car back in two hours. Get moving.

CLAUDE: Excuse me, sir . . .

FRANÇOIS: What!

CLAUDE: It might save you some money if you showed me exactly what the problem is. You know. Mechanics.

FRANÇOIS: Don't worry about the money.

CLAUDE: But it might be something I can fix myself.

FRANÇOIS: Jesus, Claude . . .

CLAUDE: Unless, of course, Monsieur is engaged in more pressing business . . .

FRANÇOIS regards CLAUDE for a moment. Then ANGÉLIQUE.

FRANÇOIS: Yeah . . . Right.

He finishes his water.

Let's go.

They exit. ANGÉLIQUE picks up a long stick and stirs the laundry.

ANGÉLIQUE: Mistah buckra
he get sick
he tak fever
he be die.
he be die

SCENE XVIII

IGNACE Gamelin in a pool of light. Delivers the following as in eulogy.

IGNACE: François Poulin de Francheville. Merchant, fur trader, seigneur, and entrepreneur in the Saint Maurice Ironworks. Son of Michel Poulin and Marie Jutras. Brother to Pierre Poulin and loving husband to Thérèse de Couagne. And, of course, my dearest friend and business partner. Born October 7, 1692. Died November 3, 1733. His early death is a grave loss to this colony.

Light expands to reveal THÉRÈSE in a black business suit and a stylish black hat with the netting pulled over her face.

THÉRÈSE: I loved him, Ignace.

IGNACE: I know, my dear.

THÉRÈSE: From the first moment I saw him. I was taking a bucket of ashes around back to the stables. We'd had a visit by *les Lutins* the night before. And I had heard that the only way to get rid of these mischievous goblins was to put a pail of ashes just inside the stable door. Because *les Lutins* hate ashes. And that would discourage them from ever coming again.

I heard someone coming to the stables. I wasn't expecting visitors. I thought the goblins were back. I didn't want them to catch me. So I hid.

She laughs at the memory.

Well, François opened the stable door—ashes went flying everywhere! And François cursed. *Mon Dieu*, I had never heard anything like it before. And then he started to stamp. I didn't realize it but some of the ashes were live and catching in the hay that lined the stable floor. All I could hear was this stamping and cursing and I thought for sure it was the goblins. So I grabbed a pitchfork and went charging out from my cache. Only to find a very strong and handsome young man stamping out the sparks. We were married six months later.

IGNACE: He loved you. He was my best friend and I know. In spite of everything he always loved you dearly.

THÉRÈSE: In spite of everything.

IGNACE: Believe it. He leaves his heart behind with you.

THÉRÈSE: What will I do, Ignace? How will I get by?

IGNACE: He left you well provided for. In addition to this property there is the farm in the parish of Saint Michel. And as his wife you inherit his interests in the Saint Maurice Ironworks, which include his own investments, the seigneury of Saint Maurice, and a small annual income derived from his having contributed to the lands as a capitol asset. Although there isn't much cash, you should never have to worry. You would receive a generous sum should you choose to liquidate any or all of these assets.

THÉRÈSE: I know. I know.

IGNACE: There is someone who would be interested in taking the Ironworks off your hands. His name is Cugnet and he . . .

THÉRÈSE: I don't want to sell the Ironworks, Ignace.

IGNACE: But it is a tricky business. And the complexities are better managed by those who are knowledgeable in the field.

THÉRÈSE: Then I will learn.

IGNACE: But it would only drain your energy at a time when you should be mourning your husband.

THÉRÈSE: I feel I must carry out his work. I know how important the Ironworks were to François. Perhaps by retaining them, I keep a part of him I never had. By working with you I will get to learn a part of him I never knew. You will advise me, won't you Ignace?

IGNACE: Well, yes, but . . . Thérèse . . . I know you're not thinking clearly with François's death so fresh in your heart. Rest. Think it over. I'll call again in a few days or so. I'm sure that in time you will see that unburdening yourself of the Ironworks is the most reasonable decision . . .

(calls) Angélique.

ANGÉLIQUE: *Oui*, Monsieur Gamelin.

IGNACE: Take care of La Dame de Francheville.

He kisses THÉRÈSE *on the forehead.*

Remember, my dear. He always loved you.

IGNACE *exits. The two women are alone. There is a long awkward silence.* ANGÉLIQUE, *her eyes downcast, stands waiting for some order, as* THÉRÈSE *regards her with a mixed range of emotions.*

THÉRÈSE: *(with a genuine desire to know)* Tell me something?

ANGÉLIQUE: *Oui*, Madame.

THÉRÈSE: *(with difficulty but without malice)* Did you like it?

Beat.

When he came to you at night?

ANGÉLIQUE: No, Madame.

THÉRÈSE: All this time?

ANGÉLIQUE: No, Madame.

THÉRÈSE: Why didn't you come to me?

ANGÉLIQUE: You have punished me for less, Madame.

THÉRÈSE: I have punished you because . . . You could have stopped him. You could have tried to stop him.

ANGÉLIQUE: So could you. He was your husband. The master only took from me what you refused to give.

THÉRÈSE advances on ANGÉLIQUE and in her anger, begins to slap her around.

THÉRÈSE: You ungrateful, jealous, slut. Black bitch. Lying whore. You liked it when he took you. You nigger girls are good for nothing else. You liked it. So don't you lie to me. You liked it.

ANGÉLIQUE grabs her hands.

ANGÉLIQUE: And you didn't. You sent him to me. The fault is yours Madame. Not mine.

ANGÉLIQUE lets her go.

I know that you have lost yourself in grief. I know the anger and the rage of loss. How hard it is to contain. How it needs to unleash itself on something. But I'm not going to let you beat it out on me. Do you understand? Do not strike me again.

THÉRÈSE collapses in her grief and tears.

THÉRÈSE: François . . . François . . .

ANGÉLIQUE: He's gone, Madame. It's just you now. So you have to be strong.

ANGÉLIQUE cradles her.

That's right. Let it out. Let it all out. I know that things haven't been good between us. But that's all going to change now. I'll serve you well. If you will let me. I will serve you.

ACT II

SCENE I

MANON in a spot.

MANON: *La negresse semble de laisser ce premier amant, César, pour tomber dans les bras d'un blanc, Claude Thibault.*

CLAUDE outside in a gentle snow. He speaks as if ANGÉLIQUE is there.

CLAUDE: The thing about snow is that even though together on the ground it all looks the same—each snowflake is different. Each has its own size, shape. Its own tiny crystal pattern.

He tries to catch one.

There. See? Aw, it melted.

He tries again.

Heat is its mortal enemy. So you have to be quick. 'Cause alone, the lifetime of a snowflake is brief. But together, one can last a whole winter. That's why two, or three, or four, or more catch on to each other and fall together. Even snow wants to live . . . as best as it can.

ANGÉLIQUE enters with her hands behind her back.

ANGÉLIQUE: I like how it makes everything quiet. But what I like most about snow is . . . snowballs!

She throws one at him.

CLAUDE: Why you . . . !

He chases her around, playfully. She squeals. He catches her. They fall to the ground, laughing. He kisses her briefly. She kisses him passionately. MANON *creeps in and watches them from the shadows.*

We should be getting back.

ANGÉLIQUE: You go. I want to stay a little while longer.

CLAUDE: I'm not going anywhere without you.

CLAUDE *sings a vibrant and raucous French folk song, such as "En roulant ma boule roulant." He claps and stamps his feet.* ANGÉLIQUE *laughs. He grabs her and tries to dance with her.*

ANGÉLIQUE: Stop! Stop! Stop! Stop!

CLAUDE: You don't like to dance.

ANGÉLIQUE: I can't dance like that. All left feet and straight lines.

CLAUDE: If you just tried a little you would get the hang of it.

ANGÉLIQUE: I have tried. My body refuses to move in that way.

CLAUDE: But I can't dance alone.

ANGÉLIQUE: Why not?

CLAUDE: I don't know. It just doesn't seem right—if there is someone to dance with.

He tries to dance with her again.

ANGÉLIQUE: No.

CLAUDE: Won't you at least try?

ANGÉLIQUE: No.

CLAUDE: Then you show me.

ANGÉLIQUE: What?

CLAUDE: Show me a dance, that you would dance, if you wanted to dance with someone.

ANGÉLIQUE: You would only find it strange.

CLAUDE: No stranger than you find my dancing. Teach me your steps so that I can dance with you.

ANGÉLIQUE: Well, for that we would need a drum, which is forbidden. How can I dance without a drum?

CLAUDE: I can beat out a rhythm for you.

He starts to beat on the ground.

ANGÉLIQUE: No, no, no . . . not like that. Like this.

She beats out a simple rhythm on her clothing. He tries. She shakes her head.

Imagine that you are a drum. Deep and resonant. And the rhythm is the beating of your heart when your spirit is in flight.

She continues beating on herself. He tries again.

Yes! You catch on quick.

CLAUDE: No flies on me.

ANGÉLIQUE laughs and beats a new rhythm which he follows.

ANGÉLIQUE: First you take off like a startled bird. Fluttering with surprise. But as your wings take you higher into the safety of the sky, they calm . . . and beat with a certain, steady pace.

As she speaks, she gradually stops beating on herself as her rhythms are taken up by the real drum.

Yes . . . Up. Up you fly. Your heart thumps loud. Deliberate. Pumping rhythm through your veins. You soar up to the sun. You spiral down to the ground. You careen on the slightest of air. You move . . . unfettered . . . through time and space. There is just the beating of your heart and the beating of the drum taking your body anywhere it wants to go.

She dances, the drums beat, the snow falls around her, and CLAUDE watches with obvious sensual delight. He goes to her and tries to move with her, but he can't keep up. CÉSAR enters and watches. CLAUDE grabs ANGÉLIQUE and kisses her.

Look. It stopped snowing.

CÉSAR: Angélique.

ANGÉLIQUE: *(stepping back from CLAUDE)* César.

CÉSAR: I went looking for you at the house. But your mistress didn't know where you were.

ANGÉLIQUE: I better go see if she needs anything.

CLAUDE: I'll go.

CÉSAR: You wait a minute.

CLAUDE pauses.

ANGÉLIQUE: César . . .

CÉSAR: I want you to stay away from her. You understand.

ANGÉLIQUE: César . . .

CÉSAR: I catch you sniffing around her again . . .

CLAUDE: You'll what? Eh? What are you going to do?

CÉSAR says nothing.

Yeah, that's what I thought.

ANGÉLIQUE: Claude . . . Please?

CLAUDE: Sure.

He kisses her while looking at CÉSAR.

You need anything, just shout.

CLAUDE exits.

CÉSAR: He the reason I don't see you any more?

ANGÉLIQUE: César . . .

CÉSAR: You haven't had enough of one white man you have to have another?

He takes out a flask of Eau de Vie.

And where are you getting this from? Is he giving it to you? No wonder you're acting like you do.

ANGÉLIQUE: And how am I acting?

CÉSAR: Like a drunken whore.

ANGÉLIQUE: Thank you, Brother.

CÉSAR: Look. It's just . . . We're supposed to be together. We have to stick together.

ANGÉLIQUE: Only reason we're together is our masters say so. My master is dead. And I don't plan on replacing him any time soon.

CÉSAR: Your mistress isn't.

ANGÉLIQUE: She doesn't pay no mind to what I do.

CÉSAR: What about me? What am I supposed to do?

ANGÉLIQUE: I don't care what you do, César.

CÉSAR: We're in this together. You can't choose that white man over me?

ANGÉLIQUE: I don't choose you at all! No more than you chose me! If there were five more to choose from you still wouldn't choose me. I'm just all there is. Better than nothing. Claude has a choice. He chooses me.

CÉSAR: Oh, I see. You think you're special. He loves you . . . Dream on. Haven't you been a slave long enough to know that there is only one thing a white man wants from a slave woman.

ANGÉLIQUE: Claude isn't like that. He's different.

CÉSAR: Yeah. Like he's refusing what you're giving out.

ANGÉLIQUE: Yes. I don't give anything. He doesn't take.

CÉSAR: Doesn't mean he don't want.

ANGÉLIQUE: Doesn't mean I won't give.

Beat.

I have been a slave long enough to realize you have to take what happiness you can when you can. Isn't that what you said César?

CÉSAR: Yeah. That's what I said. You're making a big mistake. There's only one thing worse than a rich white master and that's a poor white who wants to be one. You think he's on your side right now. But watch out. 'Cause in the end they are all white together.

CÉSAR exits. MANON follows him. He pushes her away.

SCENE II

ANGÉLIQUE in light. CLAUDE in shadow.

CLAUDE: Deep.

ANGÉLIQUE: I want to be close. To feel love. Choose love. Give . . .

CLAUDE: Rich.

ANGÉLIQUE: Dare I? Trust? Hope?

CLAUDE: Dark.

ANGÉLIQUE: Dare I? Give?

CLAUDE: Ripe.

ANGÉLIQUE: Yes!

CLAUDE comes into the light.

CLAUDE: Mine!

SCENE III

THÉRÈSE, in a red power suit, plays a tug of war with IGNACE Gamelin. They are at the height of their argument.

IGNACE: I tell you, Thérèse, productivity at the Ironworks is down! Way down! And the quality of the iron is plummeting with it!

THÉRÈSE: Then perhaps we are trying to accomplish too much in too short a time. If we just focused on producing in smaller volumes we may find that the quality of the iron we do produce is of a higher standard.

IGNACE: It doesn't work like that, Thérèse. We make a little, we make a lot. The problem is the same. Our castings crack!

THÉRÈSE: Maybe it's as simple as too much sand in the mouldings or . . .

IGNACE: Why do you go on about things you know nothing about and couldn't possibly understand.

THÉRÈSE: Be patient with me, Ignace. I'm just trying to help.

IGNACE: I'm sorry, my dear. But I am running out of patience. And we are running out of time. The bottom line is this. We're losing money. And at the rate we're going, we're not going to make the king's quota. We default on the quota, we lose the king's patronage. We lose Louis's patronage, we lose the Ironworks!

THÉRÈSE: What do you want me to do!?

IGNACE: Sell! Sell your shares in the Ironworks to François Etiennes Cugnet.

THÉRÈSE: I can't, Ignace!

IGNACE: We need him, Thérèse.

THÉRÈSE: I can't, Ignace. I just can't. You need him so badly then why don't you sell.

IGNACE: Because I built this Ironworks! From the ground up! Together with François! And I have invested more than sentimentality. If you loved your husband, you would respect what he was trying to achieve with this enterprise. Instead of trying to destroy it.

THÉRÈSE: I'm not trying to destroy it!

IGNACE: Then sell your shares to Cugnet! And I promise you, you'll be handsomely rewarded.

THÉRÈSE: I can't! I won't!

THÉRÈSE appears to be winning.

IGNACE: Then you will be the ruin of us all!

He lets go. THÉRÈSE falls back on her behind. ANGÉLIQUE helps her up.

SCENE IV

The kitchen.

MANON: I've come for the fish.

ANGÉLIQUE: The fish? What fish?

MANON: The fish you made.

ANGÉLIQUE: I don't make the fish. I just cook it.

MANON: Madame de Francheville promised my mistress some fish.

ANGÉLIQUE: Well, if Madame de Francheville promised . . . Here.

She holds up a fish skeleton but with the head and tail still attached.

It's little thin but it's really tasty. As big as ol' Madame de Beray is, she doesn't need much more.

Beat.

Kinda looks like her, doesn't it? Only prettier.

She uses the fish head to speak.

Eh, *Manon. J'ai faim. Va me chercher un poisson. Je veux manger du poisson. Je suis un poisson. Je vais me manger moi même! (fish wrestling)* Aghhhhh!

She sees that MANON is not amused.

Oh, come on. Laugh, Manon. I'm only trying to have some fun. Life is what it is but we can always share a laugh. Yes?

MANON doesn't reply.

Well, I guess not.

ANGÉLIQUE gives MANON a Corning casserole dish.

Here. Angélique's famous fish stew. I hope the old bitch doesn't choke on it.

MANON takes it and starts to exit. ANGÉLIQUE stops her.

Manon . . . I am only trying to be your friend. I know I get lonely sometimes. Don't you? So far from home. I wish I had a friend, to make the time go lighter.

MANON: César was my friend! He made me laugh. He spoke my language.

ANGÉLIQUE: I didn't know you felt that way about him.

MANON: He was good to me . . . until you came. Maybe when you go he will be good again.

ANGÉLIQUE: It was you he . . . Oh, Manon. I am so sorry. I didn't know . . . Maybe he will make you laugh again. César is free. At least, he's free of me.

MANON: He will never be free of you.

ANGÉLIQUE: But that's not my fault. That wasn't my fault, Manon. You can't blame me . . .

MANON: When you go . . .

MANON exits.

ANGÉLIQUE: But I'm not going . . .

SCENE V

THÉRÈSE at her computer.

THÉRÈSE: As of Monday, you'll be staying at the home of my brother-in-law, Alexis Lemoine Monière.

ANGÉLIQUE: Madame . . .?

THÉRÈSE: You will stay there until the first canoe leaves for Quebec—where I have made arrangements for you to be sold to Monsieur Cugnet.

ANGÉLIQUE: Sold . . .

VOICEOVER: *(whispered)* Angélique . . . Angélique?

ANGÉLIQUE: Madame . . . No . . . Madame, please . . . you can't . . .

THÉRÈSE: I can. And I have.

ANGÉLIQUE: But I belong to Monsieur.

VOICEOVER: *(whispered)* Angélique . . . Angélique?

THÉRÈSE: You belong to me. Did you think you were freed by his death?

ANGÉLIQUE: But why, Madame? Why? I thought things were better, Madame. I thought I was serving you better . . . No one ever served you better.

THÉRÈSE: *(calmly)* I don't want you. I have never wanted you here. And I welcome the opportunity to be rid of you. You have brought nothing but unhappiness and misery into my home. You will lie with anyone. César. My husband. Now Claude. Gamelin is right. You are like animals. *Vous êtes trop matinée.* I cannot live with that. I have had no choice but to endure your presence while François lived. But now that's over.

ANGÉLIQUE grovels at THÉRÈSE's feet.

ANGÉLIQUE: You can't sell me, Madame, please don't sell me.

VOICEOVER: *(whispered)* Angélique . . . Angélique?

ANGÉLIQUE: I can't take another master. I can't. Master after master. Never knowing which one will be the death of me. I can't go though this all over again.

THÉRÈSE: It is too late. The arrangements have been made.

ANGÉLIQUE: No! Madame. Please. Please . . .

THÉRÈSE exits.

SCENE VI

Fury.

ANGÉLIQUE: YOU BITCH! I WON'T TAKE ANOTHER MASTER! I'LL KILL BEFORE I HAVE ANOTHER MASTER! I'LL KILL YOU! I'll strangle you in your sleep! I'll poison your food! You stingy whore! I'll make you rue the day you sell me! I'll . . . I'll . . .

CLAUDE: Calm down . . .

ANGÉLIQUE: Take me to New England! Now!

CLAUDE: But that's impossible.

ANGÉLIQUE: You promised me, Claude.

CLAUDE: But we can't just pick up and leave like that.

ANGÉLIQUE: Then I will go alone!

CLAUDE: You'll never make it.

ANGÉLIQUE: I don't care!

CLAUDE: Wait. Listen.

She struggles with him.

Listen to me. I'll take you. I made a promise and I won't break it. But we can't leave now. I have to plan our escape carefully. 'Cause we'll only get one stab at it. We get caught we're as good as dead. Until then, just sit tight.

ANGÉLIQUE: How will we know when the time is right?

CLAUDE: Don't worry. You'll know.

SCENE VII

MANON works outside, singing quietly to herself. ANGÉLIQUE enters and works at her separate tasks. There is some distance between them. There is a large cracking sound.

ANGÉLIQUE: What was that?

MANON: The ice.

CLAUDE walks through with a sack of potatoes.

CLAUDE: It's certainly warming up.

(to ANGÉLIQUE) Soon.

He begins to whistle a lively tune.

ANGÉLIQUE: *(softly to MANON)* When we crossed the great river, some leapt into the water to become froth upon the waves. Some hunkered on their haunches and simply willed themselves to sleep. 'Cause when the spirit leaves the body it flies home to the motherland. What do you see when you look to the river?

MANON does not respond.

What do you hear?

They look at each other.

How fast your heart must beat when you look in that direction. Knowing home is close and yet impossible to reach. Does not your spirit yearn to fly this place? Are not your memories still fresh? How do you stop your feet from taking you to where you belong?

MANON: I am where I belong.

THÉRÈSE and IGNACE crossing through the scene.

THÉRÈSE: . . .six hundred pounds!

IGNACE: For her? *(referring to ANGÉLIQUE)*

THÉRÈSE: Yes. Have I done well in my negotiations?

IGNACE: Not bad.

THÉRÈSE: Perhaps I will be a good entrepreneur after all.

IGNACE: Well, I wouldn't go that far.

THÉRÈSE: *(laughing)* Oh, Ignace.

They exit.

ANGÉLIQUE: Bitch!

MANON laughs.

You think that's funny? You won't be laughing when the same thing happens to you.

MANON: They say you come from the land of the devil. That the Blackness of your skin is the blackness of your soul scorched by the fires of hell.

ANGÉLIQUE: They say that you are bloodthirsty savages. Pagan children, shameless in their nakedness. What does it matter what they say. We are here. Today!

MANON: We are not the same. I serve. I do not slave.

ANGÉLIQUE: A dog and a jackal meet in the forest. "How is it," asks the jackal, "that you are so fat and I am so poor and we are both the same animal?"

The dog says, "I lay around my master's house and let him kick me and he gives me food." "Better then," says the jackal, "that I stay poor."

MANON: Look. Just leave me alone. Okay? Our ways are different. Our stories. Our paths.

ANGÉLIQUE: I'm sorry. I thought I recognized something old and familiar.

MANON: I don't follow you. Do not follow me.

ANGÉLIQUE: I won't. You have forgotten the way.

SCENE VIII

All voices in unison: "April 10, 1734."

MANON is shovelling hot coals into a bucket.

MANON: My raging heart,
Wey a hey a
Is filled with pain,
Wey a hey a
My César's frost,
Wey a hey a
is searing me,
Wey a hey a.

My blood flows hot,
Wey a hey a
My breath blows cold,
Wey a hey a
Memories of his love,
Wey a hey a
Still burn in me,
Wey a hey.

She ululates. CÉSAR *enters with a cigar, matches, and cigar scissors. He takes the bucket from* MANON *and prepares the cigar for smoking.*

CÉSAR: I smile. I grin. I keep my eyes averted. I "*Oui*, Monsieur." "*Non*, Monsieur." "Right away, Monsieur." I do whatever I have to do to "just get along." It's survival in the white man's world. And I get by. Why fight what I can't change? But don't think that makes me any less a man.

Don't look at me too closely. You'll see the smile is on my lips not in my eyes which see everything. And though my head is bent, my backbone's strong. My shoulders broad and powerful. And these hands could crush a windpipe just like an autumn leaf. But I don't fight. I'll do whatever I gotta do to "just get along."

Claude thinks that he can beat me with a word. 'Cause in this world where white is might a word is all it takes to silence. But I am a patient man. I'll wait it out. And when the time is right.

He hands the cigar to IGNACE *and lights a match.*

I'll strike!

He hands the cigar to IGNACE, *who takes a light from* CÉSAR. *He puffs on the cigar a bit, with satisfaction, before speaking.* CÉSAR *puts the pail beside him.*

IGNACE: Women have no place in business. Their minds can't seem to get around their emotions. And there is no room in business for emotion. I let Thérèse have her way. But she will sell.

He puffs.

Eventually, she'll have to sell.

He flicks his ash into the bucket.

THÉRÈSE *enters with a candle and slowly makes her way across the stage, occasionally stopping and looking behind her, as if she is being pursued by something which isn't there.*

She stops.

THÉRÈSE: Who's there? Angélique?

Silence.

There are too many noises in this house. Creeks and bumps. Sounds I can't identify. Hear that?

She stops, listens, whispers.

Angélique?

She continues.

This is my house! I know this house. I love this house. But everything sounds strange to me. Cats cry each night. Dogs howl. Horses stamp their feet. They sense it too.

She stops.

Who's there? Angélique?

Pause.

Les Lutins. Yes. Goblins. They're back. I didn't think they could stray so far from farms. But yes! *Les Lutins.* That makes sense.

She relaxes.

Yes. Goblins. I can deal with goblins. Goblins and Angélique. Both, I can be rid of.

She takes the bucket and hands it to CLAUDE, *who enters with an oil lamp.*

CLAUDE: I'm going to be somebody someday. You think I'm going to be hauling buckets and shovelling horseshit all my life? Not me. I'll be as big as de Francheville one day. Bigger. You see, I am. I am more than . . . I am more than this!

In New France, I'll never be more than peasant scum who signed five years of his life away for some new clothes, a few bags of grain and a stony piece of land that may never bear fruit. But in New England or farther south, there's no telling what a man could make of himself! Yes. There's money to be made in the colonies. And, you know what . . .?

He puts the bucket down and gives ANGÉLIQUE *a passionate kiss.*

I'm going to make me some.

ANGÉLIQUE: Love. I had almost forgotten it felt like . . . freedom.

CLAUDE: Soon.

He exits, leaving the pail with ANGÉLIQUE.

ANGÉLIQUE: How long can I wait? Each minute brings me closer to a living death. And I'm alive. I am alive!

His touches burn, sear, scorch, igniting fire deep inside where pain and ice had been. And I feel . . . heat, life, force, power; Black and strong.

She envies that. Cold, passionless bitch! Just like her bastard husband. Both sucking. Sucking life. Denying life.

No! I am not a chair, a sack of grain, or a calf to be fattened and sold for slaughter! I am alive. And loved. And I can't wait . . . any longer.

Smoke begins to fill the stage.

THÉRÈSE: Fire!

ANGÉLIQUE: Fire!

IGNACE: Fire!

CÉSAR: Fire!

Pandemonium breaks out. Church bells ringing, people shouting, panicking. The actors run around and organize themselves into a line in which buckets pass from person to person. ANGÉLIQUE *is at the end of the line. Buckets pass swiftly and desperately from person to person.* CLAUDE *enters, picking his teeth. Watches silently for a moment.* ANGÉLIQUE *turns to grab another bucket, sees* CLAUDE *and, instead, grabs* CLAUDE*'s hand.*

ANGÉLIQUE: Now?

CLAUDE: Now!

They run. The line continues to battle the flames which mount higher and higher. They turn and speak rapidly.

ANGÉLIQUE: The fire was set at the St. Paul Street house of her mistress, in the evening of April 10, 1734.

CLAUDE: The flames travelled quickly from one house to another and, later, to L'Hotel Dieu where the neighbours had started to transport their furniture and belongings.

ANGÉLIQUE: The convent and the church were destroyed.

CLAUDE: This was the third time L'Hotel Dieu had been engulfed by flames.

ANGÉLIQUE: By the time the fire died, forty-six homes would be consumed.

SCENE IX

Reporting not unlike "Current Affairs." These scenes are a series of sound bites that play over or are intercut with the ensuing scenes of ANGÉLIQUE *and* CLAUDE.

REPORTER: It's been determined that yesterday's fire was set by the negress slave of the widow de Francheville, who has escaped with a man named Thibault, also working for de Francheville.

Rumour has it that the negress has often threatened her mistress and the city with the setting of a fire, and that on the same day said that neither her mistress nor many more would sleep in their houses that night. The King's Attorney is calling for the arrest of the negress and the said Thibault.

SCENE X

ANGÉLIQUE *and* CLAUDE *at a barn near Longueuil. The wind whistles.*

CLAUDE: This way . . . quick . . . get down.

ANGÉLIQUE: Why are we stopping . . .?

CLAUDE: Here. Stuff these in your bag . . .

ANGÉLIQUE: Bread . . .?

CLAUDE: Six loaves. I hid them two days ago when Madame sent me to Longueuil. It's not much but . . .

ANGÉLIQUE: Two days ago? Which way now?

CLAUDE: That way. Chemin Chambly.

They run off.

SCENE XI

THÉRÈSE *testifies among the ruins.*

THÉRÈSE: Thérèse de Couagne. Age thirty-seven. I don't know who set the fire in my house. I did not see the negress go upstairs to the attic unless it was between noon and one o'clock when I went to church for the blessed sacrament. Thibault did come to me the night before and asked to be paid for the time he had worked as my farmer. I told him that I sold the negress and that I didn't want him back in my house either. But I cannot, in all honesty, suspect the negress because there were no fires in my chimneys that day.

SCENE XII

ANGÉLIQUE and CLAUDE off Chemin de Chambly. They are wrapped in a thick black blanket. Covered by darkness. We hear the thundering sound of horses, wooden wheels turning on a rocky road, throwing the shadow of its spokes on the mound of the blanket where we see just the faces of ANGÉLIQUE and CLAUDE frozen with fear, panic, desperation. The sound subsides as it moves into the distance. They remain immobile until there is stillness. Then ANGÉLIQUE and CLAUDE slowly emerge out of the darkness into the dim cast of moonlight.

SCENE XIII

IGNACE sits comfortably in an armchair. He is obviously at home and untouched by the fire. CÉSAR stands by him. He testifies.

IGNACE: Ignace Gamelin. And I am old enough to be your father!

Slaves are notoriously inefficient and unwilling. A horse—if it is well treated and cared for, will gladly return all the effort which a well-loved master demands. Some slaves are like horses in this respect.

He smiles at CÉSAR.

But most are not. Their sense of freedom chafes at restraint. To kindness and forbearance they return insolence and contempt. Nothing awes or governs them but the whip or the dread of sale.

It's fascinating . . . While kept in subjugation, they are submissive and easy to control. But let any of them be indulged with the hope of freedom. Then they reject all restraint and become wholly unmanageable: as is the case with this heinous act of arson. It is by the expectation of liberty, and by that alone, that they can be rendered a threat to the population.

SCENE XIV

The woods. ANGÉLIQUE sits in frustration.

ANGÉLIQUE: The same. Everything looks the same. Those trees, this rock . . . Are you sure we're not just running around in circles?

CLAUDE: *(angrily)* Look. I know where I am going! Okay?

ANGÉLIQUE: *(surprised)* Okay, Claude. *(as he stalks off)* Okay.

She follows.

SCENE XV

Testimony.

MANON: Manon, Huron. Age, nineteen. Just hours before the fire, Angélique came over to me and tried to make me laugh. But I wasn't in the mood. She said, "You really don't want to laugh? You see Madame de Francheville there laughing with Monsieur Gamelin? Well, she won't have a house to sleep in." Angélique thought that was funny.

SCENE XVI

ANGÉLIQUE and CLAUDE in the woods. Cold, dirty, tired.

ANGÉLIQUE: I don't want to take the chance.

CLAUDE: But we're so far away. They have probably stopped looking for us by now.

ANGÉLIQUE: What if they haven't? If we light a fire the smoke will lead them right to us.

CLAUDE: Angélique. It's been days since we've been indoors. We'll freeze to death.

Beat.

ANGÉLIQUE: No we won't. Come here.

He goes to her and she wraps herself around him and kisses him.

We're going to make it.

She starts to make love to him.

SCENE XVII

The testimonies continue. The following testimonies are doubled by the remaining cast. These are like the specious and ridiculous eye-witnesses often seen on many sensational news programs.

MARGEURITE: Margeurite de Couagne. Age ten. I don't know who set the fire in my aunt's house but just before the fire Angélique was sulking in the kitchen and then I saw her leave by the door on the street and go talk to Mr. de Beray's Indian, Manon. Since then I have heard say that the negress said to the *panisse* that neither she nor her master would sleep in their house. That's all I know, except that two or three times before the fire, the man named Thibault was with the negress in Madame de Francheville's kitchen.

HYPOLITE: Hypolite Lebert, esquire. Age fifteen. I don't know who set the fire in Madame de Francheville's house. But I heard Monsieur de Beray's Indian say to Madame de Francheville that her negress said to her that Mrs. de Francheville would not sleep in her house.

JEANNE: Jeanne Taillandier de la Baume. Age forty-one. I can't positively say that the fire was started by the negress but when it started I thought for sure it was the negress who started it. I have heard from some children that the negress was threatening to burn her mistress and strangle her and that the negress has said that if she could go back to her country and there were Frenchmen there—she would make them all perish.

The testimonies begin to overlap.

MARIE: Marie Louise Poirier. Age twenty-five. I cannot say anything about the fire but I have heard that the negress said that if she ever returned to her country and there were white people there she would burn them like dogs. That we were worthless. I also know for a fact that the negress stole three deerskins from Madame de Francheville.

JEAN: Jean Joseph Boudard—forty-one. All I know are the rumours I've heard that it was the wicked negress of Madame de Francheville who set the fire. But sometimes I would see her drinking *Eau de Vie* . . .

FRANÇOIS: François de Beray. All I know is what Manon told me. That a short time before the fire, the negress told her that her mistress would not sleep in her house . . .

The REPORTER *cutting though the cacophony.*

REPORTER: In dramatic new developments in the O. J.—I mean M. J. Angélique—case, four-year-old Amable Lemoine was brought before the court. Amable, daughter of Alexis Lemoine Monière and brother-in-law of Madame de Francheville, who swore under oath to tell the truth, testified that on the day of the fire she saw the negress, Marie-Joseph Angélique, carrying a coal shuttle up to the attic.

SCENE XVIII

Black. The sound of two wild animals fighting. In the ensuing silence we hear . . .

CLAUDE: I'm afraid.

SCENE XIX

CLAUDE and ANGÉLIQUE, wet, ragged, dirty, tired, in the woods.

CLAUDE: If we don't find food, we'll starve to death.

ANGÉLIQUE: We'll be in New England soon. It's been almost two weeks.

CLAUDE: I don't know. I don't know. I was thinking. We passed a cabin a little while back . . .

ANGÉLIQUE: That was days ago . . .

CLAUDE: There could be food . . . warmth . . .

ANGÉLIQUE: You want to go back?

CLAUDE: Go back . . .?

ANGÉLIQUE: We can never go back.

CLAUDE: Not after what's happened. Not after . . .

ANGÉLIQUE: What?

CLAUDE: You know. The fire.

ANGÉLIQUE: What's that got to do with us?

CLAUDE: It doesn't matter now.

ANGÉLIQUE: Claude, you didn't start that fire? Did you?

CLAUDE regards her for a long moment.

CLAUDE: No.

ANGÉLIQUE: Then what do we care! Let's just try to leave it all behind.

She tries to raise his spirits.

It's hard. I know. Sometimes I doubt we're ever going to make it. But we've come this far. We're still alive. And close. New England feels so close. If we can just keep pushing forward . . .

CLAUDE: Angélique . . . ?

ANGÉLIQUE: Yes . . .

CLAUDE: . . . you're right.

He pulls her closer to him.

And when we get to New England, we'll dine on pheasant and roasted potatoes and wash it all down with tankards of beer . . .

ANGÉLIQUE: Stop. Stop. You're making it worse.

CLAUDE: I know. My stomach is cramping at the thought.

ANGÉLIQUE: Will they have ships there?

CLAUDE: Maybe . . .

ANGÉLIQUE: Then I will take you home. You will like my land. It's warmer there. And always green. And food hangs from the trees.

CLAUDE: Just like the Garden of Eden.

ANGÉLIQUE: You will see. You'll see.

She curls up against him and sleeps.

SCENE XX

ANGÉLIQUE sleeps.

CLAUDE: I remember watching my mother's back—always bent, her shirt sleeves rolled above the wrinkles on her elbows. The skin on her arms and hands—rough and red and flaky. She scrubbed laundry for the rich . . . for pennies. Some days I would beg more than she earned.

And I promised myself that before I left this miserable world, I would become something more than just another hungry peasant or a common petty thief.

So I jumped at the chance to come to this new world. There are opportunities here that I can't even begin to imagine. Just sitting there waiting to be discovered.

I've done everything for you. I've burnt . . . I've burnt down my dreams for you. But with you, I'll always be running. And I can't run anymore. I can't. I'm sorry. I just can't do it. Please . . . understand. I can't. I can't. I can't.

He runs off.

SCENE XXI

ANGÉLIQUE wakes up alone in the woods to the lonely whistling of the wind through the trees.

ANGÉLIQUE: Claude . . . Claude . . . ? I had a dream. Claude? We were in New England. But it wasn't New England. It was my village, Claude. Home! I was home. And the sun was setting below the water just as the fire was rising. And you were there. Claude? That's a good sign . . . Yes? Claude?

Pause.

Where are you?

Pause.

Claude, are you there?

Silence.

Claaaude!

No response. ANGÉLIQUE *listens. Searches for him in all directions with the growing realization that she is alone in the woods. Somewhere, she doesn't know where. Abandoned. No food. No idea of what direction she should follow. She sits, refusing to cry.*

It was a good sign. Claude. We could have made it.

SCENE XXII

The lights slowly fall and rise like the setting and the dawning of the sun. ANGÉLIQUE *sits in the same place staring out into space. She begins to softly sing a long-forgotten song of her homeland—accompanied by the muted beating of a drum. Over the course of this speech, two men come and drag her off.*

She does not resist.

The speech continues on an empty stage.

VOICEOVER: Marie-Joseph Angélique is declared guilty of setting the fire to Madame de Francheville's house, which proceeded to burn down the city. For redress of the damages caused by the fire, and other facts mentioned at the trial, she will make public amends by wearing a shirt only, with a noose around her neck, holding in her hands a burning torch weighing two pounds, in front of the main door and entrance of the parish church of this city, where she will be taken by the executioner of the high court in a tip cart used to pick up garbage and wearing a sign inscribed with the word "arsonist" on her front and back. There, on her knees, will she declare in a loud and clear voice that she wickedly and ill-advisedly set the fire, for which she repents and asks God, the king, and justice for forgiveness. This done, she will be taken to the public place of the said city of Montreal, to be hanged and strangled to death from the gallows erected for that purpose, her body burned at the stake, the ashes scattered to the wind, and her belongings seized in the name of the king. Prior, the accused will be tortured in both the ordinary and extraordinary means to reveal the identity of her accomplices and concerning the said Thibault.

SCENE XXIII

FRANÇOIS enters, dressed in neutral modern clothes, and reads from a book.

FRANÇOIS: Monday, June 21, 1734. Seven a.m. The accused had her shoes taken off and was put on the torture seat by the torturer, and after she'd been strapped in the usual manner with the buskins tied, the accused said . . .

During this CLAUDE enters dressed in the same fashion, as do all the actors.

CLAUDE: She has no knowledge of anyone and that it's not her. She said "no one helped her because she didn't set the fire."

FRANÇOIS: After the wedge was tightened she said I want to die . . .

CÉSAR enters.

CÉSAR: At the second blow, she said I'd rather die. No one set, or has helped me set the fire.

MANON enters.

MANON: At the third blow, she said the same.

THÉRÈSE enters.

THÉRÈSE: At the fourth blow she said to hang her, that it was her alone.

IGNACE enters.

IGNACE: After that, for the extraordinary torture, we had a second wedge put in and hit . . . and hit . . . and hit . . . and hit . . .

FRANÇOIS: She said . . .

CÉSAR: Kill me.

MANON: It's me alone.

THÉRÈSE: Hang me. It's me.

ANGÉLIQUE enters. She is barefoot and naked under a rough raw cotton period shirt.

THIBAULT: It's me with a hot plate. No one did it with me.

ANGÉLIQUE: No one helped me, nor suggested it. It was my own initiative.

She takes the book.

It's me, Monsieurs. Let me die.

She closes the book.

SCENE XXIV

ANGÉLIQUE steps up to a microphone.

ANGÉLIQUE: My name is Marie-Joseph Angélique.
I am twenty-nine years old.
I came from Portugal, from the island of Madiere
where I was sold to a Flemish,
who brought me to this New World
and sold me to Monsieur de Francheville.
But before . . .
before . . .

Look!
The view is clear . . .
So clear from here.
In the vista of tomorrow
stretching out before,
I can see this city . . .
swarming with ebony.
There's me and me and me and me . . .
My brothers and my sisters!

My brothers and my sisters . . .
Arrested for their difference.
Their misery
a silent scream,
rising to crescendo
and
falling on deaf ears.

There is nothing I can say to change what you perceive.
I will from twisted history,
be guilty in your eyes.
If thought is sin
then I am guilty.
For I wish that I had fanned the flames that lead to your destruction.
But though I am wretched,
I am not wicked.

Almost ecstatic.

Take my breath.
Burn my body.
Throw my ashes to the wind.
Set my spirit free.
The truth cannot be silenced.
Someday,
someone will hear me
and believe . . .
I didn't do it.

Until then . . .

Drums start beating softly and grow.

I am going home.

The hangman goes to put the noose around her neck. She takes it from him.

Can you see the fires rise to greet the sunset?

She puts the noose around her own neck. A male voice calls softly from the crowd.

CLAUDE: *(whispered)* Angélique. Angélique.

The soft sound of drums building.

ANGÉLIQUE: Do you hear it? Drums!

The sound of the platform giving way beneath her. Her silhouetted figure dancing on wall. The overpowering sound of drums. Black.

The end.

PLEASE DO NOT TOUCH THE INDIANS

JOSEPH A. DANDURAND

A JOURNEY THROUGH ANTI-COLONIAL DRAMATURGIES AND SPIRITUAL TIMES IN JOSEPH A. DANDURAND'S *PLEASE DO NOT TOUCH THE INDIANS*

LINDSAY LACHANCE

The structures and discourses that make up the field of Canadian theatre studies originate in Eurocentric traditions that do not automatically consider Indigenous worldviews and ways of knowing. Similarly, Canadian theatre historiography often overlooks the political, artistic, and cultural importance of the Native Theatre Movement of the late 1970s.[1] In our current era, constantly surrounded by discourses around reconciliation, *Please Do Not Touch the Indians* reminds readers about the significance of testimony, storytelling, community, and sharing; the play lays a path for Indigenous peoples both to remember and to mobilize. Joseph A. Dandurand, a member of the Kwantlen First Nation (Stó:lō), challenges stereotypes of the stoic / warrior / drunken Indian by weaving Indigenous cultural and spiritual knowledge through the play's non-linear, episodic scenes.[2]

Indigenous theatre historiography is not clearly mapped or neatly summarized in a book somewhere. It is alive—it is shape-shifting and developing as we continue to learn, make, and share with one another. Fortunately, artist-scholars like Carol Greyeyes, Yvette Nolan, Jill Carter, and Marrie Mumford, have shared their experiences during the early development of the Native Theatre

1 Features of the Native Theatre Movement include Indigenous peoples' political resistance to Trudeau's 1969 attempt to implement "The White Paper," the 1972 founding of the Association for Native Development in the Performing & Visual Arts (ANDPVA), and the 1974 creation of Native Theatre School (Centre for Indigenous Theatre).

2 For biographical information on Dandurand, see Monique Mojica and Ric Knowles, eds., *Staging Coyote's Dream: An Anthology of First Nations Drama in English,* Volume II (Toronto: Playwrights Canada, 2008), 285.

Movement on Turtle Island in the 1970s. They acknowledge the significance of claiming space to tell our stories, play our characters, direct our plays, and hear our languages onstage. In her article "On the Trail of Native Theatre," Carol Greyeyes traces her own artistic journey alongside the emergence of Native theatre in Canada, framing the theatrical movement as a political act of cultural resurgence. Greyeyes explains, "at the time Canadian Native Theatre was beginning to emerge, the standard definition of theatre had become so codified that any type of cultural expression or performance that didn't fit within those narrow parameters was not considered real theatre in the Eurocentric western tradition of theatre."[3] Greyeyes highlights how, although Indigenous characters appeared on stage in professional theatre productions throughout the twentieth century, it was not until the late 1970s and early 1980s that Indigenous theatre practitioners were cast in or creating those roles.[4] The Native Theatre Movement initiated the shift to a "by us, for us" model.

Algonquin theatre practitioner Yvette Nolan identifies 1982 as the year that marked the beginning of formal, contemporary Indigenous theatre in Canada.[5] In Toronto, a group of Indigenous and non-Indigenous artists founded a "place where Native writers, actors, directors, designers, and technicians could work together to create theatre that expressed the Aboriginal experience in Canada: Native Earth Performing Arts."[6] Meanwhile, Métis artist-activist Maria Campbell worked with non-Aboriginal actor and playwright Linda Griffiths and director Paul Thompson on the play *Jessica*. Then, in 1984, Shirley Cheechoo founded De-ba-jeh-muh-jig Theatre[7] on Wikwemikong unceded territory (Manitoulin Island). Seeing this work devoted to the creation and wider exposure of First Nations theatre, Indigenous artists began to generate works they believed would better reflect their artistic goals and political interests.

I see Indigenous theatre on Turtle Island developing within a historical framework of four waves, the first two of which were dominated by settler artists and the second two of which saw Indigenous artists taking control of how Indigenous peoples were represented. During the first wave, Indigenous peoples

3 Carol Greyeyes, "On the Trail of Native Theatre," in *Performing Indigeneity*, ed. Yvette Nolan and Ric Knowles (Toronto: Playwrights Canada, 2016), 99.

4 Some of these include *The Ecstasy of Rita Joe* (1967), *Jessica* (1982), *Shadow People* (1984), and *The Rez Sisters* (1986).

5 Yvette Nolan, "Aboriginal Theatre in Canada," *NAC-CAN*, 2008, http://www4.nac-cna.ca/pdf/eth/aboriginal_theatre.pdf.

6 Ibid.

7 Now called Debajehmujig Theatre Group at the Debajehmujig Creation Centre.

were depicted in ways that did not accurately represent—and often actively damaged—their cultures and worldviews. A very early example of this is Marc Lescarbot's *Le Théâtre de Neptune en La Nouvelle-France*, written in 1606, which portrays Indigenous characters in stereotypical ways. Characters like "Indian" and "Second Indian" represent widespread clichés like the "Noble Savage" or the "Wise Elder," creating conditions for active misrecognitions.[8] These stereotypes and misrecognitions continued to be used by playwrights for generations, leaving Indigenous characters to be fetishized by non-Indigenous creators.

In the second wave, non-Indigenous scholars and artists began to research Indigenous identity, culture, and spirituality, and started to reflect that research in their writing. The main critique levelled at second-wave writing is that authors distorted people or events in order to tell emotionally effective stories or to make political points, often leading to an overemphasis on victimization. George Ryga's *The Ecstasy of Rita Joe* (1967) epitomizes second-wave writing, reflecting non-Indigenous perceptions. Initial performances of this play included a few Indigenous actors (Chief Dan George and Margo Kane), but Indigenous peoples were not involved in character or plot development. *The Ecstasy of Rita Joe* had the potential to stimulate critical thought about social issues affecting urban Indigenous people and to expose the effects of settler colonialism, urbanization, and forced religious conversion on Indigenous peoples. Instead, by setting the bulk of the play in courtrooms and by having it culminate in Rita Joe's violent murder, Ryga's play perpetuates stereotypes about Indigenous people and themes of victimization that characterize second-wave writing. Despite this, Ryga's work continues to be performed. Theatre historians and scholars might reconsider Ryga's play today by contextualizing it in relation to the Murdered and Missing Indigenous Women crisis, specifically considering Canada's insufficient uridicial and political action to resolve this crisis, and in relation to the intergenerational effects of settler colonialism on Indigenous peoples. Fortunately, Indigenous playwrights like Margo Kane, Floyd Favel, Marie Clements, Yvette Nolan, and Joseph A. Dandurand are challenging the stereotypes that linger from first- and second-wave writings.

While first- and second-wave writings are essentially settler representations of Indigenous arts, cultures, and lives, third- and fourth-wave writings exemplify Indigenous self-representation and sovereignty. Examples of third-wave writing began to appear in the late 1970s with the arrival of the politically charged Native Theatre Movement. Influenced by socio-political movements of

8 Brian Kennedy. *The Baron Bold and the Beauteous Maid: A Compact History of Canadian Theatre* (Toronto: Playwrights Canada, 2004), 8.

that time,[9] Indigenous artists began to use their bodies and voices to manifest their experiences on contemporary stages. Because of the groundwork laid by these founding artists, we see Indigenous practitioners consciously privilege and politicize Indigenous ways of knowing in contemporary theatre. The third wave is ongoing today, and occurs in conjunction with the fourth wave: the primary difference between the two is that the fourth wave marks the arrival of Indigenous critical reflection on creative practice and performance. Indigenous peoples are producing a tremendous amount of work, on urban and community stages, in public spaces and art galleries, which foregrounds and evaluates questions of aesthetics, performance, and reception. Indigenous scholars are expanding Indigenous theatre studies into a distinct critical field. This is clearly seen in Yvette Nolan's book *Medicine Shows: Indigenous Performance Culture,* as well as her anthology *Performing Indigeneity,*[10] which demonstrate the diverse ways Indigenous theatre practitioners have been reclaiming creative and spiritual practices in order to articulate culturally specific worldviews and discourses.

Beginning by overviewing Indigenous theatre's presence and history on Turtle Island allows us to see how theatre is politically connected to the colonial past and the ongoing manifestations of this history in the present. The emergence of Indigenous dramaturgies is of particular importance because culturally specific dramaturgies allow writers to create fictional worlds that work in relationship with Indigenous knowledges, worldviews, experiences, and futures. The non-linear and disjointed use of time, place, and space in *Please Do Not Touch the Indians* embody Indigenous protocols, ontologies, and politics. The play, furthermore, demonstrates how an anti-colonial dramaturgical structure can contest and challenge the misrepresentations and misunderstandings that surround past and present Indigenous identities.

Indigenous dramaturgies differ from other dramaturgical structures as they are thematic rather than narrative or plot driven. This means that the content—Indigenous ideologies, worldviews, and protocols—manifests in *how* the story is told and holds meaning in terms of *why* it's told in such a way. In the case of *Please Do Not Touch the Indians,* Dandurand's use of non-linear dramaturgy

9 Such as the American Indian Movement, Constitution Express, and Red Power Movements. For more information see Arthur Manuel and Grand Chief Ronald M. Derrickson, *Unsettling Canada: A National Wake-up Call* (Toronto: Between the Lines, 2015).

10 See Yvette Nolan, *Medicine Shows: Indigenous Performance Culture* (Toronto: Playwrights Canada, 2015) and Yvette Nolan and Ric Knowles, eds., *Performing Indigeneity: New Essays on Canadian Theatre Volume 6* (Toronto: Playwrights Canada, 2016).

allows readers to deeply engage with the specific themes of cosmology and spirituality that the play explores. Divided into two acts, the scenes appear in repetitive cycles that begin with a tourist observing and meddling in a world of characters that he never cares to get to know fully. This non-linear structure includes visions, dreams, and memories that allow theatre to connect audiences to the natural world, Indigenous protocols, and ways of life. A dominant theme in the play is the idea that Indigenous cosmology is constantly present, that the spirit world and the living world exist simultaneously. This notion of co-existing time is privileged in Indigenous worldviews, allowing peoples to maintain their relationships with those in both the real and the spirit worlds. Indigenous worldviews presuppose a fundamental link between humans, spiritual figures, and the earth—an "all my relations" philosophy. This philosophy manifests in the play through storytelling, testimony, teachings, relationships with the animal and spiritual worlds, and the courage to move forward. Manifesting these traditions makes up the actual structure of *Please Do Not Touch the Indians.* Indigenous cosmology and identities are also presenced in the play's ambiguous and cyclical setting.

Set somewhere in the spirit world, at times within the memories and visions of the characters, and at others in an ambiguous present, relations gather to tell their stories and to generate a new one together. Although Dandurand does not explicitly state where or when the play takes place—the passing of time is only indicated by the natural cycle of leaves falling or found on the stage floor—this ambiguity is a strength, making visible the shared reality to which all of the characters belong. This also allows for the embodying of multiple temporalities (spiritual time, natural time) rather than limiting the play to the representation of the singular or "real" time of western dramaturgy.

The play's cosmological perspective manifests in its gathering of a woman, a man, a coyote, a raven, and a wolf who offer tobacco, share stories, and play marbles as a form of resistance to the visual, physical, and emotional violence that have been enacted against them by strangers, adopted families, and institutionalized colonial powers. The characters, Sister Coyote and Brother Raven, "possess the qualities of their trickster namesakes," which indicates a visual form of Indigenous sovereignty as the characters wear the animal names and navigate their physical traits.[11] Indigenous peoples have relations with animal and spiritual beings that are not always visible in our day-to-day lives and Dandurand manifests these relations throughout his play. Indigenous worldviews are seen through the aesthetics of this playtext, in the animal characters, the vision

11 Christy Stanlake, *Native American Drama A Critical Perspective* (New York: Cambridge UP, 2009), 22.

scenes, and the use of offstage voices. This activates Indigenous dramaturgies by pointing directly to the co-existence of the spiritual and living worlds and allowing for relations from different times or places to be together in the same scenes. *Please Do Not Touch the Indian's* non-linear structure works with the play's language and content to remind readers of Canada's omnipresent colonial impacts.

In the play's dialogue, Dandurand speaks to a wide range of events in Canada's colonial past and present that affect the lives of Indigenous peoples; the temporal and physical ambiguity allows for all these events to be present together on stage. Throughout, references are made to the sexual, physical, emotional, and spiritual violence inflicted upon children at residential schools, to abuse at the hands of foster parents and the impact of the Sixties Scoop, and to the damaging effects of stereotypes promoted in mainstream media and Eurocentric education systems. Through monologues and flashbacks, Dandurand allows his characters to share their stories of violence and trauma as a means of having their experiences remembered. The characters claim space for their realities and ensure that their experiences are not forgotten or erased.

In particular, the tourist's repeated action of taking photos of "Wooden Man" and "Wooden Woman" draws attention to exploitation by non-Indigenous people. The play's ambiguous temporality allows Dandurand to suggest neither that colonialism is in the past nor that the past must determine the future; instead the play ultimately embodies a political call to resist stereotypes and cultural violence through the resurgence of community gatherings, storytelling, and political mobilizations. The textual violence reminds us that although Indigenous peoples across Turtle Island have faced attempted cultural genocide, we are still here, still writing, and still performing. The colonial past is not yet behind us, and for Indigenous peoples, its residue still lives in memories, dreams, and in the intergenerational effects of our blood memories. Theatre is one political tool that Indigenous peoples across Turtle Island use to promote artistic resurgence and to honour, build, and share our cultural practices.

Indigenous theatre reclaims space for political, cultural, and artistic acts of resurgence through playwriting, directing, acting, and other forms of theatrical creation. Indigenous theatre practitioners are claiming space and exposing the truth of Canada's colonial past—and present—allowing for Indigenous and non-Indigenous audiences to sit with these truths and encouraging them to grapple with how to move forward. Dandurand gifts us with a play that encourages us to understand that Canada's colonial heritage is not strictly in the past and to consider how this heritage affects our present and our potential futures.

Please Do Not Touch the Indians was first produced by Native Voices in March 2004 at the Autry Museum of the American West's Wells Fargo Theatre in Griffith Park, Los Angeles, with the following cast and creative team:

Wooden Indian Man: Andrew Roa
Wooden Indian Woman: Arigon Starr
Tourist: Stephan Worfert
Sister Coyote: Tonantsín Carmelo
Brother Raven: Kalani Queypo
Mister Wolf: Uzziel Martinez

Directed by Randy Reindholz
Dramaturgy by Bryan Davidson
Set Design by James Ferguson
Costume Design by Christine Wright
Sound Design by Spencer T. Hill
Production and Lighting Design by R. Craig Wolf
Music by Vincent H. Whipple
Videography by Ian Skorodin

CHARACTERS

Wooden Indian Man
Wooden Indian Woman
Sister Coyote
Brother Raven
Mister Wolf
Tourist

SETTING

A painted backdrop of the Hank Williams, Sr.'s Bait and Gift Shop. There are some fallen leaves on the ground. Centre stage there is a wooden bench and sitting on the bench are two wooden Indians. Their clothing is simple and not quite traditional, but more of a Hollywood taste. Wooden Woman is holding flowers that someone has put in her hand. Wooden Man sits with his eyes closed, and around his neck is a sign that reads: PLEASE DO NOT TOUCH THE INDIANS.

ACT I

SCENE I

Lights come up as music begins: Hank Williams, Sr.'s "Kalajah." Music ends as a French TOURIST *comes out and sets up a camera and tripod. The French* TOURIST *sets the timer and sits between the two Indians. As the timer beeps, the* WOODEN MAN *opens his eyes and sticks out his tongue. The French* TOURIST *looks at* WOODEN MAN*, but he has already closed his eyes and has returned to being wooden. French* TOURIST *stands, gathers the camera and tripod, and exits as lights fade to black.*

SCENE II

Lights come up. Night. More fallen leaves on the ground. In the distance we hear squealing tires and screams from teenagers as they cheer on the dragging cars. WOODEN WOMAN *begins to move as noise fades.* WOODEN WOMAN *looks at flowers in her hand and screams as she throws them to the ground in front of her.*

WOODEN WOMAN: Geez, who put flowers in my hand? Don't they know that's bad luck. Holding flowers is a sign of death. Hey, you listening? Are you awake?

WOODEN MAN *does not move, nor does he speak.*

You just going to sit there all night and not say a word? Don't you get tired of not moving your mouth? Geez, I'd go crazy not being able to talk. You better move your mouth or else you'll never be able to talk. That's what happened to old Charlie Ketchup. He never spoke to a soul for the last twenty years of his life. When the doctor went to see him on his deathbed, Charlie couldn't even tell him where it hurt. I bet he's talking up a storm in the spirit world. Old Charlie Ketchup. I knew his wife; she was crazier than he was. Betty Ketchup. A big woman, she must've weighed about three hundred pounds. No wonder Charlie never spoke, she'd come screaming out of the house after him if he ever spoke a word against her. Never seen a woman move so fast, never seen a man move faster.

WOODEN MAN scratches his nose as a raven caws in the distance.

Betty Ketchup sure was a big woman, but she would never hurt anyone. I remember going to her house to borrow some wood one day and she was running around trying to catch every fly that came into her dirty house. I'd say, "What'cha doing with them flies, Betty Ketchup?" And she'd turn and look at me with that little mouth of hers trying so hard to suck in enough air to breath, and she say, "I'm catchin' 'em for my supper." And she laughed so hard, I was always afraid she'd swallow more than she caught.

WOODEN MAN scratches his left knee.

She never did eat any of them. She was really catching them because she could never kill a fly. She'd spend the whole day catching them and storing them in an old jar that she kept on the kitchen sink right next to her set of teeth. I followed her one day, you know to see where she went with them flies. She must've had a hundred in that jar that day. She waddled her way to the cow field and here she came across the biggest cow patty that she could find. It was real fresh, the steam still rising. Betty Ketchup opened up her jar of flies and let them fly right onto the patty. A hundred flies with a new home. Those flies never came back to Betty Ketchup's house. They stayed on that cow patty for the rest of their lives. Betty Ketchup saved millions of lives in the ten years that I knew her. Never a dead fly in her dirty kitchen. A place to live was all they wanted. She was a big woman and her heart was just as big.

Lights fade as a coyote barks. Blackout.

SCENE III

Stage lights come up. Night. More leaves on the ground. WOODEN MAN snaps awake and stares at WOODEN WOMAN.

WOODEN MAN: Are you awake? I had a vision: I was on the river, my boat was filled with fish, I had started home when a coyote began to follow me from the shore, he was smilin' at me, you know, with them yellow eyes, he's smilin' with his crooked teeth. He took his time, stopping every so often to rest his ragged paws, he knew my boat couldn't get very far with all that fish. My boat was pushing slowly up to our home, the coyote watched from the shore and then the raven came and joined the coyote, they both watched from the shore: the raven with his red eyes and his torn feathers, the coyote lights a cigarette and blows the smoke toward me and my boat. The raven smiles as coyote offers him a drag. They both sit there on a log and they laugh at me. The fish begin to dance, they want to go back to the river, they do not want to be eaten by the coyote nor do they want to be picked at by the raven. The fish begin to sing to me, they tell me to throw them back: "Please throw us back, we will come back next year." Over and over they sing this to me. The raven and the coyote are laughing at me as they begin to share their bottle. And then I begin to throw the fish back to the river, the fish throw kisses to me as they swim back to their homes, they promise to name their children after me, they turn and disappear. The raven and the coyote stand there on shore, their mouths open with confusion. They try and catch up to me but my boat is empty and goes like the wind. I hear them howlin' and cawing at me as I disappear around the mountain . . . I don't think they will name their children after me, I thought to myself, and then I woke up. Hey, are you awake? Did you like the flowers?

An English TOURIST *enters and sets up a camera. He sets the timer and sits between the wooden Indians. As the timer beeps the* WOODEN MAN *and* WOODEN WOMAN *open their eyes and smile.* WOODEN MAN *also puts his arm around the English* TOURIST*, he puts a sign on the English* TOURIST*'s back. Both Indians freeze as the English* TOURIST *looks at them as if they did truly move, he shakes his head and goes to gather his camera, he turns his back to the audience and we see the sign on his back:* KICK ME! *Blackout.*

SCENE IV

In the dark we hear a coyote bark followed by a voice yelling: "Get outta here, you stinking coyote!" A spot comes up downstage centre. SISTER COYOTE *walks into the spot, she is beautiful, but she has been crying and her makeup has run down her face, so now she looks somewhat clownish and sad. In the background we hear sounds and music that you would hear at the circus or the carnival.* SISTER COYOTE *reaches into her purse and pulls out a cigarette, lights it, takes a huge drag and exhales it into the air. She does this again and tries to act cool and special, but inhales down the wrong pipe and begins to choke, and her eyes bug out and she appears even more clownish than before.*

SISTER COYOTE: Nothing like a good smoke. You know I first started smoking when me and my sister went to the carnival that would come to our reserve every summer. We really went with our parents but as soon as we got there we would run away and disappear into the crowd, and our parents were going to the beer tent anyway so they didn't miss us much. We would run straight for the far end of the carnival grounds. We would always go to the far end of the grounds, you see, this is where the freaks and the scary rides were.

She puts cigarette out and takes out a mickey from her purse, looks around to see if anyone is looking, and takes a sip. Puts the bottle back into her purse and smiles.

My sister and I had both started to wear makeup, not very well I may add, not like I wear mine now. We didn't know a thing back then, but we didn't care because we were thirteen and we were away from the rez for a day, and we had a pack of Marlboros that we had stolen from Dad and we were looking to smoke and act cool and we were looking to see if there were any cute guys that had come with the carnival. We didn't see any, they were all fat, ugly guys with a lot of tattoos and they smelled like horses. We walked around and smoked our cigarettes, and we ate junk food and sipped Cokes, and we walked like we owned this land, well we did, well our people did, but we walked like we owned it, and we let people know that we were smoking and we were cool.

Spot changes to blue and SISTER COYOTE *sits down in the pool of light. She digs into her purse for a compact and begins to fix her makeup.*

As the day wore on and the sun got hot and we became kind of sick from all the food and the pop and the Marlboros, my sister said she was going to find Mom and Dad, and I told her I wanted to check out more of the freak shows and maybe see if there were any cute guys hiding in the haunted house. I was making my way toward the haunted house when I saw IT.

Stage lights come up as SISTER COYOTE *still sits in the blue spot.* WOODEN MAN *stands and stretches and reaches underneath the bench and takes out an old baseball glove and ball and begins to throw the ball up into the air and catch it.*

There it was in big red letters on a black sign: SEE THE TWO-HEADED BABY. I freaked out. I reached into my pocket and dug for the quarter that I knew was there and then I ran up the stairs that led to the TWO-HEADED BABY. When I got to the top of the stairs, a man who smelled like horses took my quarter and told me to go on in and to leave out the other side when I had had enough. I went in and it was dark and smelled like horses and over in the corner there was a table and on the table there was a jar and in the jar was the TWO-HEADED BABY. And

I walked up to it and I looked at it and it turned and it looked at me. I screamed but no one could hear me over all the noise on the rides outside. I wanted to run but I couldn't look away so I stood there and it stared back at me and I stared back at it. I moved closer to see if it was really alive but how could it be alive, right? I mean it was floating in some sort of liquid in a jar and it was a two-headed baby, so how could it have lived in the first place, right? But when I went up to it, it moved again, but not real movement, more like floating movement like it was in space or something, and it just spun around and around inside that jar and I just stared at it and stared at it and as its heads would spin around, the eyes would stare at me and they were looking at me like they wanted to come out of that jar and play. I wanted to run and I wanted to scream but I just stood there and stared, and then someone else came in and they wanted to stare at the two-headed baby and I let them and I went outside and I never went back, and as I went down the stairs I threw up all over some cute guy who was combing the BEARDED LADY's beard.

WOODEN MAN drops the ball and it rolls over beside SISTER COYOTE. Blue spot fades as she picks up the ball and walks toward the WOODEN MAN.

You dropped your ball.

WOODEN MAN stares at her and reaches for the ball.

WOODEN MAN: I could never throw a curveball. All my life I couldn't throw a curve to save it.

SISTER COYOTE: I could show you mine. I was pitcher for the Redhawks. We were the meanest team you ever set eyes on.

WOODEN MAN tosses her the ball, goes stage right, and crouches like a catcher and shows her the glove.

WOODEN MAN: My dad tried to show me how to throw a curve, but the ball just wouldn't curve for me. He'd get so mad, his face would get all white and he would spit a little out of the corner of his mouth and he would swear and go in the house and turn the TV on, and he would mumble: "Kid's arm is useless."

SISTER COYOTE walks over to the opposite side of the stage and faces him and tosses the ball up into the air and feels it in the palm of her hand. She scratches out her mound with her foot and she readies herself to throw a pitch.

SISTER COYOTE: Our coach was the chief and he made the rules because he bought all the uniforms and he supplied the equipment. He pretended like he was BIG LEAGUE but he didn't know a thing about baseball and the only thing BIG about him was his belly and his big belly stuck out of his shirt and he would just sit in the dugout and pretend like he was giving us secret signals. We all would look at him and pretend that he was running the show but really it was Lucy, the third baseman, who was making the calls, and she called for a fastball and I would wind up and give her my best fastball.

She throws him a fastball with some smoke behind it and it makes a hard snapping sound as it hits the glove.

WOODEN MAN: STRIKE ONE!

WOODEN MAN tosses it back at her and resumes his catcher position. She does her ritual and prepares herself for another pitch and she awaits his signal this time. WOODEN MAN shows her two fingers and readies himself again for the next pitch. She throws it and it hits the glove just like the first one.

STRIKE TWO!

He stands up and walks toward her as if he is the catcher walking toward the mound in an important game. He gives her the ball and kicks at the dirt.

SISTER COYOTE: Okay, I've given two of my best pitches and all I have left is my curve, and I've been working hard on it all week but it just sort of hangs there and doesn't curve that much and the chief is getting all mad and he's threatening to pull me out of the game, and all my friends are there and that cute guy in grade twelve is there with all his friends and he's come to see my great curveball and this is the time for it, right?

WOODEN MAN: The CURVE.

He walks slowly back to home plate as she continues to talk to herself.

SISTER COYOTE: Was there any other choice? You had thrown the fastball on the first pitch and that batter just sat there and she knew, yes, she knew that the curve was coming up, everyone knew that the curve was going to be the last pitch, so she just sat there and she chewed her big wad of gum and she just waited for the third pitch because she knew it was going to be my weakest pitch.

WOODEN MAN crouches in his catcher position and shows her one finger, the middle one, and he smacks the dust out of his glove and readies himself for the next pitch. SISTER COYOTE sees the sign and she winds up, checks the bases, looks back at the catcher, and she throws the most perfect curveball that she could ever throw, and it hits the glove with a resounding smack.

WOODEN MAN: STRIKE THREE, YOU'RE OUT!

SISTER COYOTE: It was the most beautiful pitch that I have ever thrown in my life, even now I could never have thrown a better pitch and everyone was screaming and yelling at me like I was some sort of hero, and the girls on my team all ran up to me and they put me on their shoulders and paraded me up and down the third base line, and all the people in the stands cheered and called out my name and the cute guy in grade twelve smiled to me and gave me the thumbs up sign, and the chief was trying to get at me and hug me but he tripped and ripped the seat of his uniform pants and everyone saw his bum and everyone started to laugh at him and he began to laugh and everyone was laughing, even the other team who had travelled all this way to try and beat us, but we had beaten them, yes, we had beaten them with the best curveball anyone could've thrown on that day.

WOODEN MAN: Nice pitch, kid.

He walks over and sits down in his spot and puts the glove and ball back underneath the bench and then becomes wooden.

SISTER COYOTE: Arm's a little tired. Not used to the distance, I guess.

She crosses over and sits down at the feet of the WOODEN MAN *and she leans against his legs and goes to sleep.*

WOODEN MAN: Nice pitch, kid.

Stage lights begin to fade. In the dark we hear a raven cawing followed by a voice yelling: "Get out of here, you stinking raven!" A spot comes up downstage centre and BROTHER RAVEN *walks into the light, lights a cigarette, and blows the smoke back at the voice.*

BROTHER RAVEN: I was picking at the apples in the garbage. Just picking at the apples. Where is the wrong in that?

Takes another long drag, it goes down the wrong pipe and he begins to cough. He stamps the cigarette out and wipes the tears from his eyes.

Never was much of a smoker.

Takes bottle out of his coat, takes a good-sized swig and puts the bottle back into his pocket.

Now drinking is more my style. Nothing like a good shot to get the earth moving. Nothing like a good shot.

The spot turns to blue and BROTHER RAVEN *sits down and takes a piece of paper and a piece of candy from his pocket. He unwraps the candy and puts it into his mouth and savours the sweet taste, he uncrumples the piece of paper and begins to read it.*

"In the morning as Mother walked to the river and all the children slept so peaceful on the floor with their little feet sticking out of the warm blankets, there would be a calm quietness that came over the land and all you could hear was the river as it moved gently to the ocean and Mother would walk down to the river and she would take off her dress and she would slip into the water and bathe herself and ready herself for the long day ahead."

He takes the candy out of his mouth and admires it and puts it back into his mouth and sucks on it some more and flips the piece of paper and continues to read.

"Mother would start the fire and me and my brothers and sisters would rise up off the floor and stare at her in wonderment and she would ask us if we had had any visions in our sleep and I would always answer yes and proceed to tell her what I had seen: I had seen a young salmon come to the shore of the river and it whispered to me that I should join her in the water and I asked her why and she giggled and said it was nice and warm, so I went in and the salmon swam right beside me, and she would whisper to me that I was cute and that I had skinny legs, and I would laugh and try and catch her, but she was a salmon and she could swim somewhat better than I could, and she would always get away before I could touch her. Mother would always laugh at my visions and my brothers and sisters would always laugh and tease me and they would always show me the salmon they had caught and say to me: 'Is this her, is this her!' And I would cry because what if it was her and they had cut her open and they had put her on the fire and I had eaten her. Mother would try and explain to them what my visions meant, but they were too eager to run out and play in the forest, and I would just sit there and Mother would tell me her visions, and I would eat tuna sandwiches because I felt too bad about eating salmon, and Mother would join me on the floor and hold me tight and she would laugh as she told her visions, and I would laugh too because she was so funny and kind, so funny and kind."

He folds up piece of paper and puts it back into his pocket as stage lights come up and WOODEN WOMAN *begins to move. She reaches beneath the bench, pulls out a spinning top, and begins to spin it about the stage as she follows it on her hands and knees.* BROTHER RAVEN *stands up, reaches into his pocket, pulls out a comb, and begins to comb back his slicked black hair.*

Always had the ability to have visions. Never know quite what they mean but they mean something and I have them every night.

He finishes combing his hair, puts the comb back into his pocket, and pulls out an old rotten apple from his pocket and begins to pick and eat away at it. WOODEN WOMAN *stops spinning the top, goes back and reaches underneath the bench, and this time she comes out with a bag of marbles and starts to play a game of marbles while still on her hands and knees.*

Just picking at the apples. Never meant any harm to no one but they think you're stealing from them even if the apples are rotten. Even if the apples are rotten . . .

WOODEN WOMAN shoots one marble and it rolls to the feet of BROTHER RAVEN. He picks it up and walks over to her and her game of marbles as the blue spot fades.

WOODEN WOMAN: Play for funsies or keepsies?

BROTHER RAVEN: KEEPSIES.

WOODEN WOMAN: Okay, okay, but I get to shoot first and you can't say funsies if I start to win, all right?

BROTHER RAVEN: All right, but I only have one marble left and if I lose it I can't play anymore.

WOODEN WOMAN: Okay, you better shoot first. Where's your marble?

He reaches into his pocket and pulls out a red marble. He holds it up to the light and stares through it. WOODEN WOMAN comes up beside him and she stares through it too.

BROTHER RAVEN: It's the prettiest marble I've ever owned. All my life I've been playing marbles and this is the prettiest one I've ever come across.

WOODEN WOMAN: It's lovely. All red and you can see right through it. Where did you get it?

He brings it down from the light and steps back away from her and kneels down and readies himself to play marbles. WOODEN WOMAN kneels down beside him and looks him right in the eyes.

Where did you get that marble?

BROTHER RAVEN: I'm not supposed to say.

WOODEN WOMAN: Why not? Is it a magic marble? Because if it is, then I don't want to play for keepsies.

BROTHER RAVEN: Too late.

He begins to win all her marbles. She kneels there beside him and watches as he makes the most amazing shots she has ever seen. The red marble banks and kicks out all her marbles and she sits there in wonderment and he collects all her marbles and puts them in his pocket.

WOODEN WOMAN: No fair. Winning with a magic marble just isn't fair.

BROTHER RAVEN: Here, have an apple.

He gives her one of his rotten apples and she bites into it without looking at it.

WOODEN WOMAN: Good apple.

BROTHER RAVEN: I picked it myself.

WOODEN WOMAN: I was good at picking cherries.

BROTHER RAVEN: Not me. I couldn't climb the trees and I was always falling out of them and landing on my head. I just ate the ones that fell to the ground.

WOODEN WOMAN goes and sits in her spot on the bench and lifts her dress up to the knee. BROTHER RAVEN goes and kneels at her feet just like SISTER COYOTE is sitting with the WOODEN MAN.

WOODEN WOMAN: See this scar right here on my shin? A spirit gave me that scar. You see, I got that one from falling down a cherry tree when I was just a little girl. The tree was on old Irving's land. No one ever went onto his land because everyone thought his land was full of bad spirits. They used to say the spirits were bad because they had all died on the same day, they had all died on the same hour and they had all died the same way, and they had all been buried together on Irving's land.

BROTHER RAVEN rests his head on her knee, listens to her story, and slowly falls asleep.

Nothing on his land but rocks and weeds anyway, so we pretty much stayed away from him and his land of bad spirits. But there was that cherry tree that everyone knew and talked about. They said that the cherries were so big and juicy that you could eat one and be full for a week. They said this tree never went a day without a new cherry growing and becoming big and juicy. As you can tell by this scar, I went on that land and I went past those bad spirits and I went up that cherry tree and I picked me the biggest and the juiciest of all the cherries on the earth. I ate maybe four or five and stuck the rest of them cherries into my pockets and I was making my way down the tree when I saw her.

She puts her dress down and puts the half-eaten apple in the WOODEN MAN's hand. BROTHER RAVEN is fast asleep as she touches his face.

I've never seen such a sight in all my life. It was a young girl. She looked to be maybe ten or eleven. She stood there at the bottom of the tree and she looked up at me. I spoke to her and I said: "Hey, would you like some cherries?" The little girl stared at me and then she touched the tree and the whole tree shook, no, the whole world felt like it was shaking and I tried to hold on but I couldn't because my hands were slippery from the juiciest cherries in the whole wide world, and I fell, no, I slid all the way down that tree and fell right at her feet.

That girl just stared at me as I ran, no, I limped all the way off of Irving's land and I never looked back. So you see, a spirit gave me this scar.

BROTHER RAVEN moves and becomes more comfortable, and as he does this his magic red marble falls out of his hand and WOODEN WOMAN reaches down and picks it up and she stares at it in the light as stage lights begin to fade.

Finders keepers.

Blackout.

SCENE V

Stage lights come up. More leaves on the ground. A wolf howls. A German TOURIST enters and sets up a camera on a tripod. SISTER COYOTE is asleep on one side of the bench and BROTHER RAVEN is asleep on the other side. WOODEN MAN and WOODEN WOMAN are in their usual spot on the bench. The German TOURIST sets the timer and quickly sits in between the two wooden Indians. When the timer beeps the German TOURIST smiles and the WOODEN MAN takes a bite out of the rotten apple that was in his hand and he goes back to being wooden. The German TOURIST looks at the WOODEN MAN and then down at the apple, he shakes his head and then rises and gathers his camera and tripod and exits. WOODEN MAN slowly begins to chew the mouthful of rotten apple. SISTER COYOTE moves and talks in her sleep.

SISTER COYOTE: Tell me a story, Poppa. Tell me a story, Poppa.

WOODEN MAN looks down at her and takes another bite from the rotten apple.

WOODEN MAN: Are you talking to me? 'Cause if you are, then you should look me in the eyes, not polite to ask someone for something and not look them in the eyes.

He takes another bite and another and another until the apple is finished and then he puts the apple core into WOODEN WOMAN's hand.

I met a man once who wouldn't look me in the eyes. He'd always be wanting something from me and he would come right up to my door and he'd ask for it without ever looking me in the eyes, and I'd tell him no every time, and he'd walk away all mad but he would come back and he would ask me for something else, and I would look him right in the eyes and I knew that I would give him whatever it was he was asking for, if he would just have the respect to look me in the eyes when he asked for it, but he never did and he hated me. That man hated me because I asked for respect.

SISTER COYOTE moves again and speaks again in her sleep.

SISTER COYOTE: Poppa? You there, Poppa? The house is so cold and all the wood is still wet and my blanket's too small 'cause I'm getting taller. Can you see that I'm getting taller, Poppa?

WOODEN MAN: Not going to look me in the eyes? Then I am unable to answer you. Sorry, but it's just a rule I have with people. If you can't look me in the eyes then I can't answer you. It's a rule I've stuck with all my life and I can't start breaking my own rules for the sake of talking to anyone so you'll have to look me in the eyes if you want me to answer you.

WOODEN MAN whistles and plays with the buttons on his shirt, this bores him and he bends down and unlaces his boots and re-ties them and repeats this and becomes bored with this, and he looks around for something to do but realizes that there is nothing left for him to do.

All right! I will speak and answer you this one time, but you can't tell anyone that I broke one of my own rules, because if people find out that you can't even respect your own rules, then why should they respect anything about you, right? Right. So I'm talking to you because there's no one else to talk to right now and I have to tell you about this vision I just had and if I don't tell anyone then I think I may have to scream and if you've ever heard me scream then you know what a loud scream that I have. So here is my vision. I was on . . .

SISTER COYOTE: Poppa, can I have another piece of bread? My belly isn't quite full yet.

WOODEN MAN: Listen, if we're going to have a conversation, then you'll have to respect that I was talking and it was my turn to tell you about my vision, so you just sit there and don't say a word, all right? All right. Anything more to say before I carry on with my vision? No?

SISTER COYOTE moves and we see her face, she smiles and continues to sleep as WOODEN MAN stands and stretches his legs and picks up a leaf and crumbles it in his hand.

I was on the river. I know, I know, I am always on the river but this time I was really on the river. I was born on the river, I bet you didn't know that. I was born and raised on that river.

He bends down and picks up another leaf and lets it fall from his hand to the ground.

I was on the river and I was on my old boat. That old boat sure could move when it wanted to. It could cut through the water and nothing, no storm, no wind, could stop her from getting me home.

He picks up another leaf, and goes and sits down in his spot on the bench and stares at the leaf.

I was on the river and I was on my old boat and we were heading home from a long day of fishing. I didn't pull in too much on that day, but I had enough for supper. The water was calm and there was no wind, and you could just make out the blue of the sky, and you could just catch a glimpse of the mountains. We were making real good time when all of a sudden the engine went dead. I tried to start it up again but she just wouldn't turn, and then the wind came out of nowhere and the rain started to fall hard, and the blue of the sky was gone and it was dark and you could no longer see the mountains, and the boat turned and started to head downriver as the river's current became strong and angry.

He drops the leaf to the ground in front of him. It becomes windy on stage and the leaves are blowing all over the place as he continues to tell his vision.

I had no idea where I was anymore. The boat seemed to have a life of its own and it took me where it wanted to go, and I had to go because there was no choice, and the boat landed itself on shore and then the wind stopped and the rain stopped and the sky cleared, and there was the blue and there were the mountains and I still had no idea where I was.

Wind stops and leaves come to rest on the ground. Offstage we hear a wolf howling followed by a voice saying: "Get out of here, you stinking wolf!"

I got off the boat and went down the shoreline trying to figure out where I was, but nothing was familiar to me and it felt like I was in a different world, and then I saw him. He was sitting on a log and he lit a cigarette and smiled right at me.

Spot comes up downstage centre and MISTER WOLF *walks into the spot, he is dressed in a three-piece suit and his hair is in two braids. He is wearing sunglasses as he lights a cigarette and blows the smoke into the air as he smiles.*

MISTER WOLF: That your boat?

WOODEN MAN stands to answer him.

WOODEN MAN: Yes it is. It's a good . . .

MISTER WOLF: I need a boat.

WOODEN MAN: She's not for sale.

MISTER WOLF: Did I say I wanted to buy a boat?

WOODEN MAN: No.

MISTER WOLF: No, I did not. I said I needed a boat. Is this one available?

WOODEN MAN: I was going home and the wind brought me here. I have to get home and cook the fish before they go bad. If you like I could take you upriver a ways.

MISTER WOLF: That would be fine.

They both sit down. MISTER WOLF puts his cigarette out and takes off his sunglasses and puts them into his pocket. The spot turns blue as the WOODEN MAN looks down at SISTER COYOTE but she is still asleep.

WOODEN MAN: This vision feels so real.

MISTER WOLF: What? What did you say?

WOODEN MAN: Nothing. You must've heard the thunder. It's been real crazy today.

MISTER WOLF: Can't this heap go any faster?

WOODEN MAN: She usually goes faster but her belly is full of fish that I caught today. See?

MISTER WOLF looks beside him and pretends to pick up fish and eat them whole until they are all gone. WOODEN MAN whispers to SISTER COYOTE.

He ate all my fish. There must've been thirty fish in her belly and he ate them all. He ate them whole.

MISTER WOLF stands and feels his full belly.

MISTER WOLF: Now you can go faster.

WOODEN MAN stands and he is angry because MISTER WOLF has eaten all his fish.

WOODEN MAN: You want to go fast, well here we go!

They both start to shake and twist as if going fast on a boat. They build and build their actions until they both meet centre stage and crash into one another, causing them to fall to the ground onto the now pile of dead leaves on the ground.

MISTER WOLF: Where am I?

WOODEN MAN: I've got to stop having these visions. They're really getting kind of weird.

MISTER WOLF: Where am I?

Both stand and stare at each other. MISTER WOLF has leaves in his hair and his suit is somewhat crumpled and creased. WOODEN MAN limps back and sits down in usual spot.

WOODEN MAN: You're right here. Where else would you be?

MISTER WOLF stares at him.

MISTER WOLF: Do I know you?

WOODEN MAN whispers to SISTER COYOTE who is still asleep on the ground beside the bench.

WOODEN MAN: Watch this one, he's very tricky.

MISTER WOLF: What? I didn't hear what you said. You're going to have to speak up, because I seem to have lost some of my hearing.

WOODEN MAN becomes wooden and silent. MISTER WOLF goes up to him and taps him on the shoulder but WOODEN MAN does not move. MISTER WOLF taps everyone else on the shoulder, but they do not move either. He goes back and sits in the blue spot as stage lights begin to fade.

Right back to where I began. No one to talk to. No one to laugh and play tricks on. Just me and the earth.

Reaches into his pocket and pulls out an old pocket watch and chain. He stares at it and he listens to see if it still ticks.

Never know if it's the right time or not. Can't tell by this old timepiece. It's only good to stare at when the sun is out. See how it glows in the light.

He holds it up to the light and watches it as it spins and gleams in the light.

Never was good for telling the right time.

He puts the watch back into his pocket.

Always had clocks and timepieces for the time at any time in my life. When I was a kid we had two clocks, one in the kitchen on top of the stove and one in Grandma's room right next to her bed. You could hear that old clock ticking just as loud as Grandma's snoring. We used to sneak in there at night and set the alarm to ring at exactly midnight and wait for it to ring and for Grandma to wake up and scream at us kids to stop fooling around, but we would be laughing so hard and she would start giggling too, and swear up and down that all us kids were crazy and that we should be locked up somewhere. We would get Grandma a tea and let her get back to sleep and we would go on to our rooms which were on the other side of the kitchen and we would pass the other clock that was on the stove and it would tell us that it was bedtime and we would all go to sleep and we would all hear the ticking of them two clocks because one was faster than the other: tick tick tock tock tick tick tock tock . . .

He curls up and goes to sleep as blue spot begins to fade.

Tick tick tock tock tick tick tock tock . . .

Lights go to black.

SCENE VI

In the black we hear horses and men screaming: CHARGE! Lights come up slowly. Night. More leaves on the ground. WOODEN MAN and WOODEN WOMAN are sitting in their places on the bench, SISTER COYOTE stands to the right of WOODEN MAN, BROTHER RAVEN is standing to the left of WOODEN WOMAN, and MISTER WOLF is standing behind and in the middle of the bench. They hold their pose as the TOURIST, now dressed as a Mountie, enters and sets up his camera and tripod. He sets the timer and goes behind the bench and stands beside MISTER WOLF. As the timer beeps, the TOURIST raises his hand and makes the peace symbol, as all the other characters each raise one of their middle fingers. TOURIST looks at each of them as if they did move, shakes his head, and gathers his camera and exits. Again sounds of horses and men screaming: CHARGE!

WOODEN MAN: He smelled like horse shit!

SISTER COYOTE: He must've stepped in it when he got off his horse.

MISTER WOLF: Smells more like he was rolling around in it, you know they do that.

BROTHER RAVEN: Do they really?

MISTER WOLF: Sure they do. Some sort of ritual. Some sort of ceremony to make them stronger when they go into battle.

WOODEN MAN: He's going to scare the other side away smelling like that. They won't be able to see him coming because he'll be covered in flies. All they'll see is a cloud of flies coming over the hill.

WOODEN WOMAN stands and walks downstage left. She takes out her red marble and stares at it through the light. SISTER COYOTE walks up to her and lights a cigarette and blows the smoke into the air and into the light that WOODEN WOMAN is staring at.

SISTER COYOTE: Did you smell the horses?

WOODEN WOMAN: All I can smell is smoke.

SISTER COYOTE: I couldn't smell the horses. I think those guys were just kidding about him smelling like horses. He did look pretty in that uniform and that big hat, they sure got big hats.

WOODEN WOMAN stops looking through her marble and puts it away. SISTER COYOTE offers her a drag from her cigarette.

Here, have a taste.

WOODEN WOMAN takes the cigarette and takes a drag. She blows the smoke toward the men who are all now sitting on the bench checking their shoes to see if they are the ones who have stepped in horse shit.

WOODEN WOMAN: Everything becomes different when you look at it through smoke. Nothing is as clear as it should be, it looks older and worn.

She hands the cigarette back to SISTER COYOTE.

Thank you.

SISTER COYOTE: You're welcome.

SISTER COYOTE takes a drag and blows the smoke at the men who are now sniffing each other trying to figure out where the smell is coming from.

The smoke makes them disappear.

WOODEN WOMAN: I know, it's like they've never existed. One minute they're talking and smiling and the next they're gone.

SISTER COYOTE: Wait till the smoke clears and then we can see and hear them again.

She puts out the cigarette and looks back at the men who are now standing and have moved away from each other.

MISTER WOLF: I had a horse once.

BROTHER RAVEN: Was he fast?

MISTER WOLF: No, not really. He would just stand there and eat and shit.

WOODEN MAN: Doesn't sound like much of a horse.

MISTER WOLF: He wasn't. I won him at a card game. I had three queens. I bet all my belongings on that hand. There was no way I was going to let that horse get away from me. Three queens won me that horse.

MISTER WOLF sits down on the centre of the bench.

BROTHER RAVEN: What did you bet for that horse?

MISTER WOLF: I bet my life.

WOODEN MAN: What did you do that for? That sounds pretty dumb to me, betting your life on three queens.

MISTER WOLF: I wanted that horse. There was no way I was going to walk out of that game and have no horse. It was like nothing else mattered and the only way I could go on living was if I won that horse. So I put down my three queens, stood up, walked out the door, and I got on that horse and rode into the night.

MISTER WOLF pretends to ride a horse.

BROTHER RAVEN: A horse is no good if he's not fast. What did you do with him?

MISTER WOLF: I rode him until the sun came up and then I sat there and just stared at him. He was one ugly horse.

WOODEN MAN: Three queens, your life, for an ugly horse?

MISTER WOLF: Yep. He was the ugliest animal I had ever seen. He only had one eye and his mouth sat there half open and his tongue hung out like a big snake.

BROTHER RAVEN: I hate snakes. They're always trying to get me with their big teeth. Sometimes I can't get five steps without one of them trying to bite me. You ever been bitten by a snake?

WOODEN MAN: No, but I did get bit by a dog before. Big dog bit me on the ass. He wouldn't let go, just bit right into my ass and stared at me with crazy eyes.

BROTHER RAVEN: What did you do?

WOODEN MAN: I tried to spin him around and knock him off but he had a hold of me good. I spun and spun but he wouldn't let go. I stopped and looked down into his eyes, I tried to warn him to let go but he held on, so I took out my knife from my pocket and I stabbed him right in the ass. His eyes and mouth opened wide enough for me to get my ass out of his mouth. I turned around and showed him the piece of his ass that I had just cut out and told him that we were even, and that he better get on down the road or I was going to cut him somewhere else. He turned and ran away leaving me there with my bloody knife and my bloody and sore ass.

MISTER WOLF stops riding his horse. WOODEN MAN sits down in his spot very carefully and on one cheek.

BROTHER RAVEN: I've never been bitten by a dog but I have been bitten by a snake before.

MISTER WOLF: Did he bite you in the ass?

BROTHER RAVEN: No, he bit me right on the heart.

He lifts up his shirt and shows both men where he has been bitten by a snake, there should be bite scars right where his heart is.

WOODEN MAN: That's gotta hurt.

MISTER WOLF: How in the heck did you let a snake bite you on the heart like that?

BROTHER RAVEN: I didn't let him, he took a bite when I was sleeping right beside him.

WOODEN MAN: What were you doing sleeping beside a snake? I thought you hated snakes.

BROTHER RAVEN: I didn't back then, I thought he was okay, he gave me some of the chicken that he had stolen from some farmer. Any snake who would give me some of their chicken must be a good snake, I thought.

MISTER WOLF: You ate raw chicken with a snake?

BROTHER RAVEN: No, he cooked it up, made a nice sauce out of some of the old berries that I had picked up along the road. We cooked it over a nice fire and sat there by the river and ate that chicken whole.

WOODEN MAN: And then he bit you on the heart?

BROTHER RAVEN: No, not right away. He told me stories about where he had come from and as it got later and later I began to fall asleep. He must've curled up beside me for warmth because I woke up one time and found him right there beside me. I didn't want to be rude and ask him to move away because he had given me his food and he had let me sleep by his fire. So I let him sleep there beside me, closed my eyes, and tried to dream.

WOODEN MAN: That's when he bit you.

BROTHER RAVEN: No, not right away.

WOODEN MAN: Geez, did he bite you at all, or are you just making this story up?

BROTHER RAVEN sits down on the bench.

BROTHER RAVEN: No, he bit me. But not right away. It was like he was trying to get close enough to me so he could bite right into my heart. I went back to sleep with him there beside me and then I woke up again and this time I found him right up my shirt and he had his head right next to my heart. I tapped him on top of the head and asked him: "What are you doing?"

MISTER WOLF: What did he say?

BROTHER RAVEN: Nothing. He looked right up at me with those green eyes and he opened his mouth up real slow and then he bit right into my chest. I let out a scream, and jumped up and tried to pull him off, but he was under my shirt and I couldn't get a good grip on him so he bit harder and deeper. His teeth felt like they were razors cutting into my chest. I tore my shirt off and now I had a hold of him but still he wouldn't let go, and all this time he looked at me with those green eyes and had those razor teeth buried into my chest. It was as if he was smiling at me. Smiling because he knew I was going to die. I tugged and tugged and slowly he started to get weak and his hold wasn't as strong as before. I pulled and pulled on him and it felt like I was stretching him. His eyes closed and he knew that he had to let go so he opened that big mouth and his teeth slowly came out of my chest and I swung him around in the air and I threw him into the river.

MISTER WOLF: Could he swim?

BROTHER RAVEN: Yes, he could swim. But not fast enough. When he hit the water the sound made a big splash and an owl who had been watching all this jumped from its tree and it glided toward the struggling snake. All I could see were those green eyes as they tried to make it back to shore but that owl came down and snapped that snake in half. Those green eyes closed one more time and disappeared with the owl as the night became quiet.

SISTER COYOTE and WOODEN WOMAN clear a small circle in the leaves by their feet and sit down beside it. They begin to play marbles as the men sit and become wooden. SISTER COYOTE shoots first, makes the first shot but misses the next.

SISTER COYOTE: Wasn't much of a marble player.

WOODEN WOMAN: This is a magic marble, watch how it moves and takes the other marbles from the circle.

She takes out the rest of the marbles and sits and stares at the red marble as a single spot lights the marble circle area. Stage lights begin to fade until only the single spot is left.

SISTER COYOTE: My brother used to play a lot of marbles. The other kids would save up their money until they could buy a couple of marbles at the rez store. They would come by all ready to take on my brother because he was the champ.

WOODEN WOMAN: Did he have a marble like this one?

SISTER COYOTE: No. But he had the magic within him. The other kids would watch as he gracefully took their favourite marbles. They watched as he took the marbles they had saved up for.

WOODEN WOMAN: Did anyone ever beat him?

SISTER COYOTE: They say he beat himself.

WOODEN WOMAN: What do you mean?

SISTER COYOTE: He had won all the marbles on the rez and no one would play with him anymore. So he gathered up all his marbles and he went into the woods to play one final game with someone who had a chance to beat him.

WOODEN WOMAN: Who did he play against?

SISTER COYOTE: They say the spirits came to his game and they brought all their magic marbles. My brother played each one until all their marbles were now his.

WOODEN WOMAN: What did he do with all those magic marbles?

SISTER COYOTE: Some say he gives them to children who have nothing. He comes late at night and leaves one red marble on their chest. When they wake up, find it, they know that my brother's spirit has come to see them.

WOODEN WOMAN: See how the light makes it glow?

SISTER COYOTE: One red marble.

WOODEN WOMAN: See the life, the power?

SISTER COYOTE: It looks like a tiny heart.

WOODEN WOMAN picks up the marble and stares at it through the light as spot begins to slowly fade.

WOODEN WOMAN: A child's heart.

Lights go to black.

ACT II

SCENE I

Daytime. An area downstage centre has been cleared and there is a raised platform. On the platform is a blanket with food and drink like a picnic. MISTER WOLF, SISTER COYOTE, *and* BROTHER RAVEN *are sitting on the platform.* WOODEN WOMAN *and* WOODEN MAN *are sitting on the bench.* WOODEN MAN *is holding a baby in his arms. Offstage we hear children playing in a park.*

WOODEN MAN: She's so pretty. Look at those brown eyes.

WOODEN WOMAN: What should we call her?

WOODEN MAN: We should wait for the spirits to show us what we should call her.

WOODEN WOMAN: She likes it here, see how she smiles.

WOODEN MAN: Let's listen to the spirits and see what name we should give to our daughter.

MISTER WOLF *takes off his dirty running shoes and begins to pick at his toes.*

MISTER WOLF: Look at these toes. Have you ever seen more perfect toes before?

BROTHER RAVEN: They look more like claws.

BROTHER RAVEN *takes off his shoes and shows them to* MISTER WOLF.

Now these are perfect feet.

SISTER COYOTE: They look more like turkey feet, all skinny and hairy.

BROTHER RAVEN: These are great feet. I can pick anything up with these.

BROTHER RAVEN *attempts to pick up a plate with his toes but is unsuccessful.*

WOODEN MAN: Turkey Feet!

WOODEN WOMAN: What?

WOODEN MAN: We can call her Turkey Feet.

WOODEN WOMAN: Turkey Feet? I don't think so.

WOODEN MAN: You're right, the other children would laugh at her.

SISTER COYOTE takes off her shoes and puts her feet in the air.

SISTER COYOTE: My feet are perfect.

MISTER WOLF: Never seen a perfect foot before, let me see.

He stands and examines her feet.

You should see these, they're perfect.

BROTHER RAVEN stands and examines her feet.

BROTHER RAVEN: They're perfect.

He begins to tickle her feet.

SISTER COYOTE: Hey, *cut that out,* it tickles.

BROTHER RAVEN and MISTER WOLF both tickle her feet as she screams and laughs.

Don't! Hey, stop! I'll pee myself!

They both stop tickling her and she tries to catch her breath.

You guys are so mean.

MISTER WOLF: Just having some fun.

BROTHER RAVEN: We were just playing. No harm done. Are you okay? I mean, did you pee yourself?

SISTER COYOTE: No. But I bet I can tickle you until you pee your pants.

She goes to him and tickles his sides as he squirms to get away.

BROTHER RAVEN: Don't! Ravens don't like to be tickled. Hey, stop it! You're ruffling my feathers.

She stops and goes and tries to tickle MISTER WOLF, but he just sits there and ignores her.

MISTER WOLF: You can't tickle a wolf.

She stops and sits down.

WOODEN MAN: Ruffled Feather!

WOODEN WOMAN: What?

WOODEN MAN: We can call her Ruffled Feather.

WOODEN WOMAN: I don't think so. She is much more beautiful than a ruffled feather.

She takes the baby from WOODEN MAN and holds it in her arms.

WOODEN MAN: You're right. Boy, these spirits sure aren't very good with choosing a name.

Offstage we hear children playing and then a voice saying: "Get out of here, you stinking kid." TOURIST enters dressed as a small boy, he's carrying a red ball and a lollipop. TOURIST goes up to WOODEN MAN and kicks him in the shin. TOURIST goes up to WOODEN WOMAN and pulls on her hair. They both do not react. TOURIST goes to picnic area and stares at MISTER WOLF, SISTER COYOTE, and BROTHER RAVEN. WOODEN MAN reaches for the TOURIST but WOODEN WOMAN pulls him back.

Rotten kid.

WOODEN WOMAN: Leave him be, he doesn't know any better.

WOODEN MAN: Just a good kick in the ass. That's all it'll take.

WOODEN WOMAN: He doesn't know any better.

WOODEN MAN: Where do they learn that?

WOODEN WOMAN: History, I guess.

TOURIST goes and pokes MISTER WOLF. MISTER WOLF howls and tries to be big and strong.

MISTER WOLF: You better get away from me, kid. I'm a big bad wolf!

TOURIST speaking as a snotty kid.

TOURIST: Wolves don't wear suits.

MISTER WOLF: Oh, yeah?

TOURIST: Yeah. Wolves have big teeth and walk on all fours.

MISTER WOLF: Well, I don't.

TOURIST: Then you're not a wolf.

MISTER WOLF: Beat it, kid, before I bite you on the ass and show you just how big my teeth are.

MISTER WOLF reaches for him but the TOURIST runs away and pokes at BROTHER RAVEN, who caws real loud and tries to flap his arms like wings.

BROTHER RAVEN: You better not mess with me, I'm a big old raven and I'll peck out your eyes if you're not careful.

TOURIST: You're not a raven. Ravens don't have greasy hair, they have beautiful black feathers.

BROTHER RAVEN: Yeah, well I'm having a bad hair day. Get going or I'll . . .

He reaches for him but TOURIST runs away and goes to SISTER COYOTE and pulls on her hair.

SISTER COYOTE: Ouch! Hey, quit it!

TOURIST: What're you going to do about it?

SISTER COYOTE: I'll bite you! I'm a coyote and my bite really hurts!

TOURIST: You're no coyote. Coyotes are beautiful and have nice eyes.

SISTER COYOTE: I have nice eyes. Hey, where do you get off telling me I don't have nice eyes?

TOURIST smiles and pulls on her hair again as he skips off stage. Sounds of children playing ends. SISTER COYOTE begins to cry.

I have nice eyes, don't I?

BROTHER RAVEN and MISTER WOLF go up to her and try to console her.

BROTHER RAVEN: Sure you do.

MISTER WOLF: Nothing more beautiful than a coyote's eyes.

BROTHER RAVEN: Except maybe her feet.

MISTER WOLF: And her feet.

SISTER COYOTE: Thanks guys.

BROTHER RAVEN: My eyes are black like the night.

MISTER WOLF: My eyes are yellow like the sun.

SISTER COYOTE: My mother told me that my eyes were like the earth and they could look at you forever. That's what she used to call me, Forever.

They sit down on the picnic blanket and begin again to compare feet. WOODEN MAN stares at his child as WOODEN WOMAN holds her in her arms.

WOODEN MAN: We shall call her Forever.

WOODEN WOMAN: Yes, that's a wonderful name.

WOODEN MAN: Look at those eyes.

WOODEN WOMAN: Yes, they look at you forever.

Lights fade.

SCENE II

Daytime. Stage is covered in dead leaves. All characters are sitting or standing at the bench. WOODEN WOMAN *is still holding the child in her arms.*

Offstage we hear a military bugle playing softly and then the sound of a marching drum, sounds of men going into battle. TOURIST *enters now dressed in a blue US Calvary uniform. He enters holding freshly taken scalps, his old camera and tripod, he places the scalps in the hands of* WOODEN MAN *and* WOODEN WOMAN, *goes and takes their picture. No one moves.* TOURIST *gathers the scalps, his camera and tripod, and exits as stage lights and sounds fade.*

SCENE III

Daytime. Only the platform area is lit. Everyone is sitting on the blanket and facing downstage. Offstage we hear: "Get out of here, you stinking Indian." WOODEN MAN *stands and faces downstage.*

WOODEN MAN: We are going into battle.

WOODEN WOMAN *stands with her child still in her arms and faces downstage.*

WOODEN WOMAN: The men have all left the village.

MISTER WOLF: This bread is real tasty.

SISTER COYOTE: Could you pass the butter? I like a lot of butter on my bread.

BROTHER RAVEN: Here you go. Could you pass the blueberries? It's been a long time since I've had any.

MISTER WOLF: It's a nice day for a picnic. Sun's out, not a cloud in the sky.

Sounds of war softly in the distance: horses, men screaming, gunfire, screams of wounded and dying men.

WOODEN MAN: I must go. I must kill those that have killed my fathers.

WOODEN WOMAN: The men have all left. It's just the mothers and the children.

WOODEN MAN steps off the platform. We should hear the crunching of dead leaves as he steps down. He walks and stands downstage right as red spot comes up.

Don't go! Don't go! They will kill you and there will be no more fathers for our children. Don't go! Our baby has only lived two days and has not met the earth and all its beauty.

WOODEN MAN: I must go. I must kill those that have killed my mothers.

WOODEN WOMAN is holding her child in her arms as sounds of battle get louder and louder.

WOODEN WOMAN: Come back! Come back! Be with us forever. We can hide in the forest and the soldiers will not find us. Come back! Come back!

WOODEN MAN: I must go. I must kill those that have killed my children.

Sounds build to a crashing end. Red spot fades as WOODEN WOMAN sits down with her child in her arms.

WOODEN WOMAN: The men have all disappeared. The Blue Coats have taken and destroyed their life. The earth has become silent. No more screams, no more screams. It's quiet now, my child. Sleep and dream, sleep and dream of days unlike this, this is a sad day, a day filled with the loss of our men. May their spirits sleep like you, my child. May they sleep with endless peace.

MISTER WOLF: It's a great day for a picnic. Not one sound, not even noisy songbirds.

BROTHER RAVEN: You got something against birds?

MISTER WOLF: Only ones who sing poorly.

BROTHER RAVEN: I wasn't much of a singer.

SISTER COYOTE: Could you pass the bread? My belly isn't quite full yet.

Lights fade to black on picnic area.

SCENE IV

MISTER WOLF, BROTHER RAVEN, and SISTER COYOTE are asleep on the picnic blanket. WOODEN WOMAN stands on the edge of the platform still holding her child. TOURIST enters. He is now dressed as a movie director. He brings out his chair and his movie camera and sets both up to the right of WOODEN MAN who is still downstage right. TOURIST sits down in his director's chair and on the back we read: "Mr. Costner." He talks into a walkie-talkie.

TOURIST: Lights! Okay, bring in the buffalo!

WOODEN MAN: The cannons fired and the earth shook as they charged toward us with their fire.

WOODEN WOMAN talks to her child.

WOODEN WOMAN: Your father was the bravest of all the men. He held his head up high when he went into battle with those Blue Coats.

TOURIST: More smoke! I need more smoke!

WOODEN MAN: The cannons killed half the men in five minutes. We had nowhere to run. My brothers were on the ground, torn and dying by that screaming hot metal.

WOODEN WOMAN: Your father was a great man, everyone listened when he spoke, they looked up to him and they respected his vision.

TOURIST: Okay, kill the buffalo! Where's the wolf? Someone get the wolf out of his trailer. I need the wolf to howl on cue. Can he do that?

MISTER WOLF howls in his sleep.

WOODEN WOMAN: Your father was so beautiful. His eyes held my spirit the first time I looked into them.

WOODEN MAN: A piece of hot metal cut into my leg and I fell from my horse as those around me died.

TOURIST talks directly to WOODEN MAN.

TOURIST: Could you talk slower? More poetically. Slowly and clearly. These words were written for a reason. Let's hear them, okay? More cannon fire! More cannon fire!

WOODEN MAN: I was there on the ground with my leg bleeding and burning with the fire of those men who were here to destroy us. My brothers had all died, and I watched their spirits rise off the ground and into the beautiful sky. They gathered above the battle and did not know what to do. They were confused and they began to cry and sing like the death they had become.

TOURIST: Okay, that's better. Now, I want you to look mean. Can we see your war face? Who did this guy's makeup? I want more paint! More paint on this one! Makeup! Makeup!

WOODEN MAN: I was alone as the soldiers charged forward with the cold steel of their bayonets. They slid the blades so easily into my brothers who were already dead. The cold blade slid into the warmth of death and then they cut off their beautiful hair. With the harshness of a cold blade they took their hair and screamed in victory. My brothers screamed from the sky as their hair was taken and shown to them, and then the battle became quiet.

Spot fades on WOODEN MAN *as he exits.* TOURIST *stands and gathers his chair, camera, and tripod.*

TOURIST: Okay, enough of this shot. Let's get some close-ups of those bleeding scalps. I want it to drip and drip. And get the women and children ready, I want to see the children and the women screaming and crying. Can they do that? Tell them we'll pay them more if there's real tears. Okay, let's go! Let's not waste this beautiful sunny day.

TOURIST *exits.* WOODEN WOMAN *puts her child down and stands on the edge of the platform as lights slowly begin to fade.*

WOODEN WOMAN: The soldiers didn't stop. They were heading for our village. They were coming to kill us all and take our hair. They were coming to kill our children so they would not grow up and avenge the death of their fathers. The spirits of the dead men had made it back to the village before the soldiers. They were above us and they were telling us to run to the forest. Where are you, Husband? I do not hear your voice. Where are you!? Wake up, children! Wake up! We must run to the forest and hide! Wake up!

WOODEN WOMAN *tries to wake up the sleeping* MISTER WOLF, BROTHER RAVEN, *and* SISTER COYOTE, *but they stay asleep as the light fades to black.*

SCENE V

Night. Entire stage is covered in dead leaves. Platform is gone. SISTER COYOTE, BROTHER RAVEN, *and* MISTER WOLF *are all sitting on the bench.* WOODEN WOMAN *is standing behind them with her child in her arms. Offstage we hear: "Get out of here, you stinking Black Robe."* TOURIST *enters now dressed as a priest. He sets up his easel and begins to paint a picture.* WOODEN WOMAN *begins to move and speak.*

WOODEN WOMAN: Your father is dead. The soldiers are here. They are killing the women and children.

SISTER COYOTE: I hate waiting for the bus.

BROTHER RAVEN: Me, too.

MISTER WOLF: This bus is always late.

WOODEN WOMAN: The soldiers took the children and they made them watch as they shot all the women. My sisters fell to the ground as their children screamed for them. The soldiers took the hair of my sisters and then they turned on the children. I had run into the forest with my child and I watched as the soldiers walked to the crying children. What had they done? Why did they want to kill the children?

SISTER COYOTE: When I was a child I was sent to a Catholic school on a bus.

The TOURIST goes to SISTER COYOTE and leads her downstage left as a red spot comes up. She stands there and continues to talk as TOURIST sits back down and continues to paint.

My mother was screaming at the priests and the nuns. She didn't want me to go with them.

WOODEN WOMAN: The soldiers took each child by the hand and they led them to a hole. "Don't kill them!" I wanted to scream but they would see where I was hiding and they would kill my child. So I stayed quiet but in my head I screamed, "Don't take them! Don't kill our children!"

SISTER COYOTE: I went with the sisters and the priests. I went to their schools and they cut my hair and told me to speak English. They told me that I was a savage and that the word of God would be my saviour.

BROTHER RAVEN: I was taken away from my mother on a bus because the government men said she was unfit to care for me. I was sent to live with a family far, far away from home.

TOURIST stands, takes BROTHER RAVEN by the hand, and leads him downstage right where another red spot comes up. TOURIST returns to his chair and continues to paint.

WOODEN WOMAN: They slit their throats, the youngest of the children, slit their throats and tossed their small harmless bodies into the hole.

BROTHER RAVEN: My mother was too drunk to realize what was happening to me. The government men came and took me away, took me to a family that would never love me.

MISTER WOLF: I was sent to prison on a bus. Sent to rot behind cold bars for a crime I did not commit. They came to my grandmother's house and they took me to their prison.

TOURIST stands, takes MISTER WOLF by the hand, and leads him downstage centre where a red spot comes up. TOURIST returns to his chair and continues to paint.

WOODEN WOMAN: The soldiers took the older children and dragged them toward the hole. They were screaming and begging for their lives but the soldiers shot them, each one with a bullet to the head. They tossed their lifeless bodies into the hole. The hole began to fill with blood.

MISTER WOLF: I couldn't stand it in there, with those steel bars keeping me away from my home, keeping me away from my grandmother.

BROTHER RAVEN: I couldn't stay there. I couldn't stay with a family that didn't want me. They never loved me. They never saw me as one of their own. But they were getting extra money from the government so they had to keep me. They had to keep me. They kept me in a little room beside the kitchen. They gave me bits of food but nothing a real raven needs to grow strong. I was getting to be a real nice bird before they got their hands on me. Look at me now, all skin and bones, you can't fly right if you're nothing but skin and bones, I tried to tell them, but they wouldn't listen to me. I am Raven, I would tell them, but they kept me in that little room until I decided that I had had enough.

SISTER COYOTE: They kept me in that school, they kept me until I decided that I had had enough. I had had enough of being beaten and kicked around. I am a Coyote, I would scream at them but they would laugh and kick me some more. I am Coyote! But they would say that I was a child of God and that he would be my saviour. I am Coyote! And I wasn't going to be kicked around anymore.

WOODEN WOMAN: My child began to cry. It was as if this child could feel the death around her. She began to cry louder than the sound of the soldiers as they yelled in victory. A soldier spotted me as I tried to run deeper into the forest.

TOURIST stands, goes to WOODEN WOMAN, takes her by the hand, and sits her back down on the bench in her usual spot. TOURIST sits back down in his chair and continues to paint.

SISTER COYOTE: My last night on earth was in my tiny bed. I was trying to dream of my family back home. The fat priest came into my room and he pulled off my little dress and he placed his fat cold body on top of me and he hurt me real bad, all the time telling me that I was his gift from the Lord and that I should never tell anyone. He raped me, and then he smacked me across the face and told me to never tell anyone or else God would punish me.

BROTHER RAVEN: My last night on earth was spent in my tiny room just beside the kitchen. The father of the family came into my room and told me that I had made a mess and that he would therefore have to punish me for this. I tried to tell him that I wasn't the one who made the mess but he came at me anyway. He took off his thick black belt and he tore off my little pants and he smacked me until I was bleeding and screaming for him to stop. He told me to never tell the government men about what he did to me or else I would never see my mother alive again.

MISTER WOLF: My last night on earth was spent in a dark cell. I hadn't eaten in days and they were telling me that they were going to keep me there until I was dead. They came into my cell and they beat me with pipes until I could no longer walk. They told me I would never see my mother again.

WOODEN WOMAN: The soldiers couldn't see me but they could hear my child crying. "Hush, little girl. Go to sleep. Hush, now." But she wouldn't stop crying. I took my hand and I placed it over her mouth but you could still hear her crying and the soldiers were getting closer and closer.

SISTER COYOTE lies down and begins to pile dead leaves on top of her body.

SISTER COYOTE: The fat priest left the piece of rope that he used for a belt in my tiny room. I placed the rope around my neck and tied it to the beam that went across my room.

WOODEN WOMAN: The soldiers began to shoot in the direction that I was hiding.

A loud gunshot is heard.

SISTER COYOTE: I jumped and I became the Coyote.

BROTHER RAVEN lies down and begins to pile leaves on top of himself.

BROTHER RAVEN: The father of the family that never loved me left his thick black belt in my tiny room that was beside the kitchen. I placed the belt around my neck and placed the belt around the beam that cut across my tiny room.

WOODEN WOMAN: They were shooting right at me, one of the bullets ripped into a tree that was right near my head.

Another loud gunshot is heard.

BROTHER RAVEN: I jumped and I became the Raven.

MISTER WOLF lies down and begins to pile leaves on top of himself.

MISTER WOLF: They placed the noose around my neck. The priest said some words to me that I couldn't understand. He didn't even look me in the eyes. He turned away and they let me fall.

WOODEN WOMAN: Another bullet hit me in the arm and I screamed real loud and my child began to scream. Another bullet hit the tree.

Another loud gunshot is heard.

MISTER WOLF: I jumped and I became the Wolf.

TOURIST stands, goes to each pile of leaves, and administers the last rites. As he does this each red spot fades.

WOODEN WOMAN: They were coming to kill me and take my hair. My child wouldn't stop screaming so I took some dead leaves and I gently pushed them into her mouth.

WOODEN WOMAN bends down and takes dead leaves and places them into the mouth of her child. TOURIST finishes the last rites and exits taking his painting and chair with him.

There now, my child. You can sleep now. The soldiers can't hear you anymore. Sleep, my child. Sleep and dream of days unlike this one. Dream of days spent playing and enjoying this earth that was given to us by the creator. Sleep and dream my child.

Lights begin to fade. Offstage we hear beautiful sounds: a coyote barking, a raven cawing, and a wolf howling. Blackout.

SCENE VI

Daytime. WOODEN MAN and WOODEN WOMAN are sitting in their spots on the bench. There are the three piles of dead leaves still on the stage but now each one has a white cross at the head of it. There is also a small pile of dead leaves right in front of the bench and it also has a small white cross. Offstage we hear: "Get out of here, you stinking tourist."

TOURIST enters, now dressed in a bright Hawaiian shirt and Bermuda shorts. He sets up his camera and tripod and sits between the Indians. As timer beeps, nothing happens. TOURIST stands and checks his camera and resets it and sits back down. As timer beeps, nothing happens again. TOURIST angrily gathers camera and tripod and exits.

WOODEN MAN: It sure is quiet here without the children.

WOODEN WOMAN: Weather's changing. Autumn's almost over.

WOODEN MAN: Are you warm enough?

WOODEN WOMAN: Yes. Are you?

WOODEN MAN: Sure. Not too much wind on this side.

WOODEN WOMAN: Are you hungry? I've got some apple left.

WOODEN MAN: No, my belly's full.

Offstage we hear the faint sound of children playing and singing.

WOODEN WOMAN: I didn't mean to kill her.

WOODEN MAN: I know.

WOODEN WOMAN: She wouldn't stop crying. Everything I did made her cry louder.

WOODEN MAN: I know. It's okay. It's over now. We just have to live on, together.

WOODEN WOMAN: I just wanted her to be quiet for a moment so I could think straight. I never wanted her to die like that.

WOODEN MAN moves closer to her and puts his arms around her.

WOODEN MAN: We still have each other. We still have our memories.

WOODEN WOMAN: I put leaves into her mouth so she would be silent just for a moment. She stopped crying when I did that. I was able to breathe for a moment and rest and try and get strong, but she wouldn't wake up when I was taking the leaves out of her mouth. She just stayed there all quiet and so beautiful.

WOODEN MAN: Rest now. She is with the spirits of the forest. They will take care of her now.

WOODEN WOMAN: I loved her so much. I would do anything to bring her back, you know that don't you?

WOODEN MAN: Yes, I do. Rest now. She is with the spirits. Can you hear them playing?

Sounds of children get louder and louder.

WOODEN WOMAN: Little child with her little red heart. She would've grown up to be a wonderful daughter. Her little red heart and those brown eyes that looked up at you forever.

WOODEN MAN takes her by the chin and kisses her softly on the lips as sounds of children get louder.

WOODEN MAN: I love you more than anything on this earth. I will never leave you alone again. Let's just sit here a while longer and go home. The weather's changing and soon the snow will come.

WOODEN WOMAN: I am at peace here. I can see her, you know. I can see her as a little girl playing with other children. I can see her playing catch with her brothers, I can see her as she plays marbles and gets dirty, I can see her as she becomes a woman, I can see her as she becomes a spirit, a beautiful spirit upon this earth.

WOODEN MAN: Rest now. We will come back tomorrow and see what spirits come to visit us. Go to sleep, my love. Sleep and dream of days like this. Days filled with wonderful and alive spirits that play and sing, forever . . .

Sounds of children build and build, and then slowly fade as lights begin to fade to black.

The end.

ACKNOWLEDGEMENTS

I owe great thanks, first and foremost, to the seven authors who wrote the plays included here: their efforts to document, commemorate, challenge, and theatricalize Canada's past made this volume a possibility. I also would like to thank their agents, families, and estates for kindly allowing us to reproduce their works in this anthology. Roberta Barker, Marlene Mendonça, Kailin Wright, Lindsay Thistle, George Belliveau, Naila Keleta-Mae, and Lindsay Lachance: thank you for your insightful introductions that shed new light on plays and demonstrate why they deserve wider readerships today. The folks at Playwrights Canada Press—Annie Gibson, Blake Sproule, Stephanie Nuñez, Mandy Bayrami, Jessica Lewis—have made the process of editing this volume and its companion anthology of essays an absolute pleasure. I'd like to thank Roberta (again) for her generous invitation to edit this volume and her unflagging enthusiasm for historical drama. At the University of the Fraser Valley I have received support from the Office of Research, Engagement and Graduate Studies in the form of teaching releases, and encouragement from the Dean's Office in the College of Arts and from my colleagues in the English and theatre departments. My students in Canadian drama and theatre courses, at UFV and at UBC, have brought many of the plays in this volume to life in the classroom and their interest in Canadian drama has been a significant motivation for this collection. Phay Gagnon, my research assistant, has provided invaluable editorial assistance in the preparation of this manuscript. Finally, I would like to thank my extended families and friends, who have generously not asked whether I wasn't finished with this collection yet. Two furry friends—Briscoe and Pickles—kept me company as I reviewed plays and worked on this collection. Jasper and Quinn: thank you for helping me keep work in perspective and making sure I take time to play. Scott: I can't list all the ways you made this book possible, but thank you.

FURTHER READING

Aikins, Carroll. *The God of Gods: A Canadian Play.* Kailin Wright, ed. Ottawa: U of Ottawa P, 2016.

Atkins, Damien, Paul Dunn, and Andrew Kushnir. *The Gay Heritage Project.* Toronto: Playwrights Canada, 2018.

Byrne, James. *Nootka Sound; Or, Britain Prepared.* Ms. Larpent Collection. Huntington Library, San Marino, California. N.d.

Clements, Marie and Rita Leistner. *The Edward Curtis Project.* Vancouver: Talonbooks, 2010.

Cooper, Beverley. *Innocence Lost: A Play About Stephen Truscott.* Winnipeg: Scirocco, 2009.

Coulter, James. *Riel: A Play in Two Parts.* Toronto: Ryerson, 1962.

---. *The Trial of Louis Riel.* Ottawa: Oberon, 1968.

Curzon, Sarah Anne. *The Sweet Girl Graduate: A Comedy in Four Acts.* Toronto: Canadian Theatre Review Publications, 1979.

---. *Laura Secord, the Heroine of 1812.* 1887. *Project Gutenburg.*

Davies, Robertson. *Question Time.* Toronto: Macmillan, 1975.

Denison, Merrill. *Henry Hudson and Other Plays.* Toronto: Ryerson, 1931.

---. *The Unheroic North: Four Canadian Plays.* Toronto: McClelland & Stewart, 1923.

Gale, Lorena. *Je me souviens.* Vancouver: Talonbooks, 2001.

Garnhum, Dennis. *The Wars.* Winnipeg: Scirocco, 2008.

Gowan, Elsie Park. *Hungry Spirit: Selected Plays & Prose by Elsie Park Gowan.* Moira Day, ed. Edmonton: NeWest, 1992.

Griffiths, Linda. *Maggie & Pierre: A Fantasy of Love, Politics and the Media.* Vancouver: Talonbooks, 1980.

Highway, Tomson. *Ernestine Shuswap Gets Her Trout.* Vancouver: Talonbooks, 2005.

Hollingsworth, Michael. *The History of the Village of the Small Huts: Pts. I-VIII.* 7th ed. Winnipeg: Blizzard Publishing, 1994.

Hunter-Duvar, John. *De Roberval.* Saint John: J. & A. McMillan, 1888.

MacKenzie, James Bovell. *Thayendanegea: An Historico-Miliary Drama.* Toronto: W. Briggs, 1898.

Mair, Charles. *Through the Mackenzie Basin.* 1908. *Project Gutenburg.*

Massey, Vincent, ed. *Canadian Plays for Hart House Theatre.* Toronto: Macmillan, 1926.

Mitchell, Ken. *The Medicine Line.* Regina: Department of Culture and Youth, 1974.

---. *The Plainsmen.* Regina: Coteau Books, 1992.

---. *Rebels in Time: Three Plays.* Edmonton: NeWest, 1991.

Mojica, Monique. *Princess Pocahontas and the Blue Spots.* Toronto: Women's Press Literary, 1991.

Moses, Daniel David. *Almighty Voice and His Wife.* 2nd ed., Toronto: Playwrights Canada, 2009.

---. *Brebeuf's Ghost: A Tale of Horror in Three Acts.* Toronto: Exile, 2000.

---. *Indian Medicine Shows: Two One-Act Plays.* Toronto: Exile, 1995.

Mummers Troupe. *Buchans: A Mining Town.* Alan Filewod, ed. *Canadian Drama* 13.1 (1987).

Pollock, Sharon. *Walsh.* Vancouver: Talonbooks, 1983.

Reaney, James. *Sticks and Stones.* Erin, ON: Porcépic, 1975.

---. *The St. Nicholas Hotel: The Donnellys Part II.* Erin, ON: Porcépic, 1976.

---. *Handcuffs: The Donnellys Part III.* Erin, ON, Porcépic, 1977.

---. *Wacousta!* Erin, ON: Porcépic, 1979.

Ryan, Oscar, E. Cecil Smith, Frank Love, and Mildred Goldberg. *Eight Men Speak.* Alan Filewod, ed. Ottawa: U of Ottawa P, 2013.

Salutin, Rick and Theatre Passe Muraille. *1837: A History, A Play.* Toronto: James Lorimer & Co., 1976.

Voaden, Herman. *A Vision Of Canada: Herman Voaden's Dramatic Works 1928-1945.* Anton Wagner, ed. Toronto: Simon & Pierre, 1993.

Scribble, Sam. *Dolorsolatio, a Local Political Burlesque.* Montreal, 1865.

Wasserman, Jerry, ed. *Spectacle of Empire: Marc Lescarbot's Theatre of Neptune in New France.* Vancouver: Talonbooks, 2006.

Wiebe, Rudy. *Far as the Eye Can See: A Play by Rudy Wiebe and Theatre Passe Muraille.* Edmonton: NeWest, 1977.

Young, David. *No Great Mischief.* Toronto: Scirocco, 2006.

NOTES ON CONTRIBUTORS

Roberta Barker is Associate Professor and Associate Director (Theatre) in the Fountain School of Performing Arts at Dalhousie University. A practising director and dramaturge of theatre and opera, she is the author of *Early Modern Tragedy, Gender and Performance, 1984-2000: The Destined Livery* (Palgrave Macmillan, 2007), co-editor with Kim Solga of *New Canadian Realisms: Eight Plays* and *New Canadian Realisms: Essays* (Playwrights Canada Press, 2012), and General Editor of the series New Essays in Canadian Theatre at Playwrights Canada Press. Her current book project, *Symptoms of the Self: Tuberculosis and the Making of the Modern Stage*, is under contract with the University of Iowa Press.

George Belliveau is Professor of Theatre / Drama Education at the University of British Columbia. His research interests include research-based theatre, drama and social justice, drama and L2 learning, drama across the curriculum, drama and health research, and Canadian theatre. His scholarly and creative writing can found in various arts-based and theatre education journals, along with chapters in edited books. His most recent book, *Research-based Theatre: An Artistic Methodology*, was published by Intellect Press in 2016.

Joseph A. Dandurand is a member of Kwantlen First Nation, located on the Fraser River. He resides there with his three children: Danessa, Marlysse, and Jace. Joseph is the director of the Kwantlen Cultural Centre and has been performing his duties for twenty-two years. He has been tasked with protecting his people's heritage from the many destructive elements of development in the Kwantlen territory. Joseph received a diploma in Performing Arts from Algonquin College and studied Theatre and Direction at the University of

Ottawa. His produced plays include *Crackers and Soup* (1994), *No Totem for My Story* (1995), *Where Two Rivers Meet* (1995), and *Please Do Not Touch the Indians* (1998), which was produced by Red Path Theater (Chicago, 1999), Algonquin Theatre (Connecticut, 2000 and 2006), Debajehmujig Storytellers (2001), and the Autry Theater (Los Angeles, 2004). He has published eight books of poetry; his latest, *The Rumour*, will be published by BookLand Press in 2017. Joseph's children's play, *The Hungry Feast Dish*, will be produced by Axis Theatre on Aboriginal Day 2017 at the University of British Columbia Amphitheatre.

Robertson Davies (1913–1995) was a renowned writer, journalist, and professor; he is widely acknowledged as one of Canada's most influential novelists. His interest for the stage began early in life when he performed in various stage productions as a child. He attended Upper Canada College from 1926 to 1932, and Queen's University from 1932 to 1935, before graduating from Balliol College, Oxford. After returning to Canada, he published his books, wrote and produced his own plays, and contributed his essays to numerous journals (sometimes under the pseudonym Samuel Marchbanks). In 1960, Davies began a career as a professor and continued for twenty-one years. His achievements include the Lorne Pierce Award for literary achievement, becoming the first Master of Massey College at the University of Toronto, and honorary degrees from various Canadian universities.

Heather Davis-Fisch is Associate Professor of English and Theatre at the University of the Fraser Valley in British Columbia. Her research interests include performance historiography and Indigenous and intercultural performance, particularly in historical paradigms. She is the author of *Loss and Cultural Remains in Performance: The Ghosts of the Franklin Expedition* (Palgrave, 2012) and editor of *Canadian Performance Histories and Historiographies* (Playwrights Canada Press, 2017). Her work has also appeared in the journals *Theatre Research in Canada*, *Canadian Theatre Review*, *Performing Arts Resources*, and *Cultural Studies / Critical Methodologies*, as well as in the books *Theatres of Affect*, *Performance Studies in Canada*, and Bloomsbury's *Cultural History of Theatre*. She is the co-editor of *Canadian Theatre Review*'s Views and Reviews section.

Merrill Denison (1893–1975) was born in Detroit, Michigan, and graduated from the University of Toronto before returning to the United States to study architecture. He was invited by Hart House Theatre to be a stage designer and art director, which led to his debut as a playwright. A key figure in the Canadian Little Theatre Movement, he is widely known for his realistic dramas and satirical comedies, including *Brothers in Arms* and *Marsh Hay*. He returned to the United States once more to produce his radio drama series *Great Moments in History* (1932-33) and *America's Hour* (1936). Productions of his plays have been featured at the Shaw Festival, with *Marsh Hay* remaining one of the most frequently produced English-Canadian dramas.

Lorena Gale (1958–2009) was an actor, playwright, and activist, known for her role as Elosha in *Battlestar Galactica* and her body of work in Canadian theatre. As an activist, she spoke out and promoted Black causes; her plays were an outlet for this activism, as seen in *Angélique* and *Je me souviens*. *Angélique* won the 1995 du Maurier National Playwriting Competition and was staged off-Broadway in 1999. Gale died of cancer in Vancouver in 2009, and the Union of BC Performers created the Lorena Gale Woman of Distinction Award as a tribute to her "nduring commitment to power, dignity, intelligence, and truth.

Naila Keleta-Mae is Assistant Professor of Theatre and Performance at the University of Waterloo where she researches race, gender, and performance. She is currently writing a book on Beyoncé's art and influence. Dr. Keleta-Mae has discussed aspects of popular culture in media outlets including the BBC, CBC, the Canadian Press, the *Globe and Mail*, and *Chatelaine*. Her scholarship appears in academic publications including the journals *Theatre Research in Canada* and *Canadian Review of American Studies* and in the books *In Defence of Theatre* (University of Toronto Press, 2016) and *Performance Studies in Canada* (forthcoming). Dr. Keleta-Mae has been awarded a Lois Claxton Humanities and Social Sciences Award from the University of Waterloo, the New Scholars' Prize by the International Federation for Theatre Research, and the Mary McEwan Award for feminist scholarship from York University.

Lindsay Lachance is of Algonquin Anishinaabe and of eighth-generation mixed Canadian ancestry. She is a Ph.D. candidate at the University of British Columbia and has a masters in Theatre Theory and Dramaturgy from the University of Ottawa. She is a sessional instructor in the Institute for Critical Indigenous Studies and Theatre at UBC. Lindsay is an active theatre professional, reviewer, and scholar, and has presented her research at five international conferences. Her areas of interest include performance as politics, the physicalization of spirituality in time and space, and the multiple creation processes of Indigenous dramaturgies. She was the dramaturge for Simon Fraser University's Mainstage production of *An Encounter with "The Unnatural and Accidental Women" by Marie Clements* in 2015, and has been a guest speaker at events hosted by the National Arts Centre, the PuSh Festival, the Talking Stick Festival, the Indigenous Performing Arts Alliance, the Museum of Anthropology at UBC, and the Audain Gallery at SFU. Lindsay is a member of Full Circle First Nations Performance and the Indigenous Performing Arts Alliance.

Charles Mair (1838–1927) was born in Lanark, Upper Canada. He is best known as a Canadian nationalist, poet, and journalist, and was a member of the Canada First movement. He published his first poems in newspapers and journals and published his first book *Dreamland and Other Poems* in 1868. His work eventually led to a position working as a research secretary for the Canadian government; his position would embed him in the Red River and Northwest Rebellions, in which he opposed Louis Riel. An advocate for Protestant immigration to western Canada, his beliefs and professional work clashed with the Roman-Catholic Métis; however he expressed strong sympathy for Indigenous peoples in his literary work.

Marlene Mendonça is a Ph.D. student in the Theatre and Performance Studies Program at York University. Her research uses historical documents to understand the often-overlooked ways in which the theatre-loving "matinee girl," and girls generally, have contributed to social and political thought in the early twentieth century. Her dissertation examines the ways in which the matinee girl challenged conventions of femininity and blurred the lines between public and private spaces in New York City.

Sharon Pollock is a playwright, director, and visiting artist. She won the Governor General's Literary Award for Drama in 1981 for her play *Blood Relations* and in 1985 for her play *Doc*. Her plays have been produced internationally and have been performed at the Shaw Festival, the 1988 Cultural Olympics in Calgary, and the Stratford Festival, which is producing *The Komagata Maru Incident* as part of their 2017 season. She has visited academic institutions as a guest and keynote speaker, been a chairperson of the Advisory Arts Panel for the Canada Council, and Executive Director of the Alberta Playwrights' Network. Her most recent work, *Blow Wind High Water*, will be produced by Theatre Calgary in 2017.

Amy Redpath Roddick (1868–1954) led a privileged life as the daughter of a sugar refiner and wife of Sir Thomas Roddick, one of Canada's most prominent physicians; however, she had a unique passion and talent for the arts. As a member of Montreal's social elite, Lady Roddick frequented Mount Royal Park,

Westmount, and Square Mile when she was not travelling to Europe or New York. After her husband died in her fifties, Lady Roddick published over a dozen volumes of her plays, verse, and verse drama. She eventually became a benefactor of McGill University and was initiated into the Bear Clan of the Iroquois at Kahnawake. After her death, her obituary focused more on her literary achievements and her generosity toward the Canadian Aboriginal community than on her privileged social standing.

Lindsay Thistle holds a Ph.D. in Theatre and Performance Studies from York University. Her research focuses on the dramatization of history, with a particular interest in representations of war and their shifting connections with ideas of Canadian identity. She is currently working as an instructor in the Canadian Studies Department at Trent University and the Communication Studies Department at Wilfrid Laurier University. She also completed a postdoctoral fellowship through the International Council for Canadian Studies at the University of Silesia in Poland.

Kailin Wright is Assistant Professor of English at St. Francis Xavier University. Her research focuses on gender, race, Indigenous culture, and spectatorship in Canadian literature and theatre. She has articles published or forthcoming in *Theatre Journal*, *Canadian Literature*, *Studies in Canadian Literature*, and *Theatre Research in Canada* as well as in the books *Making Canada New: Editing, Modernism, and New Media* and *Shakespeare and Canada: Remembrance of Ourselves*. Her critical edition *Carroll Aikins' The God of Gods: A Canadian Play* was published by University of Ottawa Press. She was also a co-applicant for the Editing Modernism in Canada Project, funded by a SSHRC Strategic Knowledge Cluster grant.

First edition: May 2017
Printed and bound in Canada by Marquis Book Printing, Montreal

Cover photo provided courtesy of Library and Archives Canada
Cover design by Leon Aureus

PLAYWRIGHTS CANADA PRESS

202-269 Richmond St. W.
Toronto, ON
M5V 1X1

416.703.0013
info@playwrightscanada.com
www.playwrightscanada.com
@playcanpress

RECYCLED
Paper made from recycled material
FSC www.fsc.org FSC® C103567

Printed on Rolland Enviro, which contains 100% post-consumer fiber, is ECOLOGO, Processed Chlorine Free, Ancient Forest Friendly and FSC® certified and is manufactured using renewable biogas energy.

PERMANENT 100% BIO GAS ENERGY Ancient Forest Friendly™